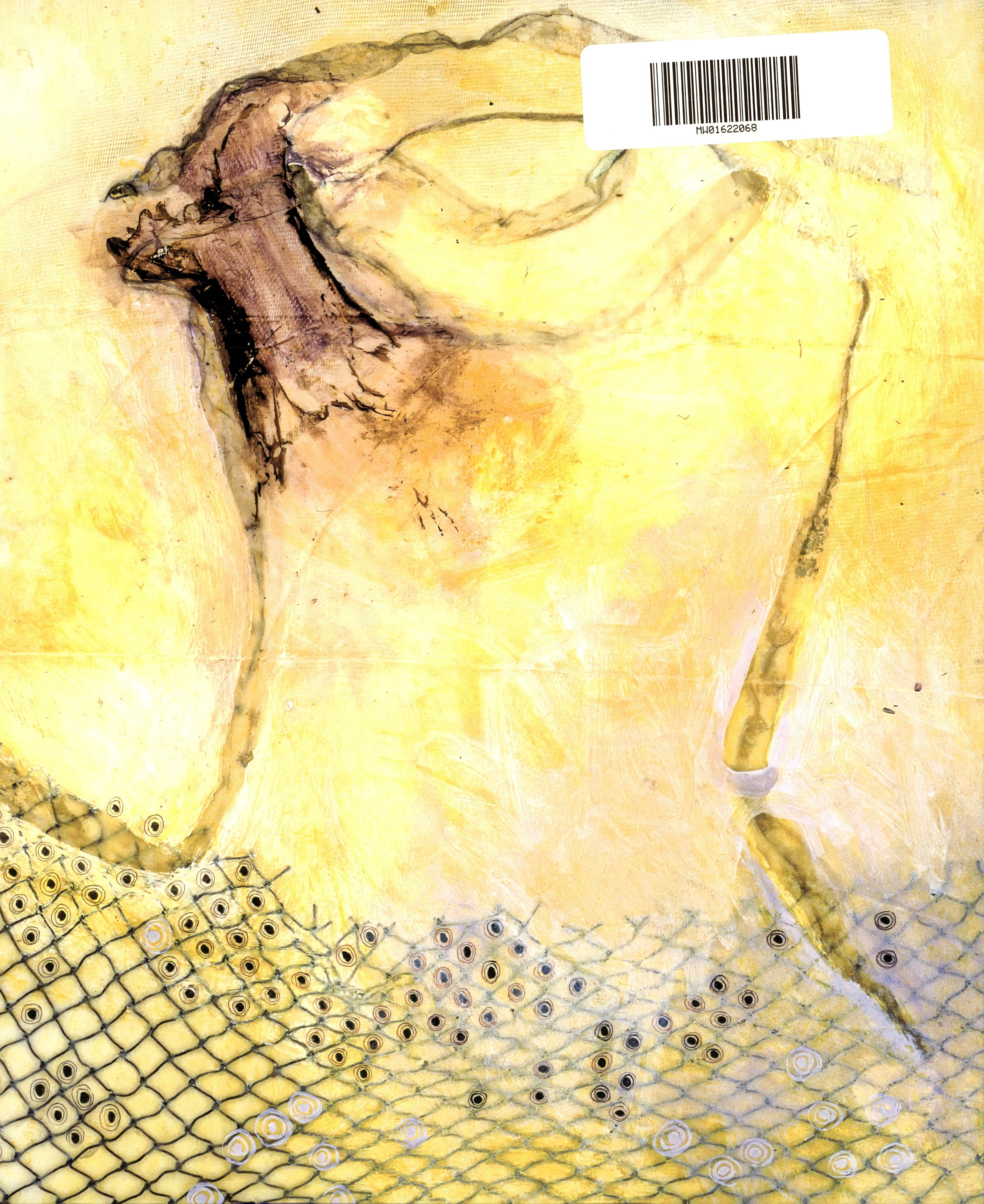

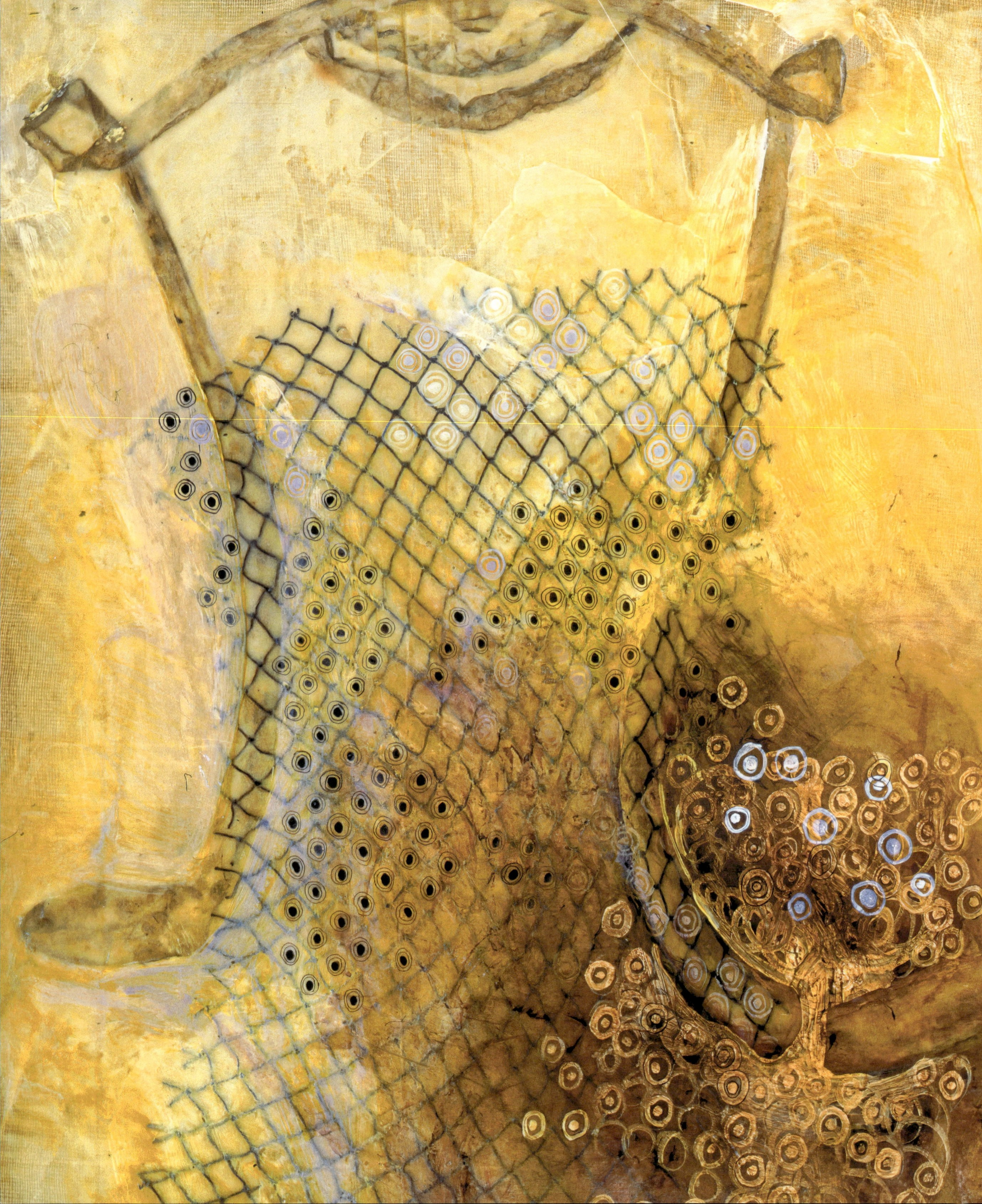

Sonya Kelliher-Combs

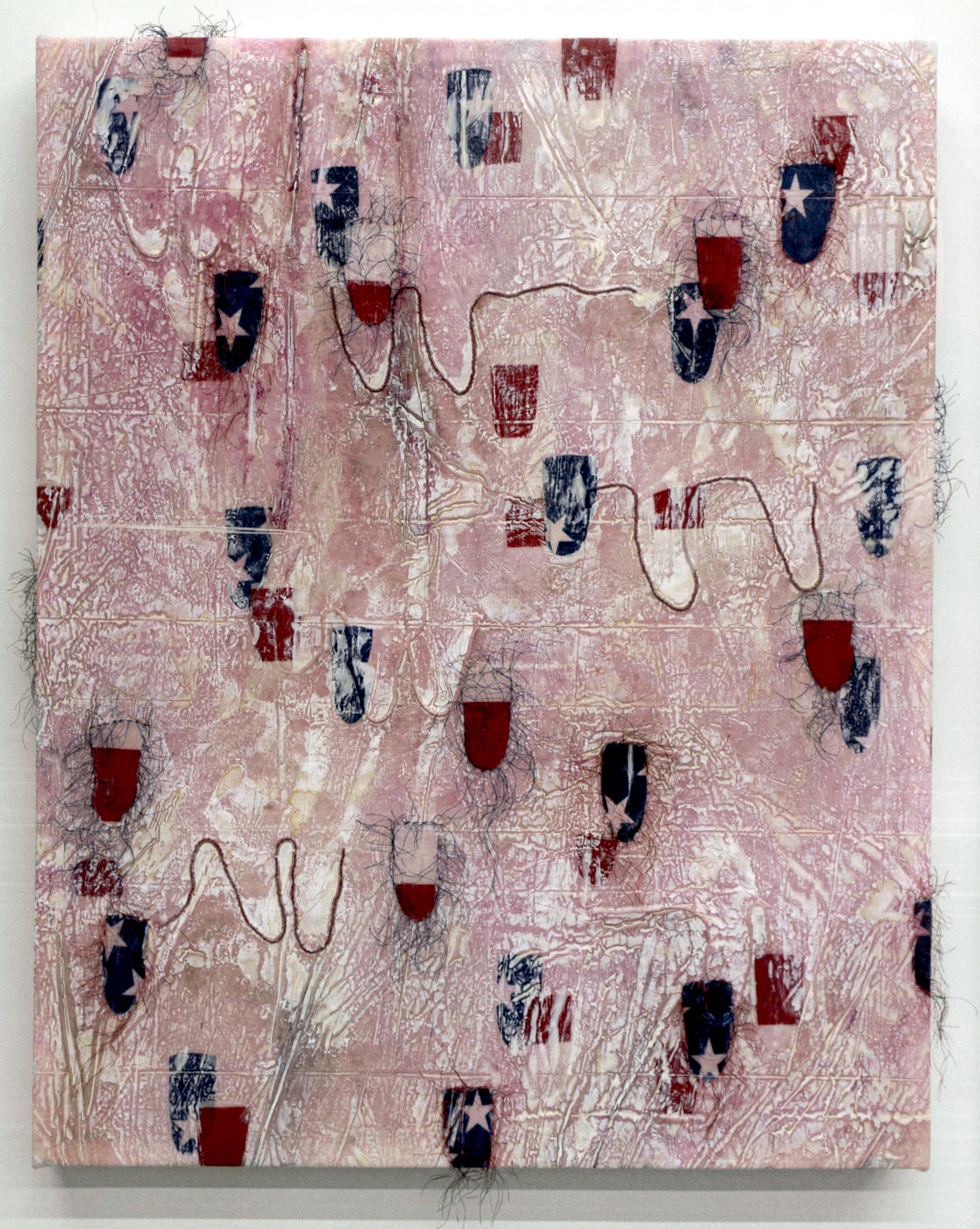

MARK

Sonya Kelliher-Combs

Edited by Julie Decker

ANCHORAGE
MUSEUM

HIRMER

ESSAYS

CONTENTS

WORKS

POEMS

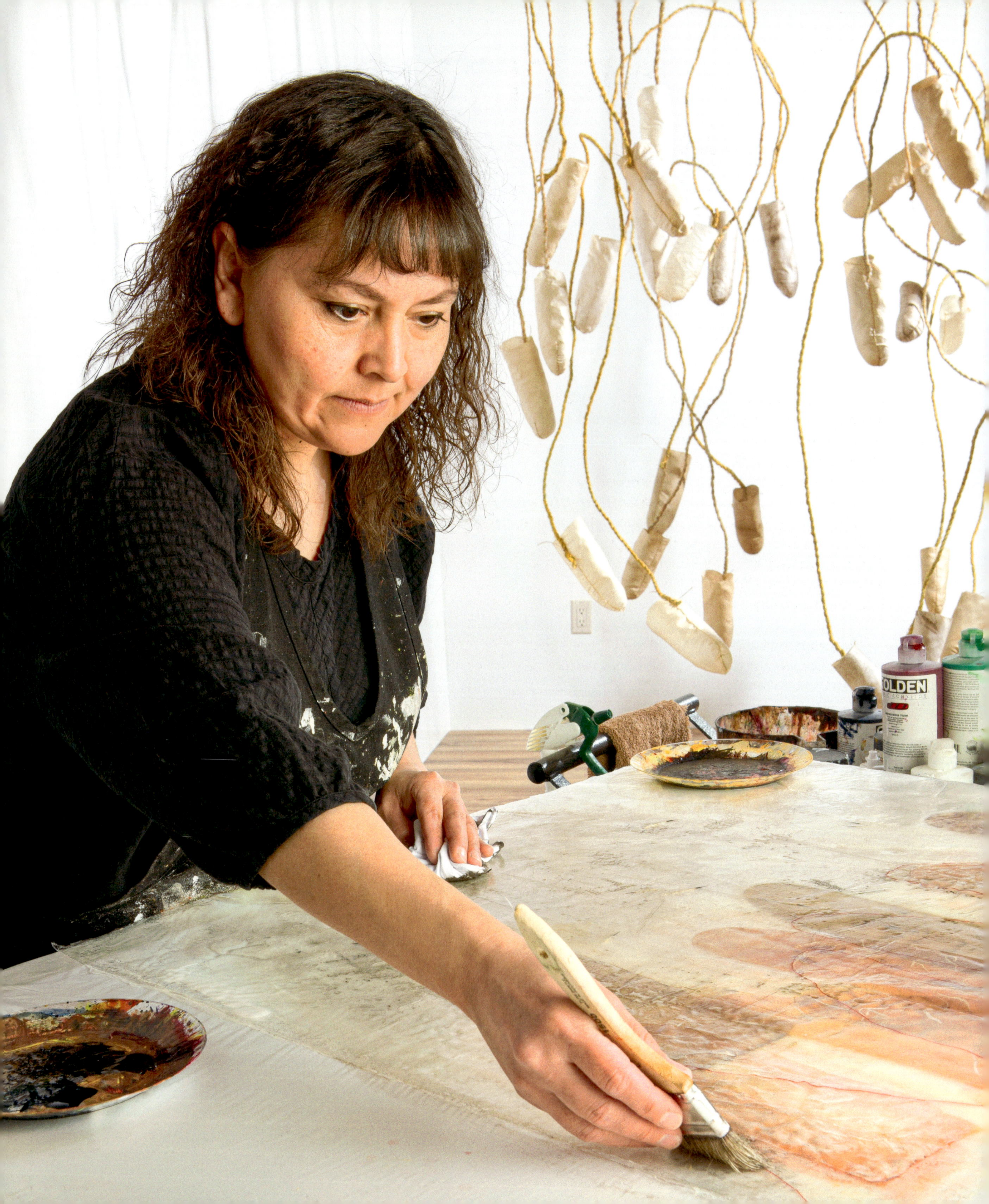
GOLDEN

ARTIST'S STATEMENT

Sonya Kelliher-Combs (Iñupiaq and Athabascan) is a mixed-media artist whose family hails from the Alaska North Slope community of Utqiaġvik and the interior village of Nulato. Her family, cultures, and relationship to the land influence all that she does. Growing up in a rural community, she observed and practiced time-honored traditional women's and collective labor—skin sewing, beading, and food preparation—that taught her to appreciate the intimacy of intergenerational knowledge and material histories. This collective knowledge deeply informs the materiality, symbolism, and structure of her artistic practice.

Through her mixed-media painting and sculpture, as well as her curation and community engagement, Kelliher-Combs offers a chronicle of the ongoing struggle for self-definition and identity in the Alaskan context. Her work's imagery and symbolism speak to history, culture, family, and the life of her people. They also speak of abuse, marginalization, and the historical and contemporary struggles of Indigenous peoples in the North and worldwide. Likewise, the materiality of her work honors the ingenuity of such ancestral practices as hide and membrane preparation while examining how materials like plastic and oil are changing the landscape. Her use of synthetic, organic, customary, and contemporary materials moves beyond the binary divisions of Western and Indigenous cultures, self and other, and man and nature to examine the interrelationships and interdependence of these concepts. Kelliher-Combs' community advocacy in turn extends these conversations beyond her individual practice. Through her curatorial work, archival research, and collaborative arts initiatives, she works to create opportunities for Indigenous artists and community members engaged in social action and customary techniques.

Kelliher-Combs is a recipient of the prestigious United States Arts Fellowship, the Joan Mitchell Fellowship, the Eiteljorg Fellowship for Native American Fine Art, and the Rasmuson Foundation Fellowship, as well as the 2005 Anchorage Mayor's Award for the Arts and 2010 Alaska Governor's Individual Artist Award. Her work is included in the collections of the IAIA Museum of Contemporary Native Arts, Whitney Museum of American Art, Denver Art Museum, British Museum, Anchorage Museum, Alaska State Museum, University of Alaska Museum of the North, Eiteljorg Museum, Smithsonian National Museum of the American Indian, and Montclair Art Museum. Her recent exhibitions include *Arctic/Amazon*, Power Plant Contemporary Art Gallery, Toronto, Canada; *Agency: Feminist Art and Power*, Museum of Sonoma County, Sonoma, CA; and *Hearts of Our People: Native Women Artists*, Minneapolis Institute of Art, Minneapolis, MN. She lives and works in Anchorage, Alaska.

ARTIST'S STATEMENT
IÑUPIAQ

Sonya Kelliher-Combs (Iñupiaġlu Athabascan-lu) supayaatigun savakłuni sanarim Ilauraaŋi iñuit Alaska North Slope-miñlu Utqiaġvigniñ suli nunamiuniñ nunaaqqimiñ Nulato-miñ. Ilauraaŋisa, iñuuniaġutaisa, suli iñuuniaġutaisa nunami nuimanaġniŋat nalunaitchuq savaaŋiñi. Iñugullaġmi nunaaqqiurami, qiñiŋagai suli piqatauŋaruq taimaŋŋaqaŋa aġnat savausiŋiññi atautchikun - miquqłutiŋ ammiñik, suŋaurriqivlutiŋ, suli niqłiuqłutiŋ - ilitchuġipkaŋagaat piqpagnaġninaglu nuimanaġniŋagli atautchikun naggutaak ilisimarapta taimaŋŋaqaŋa suli savalġutipta allaŋŋuutaat. Tamaġmiŋ ilisaŋisa ilumun sivunniqsupiaġataġaat savalġutiksraŋisigun, isummiqsupiaġataġaat suniñ naakka qanuq qiññaksraŋisigun savaaŋisa.

Supayaatigun savaaŋisa qiñiġaaliatigun miŋuliqługit suli suliat argagnik savakługu qiruk, uyaġak, naakka ammit, suli taputivlugu naligagniŋisigun, suli savaqatigivlugit nunaqqiqatiini suli qaunaginiŋisigun savalġutimi, Kelliher-Combs salapqiġaa siġġaqqutini nalunaiqsaqługu kisuutilaani suli kitkuayaagutilaani Alaska-mi. Savaaŋisa qiññaŋisa suli savaaŋisa sivuniŋisa uqausiġigait inillaaniŋaruat, iñuuniaġusit, ilauraaġiigñiq, suli qanuq iñuuniŋat iñumi. Uqausiġimmigait pimaqłuktausiq, piqatauŋiññiq, suli taputivlugit taimaŋŋa inillaŋaruat suli pagmapak siġliqqutaŋit iñuqqaat nunamigni, Irriliqsuami suli tamaan nunaqpagmi. Tainnaptauq, savaaŋisa nuimagigait sanatuniŋit taimaŋŋaqaŋa savausiŋit sivulliipta amiŋisigunlu mamiŋisigunlu niġrutit qimilġuullaisa qanuq makua plastic-gillu uqsruġruallu allaŋŋuqtittaŋat nunam qiññaŋa. Atuqługit savaamiñi nunam savaaġiŋisaŋillu, nunam savaaŋillu, suli pagmapak savalġutinik qaaŋiluaġaik avgutaak ukuak Tanŋillu Iñuqqaallu iñuuniaġusillaaŋiksa, inmiunikunlu allaunikunlu, suli iñuunikunlu nunakunlu qimilġuuġamigik qanuq akurrutigiiksilaaŋigñik suli qanuq sapurrutigiiksilaaŋigñik.

Kelliher-Combs nunaaqqiurani savaamigun sivunmuktaaġai tamakua isummatigirani uqausiġivlugit. Savaamigun naliġaivluni tutquqtuivlunilu, qimilġuivlunilu katiqsramiñik, suli ilauvluni savaqatigiigñiġni piviksritchuugai iñuqqaat sanarit suli nunaaqqiñi savaaqaqtuaq iñuuniġum allaŋŋuġniksraŋagun suli taimmaŋŋaqaŋa savalġutit atuġniŋisigun. Kelliher-Combs nanġaqtauŋaruq United States Arts Fellowship-mik, Joan Mitchell Fellowship-mik, Eiteljorg Fellowship for Native American Fine Art-mik suli Rasmuson Foundation Fellowship-mik, suli 2005 Anchorage Mayors Art Award-mik suli 2010 Alaska Governor's Individual Artist Award-mik.

ARTIST'S STATEMENT
KOYUKON ATHABASCAN

Sonya Kelliher-Combs nelo et'aanh. Iñupiaq yeł tl'eeyegge hut'aane nelaanh. Noobaaghe Utqiagvik hʉt'aan nelaanh ts'e Noolaagh Doh koonh. Ts'ʉh go beyee teyaay kkaa ts'e kko hebenenh dohudeełt'aa ts'e detlekts'e det'aanh. Ts'e go kkaayeh naalyonh ts'e dohedel'eeh ts'e eego sołten kk'o'eedeneyh ts'e eego uhdeton' ts'en' huk'uhts'en' baabe kk'o'eedeneeyh ts'en'. Ts'ʉh detlekts'e gonh yuh dehoon hebedełnekkaa kk'oheedeneeyh go nen' go hudetlaa detlekts'e bʉgh hoonaaneek. Ts'ʉh ohde hookk'aat toh eego det'aanh eego kk'o'eedeneeyh belo' hoolaanh.

Ts'ʉh eego kk'onaalyonh ts'e kk'aatoh, eego nek'edetlekts'e eego yʉgh kk'o'eedeneyh eego haash te yʉgh netsen nee'elaayh k'ełnee'elaayh ts'en'. Eego kkaayeh kk'o'eedeneeyh ts'en'. Eego yekk'o'eedeneeyh detlekts'e eego naalyonh ts'e hukkaatoh. Eego Alaska hʉt'aan nelaanh ts'e det'aanh hebeno detlekts'en'. Ts'ʉh yʉgh kk'o'eedeneeyh eego henaayh ts'en' go Alaska det'aanh tleeyegge hʉt'aan kkaa kk'aatoghe. Ts'ʉh huyego tleeyegge hʉt'aanh kkaa k'ets'e hebek'ononaadle t'aanh ts'en' ts'e eego hoozoonh ts'e hebeneełaanaa ts'en' ts'e k'uh hu eego hoodetaayh eego tleeyegge hʉt'aanh kkaa tlee k'uhts'e deheełt'aa. Ts'ʉh eego tleeyegge hʉt'aanh kkaa kk'olts'eneek ts'en' eego uhdegheelaah ts'en' eego k'ʉhneets ts'en' boho hoozoonh dehoon eego et'aałt'un' dehoon plastic yeł oil yeł aahaa eego nen' edetugh de'eełtaa'aa ts'en' doneeł. Ts'ʉh eego edaał doo' hedodeełt'aay yoogh plastic yeł gen eey yoogh nen' kkokk'e yoodoon haay dodeełt'aa'elaay et'aałdoo'tuh te hedeełt'aa. Eego Kelliher-Combs oodee koonh et'aałdoo' dehedenaayh ts'e hooghaa dodeełt'aa kk'o'eedeneyh hu ts'e eego noho kk'o'eedeneyh ts'en' huyeet'aayh. Eego kk'o'eedeneeyh ts'en' ts'e eego archives kk'o'eedeneeyh ts'en' ts'ʉh eego kk'o'eedeneeyh kkaa et'aałodeet'aa eego kk'o'eedeneeyh ts'en'.

Ts'ʉh tl'eeyegge hʉt'aan kkaa eego tlohaayeghok'aan kk'o'eedeneeyh tlogho bets'e hoolaanh ts'e kk'o'eedeneeyh ts'e haayo ts'ʉh eenegho k'e'aan nʉgh tl'eeyegge hʉt'aan kkaa detlekts'e det'aanh kkaa United States Arts Fellowship, the Joan Mitchell Fellowship, the Eiteljorg Fellowship for Native American Fine Art, and the Rasmuson Foundation Fellowship, as well as the 2005 Anchorage Mayors Arts Award and 2010 Alaska Governor's Individual Artist Award kk'o'eedeneyh ts'e hughunh. Detlekts'en eego kk'o'eedeneeyh hʉts'e haayegho k'e'aanh ts'e IAIA Museum of Contemporary Native Art, Whitney Museum of American Art, Denver Art Museum, British Royal Museum, Anchorage Museum, Alaska State Museum, University of Alaska Museum of the North, Eiteljorg Museum, Smithsonian National Museum of theAmerican Indian, and Montclair Art Museum neeheneelo. Eego kk'odeet yok'ołeneegee Arctic/Amazon, Power Plant Contemporary Art

Gallery, Toronto, Canada; Agency, Feminist Art and Power, Museum of Sonoma County, Sonoma, CA; Hearts of Our People: Native Women Artists, Minneapolis Institute of Art, Minneapolis, MN. Anchorage ledo ts'e eego Anchorage kk'o'eedeneyh.

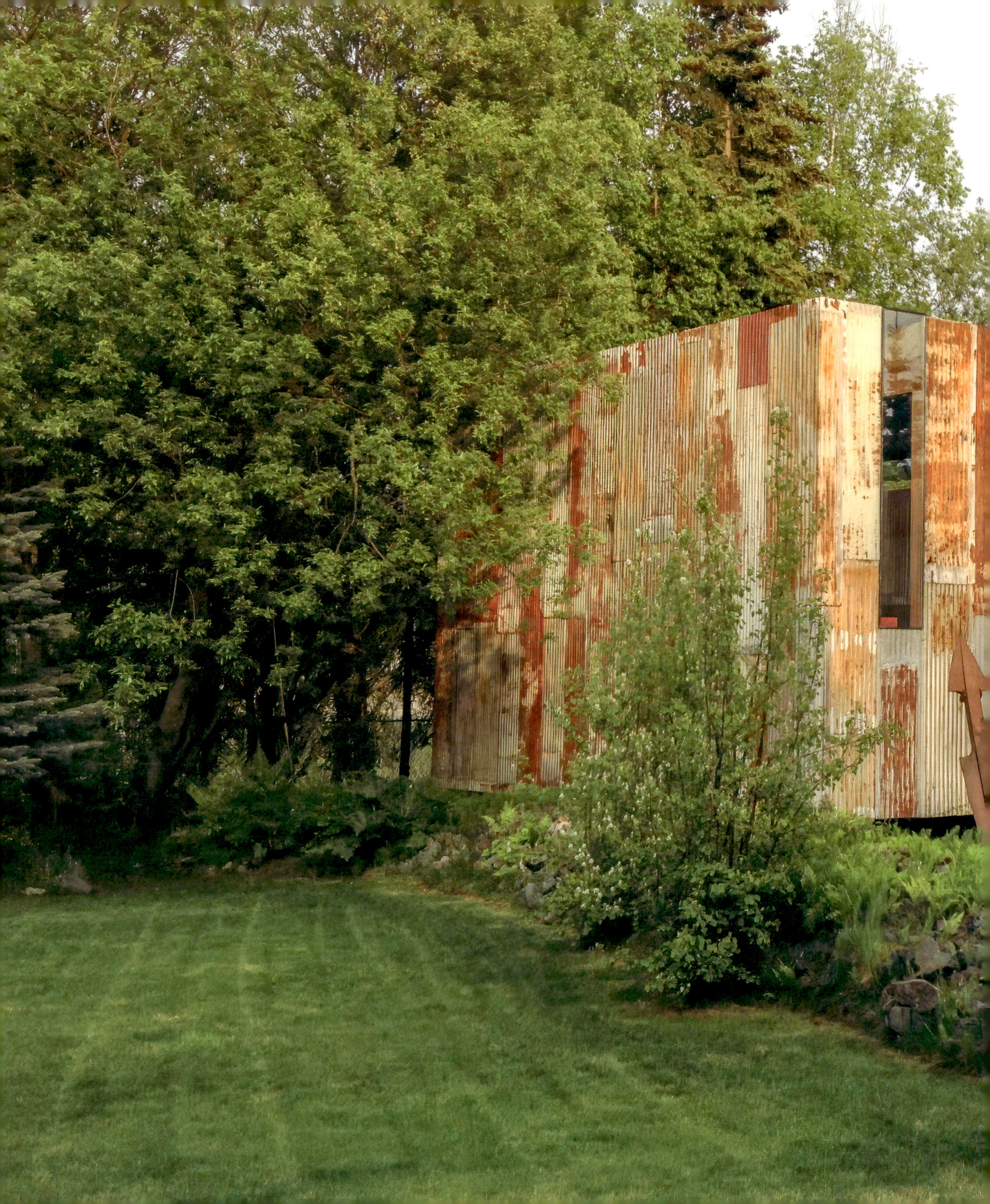

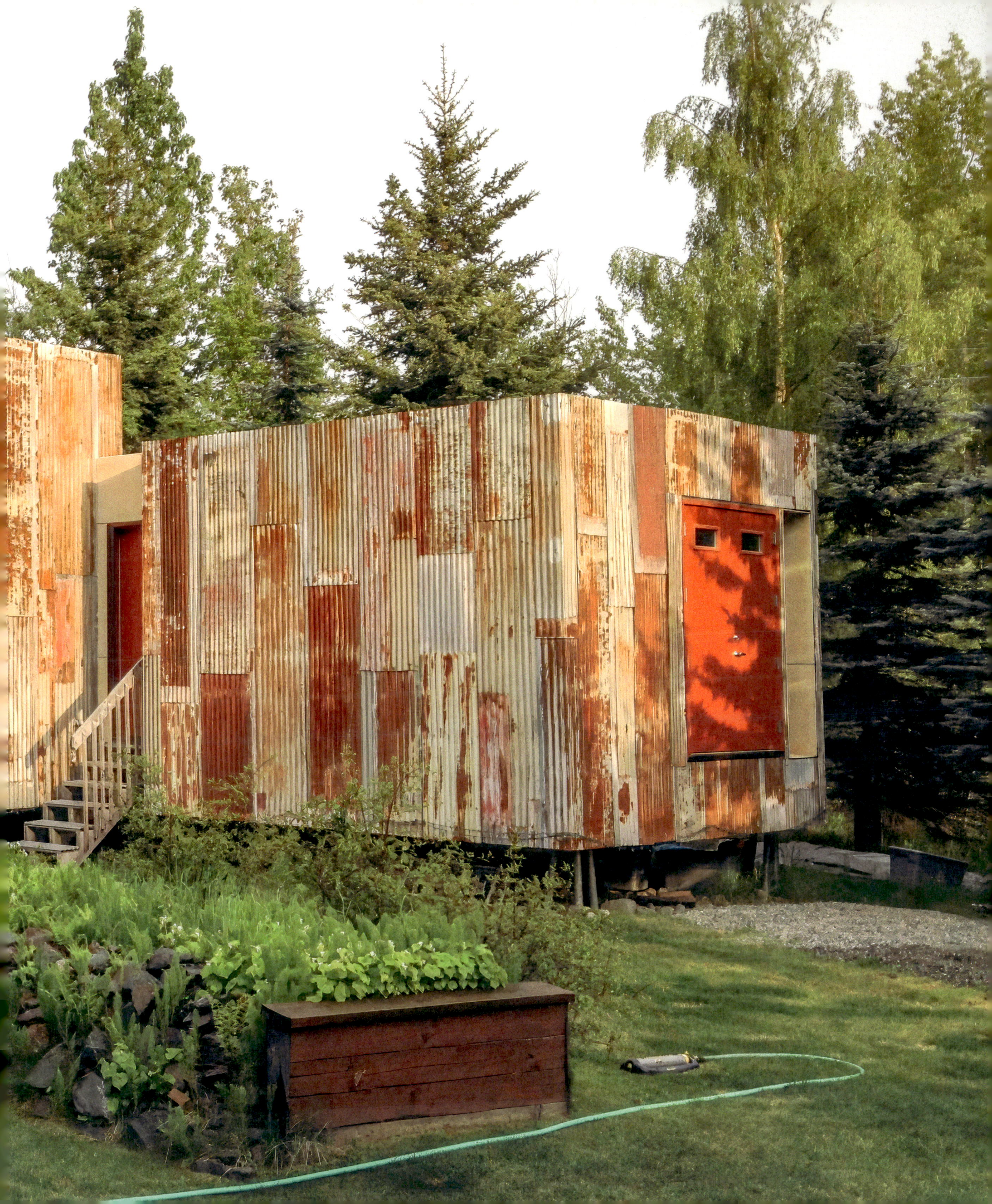

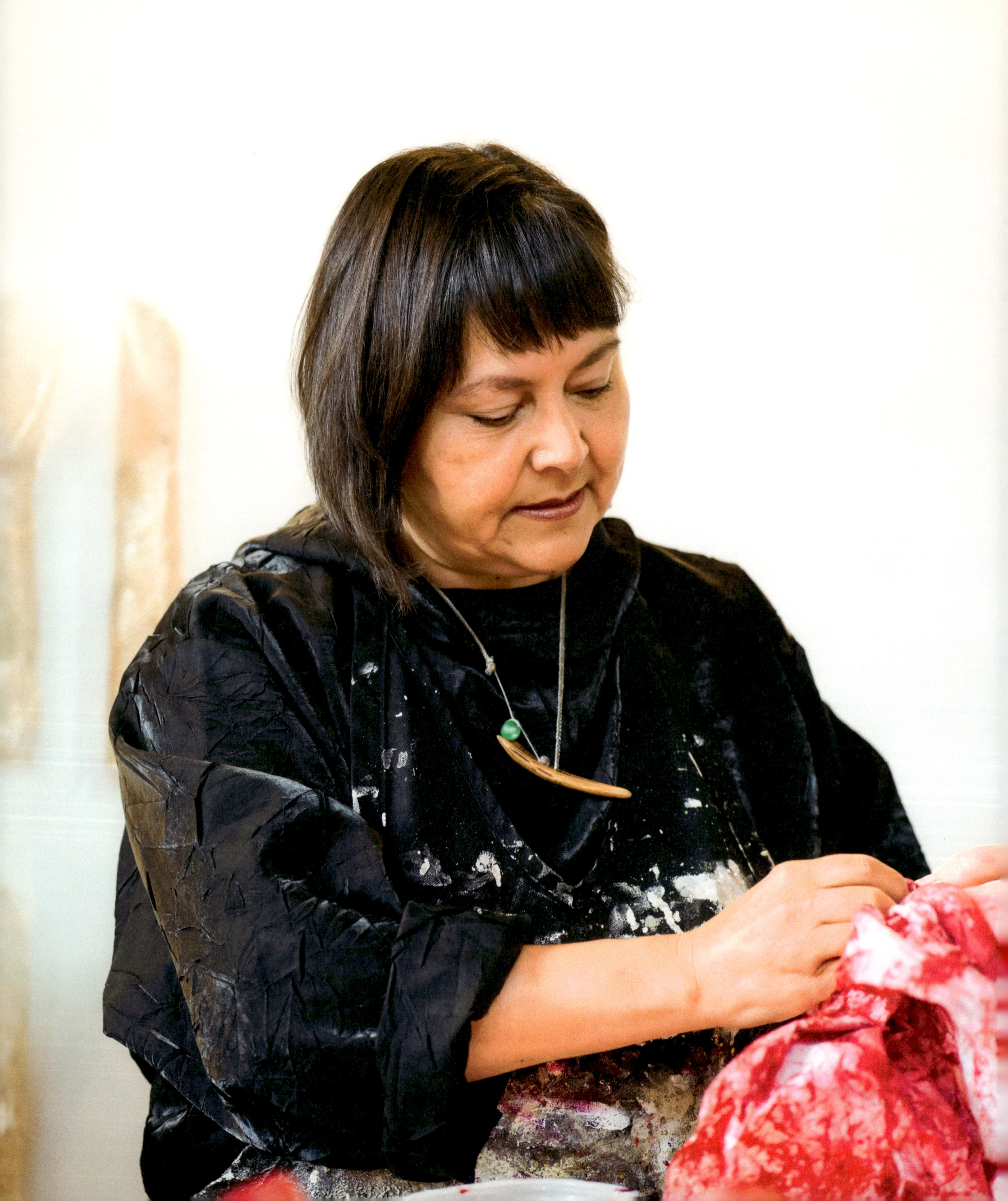

INTRODUCTION

Mark

noun	verb
a boundary land something (such as a line, notch, or fixed object) designed to record position an impression (such as a scratch, scar, or stain) made on something a distinguishing trait or quality: characteristic a symbol used for identification or indication of ownership a written or printed symbol (such as a comma or colon)	marked; marking; marks to fix or trace out the bounds or limits of to plot the course of: chart to set apart by or as if by a line or boundary to make or leave a mark on register, record characterize, distinguish signalize to take notice of: observe

Mark is the first major monograph publication on the work of Sonya Kelliher-Combs (b. 1969). Kelliher-Combs creates works embedded in cultural values and knowledge, using both synthetic and natural materials to center Indigeneity. The term "mark" speaks to Alaska, harmful colonization, and the resilience and sovereignty of Indigenous people. It references marking time, marking place, and leaving a scar on an individual or a population. Marks are dividing lines of nations and histories. A mark is the central element from which art emerges. It is not neutral territory.

Kelliher-Combs' work embodies her family, cultures, and relationship to land and sea, which provide the resources to sustain a healthy life, both spiritual and physical. Land is at the center of the work; organic materials derived from subsistence are marked by the artist. The marks are experiences, historical tragedies and traumas, lost lives, mourning, grievance, human and non-human agents, and self. Kelliher-Combs' work reflects the individual artist as maker as well as the community as a collective creator. She brings together land-based and nonnatural, narrative and abstract. She challenges Western ideologies and exposes and reflects upon the impact of setter society on Indigenous land and people.

Often inviting interventions from family and community members, Kelliher-Combs' work represents her values and truths.

Sonya Kelliher-Combs grew up in Sitŋasuaq (Nome), Alaska, and currently lives in Anchorage. She graduated cum laude from the University of Alaska Fairbanks with a Bachelor of Fine Arts in 1992, and from Arizona State University with a Master of Fine Arts in 1998.

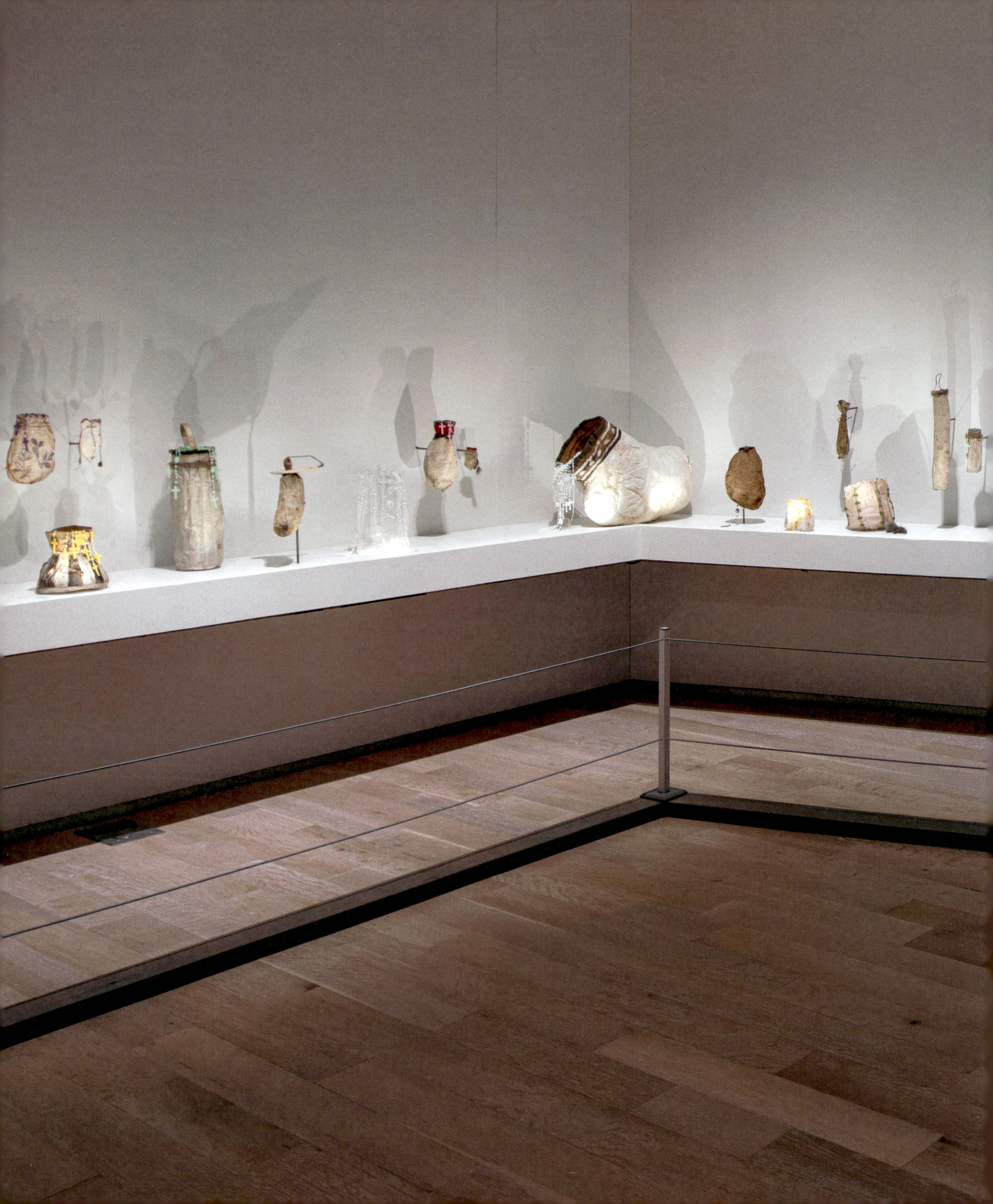

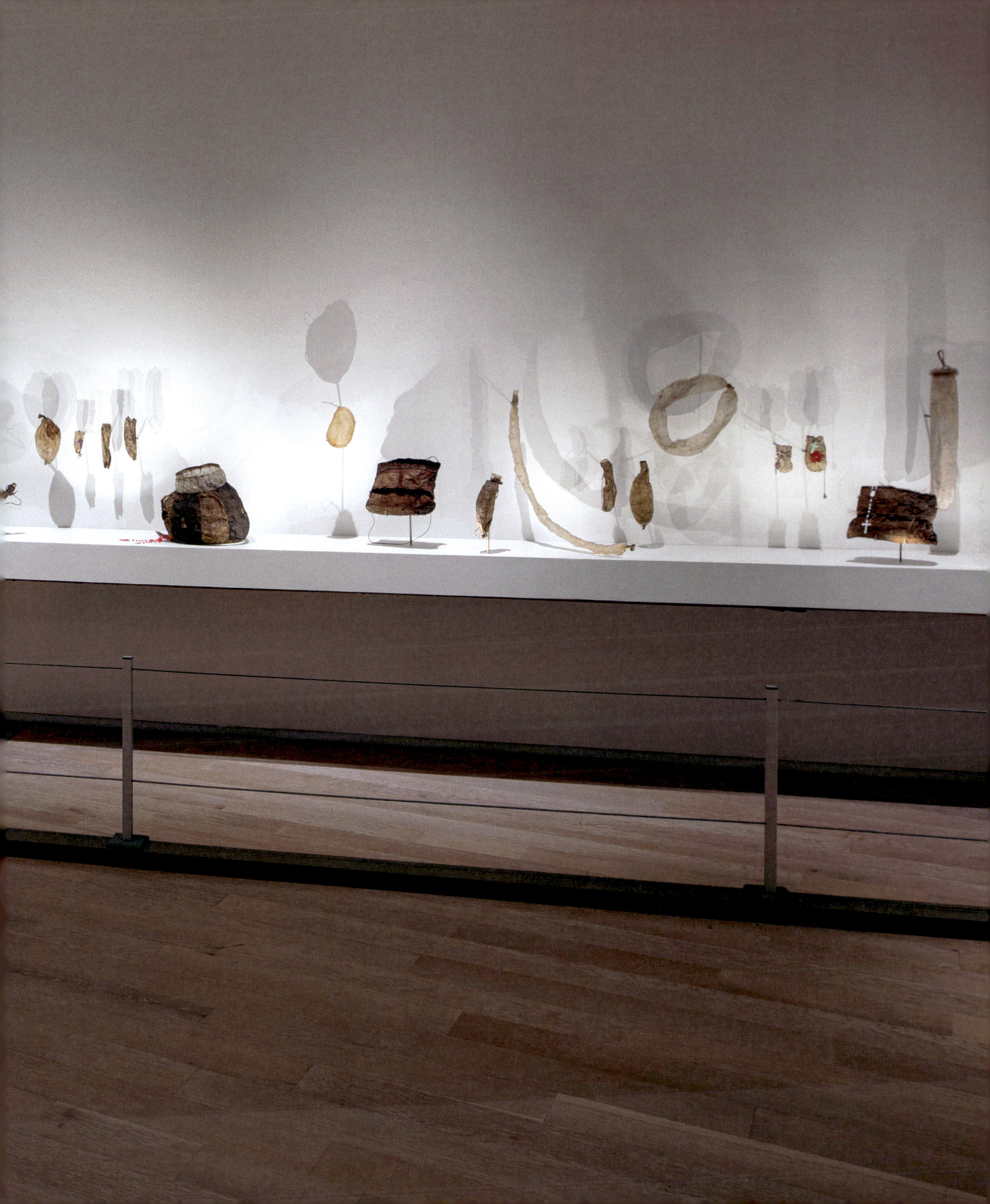

BURIED AND EXPOSED

Land in the Work of Sonya Kelliher-Combs

by Julie Decker

In a globalized world experiencing a homogenization of culture, local knowledge and perspectives have deep value for place and people. We are living through a time of war, polarization, and the dawn of artificial intelligence. The things we can see, hold, and touch are imbued with authenticity, hold meaning, and become both nostalgic and futuristic. The object: now both virtual and real.

Art has always reflected place and time; artists highlight, critique, respond, pose questions, demand answers, challenge systems, offer hope, or suggest demise. Materials for making can evoke and aid meaning. To artist Sonya Kelliher-Combs, the tactile and visual qualities of the work are visceral, born of place and person, each element chosen for its connection to land and culture, to representations of memory, of story, of what was lost and what is held.

Kelliher-Combs was raised in the Northwest Alaska community of Sitŋasuaq (Nome) and is of Iñupiaq from the North Slope of Alaska, Athabascan from Interior Alaska, German, and Irish descent. Arctic landscapes are imbued with Indigenous knowledge. Amid today's manufactured spaces, they are places of dramatic changes in migration, energy, economy, and ways of being.

Events that used to occur once in 100 years—flash floods, droughts, heat waves, coastal erosion, melting permafrost, hurricanes, bomb cyclones, polar vortices, atmospheric rivers, fires, and pandemics—are now happening annually. In Alaska, it is not about anticipating change, but about responding to it in real time. The Arctic habitat, a home and a bellwether for the future, sees ways of life in flux, as icebreakers give way to cruise ships and warships. As it warms, the land has become present again in a collective imagination, at the center of creative visions, political disputes, social speculation, scientific observation, and cultural sovereignty.

Indigenous peoples have sustained their knowledge systems for millennia, even while undergoing social and environmental upheaval. For Alaska Native people, the Circumpolar North represents a continuous habitation of place, an intimate understanding of the relationship between humans and the ecosystem, and a balance maintained with respect for nature. Use only what you need and not more. Land is pharmacy and library, sustaining. Land is identity. It is inseparable from the life and artistic practice of Kelliher-Combs. In her work, layered histories are both buried and exposed. Ties to family and tradition are strung painstakingly through the eyes of needles. Surfaces are organic and synthetic, real and imagined. The resemblance of works to skin refers to skin as a medium used to educate people about culture. It reveals, marks, categorizes. Transparency is an investigation of identity, self-definition, kinship, and nature, both revelation and material.

Kelliher-Combs began her career in art as a painter with an interest in abstract art, the animals of Alaska, the conflict between nature and man, and the formline designs of Southeastern Alaska. Later, she became interested in repetition and serialization, exploring something as many times as necessary to capture a single idea, whether it is in the form of mittens, tusks, pores, nets, or secrets. Completed works are often installed in rows and grids, highlighting the repetition and serialization of the images and the idea. The work has become difficult to classify in traditional art disciplines and Western canons, as it combines principles of painting, sculpture, drawing, sewing, installation work, and social practice. It is domestic and industrial, feminine yet fluid, organic and synthetic.

At the 2019 Venice Art Biennale, Nunavut filmmaker Zacharias Kunuk and Norman Cohn of the Isuma collective webcast footage from Igloolik in Arctic Canada to the exhibition's Canadian pavilion in Italy. The project *Silakut: Live from the Floe Edge* marked a shift. In past narratives, human experience was overlooked and exempt from its own knowledge. Isuma forces the perceived center to look North for its truth. Western European and American views seldom distinguish the different cultural spaces of the North; instead, it is one Arctic, one pole—

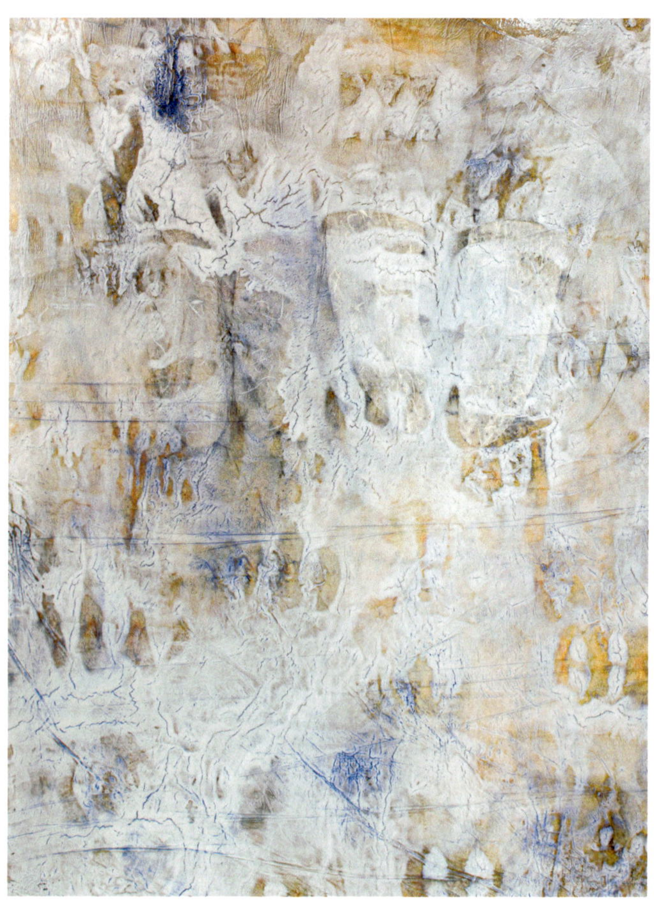

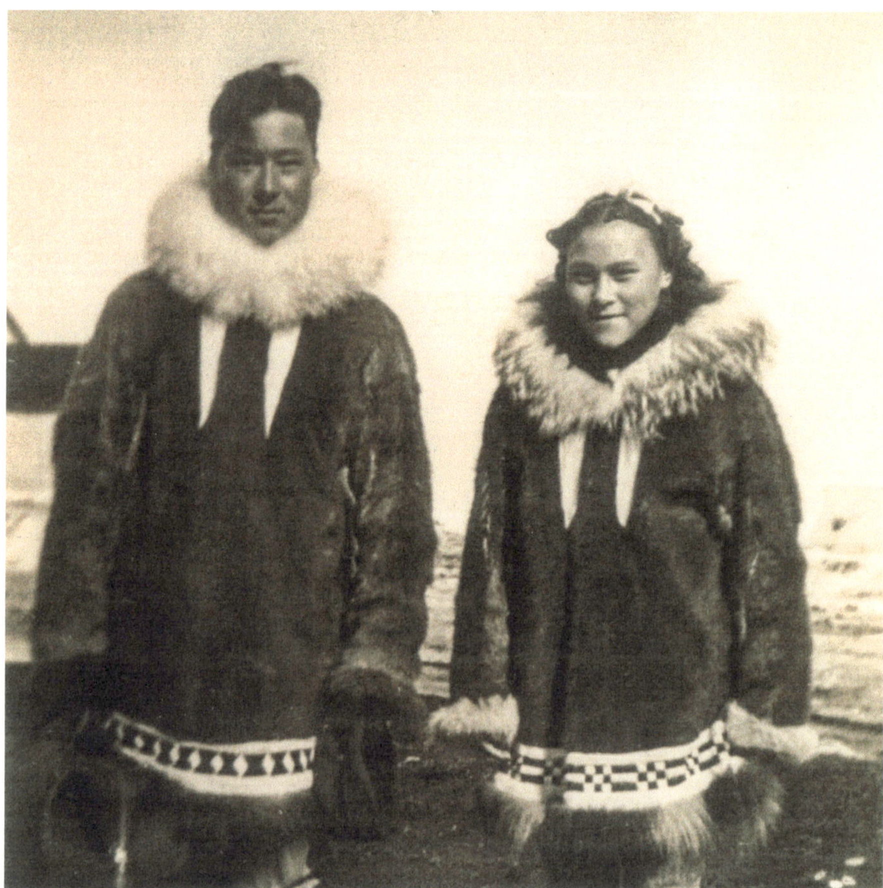

left: *Buried Walrus Family Portrait*, 2008. Paint and mixed media, 30 × 48 in. Private collection. Photograph by Kevin G. Smith.

right: Kelliher-Combs' great-uncle Harry Brower and grandmother Marry Brower Stotts, 1941. Photograph courtesy of the artist.

monolithic rather than displaying the rich, varied, and distinct qualities of each place, each people. The Western canon has left out crucial voices, materials, and depictions, substituting an uninhabited and uninhabitable Arctic—rarefied.

Through her work, Kelliher-Combs finds spaces between conflict and resolution, between generations, between art and activism. Her combination of shared iconography and personal imagery holds home and identity, subsistence and sustaining. It also points to colonization and injustice. Kelliher-Combs' work is tied, through language and values, to people and landscape in a reciprocal relationship.

With her parents and five siblings, Kelliher-Combs spent her childhood summers at an Alaskan camp, living a subsistence lifestyle of hunting and gathering. Her work comes from her lived experience and family iconography. The tusk forms reference a familial patterning and parka trim of her grandmother. Circular "pores" and pouch-like or cocoon shapes form her "secrets" and "walrus family portraits." Spiral forms are "eddies" and tally marks "tattoos."

These are metaphors. The pores suggest openings or passages; the secrets represent things that are hidden, often just beneath the surface, suggesting individual family or cultural secrets contained within the vessels. Eddies and tattoos suggest pathways, journeys, and the marking of time. While her artistic process allows each work to evolve on its own, these patterns and symbols form the beginning of each piece. Knowing which series the pieces will come from defines the genesis of each work. Within the iconography are the various dichotomies Kelliher-Combs confronts, such as the relationships between Western culture and Alaska Native culture. She says some subjects

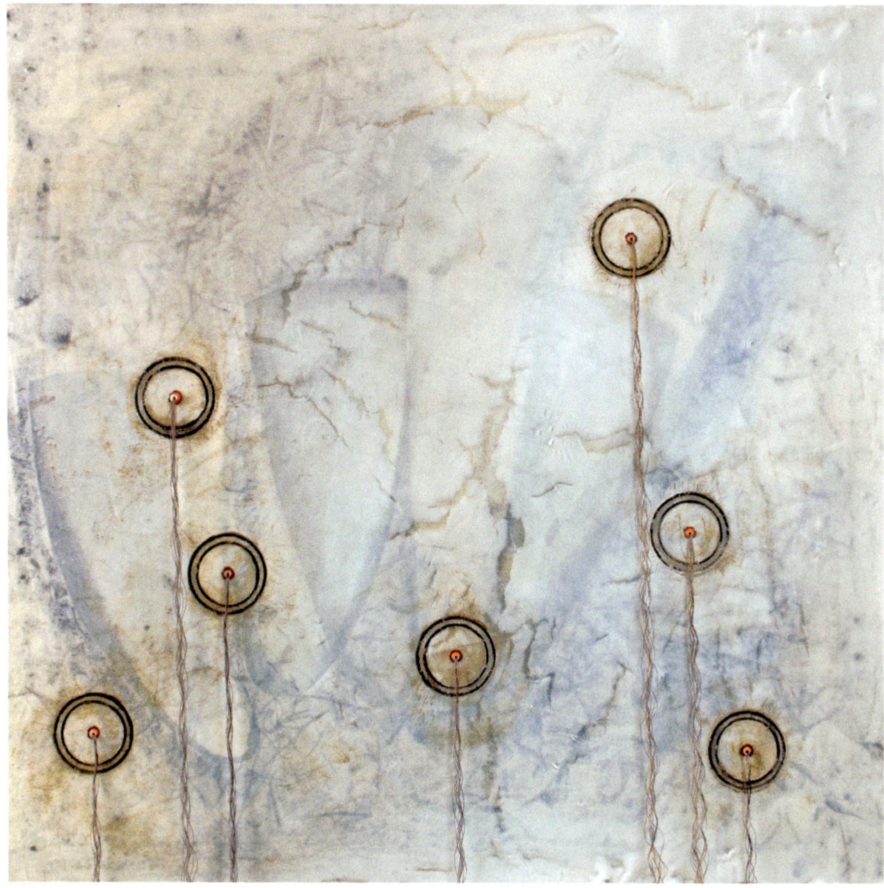

Buried Walrus Family Portrait with Brown, 2008. Paint and mixed media, 24 × 24 in. Private collection. Photograph by Kevin G. Smith.

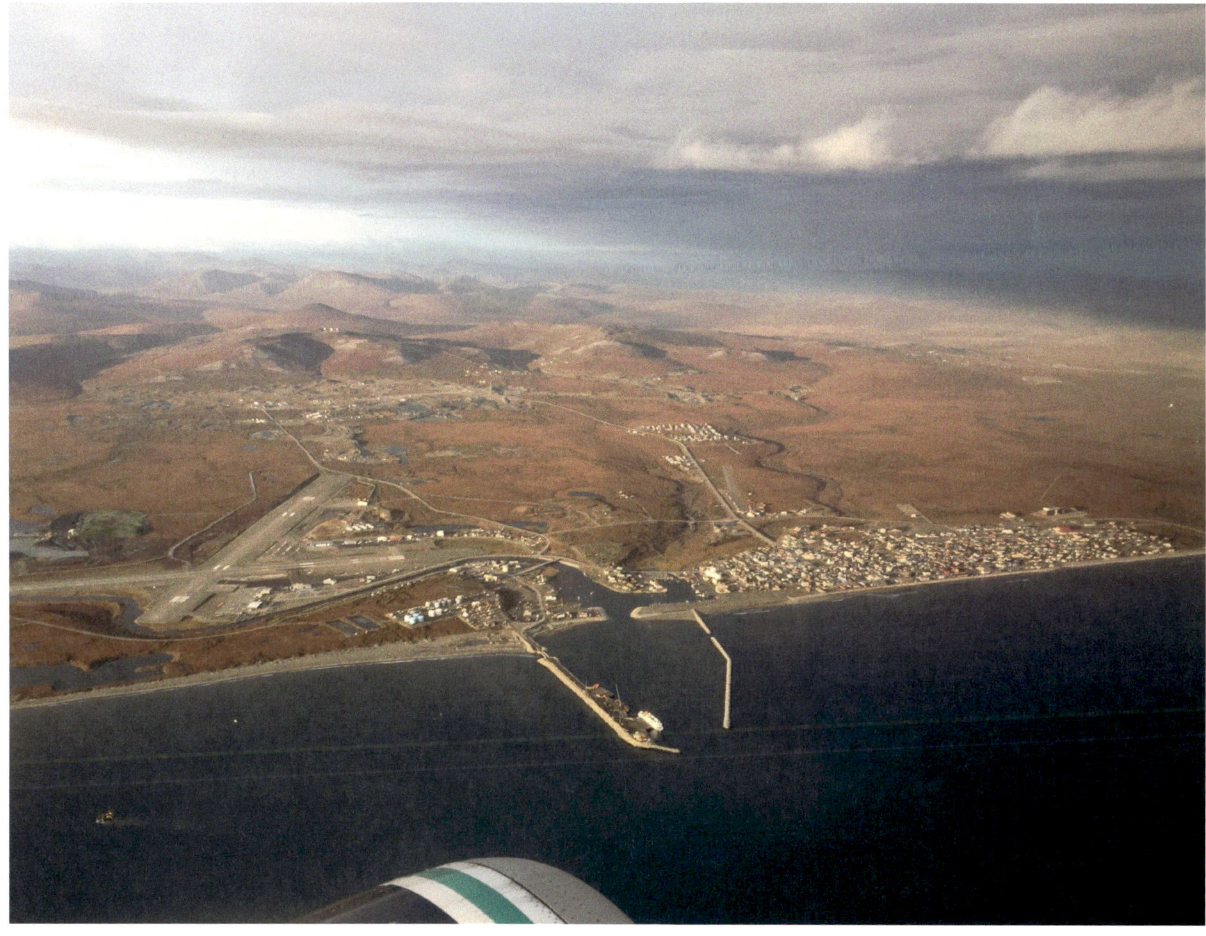

Nome, Alaska, from the air. Photograph by the artist.

need to be revealed slowly because they are so painful.

The climate and resulting cultural changes affecting lifeways in the Arctic have brought increased attention to and interest in the area, ranging across science, art, literature, geopolitics, and cultural history. Creative practitioners in Northern places move beyond nostalgia and warning bells. Local knowledge encompasses the values, understandings, skills, and philosophies developed by societies with long histories, stories, and memories of interaction with their natural surroundings. These are just as embedded in Kelliher-Combs' work as the human hair, the child's kuspuk, or the colonial map.

Kelliher-Combs uses synthetic, organic, traditional, and modern materials to examine cultural traditions. Surfaces are composed of many layers of acrylic polymer, spread flat using a rubber spatula originally intended for applying putty to the body of automobiles. Elements are added to each layer. Buried in the polymer might be thread, sheep intestine, bedsheets, undergarments, nightgowns, paper, net, fur, and walrus stomach. When the medium dries, some of these elements might then be removed, pulled, or carved from the surfaces and layers to create scar-like forms and textures. Human hair (the artist's or other family members'), sewing, and beadwork reference the history, intimacy, and repetition of "women's work," much a part of Indigenous cultures and the artist's own experience.

Pigmentation is created from acrylic paint as well as from adding nontraditional elements to the polymer, such as grass, wine, coffee, and dirt. Often each work in a series is differentiated by its color and reflected in the titles; sometimes the colors are sharp and primary, but often they are muted, lending themselves to the qualities of translucency. The resulting skin is pockmarked with circular pores, spiral eddies, and beaded loops, a surface imbued with secrets. For Kelliher-Combs, it is the nature, power, and impulse of secrets, not the content nor the material, that compels. Secrets are individual burdens. Kelliher-Combs' two- and three-dimensional secrets are lightweight, intimate, delicate, and portable, often constructed of gut and sewn together at the edges. Some are pierced through with porcupine quills, becoming less about hiding secrets than about bringing them to light. It is not about illicit exposure, but rather about observation and commonality, about revealing the universal nature and acquisition of secrets. Similarly, the personal effects buried in her work are a response to shared loss and neglect rather than a narrative of one person or experience. Other times, walrus bones and seal intestines are submerged within translucent resin, inseparable from ideas of place, sea, land.

In her series of works such as *Idiot Strings* (a term used to describe the strings that connect a pair of mittens to prevent loss), one can find a memorial to three uncles who committed suicide, but also memorials to generations affected by suicide, coaxing issues to the surface—the surface of the work and the surface of awareness—to overcome the sense of taboo associated with speaking about suicide in Indigenous cultures. Kelliher-Combs does so in a way that symbolizes sorrow and loss, in order to speak of the perseverance of her cultures and to promote healing. The idiot strings evolve into symbolic ties to the past, ties that bind, ties that offer comfort, and ties that cannot be severed.

The poise of the artist and her work is fluent. The work's messages are complex, challenging Western norms, histories, assumptions, systems, and institutions. Recent work embeds the American flag, revealed through the edges of polar bear and seal fur. Red, White, and Blue was a 2023 exhibition that included works incorporating the flag to recognize the history of a nation built on enduring foundations of marginalization and violence. Continuing the *Idiot Strings*, begun in 2005 as a project engaging friends and family to memorialize three uncles who died by suicide, Kelliher-Combs created pouches from the flag, maps, walrus stomach, sheep, reindeer hide, found bedsheets, clothing, and other raw materials. The mittens are devoid

Red Secrets, 2005. Mixed media, 42 × 72 in. Private collection. Photograph by Kevin G. Smith.

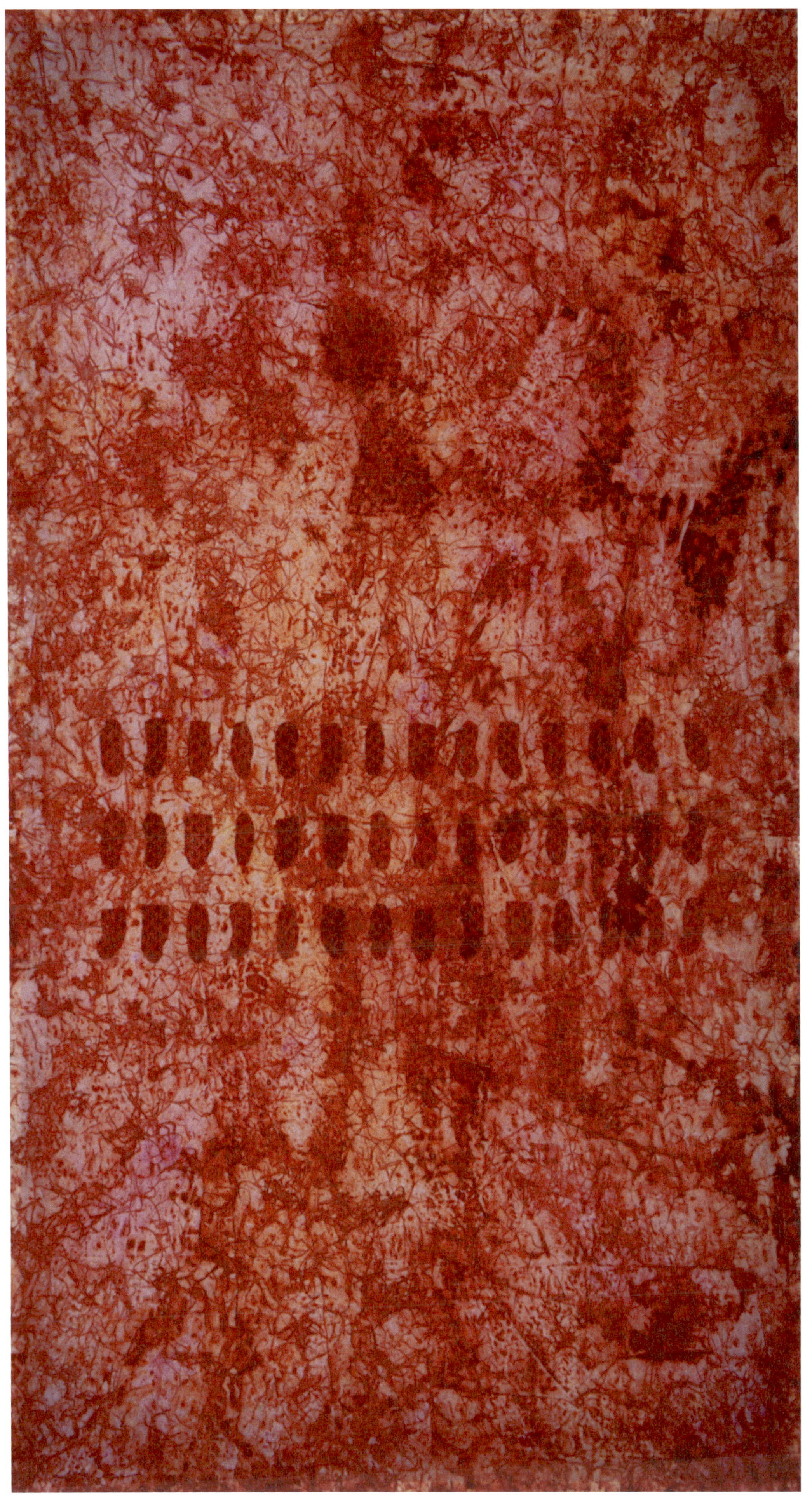

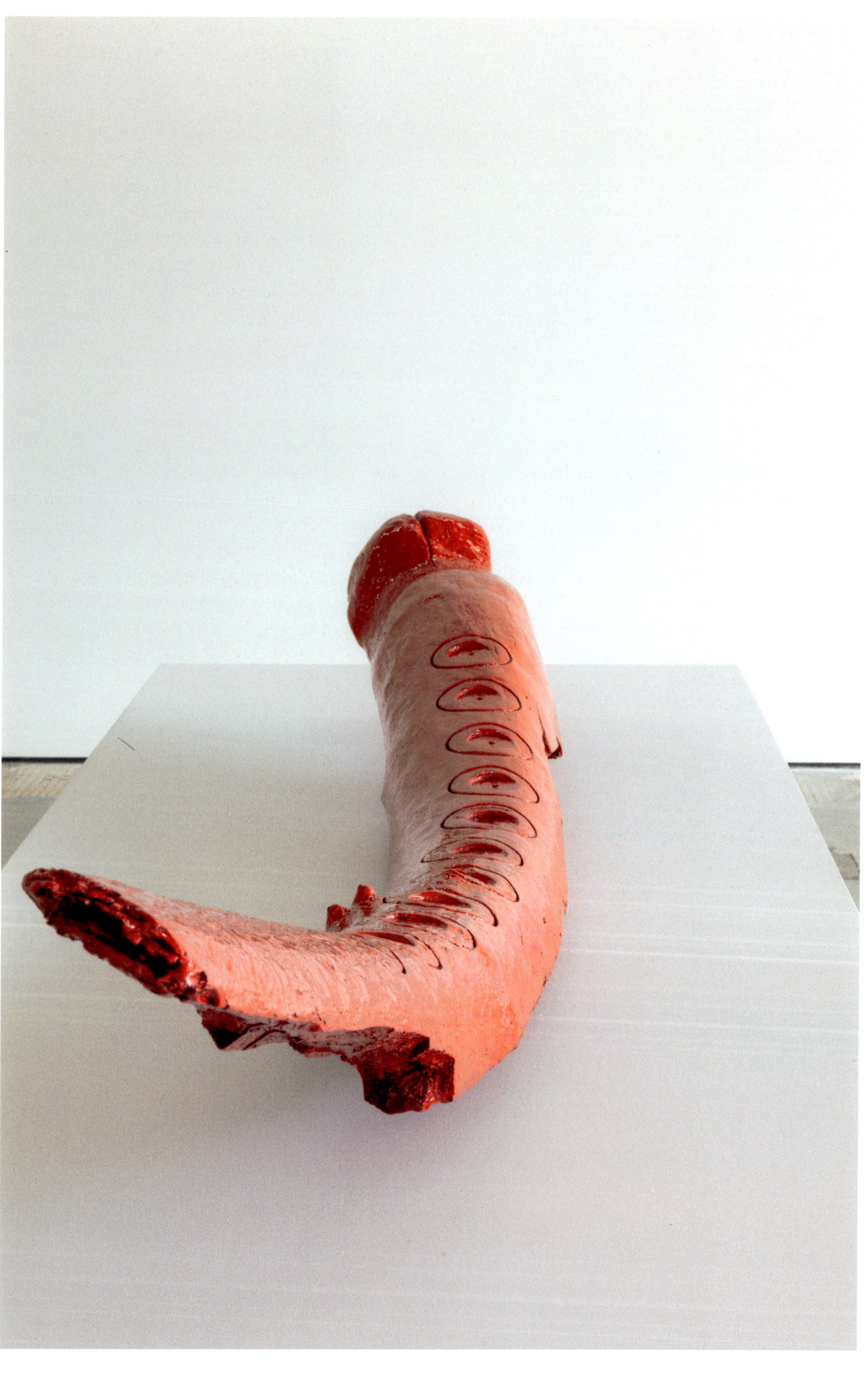

New Artifact (Red), 2023.
Found object and
auto-body paint,
16 × 103 × 15 in.
Photograph by
Kevin Todora.

of the body, sculptured in the shape and size of a collective of hands.

Kelliher-Combs' voice is one that is empowered, strong in its commentary, representative of a persistent, resilient people and culture, of lifeways that are adaptative and sustained. She pushes back against fetishized narratives and perceptions. She exposes intergenerational traumas and celebrates intergenerational knowledge and belonging.

Her work with museum collections reveals this tension. In exhibitions she has curated and designed at museums such as the Anchorage Museum and the Alaska State Museum, cultural belongings are highlighted for their materiality, technique, care, and joy. At the same time, the artist reveals the histories of colonization, of cultural belongings taken from land and people, collected, and exotified. She sees these objects as stories and memories that reveal histories of trauma and injustice. In a 2023 exhibition at STARS gallery in Los Angeles, titled *Mark*, Kelliher-Combs included her *New Artifacts* series, initiated during the 2021 lockdown, when she was collecting various objects from nearby beaches and dialoguing with artist Maureen Gruben. The work references museum and anthropology practices that appropriate Indigenous culture—and Indigenous bodies—as artifacts from a "dying people." The found objects from the beaches, made of materials such as rope and wood, had been reshaped by natural forces. Kelliher-Combs added marks and automotive paint, suggesting artifact, artifice, history, and future. She is interested in ideas of containment: "Containment is what Western cultures did to Indigenous cultures in awful ways, but containment can also reference something precious or safe." Her series about modern artifacts questions who has the power to make and define precious objects. The series has similarities to her *Remnant* works (2016–ongoing), which address what remains when the world changes rapidly.

Her *Credible* series addresses the abuse by the Catholic Church in the state of Alaska, a subject Kelliher-Combs has explored since 2007, including in exhibitions at the Anchorage Museum, Mattress Factory, Denver Art Museum, The Power Plant, Minus Space, the Alaska State Museum, and other venues. In paintings, she represents the 35 villages that have put forward credible claims of abuse "by the hand of those sent to save them." Below each work is a list of those accused. The information comes from reporting by the *Anchorage Daily News*. In her artist statement, Kelliher-Combs writes, "These are the credible claims the Church acknowledges. We all know there are many more victims all around the world who died of countless diseases—mental illness, suicide, alcoholism, and drug abuse—before this information came to light." Kelliher-Combs' work is powerful, as it addresses abuse, marginalization, and the historical and contemporary struggles of Indigenous people.

Kelliher-Combs combines her practice of painting and sculpture with jewelry-making and with social practice. Recently, *The Visceral Trilogy* explored contemporary and historical Alaska Native issues, spotlighting gut as a conduit for Indigenous voices. In exhibitions across the United States and the world, Kelliher-Combs centers Indigenous values amidst destructive settler practices, both in Alaska and beyond. Her work, in all its forms, speaks to the history, power, innovation, and dignity of Indigenous people and culture. It is a vision embedded in the landscape, born of knowledge and offering a passageway to tomorrow.

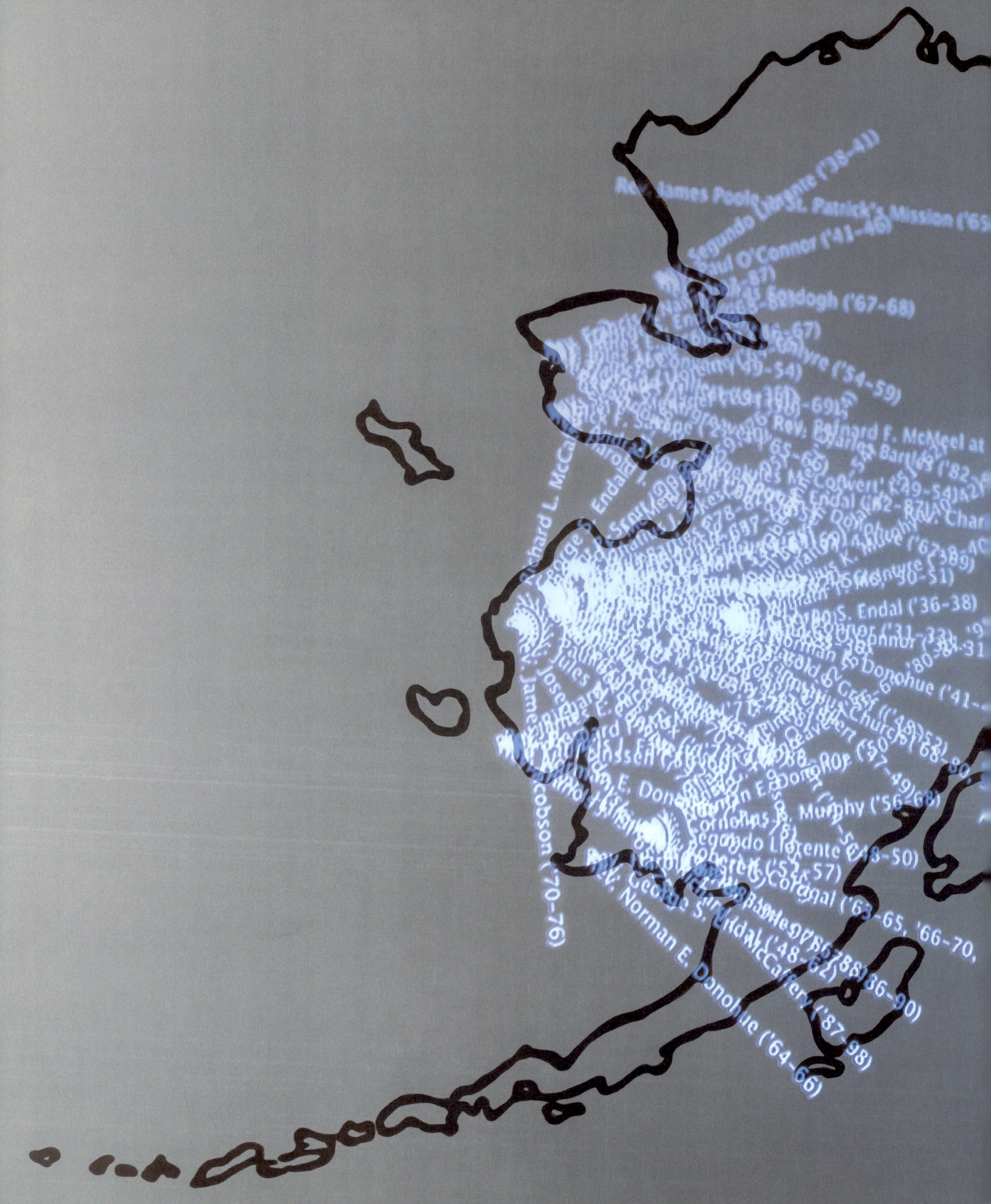

Rev. James Poole
Segundo Llorente ('38-41)
St. Patrick's Mission ('65
Paul O'Connor ('41-46)
Sourdough ('67-68)
Rev. Bernard F. McMeel at
S. Endal ('36-38)
Donohue ('41-
Murphy ('56-68)
Segundo Llorente ('48-50)
Norman E. Donohue ('64-66)
McCaffery ('87-98)
cobson ('70-76)

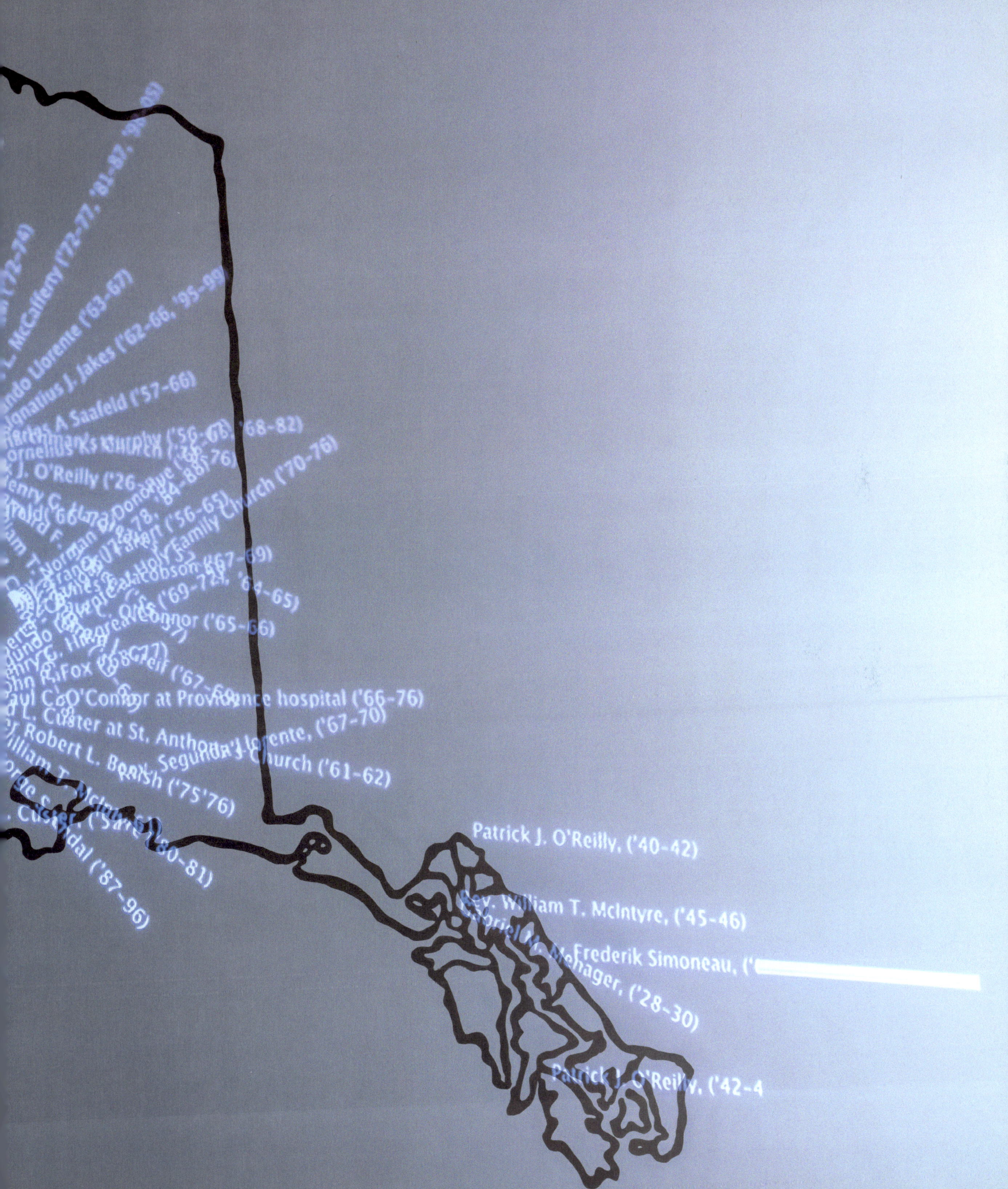

Ignatius J. Jakes ('62-66, '95-99)
Saafeld ('57-66)
J. O'Reilly ('26-
Paul C. O'Connor at Providence hospital ('66-76)
L. Custer at St. Anthony's
Robert L. Boal
Segundo J. Llorente, ('67-70)
Church ('61-62)
Parish ('75'76)
('80-81)
('87-96)
Patrick J. O'Reilly, ('40-42)
Rev. William T. McIntyre, ('45-46)
Frederik Simoneau, ('
('28-30)
Patrick J. O'Reilly, ('42-4

PERSEVERANCE, CONTINUITY, INGENUITY

Sonya Kelliher-Combs' Community-Centered Practice

by Heather Igloliorte

Sonya Kelliher-Combs is an internationally celebrated artist whose career spans over thirty years and whose work has been widely exhibited across North America and Europe. Yet while her work is deeply admired and appreciated in global contemporary art spaces, her artistic practice has always been not only grounded in, but focused on, the communities and network of relations found throughout the lands and waters now known as Alaska. This becomes evident as you examine her oeuvre, from her earliest works right up to the present, and will undoubtedly continue into the future. Despite working across various natural and synthetic media on fluctuating scales and on wide-ranging topics, her works all share a common, careful attention to her kin: her ancestors, relations, family, and forthcoming generations; what they've passed down, shared, survived, and revived; and how to protect, respect, honor, learn from, and reciprocate the gifts they have provided.

Whether she is making art alone, in collaboration with other artists, or with a small constellation of community co-creators that include her family, friends, and relatives, Kelliher-Combs is always working in relation. Either sitting around a kitchen table and working on a sewing project, preparing walrus gut with youth and elders on the heritage center floors, or crafting a tiny, delicate container to hold a fading memory or whispered secret, Kelliher-Combs imbues her works with her deep connections to and care for the people and places that have long supported and informed her practice. Her many series of works constitute little communities of similar forms—mittens, pouches, vessels—replicating the close-knit networks of kinship that exist throughout the North but also signaling those we've lost. In contemporary art settings, her works may seem ambiguous at times, their meanings either open to subjective interpretations or deliberately obscured and hidden from gallery-going audiences in the South; yet to Northerners, her connection to the land and its people is apparent in all her works. As an Iñupiaq and Athabascan woman who was raised in the community of Nome and who now makes Anchorage her home, whether she is making reference to customary clothing practices, the "idiot strings" on mittens, or using carefully harvested porcupine quills to pierce the surface of her hollow-formed "guarded secrets," she is always working from and for community.

Her works thus share the common concerns about her people and their land, sky, and waters, and the deep knowledge passed down through millennia about how to live from and coexist with her environment. As Kelliher-Combs recently explained in an artist statement, what she learned from that upbringing in the lands now known as Alaska is that she was taught that the land provides:

> "We have unspoken truths: honor all that you harvest; respect the natural world that provides for you, your family and community; take care of one another; and do not take more than you need. Nothing is more beautiful than growing up on the land, harvesting with your family and understanding that you are a part of this place."

These guiding principles around how to be in good relation with land and kin define her entire practice. While this may seem like a radical strategy in the international art world, which has long been founded on individualism and Western ideas of the solitary genius, what makes Kelliher-Combs such a remarkable artist is that she is able to infiltrate those art world spaces by refusing to leave her community at the door. For millennia, Indigenous peoples' existence has been predicated on collaboration and working together for the greater good. From whale hunts to sewing circles, many hands are needed to accomplish great things. Her work is a continuity of this long-held way of being in community.

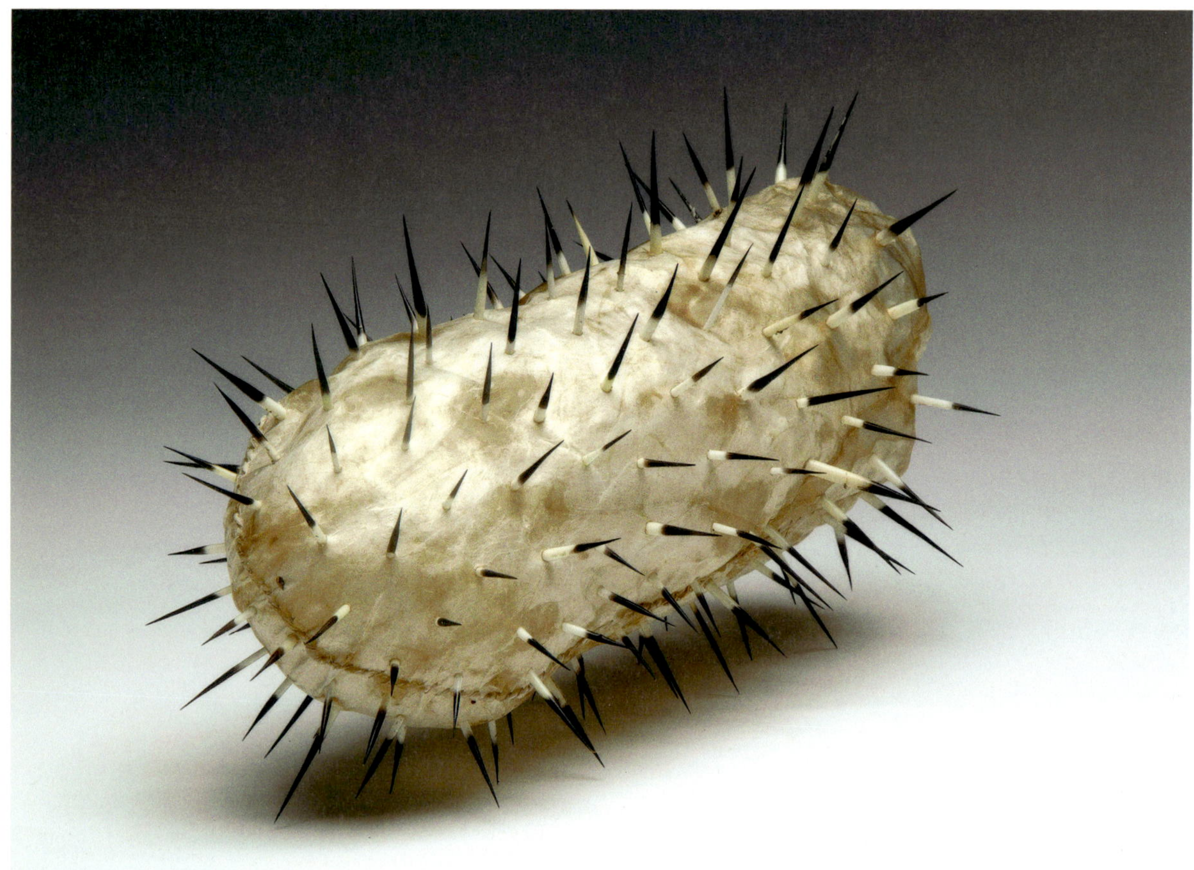

Guarded Secrets, 2004. Walrus stomach, porcupine quills, archival ink, nylon thread, dimensions variable. Collection of the Museum of the North, University of Alaska Fairbanks. Photograph by Kevin G. Smith.

Investing care in her community also means addressing the historical and ongoing traumas that continue to cause harm. Many of Kelliher-Combs' artworks—from early in her career to the present day—act as a voice for the voiceless and silenced. She has fearlessly taken aim at the abuses wrought upon her people by Church and State. While celebrating her Alaska Native continuity, she also grapples with their pain in equal measure—the trauma caused by the intertwined legacies of colonialism and evangelization, from boarding schools and churches, and conflict, famine, abuse, and loss. As such, she has created many artworks that deal with her community confronting hard truths and mourning, hurting, recovering, and healing. The stories, secrets, and hurts shared about the shameful behavior of those who abused their power in Northern communities are made raw and tangible in Kelliher-Combs' thorny manifestations in the *Small Secrets* and *Guarded Secrets* series, among many other of her ongoing works.

Furthermore, Kelliher-Combs' decades-long social practice in the art world does not just include art-making, but also curating exhibitions, organizing events, making connections across international borders, and creating opportunities and spaces for dialogue and exchange between artists and community members. This has extended to the creation of a series of curated conversations featuring Indigenous artists, scholars, curators, and community members. Organized through the Anchorage Museum's *Polar Lab* series, Kelliher-Combs invited a diverse and provocative international selection of speakers to engage in dialogue and exchange ideas with one another both onstage and online, disseminated through YouTube, building community between Alaska Natives and the international Indigenous art world

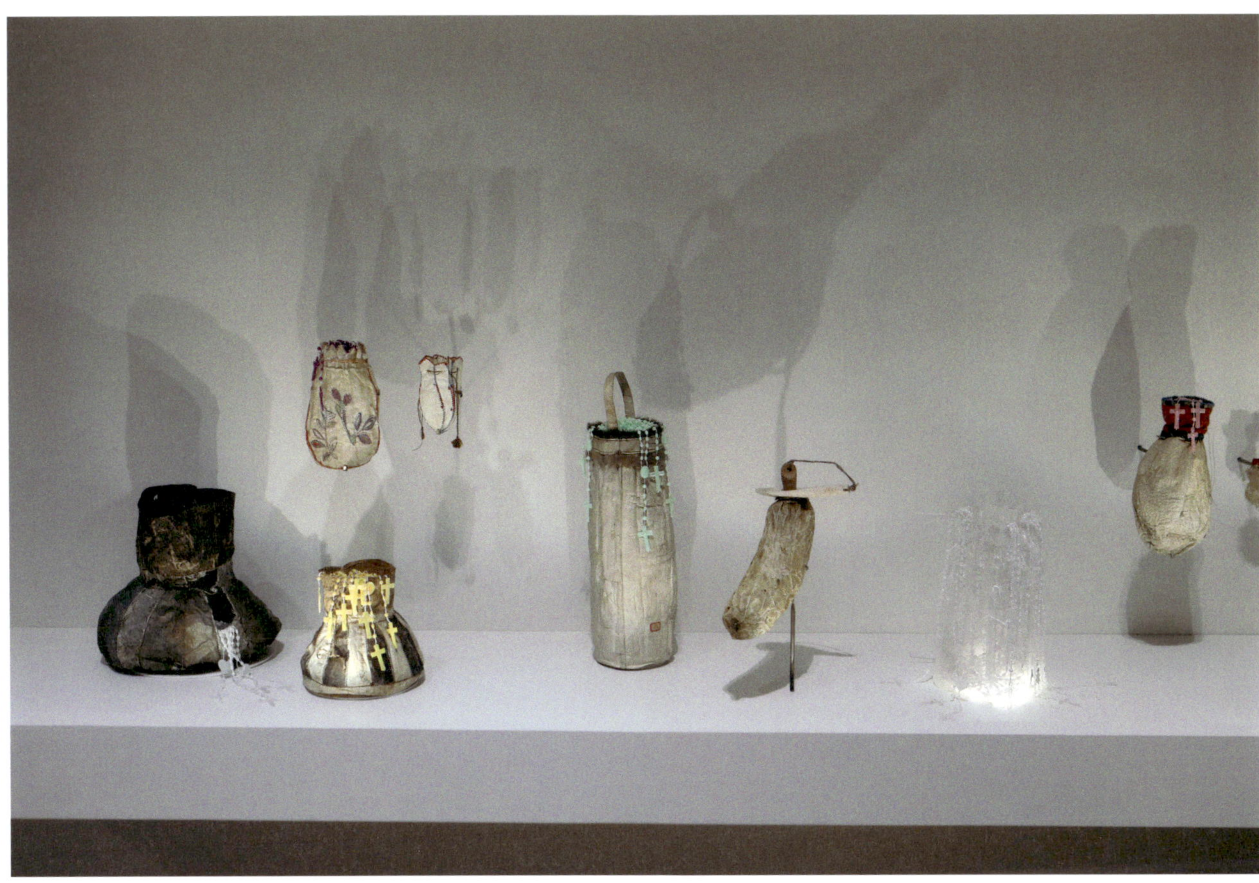

Visceral Verity installation at the Alaska State Museum, 2023. Photograph by Brian Wallace.

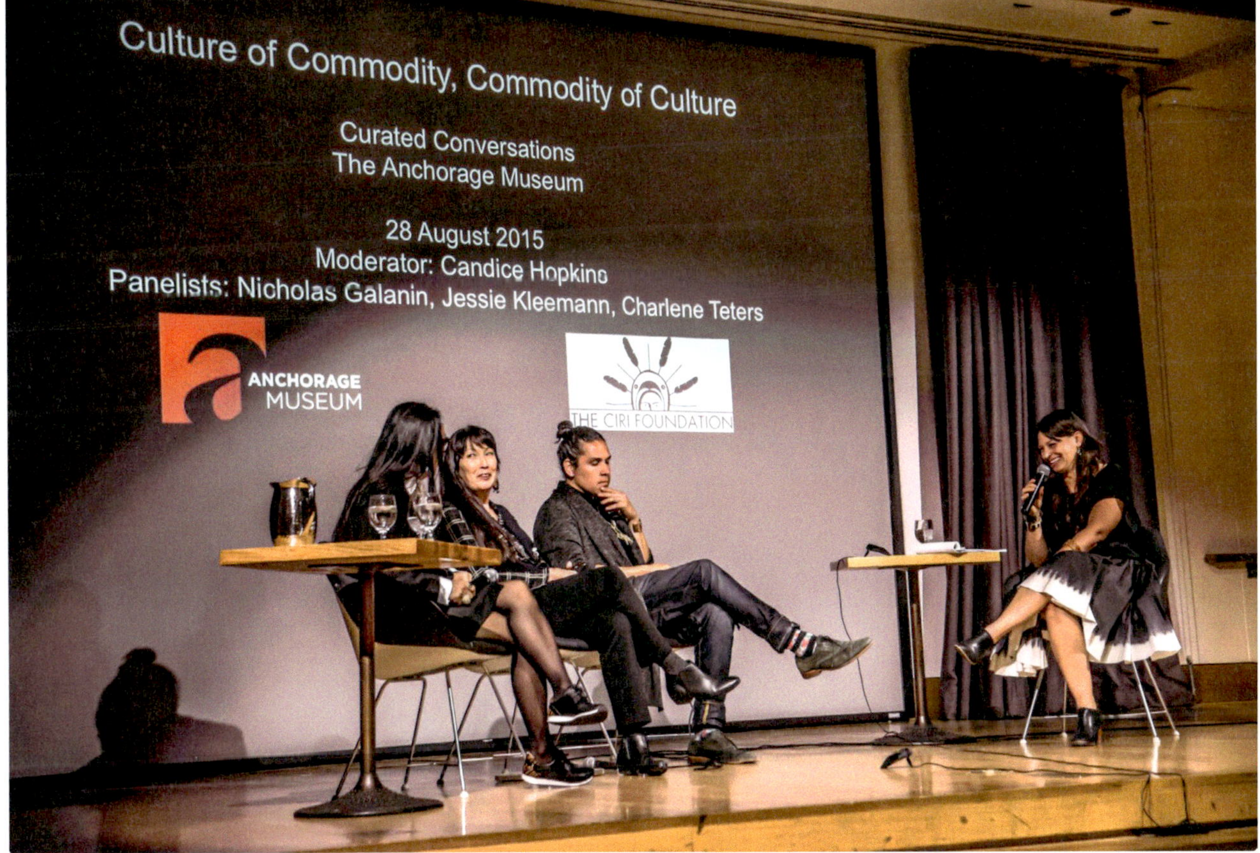

Curated Conversation, Culture of Commodity / Commodity of Culture, Anchorage Museum, 2016. Photograph courtesy of the Anchorage Museum.

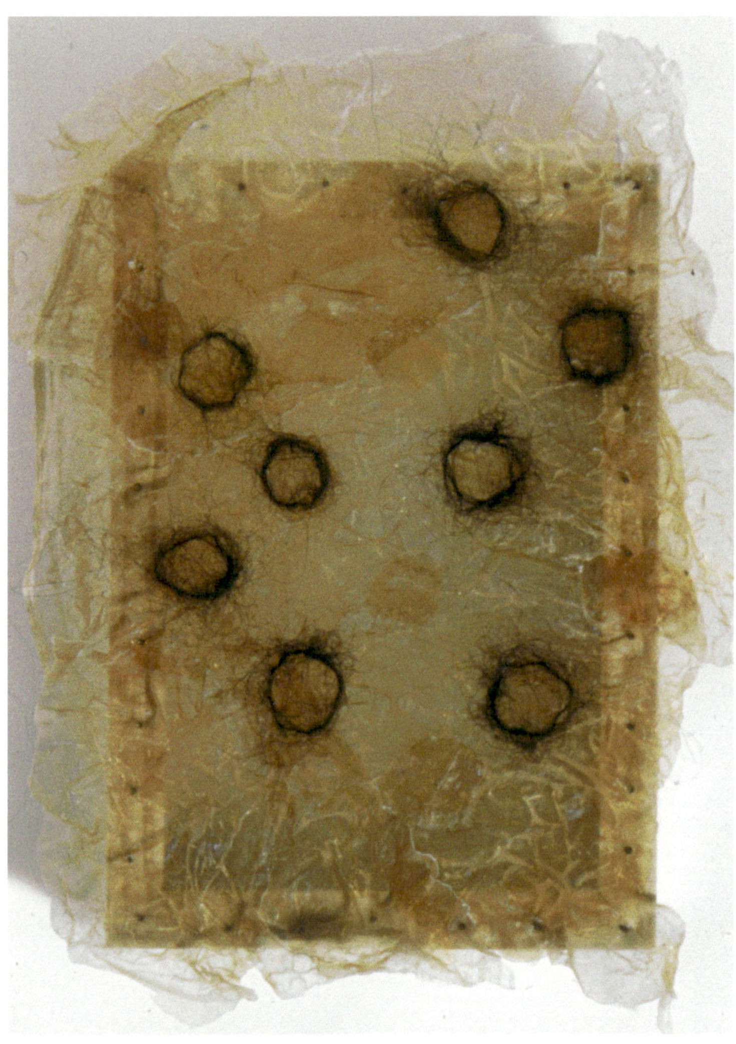

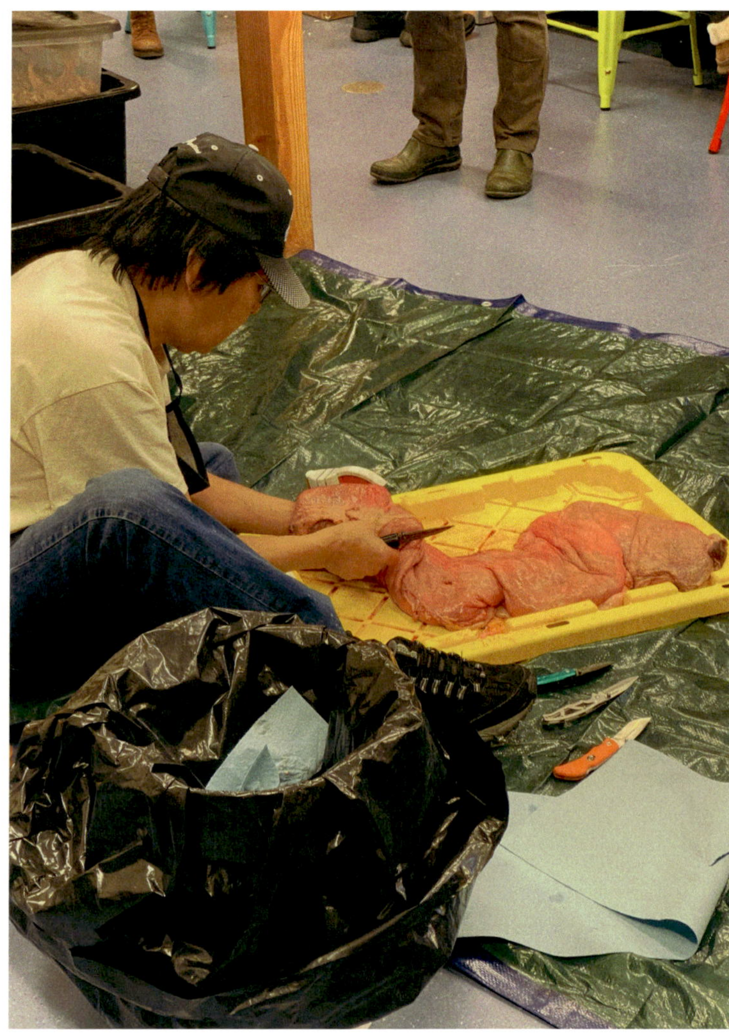

left: *Walrus Stomach Pore,* 2005. Painting and mixed media, 8 × 11 in. Private collection. Photograph by the artist.

right: Eugene Tiulana, master artist, conducts a walrus stomach processing workshop. Photograph by the artist.

across nations and knowledges, disciplines, and geographical divides. Similarly, in a forthcoming exhibition highlighting circumpolar Indigenous women's responses to climate change, Kelliher-Combs brings together a community of concerned artists, united in their concern to foster first peoples' authorship and voice, create increased community participation, express their concerns for the environment, and empower Indigenous women artists both through and beyond the physical exhibition.

Sonya Kelliher-Combs' social practice has recently culminated in an ambitious initiative centered on celebrating, appreciating, and preserving her peoples' extensive knowledge of working with gut. Gut, when cleaned and prepared for sewing, is an ingenious technology, a lightweight, waterproof, and watertight material that can be used to make a wide variety of clothing and other useful creations. For the exhibition she created, *Visceral: Verity, Legacy, Identity* (2023) held at the Alaska State Museum, Kelliher-Combs, in collaboration with Alaska State Museum conservator Ellen Carrlee, selected a vast array of gut items to be installed in a massive exhibition uniting the translucent works in a conceptual installation. Subtitled *Alaska Native Gut Knowledge and Perseverance*, the pair dug deep into the collections to find examples of gut works from each region, and then paired these installations with contemporary gut objects. These pairings of historical

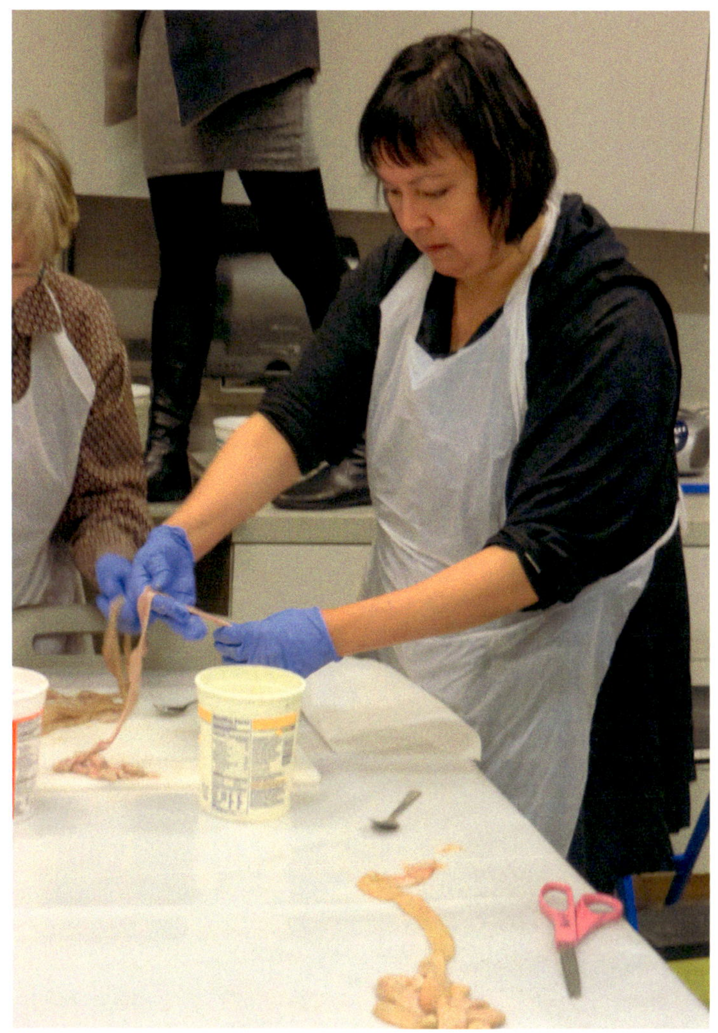

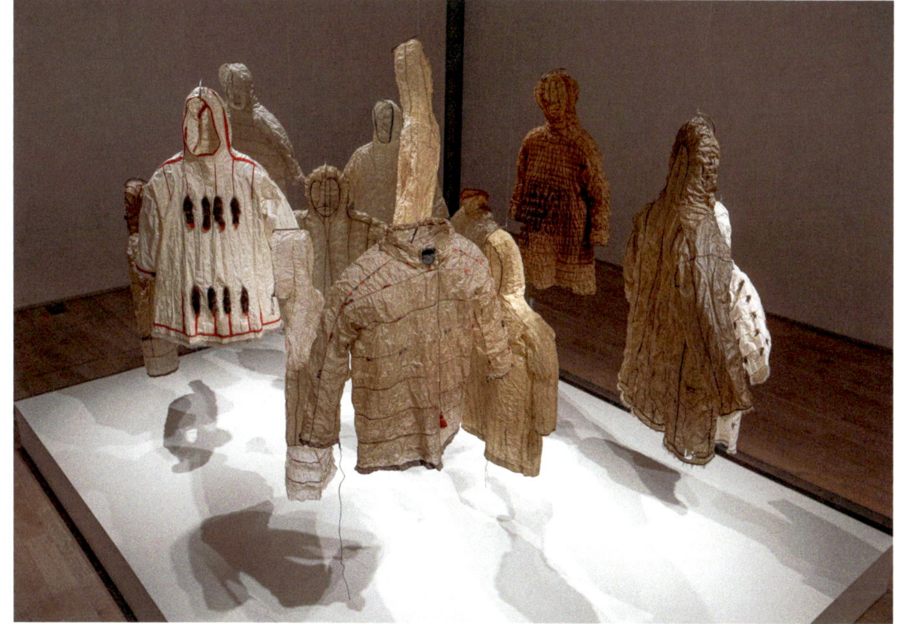

Legacy: Transcend, an installation of cultural belongings from the Alaska State Museum collection as part of the *Visceral: Verity Legacy Identity* exhibition, 2023. Image courtesy of the Alaska State Museum.

Sonya Kelliher-Combs participating in Smithsonian Arctic Studies Center *Material Traditions: Sewing Gut* Workshop, 2015 at the Anchorage Museum. Photograph courtesy of the Arctic Studies Center.

items and her contemporary artworks were strategically installed to communicate to visitors the theme of perseverance, making symbolic connections that highlight cultural continuity despite concerted colonial and evangelical efforts to oppress Indigenous peoples.

Making these historical collections accessible was a key feature of *Visceral*, which speaks to the ethos of Kelliher-Combs' social practice writ large. For the *Visceral* trilogy, the Alaska State Museum and Kelliher-Combs received a grant to reconstitute some of the parkas for the exhibition, so that works that had never been able to be exhibited before, due to their condition, could be reawakened and thus shared with her people. The tremendous amount of care and thought put into *Visceral* extends even beyond the exhibition, as Kelliher-Combs continues to further knowledge once threatened around the preservation of this practice, by creating new and ongoing opportunities for Alaska Natives to learn how to prepare gut for use. She has noted that the skills and understanding, both material and immaterial, are profound. This work, like all her works in some way, forms an homage to her ancestors, an expression of gratitude and respect for their knowledge. It is their perseverance and ingenuity over millennia that provided for her community's existence today.

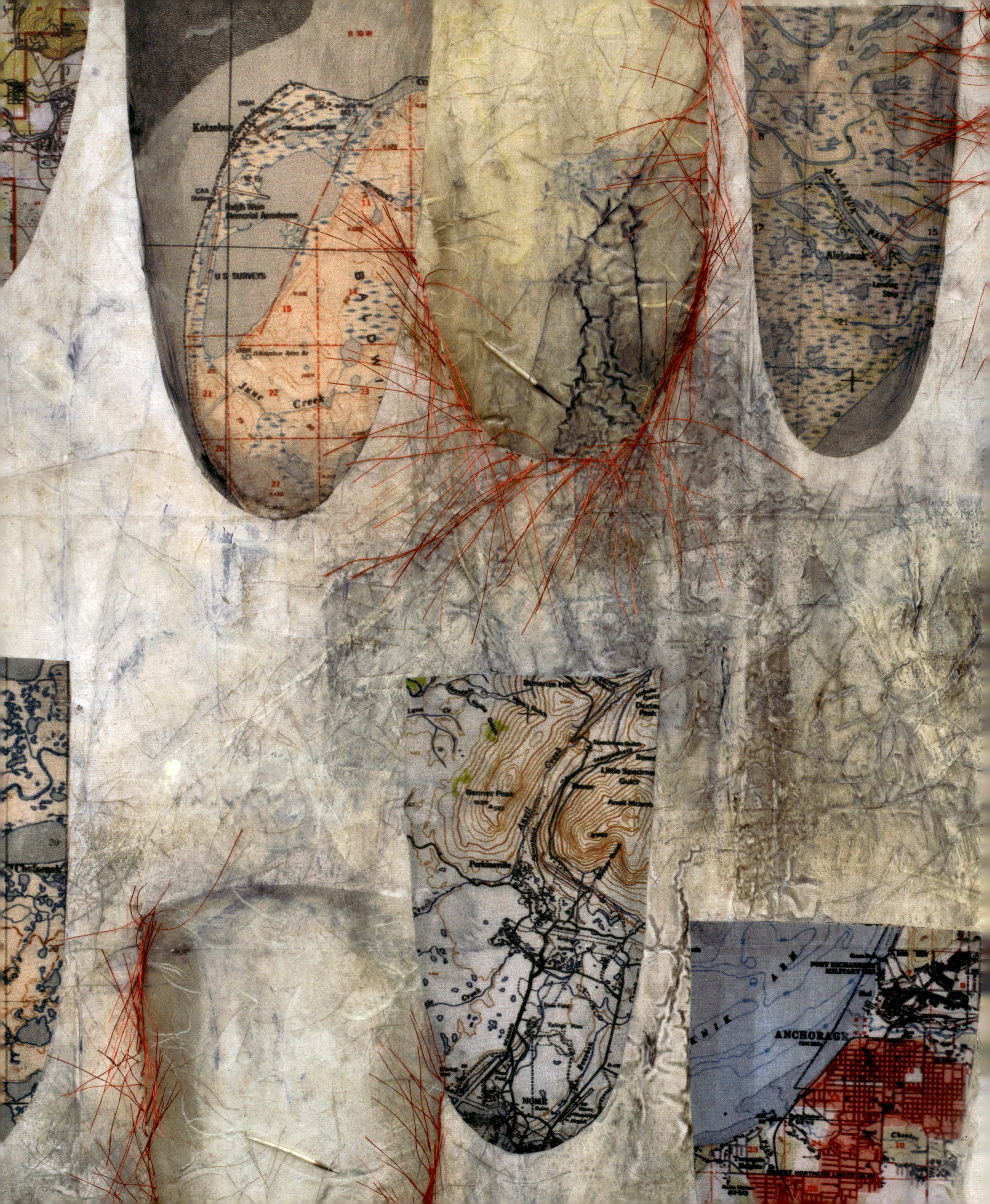
U S SURVEYS
June
Creek
Perkinsville
ANCHORAGE

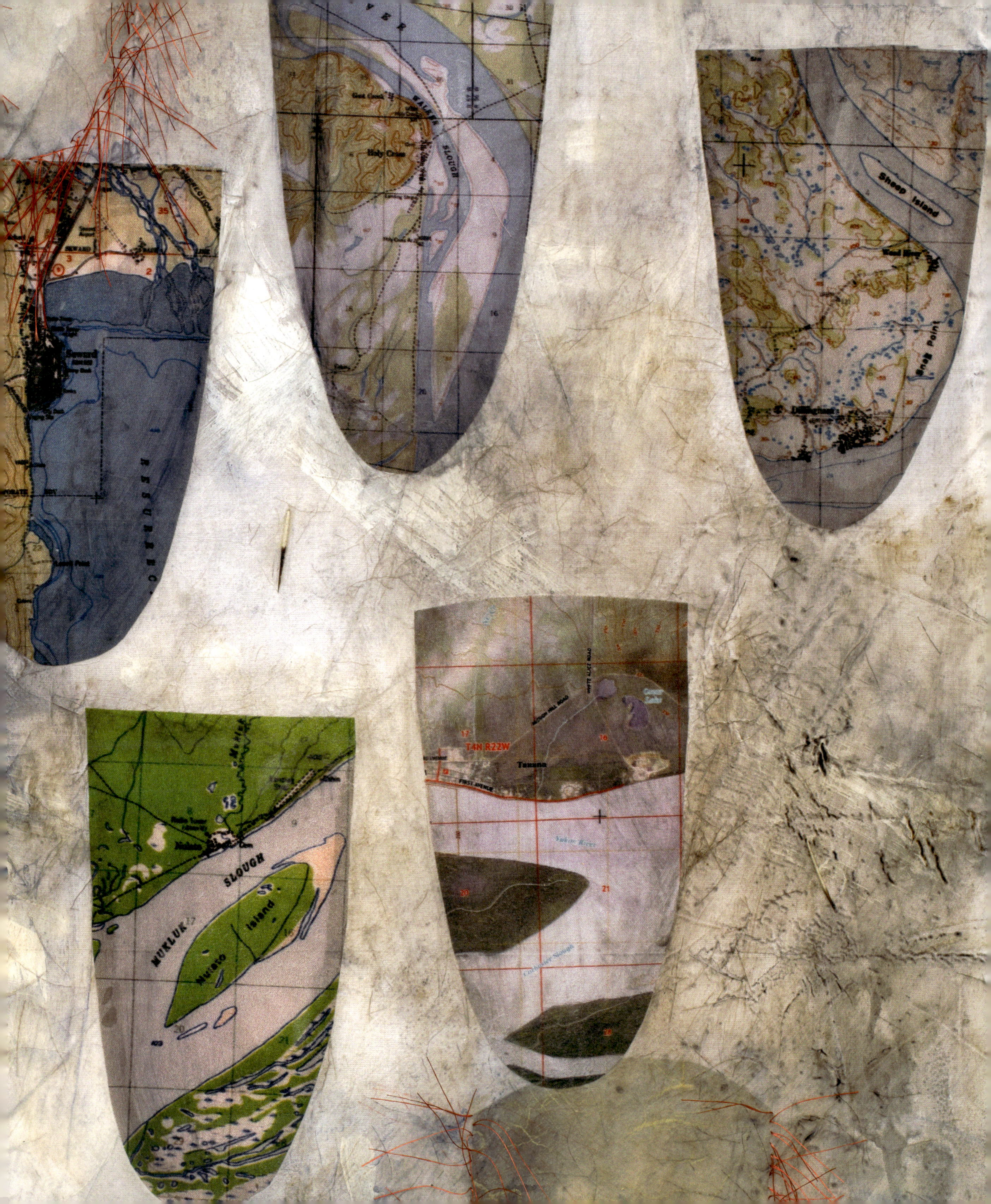

Sheep Island
SLOUGH
MUKLUK
T4N R22W
Tanana

SONYA KELLIHER-COMBS

"There is no line between the land, animals, and myself. There is no separation or segregation."
— SONYA KELLIHER-COMBS[1]

by Laura Phipps

This quote is in response to a prompt to describe her relationship to the land, animals, and herself as an artist, lays bare the project of Kelliher-Combs' work. For over 30 years, Kelliher-Combs' practice has gently, but relentlessly, tinkered with the notion of hierarchies—not only those often presumed of human and nonhuman relations, but also those between humans and between institutions.

Kelliher-Combs grew up with a strong understanding of her place in relation to the natural world, much of it influenced by her Iñupiaq and Athabascan heritage. Raised in Nome, Alaska, she spent summers with her family at their remote camp and participated in hunting and gathering food and supplies for the winter. Kelliher-Combs says she was taught that "the land and the sea would provide resources—spiritual and physical—necessary to sustain a healthy life."[2] Throughout her childhood, she learned much of the ways the land and sea did this through observing: by watching, listening, and eventually participating in the skin sewing, beading, and food preparation practiced by her relatives. These early experiences came to resonate deeply within Kelliher-Combs' practice and within works that refuse hierarchies of beings and of material.

In her early practice, Kelliher-Combs' acrylic-on-canvas paintings from the early 1990s hint at the artist's interest in abstraction as a means for potent content, which continues to be a strategy in her work. In graduate school at Arizona State University, she was drawn to some of the formal approaches of such art-historical figures as Robert Motherwell and Willem de Kooning; however, her interest in these artists lay not in their bombastic expressionism, but in the intimate details of surface- and mark-making in these artists' work. Kelliher-Combs focuses on the grounding that can occur even in abstraction and centers the idea that even on the flat surface of a canvas, artists have a relationship to a place, to the world around them. Reading through Kelliher-Combs' interest, the human touch inferred in the works of Motherwell and de Kooning points to a dialogue between human movement and place. To continue establishing these relationships between touch, abstraction, and the natural world, as well as to cultivate an intimacy, Kelliher-Combs began exploring the flexibility of watercolors and different strategies to create translucence in her work. She often uses the properties of paint to obscure areas of canvas or legible forms, characteristics that come to define much of her work even beyond painting.

During her years in college, Kelliher-Combs continued her informal education in cultural traditions.[3] In particular, she learned from cultural bearer Anna Golgeregen about processing marine mammal gut, an endangered process that informs Kelliher-Combs' understanding of medium specificity and that eventually became inextricable from her material practice. The product of this process has the appearance of fragility because of its translucence, but it is an incredibly durable material that had historically served an important function as clothing because of its waterproof property. Kelliher-Combs' use of processed guts and her exploration of inorganic simulacrum through polymers came about after she returned to Alaska from Arizona in 1998. She was drawn back to a land and to a place of sacred and familial connection, and her return allowed her to be in community with Alaska Native artists. Her process of watching, listening, and participating within the community resumed. It was in this space that Kelliher-Combs' relationship to material shifted, and the practices she had learned throughout her early life became intertwined in her studio.

In particular, Kelliher-Combs uses elements that had a life before they came to her—materials like walrus stomach, polar bear fur, beads, and thread that were harvested, salvaged, purchased, and gifted to and by her. As she says, "there is often a long process they [these materials] go through before becoming a part of a work of art. Working with these resources makes me appreciate the thread that bonds us to the natural world."[4] Kelliher-Combs' practice is not solely about organic matter, as she also embraces the use of commercial materials and creates those that allow for mimicry and expansion across media. She developed techniques to form skin-like surfaces for paintings and sculptures using layers of acrylic polymer, continuing to focus on flexibility and translucence. These techniques and the synthetic results are extensions of Kelliher-Combs' communion with and respect for nonhuman beings and nature and reflect her attempt to eliminate the assumed hierarchies between these entities.

The connection between the art Kelliher-Combs learned about in school and saw in Western-centric art history books and museums and the art that she experienced as a child also coalesced as she established herself back in Alaska. Material was a key to this shift, and despite Kelliher-Combs' inattention to their oeuvres, mid-century artists like Eva Hesse, Louise Bourgeois, and Bruce Nauman, who worked in rubber or latex, are often referred to in relation to her work with similar materials.[5] While certainly none of these artists' practices are in opposition to the others, it would be a mistake to assume a lineage between them, given their distinct and divergent intents and interpretations. Bourgeois used latex in a number of her sculptures, including *Fillete* (1968) and *Avenza* (1968–69), which directly and indirectly allude to human body parts and were interpreted as obliquely erotic. They were reviewed in evocative terms: "like living flesh, the rubber quivers and flaps," having a "viscous sheen like the inside of a mouth."[6] In contrast to the way that Bourgeois' use of natural-looking unnatural material is read as explicitly and solely human, Kelliher-Combs' use of similar material—in a congruous manner, even—invites references to both human and Nonhuman beings and relationships between them. Throughout Kelliher-Combs' community of works called "Curls" (2013–ongoing), she uses acrylic polymer along with animal fur to make forms that toggle between recognition of human and animal bodies.[7] For example, *Orange Curl* (2013) comprises a row of polymer cuffs with reindeer fur and thread that present as delicate arms or parka cuffs but also recall a line of drying salmon, an important food source that is threatened by the effects of climate change. The bifurcated reference in works like *Orange Curl*, as well as those like *Polar Bear Curl* (2017) made with polar bear fur, implicates humans in the environmental changes that imperil the natural world. As Kelliher-Combs has said, "We are a part of this environment. We all are impacting the land, the Earth. It's not just a commentary about the animals, the fish, the birds. It's about our place in this world."[8] The expansive signifiers of Kelliher-Combs' material choices stand out when facile visual comparisons of material are employed—it becomes obvious that her formal decisions are multifaceted and that history is held in material. The recognition of ancestral knowledge is held in Kelliher-Combs' material choices even when the reality of the material is unnatural.

There are other artists Kelliher-Combs notes as inspiration whose formal approaches are not evident in her work, but whose conceptual and cultural approaches lie below the surface of her thinking. She cites her love of the art of Jim Schopert (Tlingit and German ancestry)—known for his expanded Tlingit style of formline[9] in sculpture, carvings, drawings, and prints—as well as his poetry.[10] Schoppert is credited with opening up ideas not only of what formline could be, but also presumptions of Alaska Native and Northwest Coast art more broadly. Kelliher-Combs recalls being seduced by formline, and though her work doesn't bear a recognizable relationship to most formline, she includes abstractions of ovoid forms and continuous, flowing lines throughout her practice.[11] Kelliher-Combs also cites James Luna (Luiseño, Puyukitchum, Ipai, and Mexican) as an important influence—his attitudes toward identity and contemporary modes of making were permission-granting for her as she considered her position as an Alaska Native and an artist. Luna,

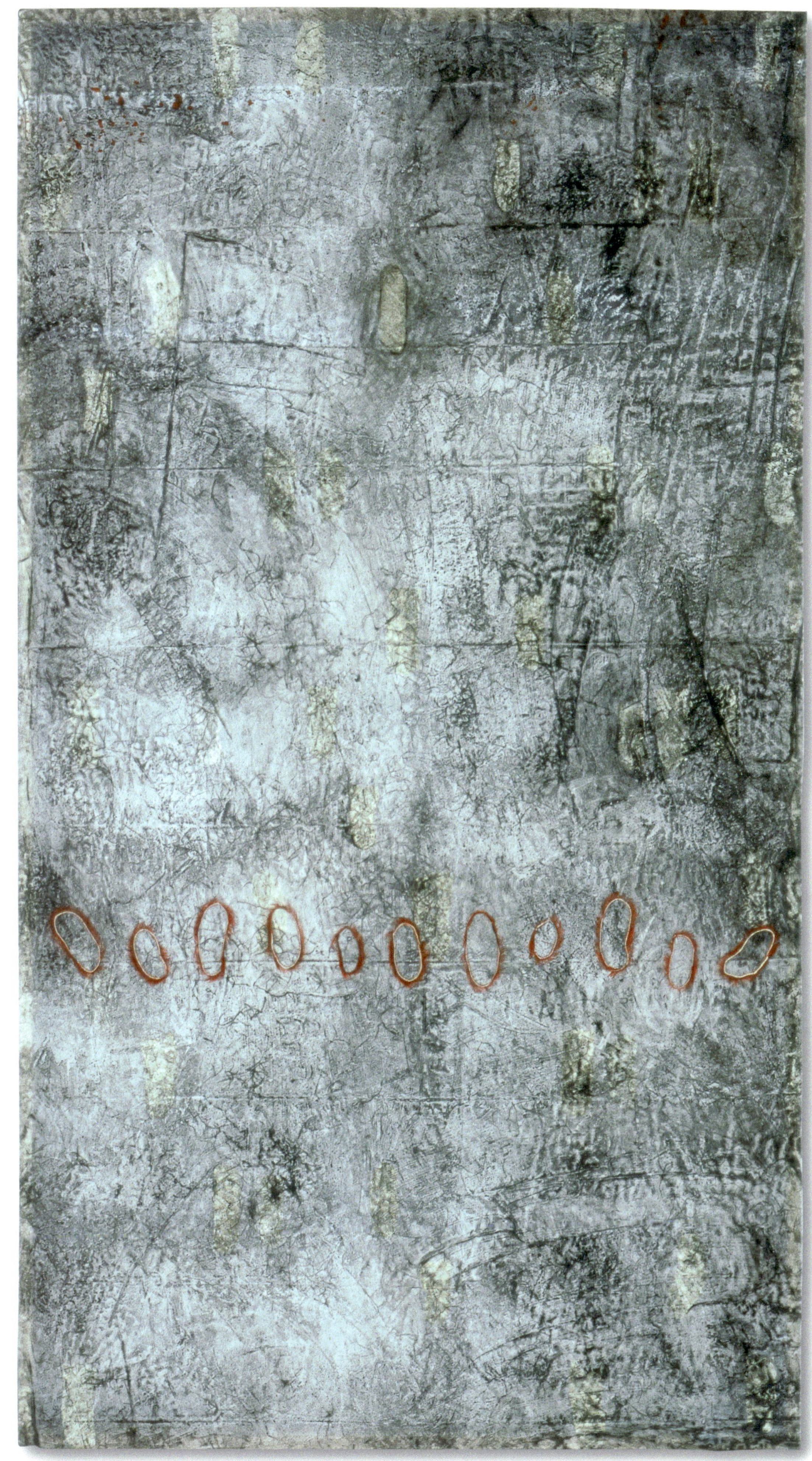

Gray with Red Sealskin Secrets, 1998. Acrylic polymer, walrus gut, thread, mixed media. 36 × 52 in. Photograph by Chris Arend.

as well as Kelliher-Combs' mentor artist Ronald Senungetuk (Iñupiaq), expressed an interest in being understood as an artist first and foremost. This desire was not meant to devalue their identity as Indigenous people—in fact, throughout his career, Luna showed a relentless commitment to centering an Indigenous experience—but to provide a way into appreciating their art that is not wholly predicated on ideas of identity or on knowing, and therefore claiming, culture. Kelliher-Combs' position as an Alaska Native artist, in a way, allows for a capacious reading that can be seen as more encompassing and liberating than limiting.

Kelliher-Combs' communities of paintings and sculptures called "Secrets," begun in the early 2000s and ongoing, echo something that Luna's proposal implies. The works speak to all of the different formations or ways of thinking about secrets—not only the things we intentionally keep secret, but also the ways that people hide aspects of themselves from others and how this kind of secret-keeping can feel imperative to artists whose culture is often cannibalized by others.

"Secrets" began in two dimensions, as in *Cream Secret with Red* (2005) and *Grey Secret with Red Seal Skin Secrets* (2005), with a repeated, sometimes overlapping ovoid form. The shape is often embedded and even spectral throughout this community of paintings. This organic ovoid form is one of many that make up Kelliher-Combs' visual iconography of symbols and materials that have deep histories in traditions of ivory and whalebone carving, scrimshaw design, and formline made personal by Kelliher-Combs' expressive hand. These "Secrets" loop loosely across and deeply within the surfaces of these paintings. Almost all of these paintings include stretched walrus stomach as well as commercial materials like acrylic paint, though there are also drawings such as *Secret Portraits* (2002 and 2007) in which the act of dipping the drawings in beeswax reveals the content of the drawings—human hair, ink, and stitching. Eventually, Kelliher-Combs pulls the ovoid free of the surface and into three-dimensional objects that morph this form into pocket-like containers. The shape of the objects in works like *Guarded Secret* (2015) creates pouches or containers, and the form is also an abstraction of the parts of an Iñupiaq parka that empower the wearer. Kelliher-Combs' use of shadows or traces of such symbols, known to her since childhood, results in a type of minimalism in mark-making that suggests the ghosts of influence. In this way, Kelliher-Combs hints that secrets are not solely about shame but can be a way to hold onto information, to power.

The complexity of secrets and power recalls stories artists Jaune Quick-to-See Smith (Confederated Salish and Kootenai) and Emmi Whitehorse (Diné) recount when speaking to the importance of Grey Canyon (the collective Smith founded in Albuquerque in late 1977) to them as they began their careers.[12] This group of young Native American artists supported each other as they navigated what it meant to be Native artists in a contemporary art space. Importantly, they were committed to changing the expectations of what constituted "Indian" art. Whitehorse summed up the prevailing expectation by recalling an experience with collectors: "'You call yourself Indians? Your work doesn't look Indian at all.' I guess they were expecting shells, feathers hanging off the work, buckskin, beads. Arts and crafts items, I guess, they were looking for, and our work just was not Indian enough to them."[13] But Whitehorse also recalled that this was not the only expectation Indigenous artists contended—or continue to contend—with. There is the more subtle, but no less essentializing, expectation that Indigenous artists' work must be freighted with sacred symbolism and lessons about their own cultural practice and traditions—and that these lessons are available for consumption by all audiences. Because of this expectation, the veiled references—to personal and cultural memory and implicitly art-historical strategies—which Kelliher-Combs employs accord power to the objects and the artist. One of the ingenuities of "Secrets" is what they imply about the desire for access to information and what they deny viewers.

The "Secrets" community is emblematic of Kelliher-Combs' practice of asking viewers to appreciate them on their own terms. However, through Kelliher-Combs' material choices, there is also an explicit statement that art is in relation to human, plants, and animals and that it is, ultimately, not separate.

1 Christopher Patrello, "Skin as Media: An Interview with Sonya Kelliher-Combs," in *Northwest Coast and Alaska Native Art* (Denver and Norman, OK: Denver Art Museum and University of Oklahoma Press, 2020), 74.

2 Specifically noted in an unpublished interview for Sharon Louden, fall 2023.

3 Kelliher-Combs had thought she would be a lawyer or an engineer, but through an influential drawing class at the University of Alaska Fairbanks, she first understood that "artist" was, or could be, a profession. Conversation with the author, April 14, 2023.

4 Patrello, 74.

5 The artist says she hadn't known of Hesse's work, in particular, until later in her career (conversation with the author, April 14, 2023), but references to Eve Hesse in relation to Kelliher-Combs' work are found in Manuela Well-Off-Man, ed., *Connective Tissue: New Appearances to Fiber in Contemporary Native Art* (Santa Fe: IAIA Museum of Contemporary Native Arts, 2017), 26 and Aleta Ringlero, "Sonya Kelliher-Combs: Secret Skin," in *Hide: Skin as Material and Metaphor*, ed. Kathleen E. Ash-Milby (Washington, DC: Smithsonian National Museum of the American Indian, 2010), 47.

6 Daniel Robbins, "Sculpture by Louise Bourgeois," *Art International*, October 20, 1964, 29–31.

7 Kelliher-Combs refers to her series as "communities," something that feels like a wonderful insight into the scope of her practice and understanding that these works are in relation to one another.

8 Michael Abatemarco, "Sonya Kelliher-Combs: Something Left Behind," *Pasatiempo*, July 15, 2016: https://www.santafenewmexican.com/pasatiempo/art/sonya-kelliher-combs-something-left-behind/article_5d6a32d0-7cdf-5f48-a820-1e68e9ccfa25.html

9 Formline is a powerful Indigenous art form and an important element of two-dimensional Pacific Northwest Native American art which involves a number of "rules" or building blocks, including the use of one continuous enclosing formline and a number of basic shapes.

10 Conversation with the author, April 14, 2023.

11 Conversation with the author, April 14, 2023.

12 In 1977, Smith and other Indigenous students at the University of New Mexico formed a collective called Grey Canyon, whose members—Larry Emerson, Whitehorse, Paul Willeto [all Navajo (Diné), Conrad House (Navajo [Diné]/Oneida)], Felice Lucero (San Felipe Pueblo), and Smith—met informally to discuss their art and support one another and also exhibited their art together through 1983.

13 See *American Indian Artist Series II: Jaune Quick-to-See Smith*, a film by the Native American Public Broadcast Consortium (now Vision Makers Media), 1982, at 00:17:50,900.

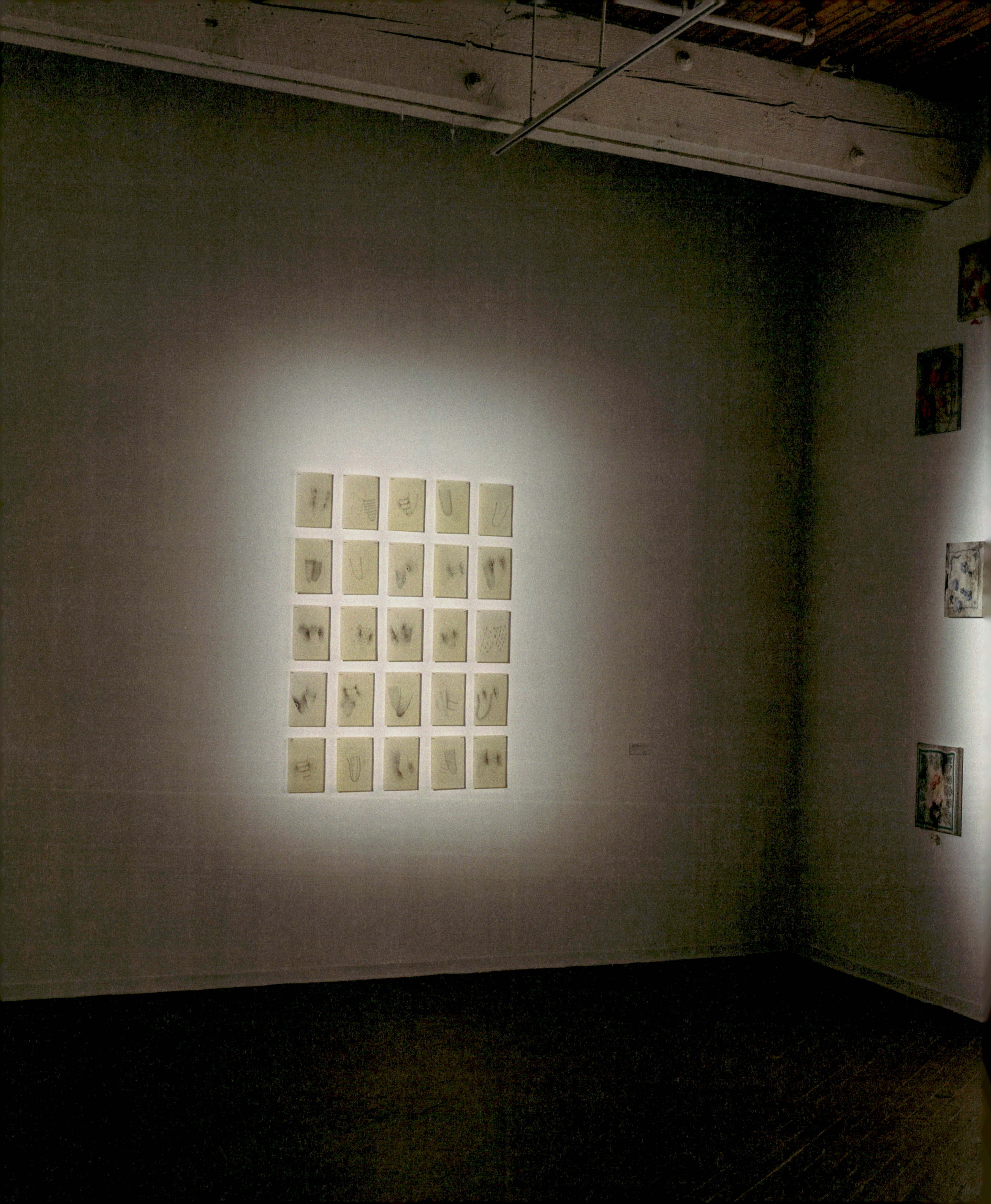

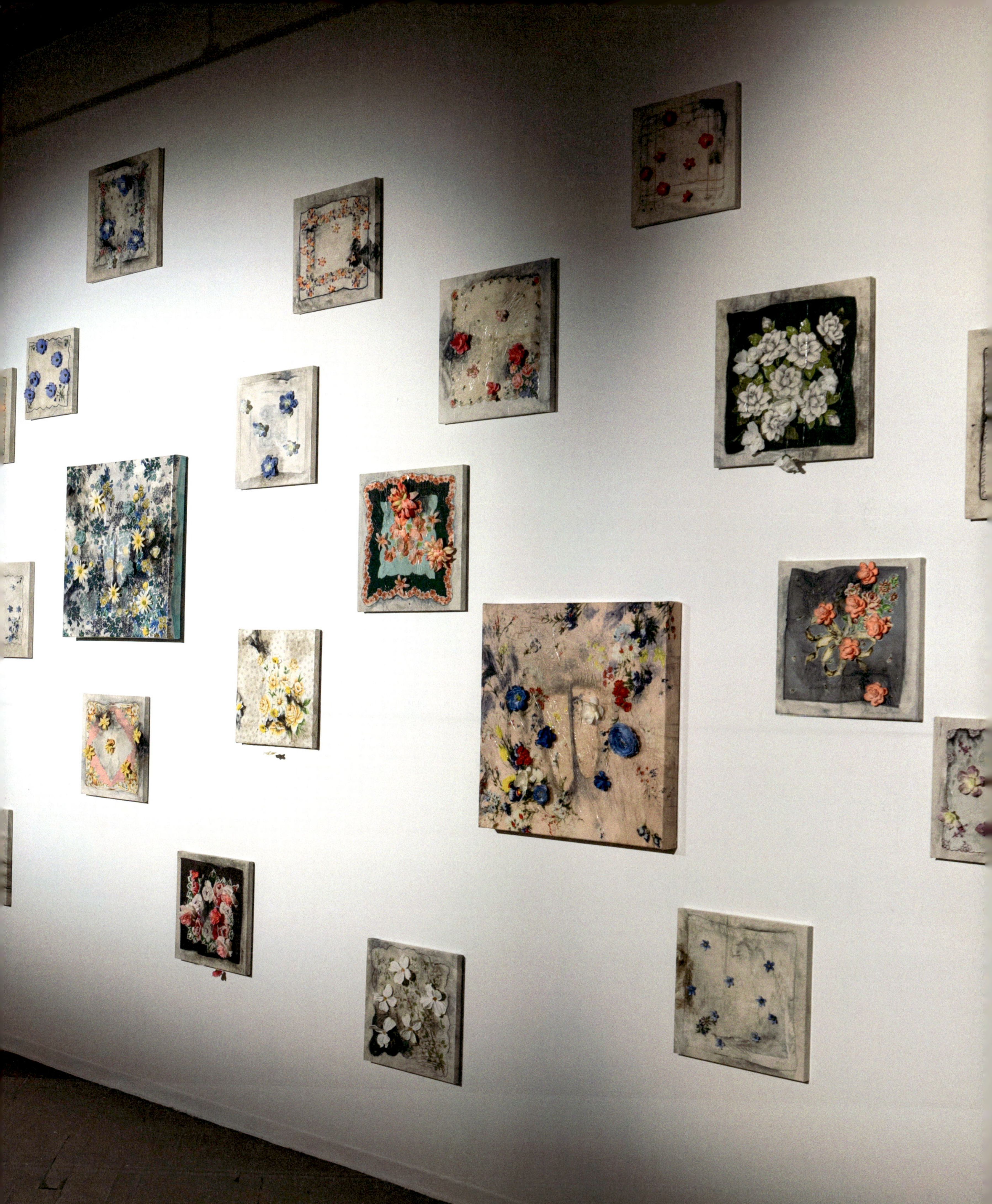

gathering buoyant

by Tanya Lukin Linklater

I am listening to Elisapie's 2023 cover album in Inuktitut, particularly "Sinnatuumait (Dreams)," "Uumamati Attanarsimat (Heart of Glass)," "Isumagijunnaitaungituq (The Unforgiven)," and "Qimmijuat (Wild Horses)." Translated into her mother tongue, these song memories are "formative to her childhood in Salluit, a village in Nunavik, Quebec," stirring within her images of cousins, mourning and healing.[1] As Elisapie sings, the sounds move skillfully through her throat, then mouth. Consonants and vowels—like thread or sinew—arc into forms, curve with lips, bend with teeth, loop with tongue as though she is sewing Inuktitut. Not an inflexible fastening or fixing.

Like gut sewn by our grandmothers in the North, the material of language and song swell. With water and heat (the weather of the body and of our surroundings), the entrails (scraped, hemmed, mended) puff up. Without our touch, these organs become brittle. Translucent gut sewn into clothing allows us to glide along the surface of water. We rebound, buoyant with air and wisps of light.

This reminds me of Sonya Kelliher-Combs' drawings, paintings, and sculptures, which gesture toward ancestral Iñupiaq and Athabascan material practices of harvesting, processing, and sewing. The small-scale forms in her singular works become phrases, lyrics, and melodies. Across time, these songs become ample compositions, in moments open like the abstracted vessels she reconstitutes again and again. In other moments, they exude needle-sharp incisiveness in their critique of the ongoing harms against Alaska Native peoples and communities. From finding material that has washed up on beaches near Nome and Kasilof, to harvesting near fish camps, or friends and relatives hand-delivering found objects to her studio in Anchorage, Kelliher-Combs' work cannot happen without gathering (in the multiple meanings of the verb.)[2]

Sherry Farrell Racette (Métis) offers writing regarding Indigenous art forms and their makers, noting that "there is a language of gestures: bundle, weave, stitch, and form" in making.[3] She writes of time in these processes, contrasting the singular stitch with the repetition of the gesture.[4] Farrell Racette brings our attention to the profound qualities of devotion and meditation that occur during sewing and beading, an inward practice that shifts the mind through the generation of a singular work, often in the space of the home.[5] Later, she further describes the energetic qualities of emotion that can be transferred into garments or other forms.[6]

I am moved by the cultivation of deep inwardness that happens in the (sometimes unspeaking of) making, marked by dwelling with and returning to ideas, devoted—a persistent and insistent staying with...[7]

"Visiting *A Million Tears* at ᐊᓚᒃᑳᔪᑦ Alakkaajut (Many Things Appear)
with Taqralik Partridge. It is November 2021 in Ottawa. We wear masks."[8]

thick smoke in church thick gold shimmering thick
poured upon us wept floral handkerchief square
worn at head or neck held in palm tucked in sleeve
phlegm unspoiled throat clothed wildflowers hand-picked clumps formed
then draped pliable soft grasses thread that fell thread that fell into her lap
the thread that fell into her

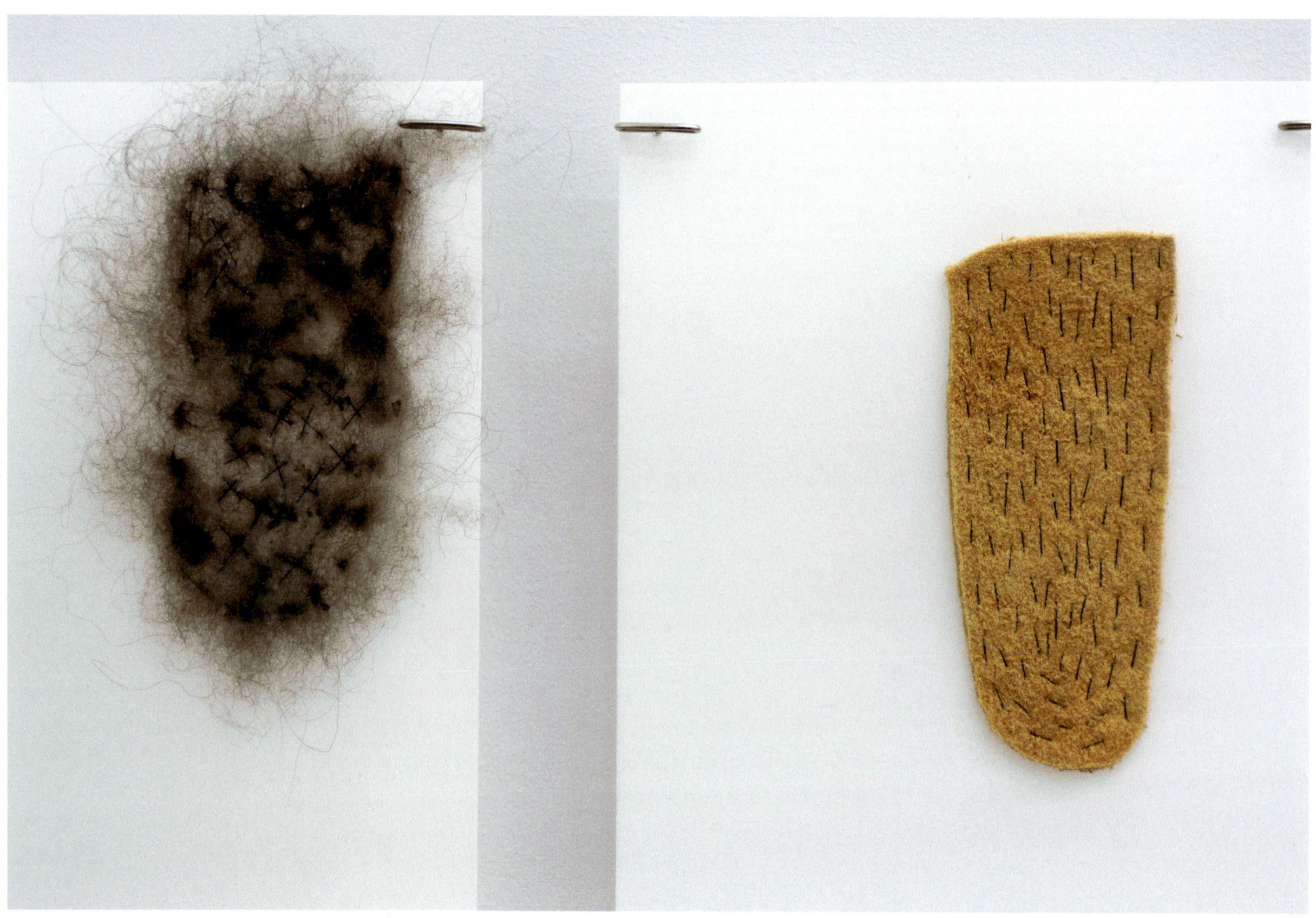

Fur and Hair Portraits (detail), 2023. Installed at Andrew Kreps Gallery. Mixed media, dimensions variable. Photograph by Kunning Huang.

"Visiting *Hair and Fur Secret Portraits* with Sonya Kelliher-Combs, Duane Linklater, and Laura Phipps. It is November 2023 in TriBeCa, Lower Manhattan. The weather is unseasonably warm."[9]

human hair drawn. seal skin sculpted. salmon skin cupped.
walrus stomach spiraled.
reindeer fur smoothed. polar bear fur fluffed. wolf fur flattened, a silhouette.
musk ox wool looped. moose hide stitched.
a drawing, a sculpture, a cup, a spiral.
smooth, fluffed, flattened.
a silhouette.
a loop. a stitch.
dipped in beeswax, no larger than my hands.

Works Cited

Cardinal, Harold, and Walter Hildebrandt. *The Treaty Elders of Saskatchewan: Our Dream Is That One Day Our Peoples Will One Day Be Clearly Recognized as Nations*. Calgary: University of Calgary Press, 2000.

Farrell Racette, Sherry. "Encoded Knowledge: Memory and Objects in Contemporary Native American Art." In *Manifestations: New Native Arts Criticism*, edited by Nancy Mithlo, 40–55. Santa Fe: IAIA Museum of Contemporary Native Arts, 2012.

-----. "Kitchen Tables and Beads: Space and Gesture in Contemplative and Creative Research." *The Routledge Companion of Indigenous Art Histories in Canada and the United States*, edited by Heather Igloliorte and Carla Taunton, 85–91. Milton Park: Routledge, 2022.

Gordon, Holly. "How Translating Classic Hits into Inuktitut Became a Healing Process for Elisapie." CBC, September 15, 2023. https://www.cbc.ca/music/elisapie-inuktitut-covers-album-release-pink-floyd-led-zeppelin-blondie-1.6966403.

Kelliher-Combs, Sonya. *Secret Portraits*, 2018. Ink, pencil, beeswax on paper.

-----. *A Million Tears*, 2020. Found items, synthetic flowers, and delicate handkerchiefs in acrylic and polymer coating, dimensions variable.

-----. *Hair and Fur Secret Portraits*, 2023. Human hair, seal skin, salmon skin, walrus stomach, reindeer fur, polar bear fur, wolf fur, musk ox wool, moose hide, beeswax on paper with steel pins, dimensions variable.

Lukin Linklater, Tanya. *Slow Scrape*, edited by Michael Nardone. Documents series. Montréal: The Centre for Expanded Poetics and Anteism Books, 2020.

-----. *On Felt Structures: Weather, Embodiment, and Materiality*. PhD diss., Queen's University, 2023.

Endnotes

1 Holly Gordon, "How Translating Classic Hits into Inuktitut Became a Healing Process for Elisapie," CBC, September 15, 2023.

2 In repetition, she rends gendered violence; she pierces shame; she pokes, then lances, generational and self-inflicted violence.

3 Sherry Farrell Racette, "Encoded Knowledge: Memory and Objects in Contemporary Native American Art," 46.

4 Short excerpts of this writing have been adapted from Tanya Lukin Linklater, *On Felt Structures: Weather, Embodiment, and Materiality*, including my extensive footnoting practice.

5 For a discussion of my relatives' sewing and beading practices, see Tanya Lukin Linklater, *Slow Scrape*.

6 "An invisible strand sometimes comes from the beader to lie alongside the thread, and each stitch can be a transformational action. The gesture of stitching—the tiny, precise movements created by the piercing needle that secures a strand of beads to a surface—can tether emotion and be a gesture of claiming or one of letting go." Sherry Farrell Racette, "Kitchen Tables and Beads: Space and Gesture in Contemplative and Creative Research," 90.

7 This reminds me of my writings on short form. "I describe short forms as garments, belongings, poems, dances, sculptures—a moment within a (lifelong) practice that is often situated in relation to Indigenous knowledges. Everyday, unseen, intellectual, embodied, and emotional labor accumulate (like sediment in riverbeds) through making over hours, days, weeks. *This labor near land, water, and weather as we harvest and gather fish skin, fur, grasses and other plants, hair, hides, quills, sinew, tusks.* For instance, while porcupine quilled works may be generated in relatively short periods of time, first, the porcupine must be harvested, quills retrieved, cleaned, and dyed. Only then can the artist hand-build the quills into a form. Short form is a visible moment within a practice that is mostly unseen except by those closest to us—those who harvest, process, and sit with us as we make.
The garment, the stitch do not tell. We marvel at precision, skill, and materiality, but we cannot access the experiences held by communities of makers or the garment itself. The garment does not explain how one harvests or processes. We do not know when (in late spring, early fall, in alignment with seasonal migrations, spring breakup, or other activities that unfold), or where (tundra, coves, mountains), or how (the techniques used) to harvest, process, and generate the garment. In this way the garment withholds knowledge. Similarly, this withholding supports the transmission of knowledge generation to generation. Withholding knowledge from those who have not inherited or earned the responsibilities for place-based and seasonal harvesting ensures an intendedness (Cardinal and Hildebrandt). These ethical boundaries and rigorous protocols allow for continuance of our structures of sustenance." Lukin Linklater, *On Felt Structures*, 55–56.

8 There are 52 canvases that comprise this work. The canvases are each 12" × 12" or 18" × 18".

9 These works initially remind me of "Secret Portraits," drawings of the same dimensions, which I first encountered at ᐊᕙᑖᓂᑦ ᑕᒪᐃᓐᓂᑦ ᓄᓇᑐᐃᓐᓇᓂᑦ *Among All These Tundras*, curated by Heather Igloliorte, Amy Dickson, and Charissa von Harringa, at OCAD University in Toronto in 2019.

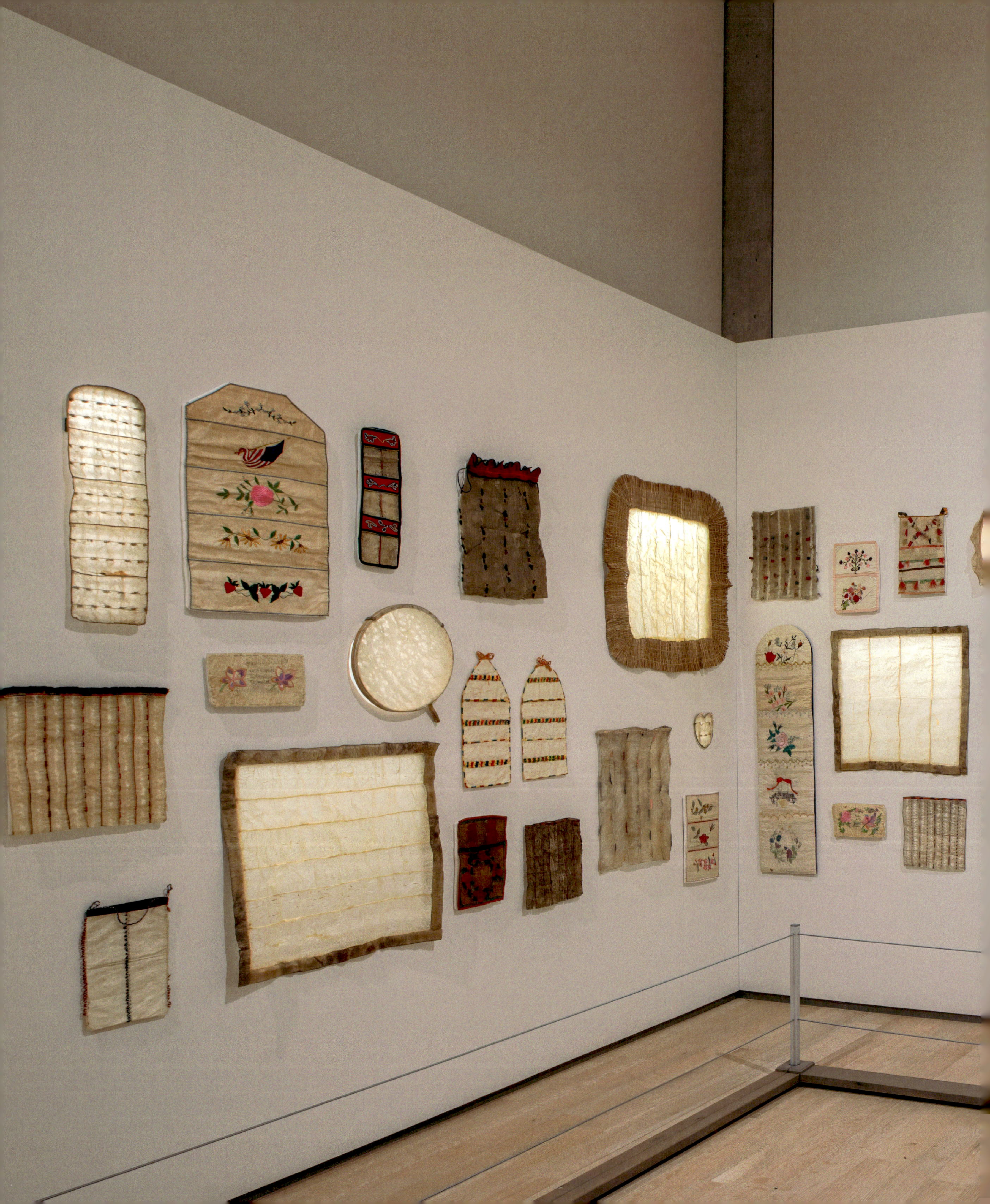

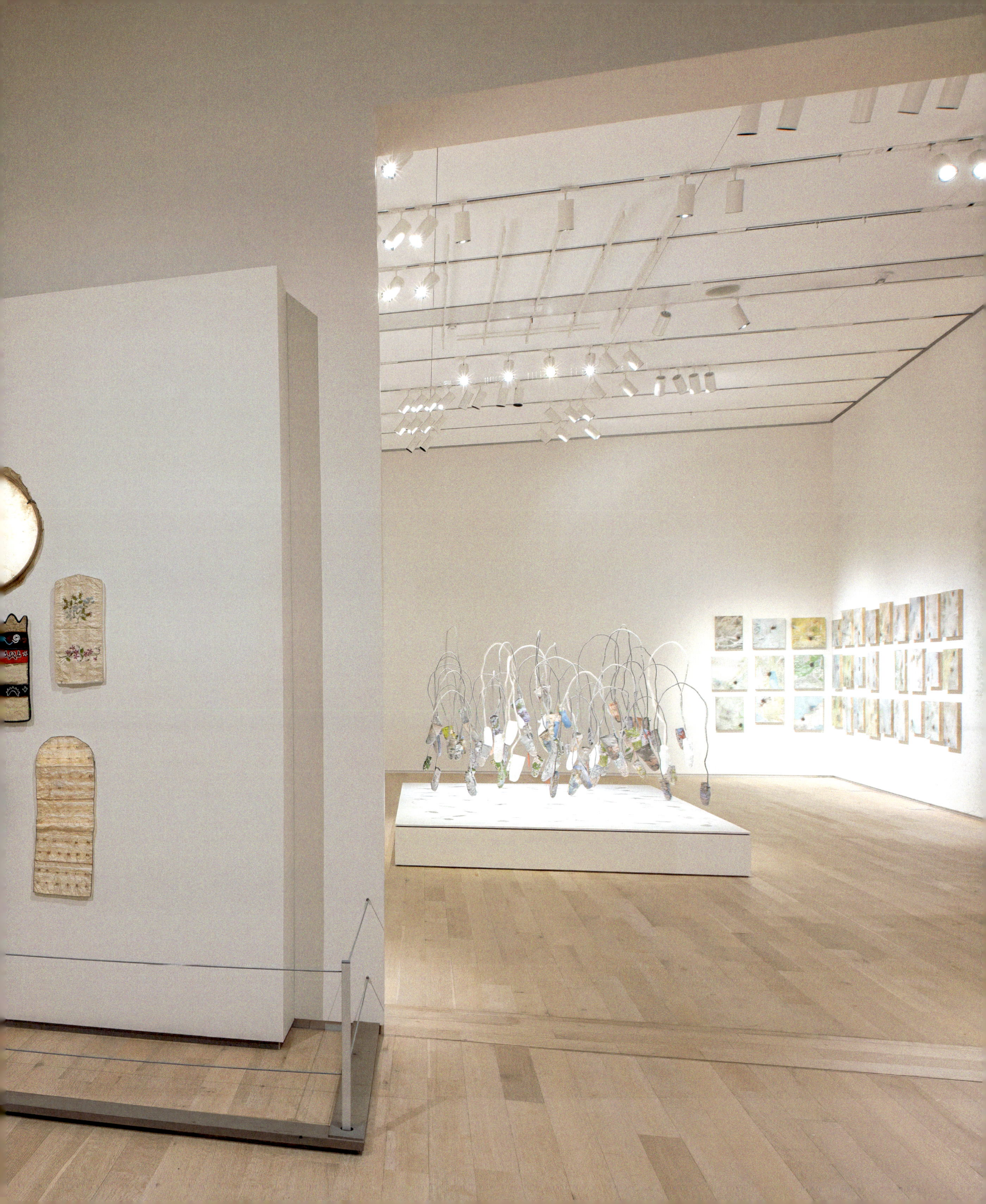

INTERVIEW

with Sonya Kelliher-Combs

by Candice Hopkins

Candice Hopkins: Sonya, as a way of beginning our conversation, I was wondering if you could share more about how you first came to be an artist or how you thought of that as even a possibility in your life.

Sonya Kelliher-Combs: Both my mother and my father had a big influence on me, as did my grandparents. They were forever collecting beautiful things. Not necessarily collecting, but they had been given things that I grew up around, baskets and some carvings and some artifacts. I took art classes in high school and art and culture in grade school. Growing up around creative people like my mom, we couldn't afford a lot of things, so she always made our parkas and our ruffs and mittens. But as a kid, I never considered being an artist. It wasn't until college that I did.

CH: Growing up in the North, I imagine it's similar. When I was growing up, my mom and my grandma made everything. My mom made her own parkas and made a little parka for me. They were constantly beading, especially later in life. I was always surrounded by women making things.

SC: Absolutely. Everyone in our community was a maker. Growing up in Nome, in wintertime especially, people were coming together, and they couldn't do it all by themselves. If someone was stretching a skin boat or something similar, there are a lot of big tasks that many people had to partake in to make it happen.

CH: And you don't classify these activities as art at the time because it's part of everyday life. Sonya, who were your early influences as an artist?

SC: When I was young, there were local artists who taught us art and culture. Harry Koozata and Marie Saclamanna taught art and culture at our high school. Edna Alvanna was an influence in grade school. There are a bunch of elders who were important influences on me. Of course, my family as well. When I went to college, I think the first artist that I was really taken with was Jim Schoppert. He was Tlingit. The way he thought and talked about the formline design with all its rules: he learned it, honed it, and then broke it apart and rethought or reimagined it. At the time, I didn't want to be limited by my identity, by my cultural background, and wanted just to be seen as an artist.

When I found Schoppert's works at the museum in Fairbanks, I would spend hours with them. I was mesmerized by them. Other artists, like Susie Bevins-Ericsen and Edna Jackson, were trailblazers using material in new ways, but still, you could tell it came from a special place—a well of history, continuity. When I met Edna Jackson in person years ago, I asked her why she stopped making that earlier gut work. She said, "Well, my work is this work I do with my community. ... That's more important to me."

It's interesting that the women who inspired me in the beginning found other ways of creating community. Susie Bevins-Ericsen is the reason that I do a lot of [this work]. It's not community engagement; it's not even activism. It's fostering community. I think it's important to create opportunities for others, so that's part of my practice.

CH: Yeah. It's interesting, too, that you're saying it's community engagement. I think that these terms come forward and almost stand in for practices that have been part of our [Indigenous] communities for a long time. We didn't name it that way because it's just how you do things in a good way. You bring people alongside you.

I think this might've been the case for a lot of people when I was in art school in the mid- to late '90s—I was discouraged from making any work that was "dealing with my identity." This was seen not only as a negative, but it wasn't art

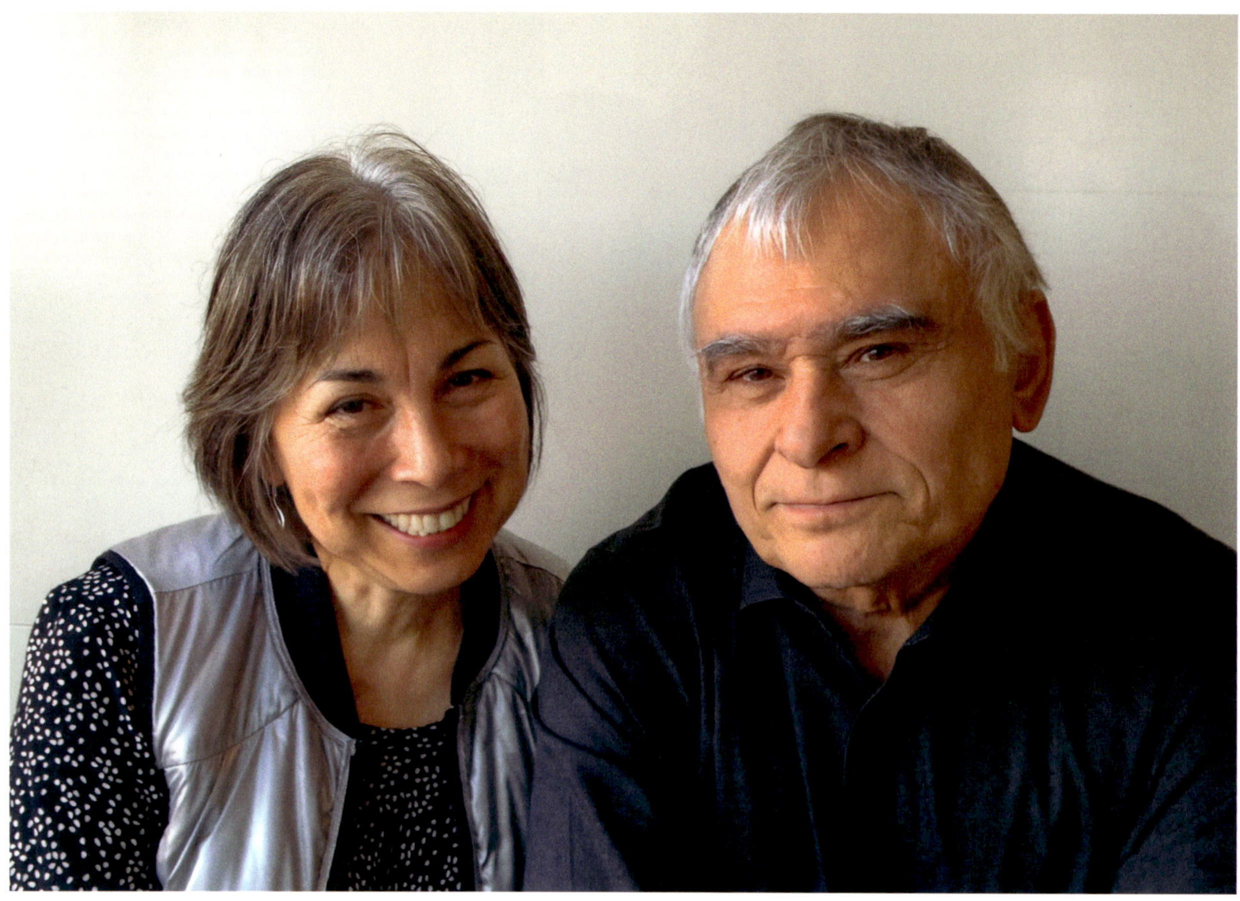

left: Kelliher-Combs' father, James Stotts, and his wife, Karoline Stotts, Anchorage, Alaska, 2018. Photograph by the artist.

for art's sake. Why do you think that's different for you now? Is there something in the greater art world that's changed?

SC: I think the audience has changed. I think demographics have changed. I think I have changed. For me personally, I think the boxes that people want to put you in have changed. Today there's more education about who we are, what we do, where we came from, and more importantly, that we're still here.

Still, when I go to the National Museum of the American Indian and I go to the African American Museum, there are very different things happening in those spaces. We need to break through that [lingering prejudice]. I am thankful that people like you are doing this important work. I am proud to see so many of our artists are not limiting themselves to mainstream locations and markets that have been a part of the old guard for so long.

CH: It's something I think about all the time. I was curious about your take on it. I think there are a few things at play right now. One is that market forces are changing, but there's also this realization that there are art worlds, and there are also Indigenous Art Worlds. I wouldn't say that there's just one, right? You just gave a whole genealogy.

I think it's because there needed to be a certain level of literacy, because we often use such specific cultural signifiers in our work, which I feel comes forward in your practice. Sometimes it's like we get the art histories we're ready for, and in saying "we," I'm saying the art

Kelliher-Combs' mother, Trudy Kelliher, and her grandfather Maurice Kelliher, Snow Gulch, Alaska, 1984. Photograph by the artist.

right: Kelliher-Combs' dad, Patrick Kelliher, Snow Gulch, Alaska, 1990. the artist. Photograph by the artist.

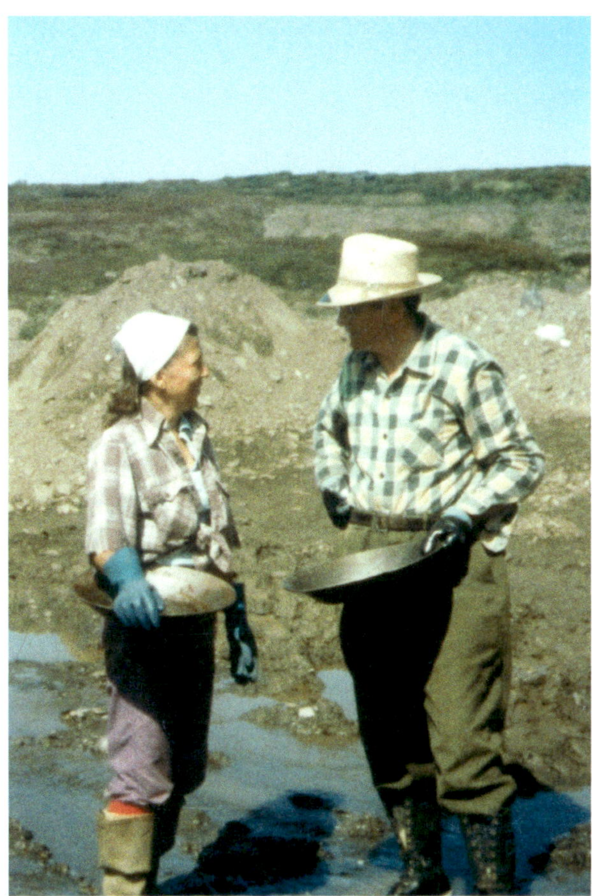

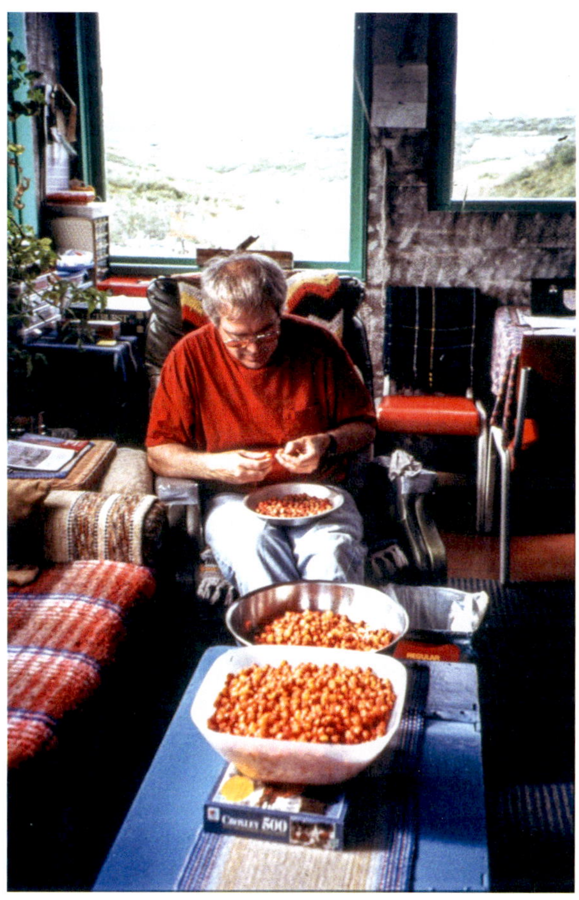

world in general. I feel that right now there's recognition that a whole part of American art history has been completely overlooked.

SC: I agree that it is about literacy. I'll go back to my grad school experience. I had two professors say literally the exact same thing: "I don't buy your imagery. You have to educate me." I was a little dumbfounded, but then I thought, well, you'd better learn a little bit more, because I'm not the only one who does this kind of work. I kind of feel that until it's the true history—when every grade school and high school textbook across the nation and around the world teaches what actually happened to our people and other populations all around the world—until that happens, people are never going to acknowledge it and understand. There are so many times I've been included in a blog or something where somebody says, "Oh, these things never happened," especially regarding boarding school and abuse by the Church. I think it is important for art to provoke, make people think. The work I want to make has to say something; I can't just have a pretty picture anymore.

CH: I've noticed that shift. One of the markers of Indigenous art is we carry our ancestors with us. And some of those ancestors are those material inheritances. I feel that that idea of material inheritance grounds your practice, because these are the tools your family uses; your ancestors used and continue to use the things in their environment. Why is it important that you bring forward these material practices I say as inheritances—the skin, the hair, the membrane, and the stitch—in your work?

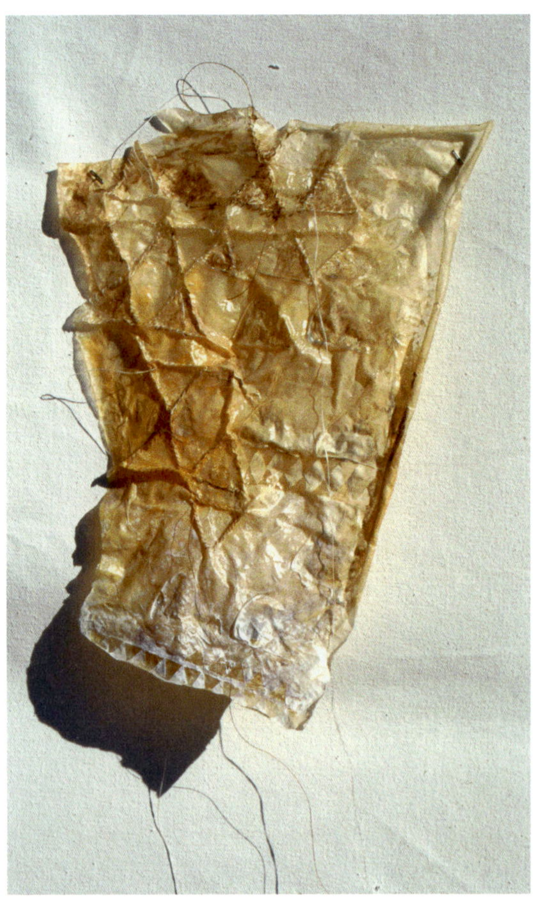

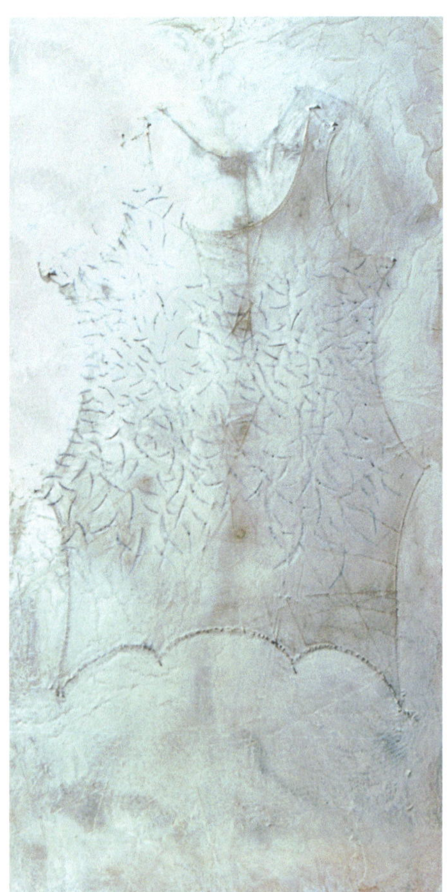

left: *Trim Three*, 1997. Paint, walrus stomach, acrylic polymer, nylon thread, 6 × 7.5 in. Private collection. Photograph by the artist.

right: *She Was Only Ten*, White 5. 2002. Paint and mixed media. 24 × 48 in. Private collection. Photograph by Kevin G. Smith.

SC: In the beginning, it was kind of a coping mechanism. [When I was in grad school,] I was living in Arizona, a place that was so different from where I was brought up. I was homesick. I brought those materials with me—like gut and hide—so that I had something that was familiar and something that I loved. That's how I started thinking about material. I never intended to use it, and then I started emulating it. My earliest pieces were the real thing, walrus stomach, stretched next to a synthetic copy. Eventually, I started to mix them together and submerge them. Sometimes they're on the surface. It's not just about using these materials, but also about gathering and processing them. The relationship of making the piece is a small part of the actual piece.

CH: Yeah. And it reminds me, too, as in the use of those materials and even in making them synthetic, and you had that revelation when you were in grad school. It's not just about the materials; it's about their meaning, right? Their meaning for where you're from, how they're harvested, and the knowledge they carry forward with them.

SC: With regard to that knowledge and the inherent power of our historical objects, I want to tell a story. I went to NMAI with Susie Bevins-Ericsen, and I had the opportunity to go to Suitland, the storage facility for the Smithsonian. We were so moved by how much of our material culture was there. It was a tearful time, but also joyous, almost like visiting family. I have since helped facilitate numerous opportunities for others to have similar experiences at other institu-

Sonya Kelliher-Combs' family summer camp, Snow Gulch, Alaska. Photograph by the artist.

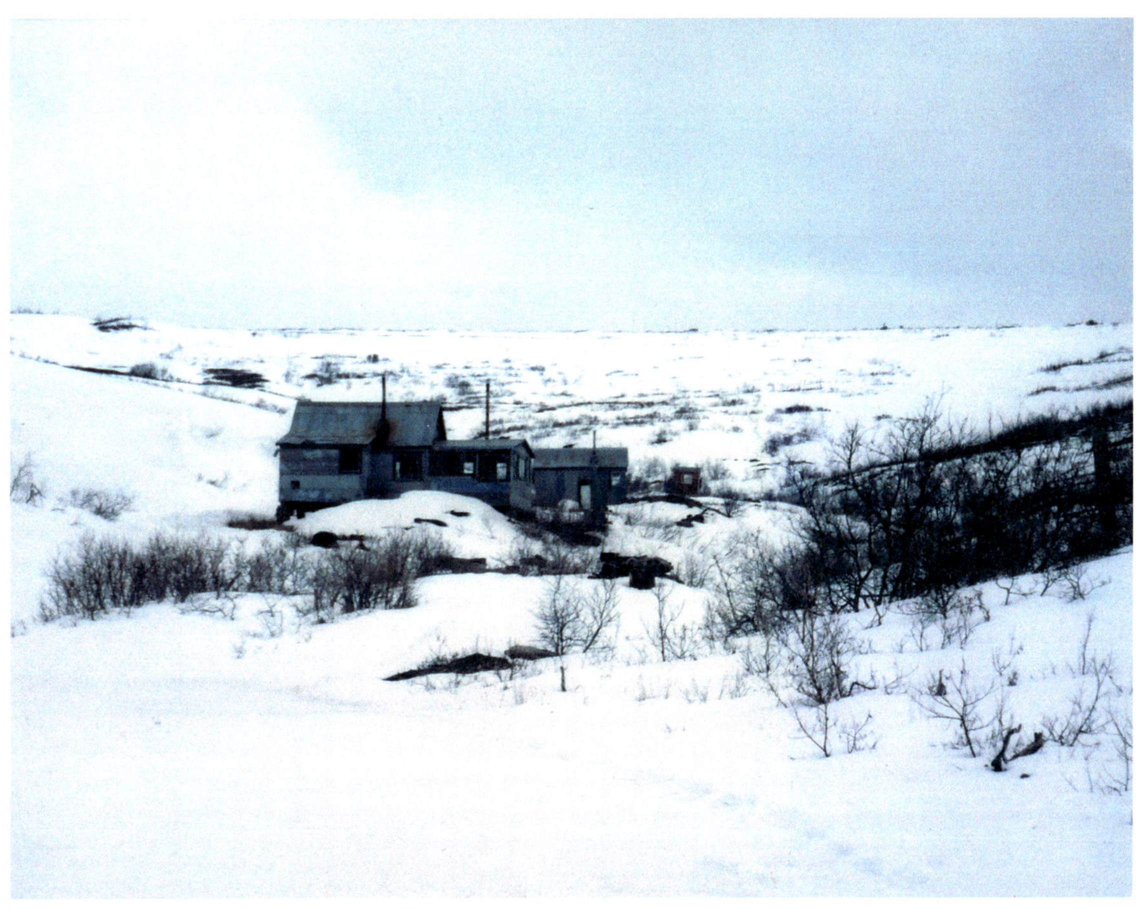

tions. My dream is to go through there and rematriate all those objects and let them come out. I'm slowly trying to do that in other places. Those are our ancestors in those boxes. That history, knowledge, and energy within those objects... you could feel it. It's tangible.

CH: Exactly. And I think that the honoring of those materials is embedded with them. They are ancestors. I've been thinking a lot lately, also in following your work and the work of other people who are spending time in the archives of other museums, like Tanya Lukin Linklater. She's originally from Kodiak Island. I've been thinking about what I've been calling "repatriation otherwise," because a lot of laws about bringing our things back are necessitated on how they were taken—if they were taken under duress or if they're funerary objects—but they can account for the masses of things that either don't have good records or were sold or were amassed in other ways, often under salvage anthropology.

With repatriation otherwise, I've been thinking about how important visiting is to us in those spaces, and how we can better share that sense of embodiment. I think we'll be getting somewhere, because the protocols around NAGPRA [Native American Graves Protection and Repatriation Act] are often set up against us. They're also predicated on things like a collections manager, or if you don't have a museum to bring them back, you're not allowed to bring them home. But their home is not on, like, a steel shelf in a basement somewhere. Their home is with people.

SC: Yeah, exactly. If our people want to go and rebury these objects, they should be able to do that. Repatriation [laws are] another form of colonialism as far as I'm concerned. They're another door that you have to break down.

CH: Thanks for sharing that with me. There are people making a difference, because they're making new protocols. They're showing that it's possible for museums to have different protocols, too, because these items are our cultural wealth. Communities aren't healthy when all their wealth has been taken away from them.

I wanted to ask you about the sense of seriality in your work. In art history, the repeated form is often related to minimalism. I don't think that's what's going on in your work. I see it as evidence of the labor of women, particularly; of preparing and drying, let's say, salmon skin, which I know you do every year, or of cutting the same patterns for mitts, of sewing the same stitches.

SC: First, just using this single form, the walrus tusk shape, which I think is very simple but represents many different things, like the idea of a secret. But that shape also represents generations, history, legacy, connection to each other—those kinds of things. Like when you were little and your mom gave you a scrap, and you kept on working on it until you got it perfect, though it's never perfect, but you just kept on working on it. It's not necessarily the finished product that's important, but it's about the process of learning and working and making. This idea of spending time is something that we talked about earlier. It is so important, something that you can't get back—something missing in much of the world today. We must treasure the time with our grandma or grandpa, mom, sister, aunt, and uncle, learning how to do these things. There's something about working on smaller things that become a larger thing in which they are related, like community. I always think about [each element] as an individual, but they're all connected to each other.

CH: So it's like they're relatives.

SC: Yes. Exactly. And it doesn't even have to be just relatives. There's one series I call *Common Thread* that is all those pouches. They're all connected by a single thread, but they're all different colors, shapes, sizes. We share common DNA, and we're more similar than we are different.

CH: That was a beautiful answer.

CH: We're living with one of your red curls at Forge Project right now, and when you look at them closely, every single one of them is different. You can also tell that you're not trying to create exact replicas of each one. I think what you're trying to do is highlight their differences.

Circling back to something that you said before, I was wondering if we could go a little bit deeper into the materials that you use. Some of your materials, including those that are synthetic or inorganic, tend to mimic parts of animals, like thin, opaque membranes that could be walrus gut. This creates a suspension of belief, particularly when you look closer and you see, actually, "Oh, there are little bits of caribou hair." And then there's this kind of slippage that happens between the organic and the inorganic. It kind of moves back and forth between the two. And it seems to me that that's very deliberate on your part.

SC: Something I'm really interested in is kind of that tension between what is real and what isn't, and a little bit of mystery. I love it when people are drawn to it, because it has this glow. It is translucent, and if [the material] is lit right, it casts a shadow through the surface of the piece. You don't only have these forms in the front, but also behind it; it touches outside of its physical form. Sometimes it's submerged beneath it, and sometimes there are multiple layers. Sometimes it's veiled. I want there to be some discovery, unearthing. The mixing and melding of material becomes a metaphor.

CH: The more that I see your work, there's often these material slippages—these productive slip-

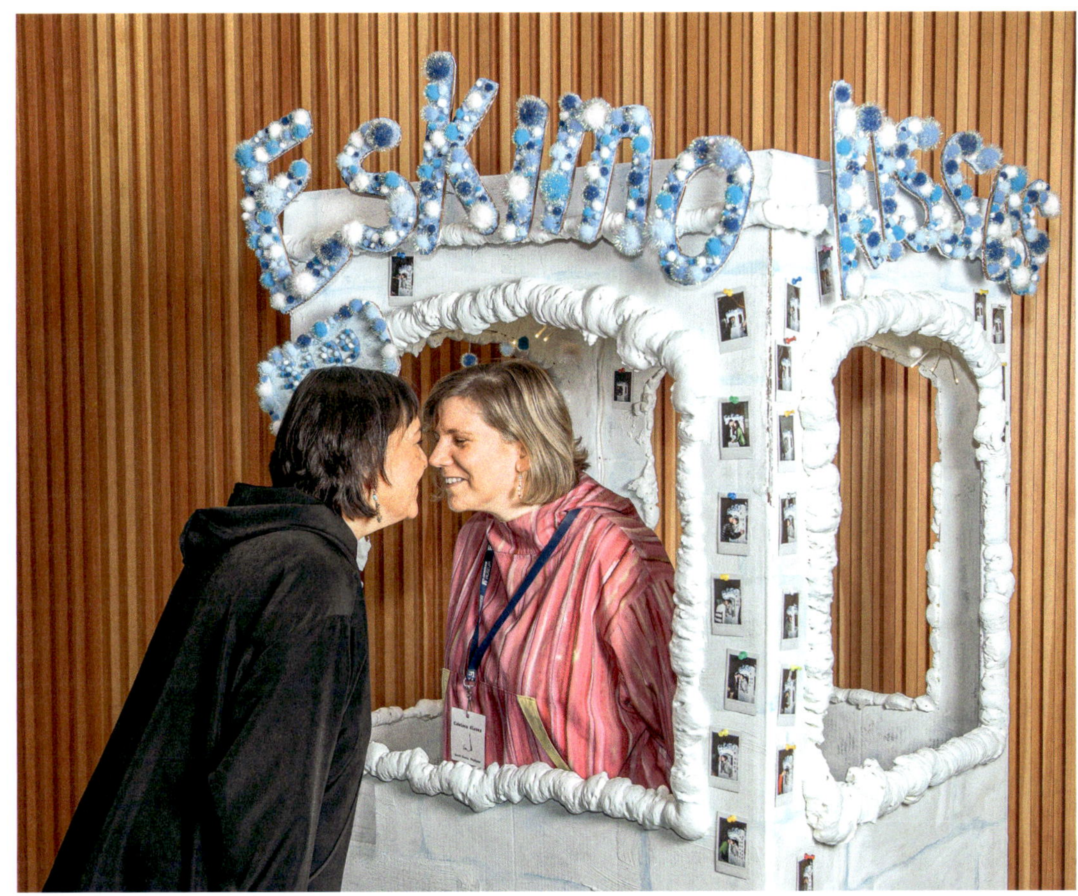

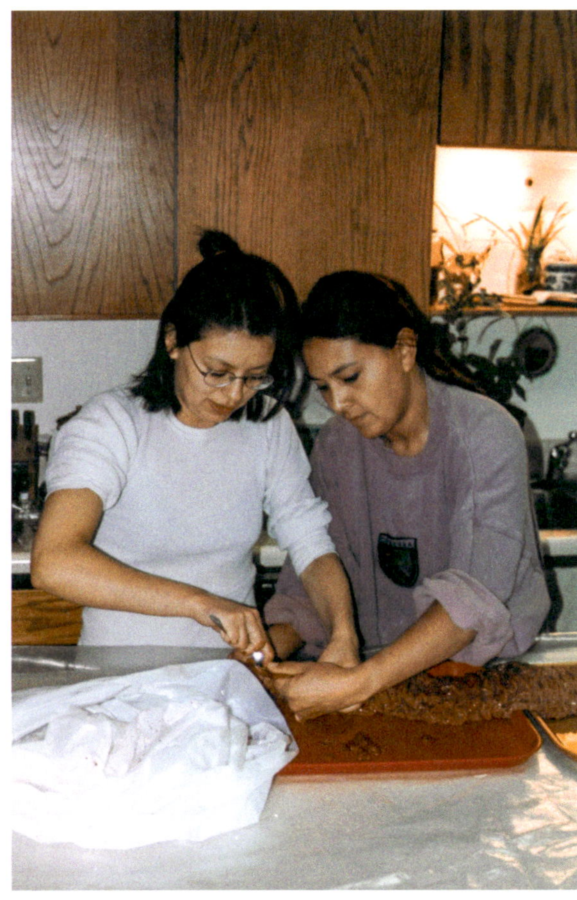

left: *Eskimo Kissing Booth* from the *Out of the Box* performance at the Anchorage Museum, 2015. Pictured: Sonya Kelliher-Combs and Sarah Owens. Photograph courtesy of the Anchorage Museum.

right: Sonya Kelliher-Combs and her sister, Allison Kelliher, de-fleshing walrus stomach, 1995.

pages between human and animal and back again. And of course, we're animals, too. And I think that inherently much of your work is reflecting the human body. We all have experiences of skin and of hide.

SC: As far as it being related to the body, I like that you said that, because things are made to the scale of the body. At one point I made parkas out of a gel medium. I was sewing them together and making them with consideration to perform in them, but I never performed them. I'm so afraid of the performance aspect of everything. But at the same time, I love the idea of performance. Once I did the Eskimo Kissing Booth, but I didn't go into the box and administer kisses. I trained a friend, who was British, to do it [laughter]. I actually had people come up to me and say they would give me an Eskimo kiss, but not her, and I asked why it was OK to kiss me but not her.

CH: I feel that your work is edgier than people realize. There's a seductive element to it which I think is part of its strength. Last time I was up visiting you, there was a piece that I considered to be a memorial of sorts. It was at the Anchorage Museum, and it was a series of suspended mitts in response to the suicide epidemic in the North. There was this real poignancy in the suspension of it, in that they were suspended from this platform as though they were floating between worlds. There's an inherent beauty in your work, and that's an avenue for you to speak about these harder subjects.

SC: Yeah. The Idiot Strings, which started out as two-dimensional forms, were memorials to three uncles who had committed suicide. They all were 27 when they did that. We've since lost a couple of cousins of the same age. Among people in the North and people in Native

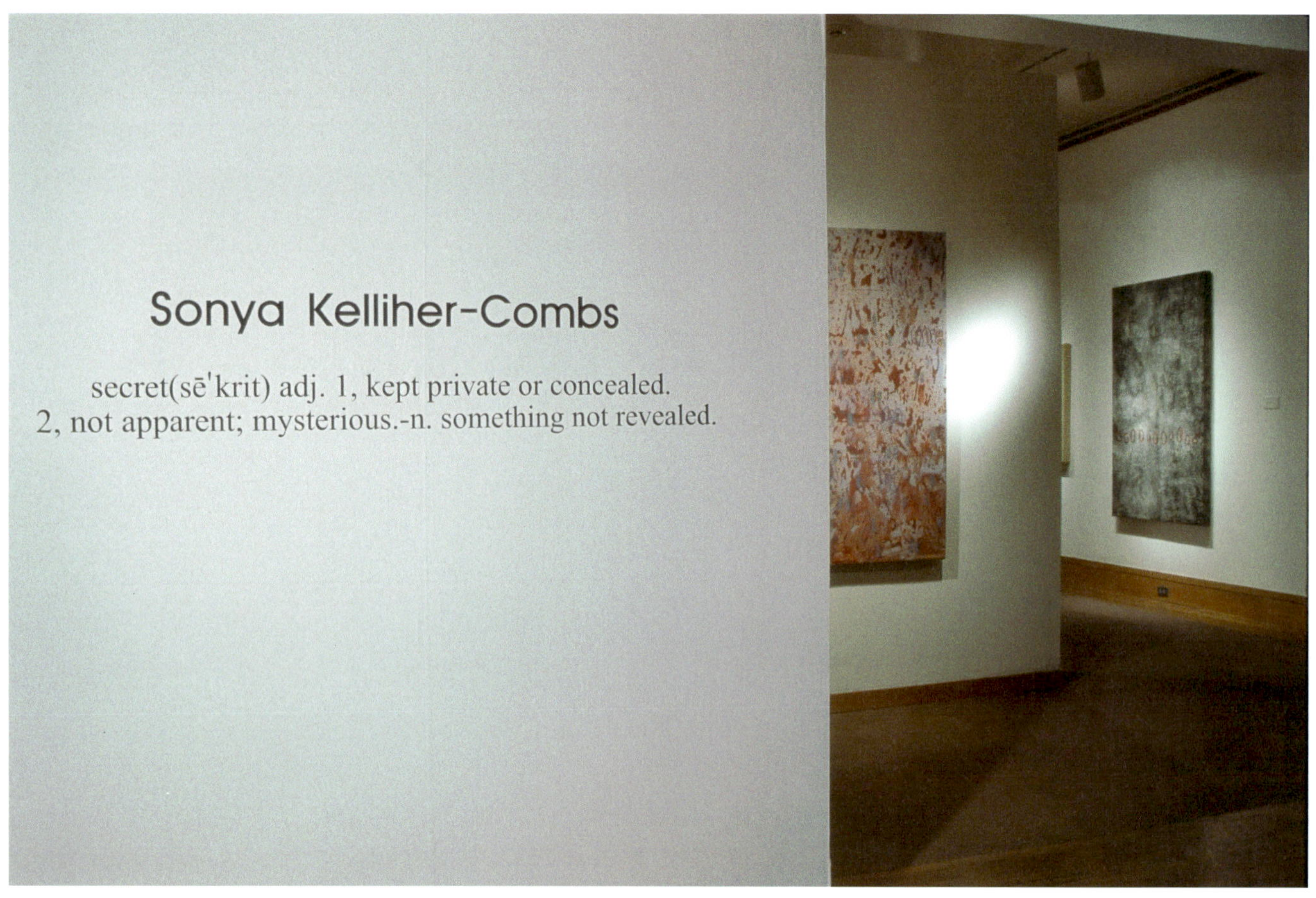

Secrets exhibition at the Anchorage Museum, 2004. Photograph by the artist.

communities, Indigenous communities, [suicide] is disproportionate to other communities. I felt like we had to talk about that, and I wanted to create an opportunity to say something—to let people feel that it's OK. Because being raised in the Church, it's not OK. You just hide that stuff away—sweep it under the rug. And even though people do have memorials or funerals for people who passed that way, until recently, they weren't able to celebrate their loved one's life the same way, especially in the Church. I feel that part of my work is about creating an opportunity for people to have a voice and not be afraid to address these difficult issues.

As far as the installation of these works goes, I wanted [the mitts] suspended. It's important for them to have a platform and good light, because shadow and movement are as important as the actual objects. Through movement and shadow, they touch, because we all know one suicide affects many, and they're not completely alone.

CH: Thanks for sharing that—how some of them are very specific. There's bravery in doing that kind of work. Also, the way that it brings people together, honoring that which under colonialism—which the Catholic Church was part of—had so much shame. We're still dealing with those, like, veils of shame.

I also feel that your work is starting to shift scale. When I saw your Pink Slips in New York at James Fuentes Gallery, they looked like larger hides. They were draping. They felt heavy. I wondered if you could share more about these newer works, including the scale of them. I think that it's significant that they're pink and they're red.

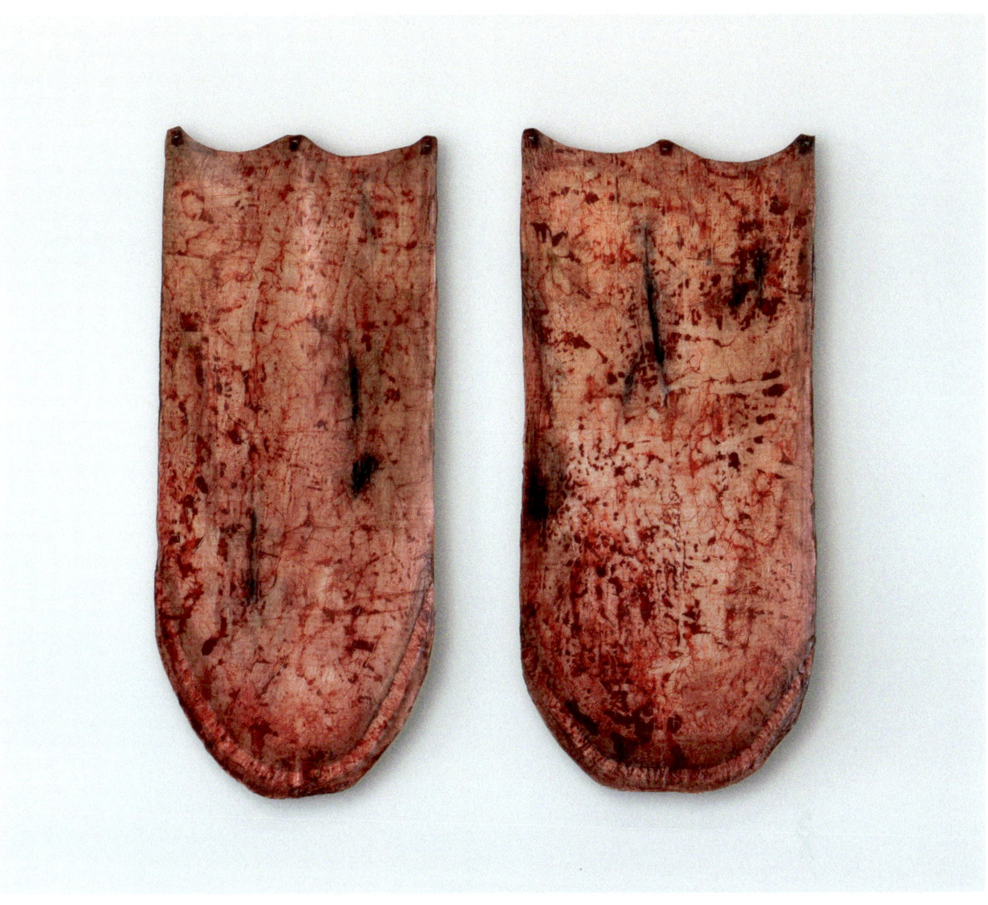

Pink Slip 2 & 3, 2023. Paint, acrylic polymer, reindeer fur, cotton fabric, plastic knitting counter, steel pin, 44 × 22 × 3 in. and 47 × 16 × 3 in. Photograph by Kevin Todora.

SC: They could be a garment; they could be a hide. I like that even though they're synthetic, the weight of them changes the way that natural hide can move, and that they are heavy. There's something that's kind of... I don't want to say violent, but something that could be violent.

I did a series of white ones; some were stretched like a hide and then submerged in white with all these scars. Submerging garments within a medium does something different. They're more obviously about trauma, but I also feel it's about resilience, because it survived somehow, even though there's all this stuff, all these scars, buried within those pieces.

CH: I think the weight is important, because it's the way that I read it, too. When I first saw them, I thought how much that would weigh if I tried to carry it on my back.

SC: It was a serious consideration, the weight of them. They are meant to be heavy. They remind me of my mom. When we were little, she would carry the youngest in her parka, amaking (carrying) the child on her back, with two others in tow, holding her hands. She is the strongest person I know. These works need a lot of weight. Our women carry so much. Lots of metaphor there.

CH: I'm sure that this comes up for you a lot: similarities with Eva Hesse's work, and her work in latex. Over time, people realized that those sculptures were incredibly fragile. I was thinking, too, in works like Pink Slips, of how you've made an inorganic medium organic, because it's constantly shifting and changing and slumping and responding to the humidity. That's kind of a source of its magic: it doesn't feel fixed; it doesn't feel inert; it's very active.

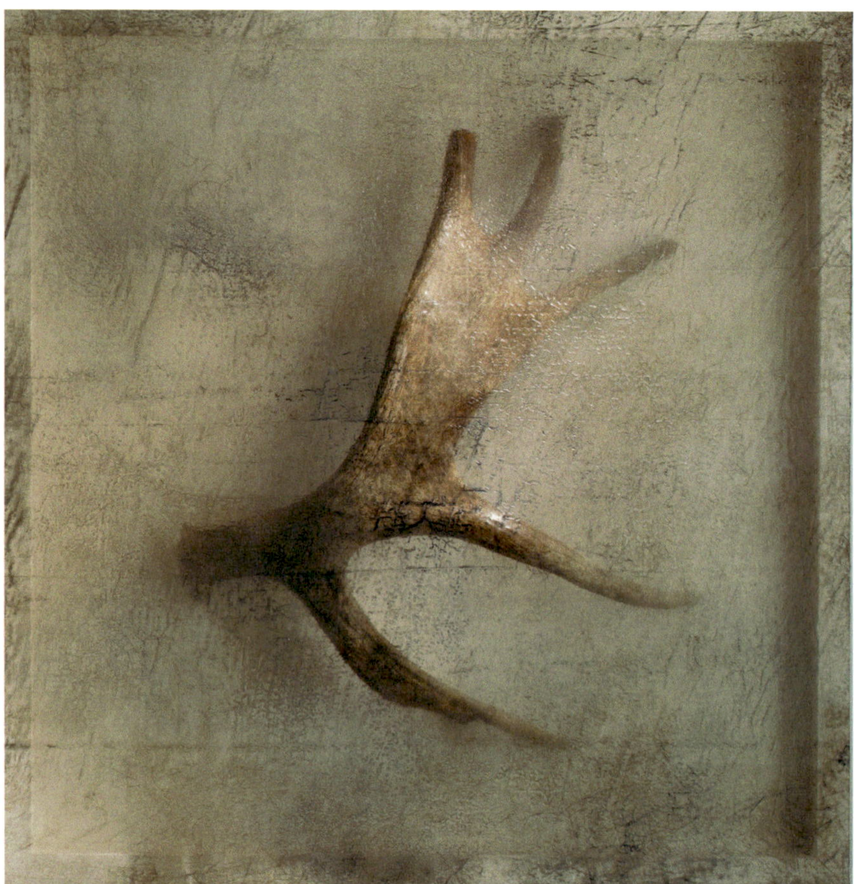

Moose Antler, 2016. Paint and mixed media, 30 × 30 in. Private collection. Photograph by Chris Arend.

SC: I like that it moves and changes, and also [the idea] that physical things aren't meant to last. I think that's why I'm so seduced by that material. The tension of them stretched to where it's pulling the synthetic skin to its limits, similar to stretching a walrus stomach for a drum—there is a perfect balance in how much you stretch it to make the perfect pitch. I've been doing this, finding the perfect balance in stretching synthetic hide over natural materials, like antlers. Trying to figure out whether I want them to break through is what I am considering now.

CH: Where do you see your practice taking you now? I feel that you're always pushing the bounds of your material and your medium.

SC: I am also thinking about a large-scale installation similar to Visceral: Verity, my show at the Alaska State Museum. I would love to do something on a much larger scale and invite other people to partake. I have also been thinking about some translucent, almost clear, works, where you can see through them—all is revealed. So many ideas!

CH: You just showed a beautiful installation of historic gut parkas, and in so doing provided that there are not only other ways to show our cultural belongings, which is our material inheritance, but to exhibit them in a way that exposes how beautiful and alive they are. I think museums inevitably show our things as though they're already dead, and I feel that you do the opposite.

SC: I want to do more of that. Curating and having that solo exhibition was such an honor. Access to our historical objects, our ancestors, is

From the *Legacy: Resilience* installation at the Alaska State Museum, 2023. Large Bag for Clothing Storage. Collection of the Alaska State Museum, Cup'ik from Hooper Bay, likely early 20th century. Winter-processed stomach (likely walrus), cotton, fish skin, hide (possibly once fur), cotton cord drawstring, thread. Collected by Alfred and Elma Milotte in 1946 during filming of *The Alaskan Eskimo*. Alaska State Museum II-A-6711. * Photograph by Brian Wallace.

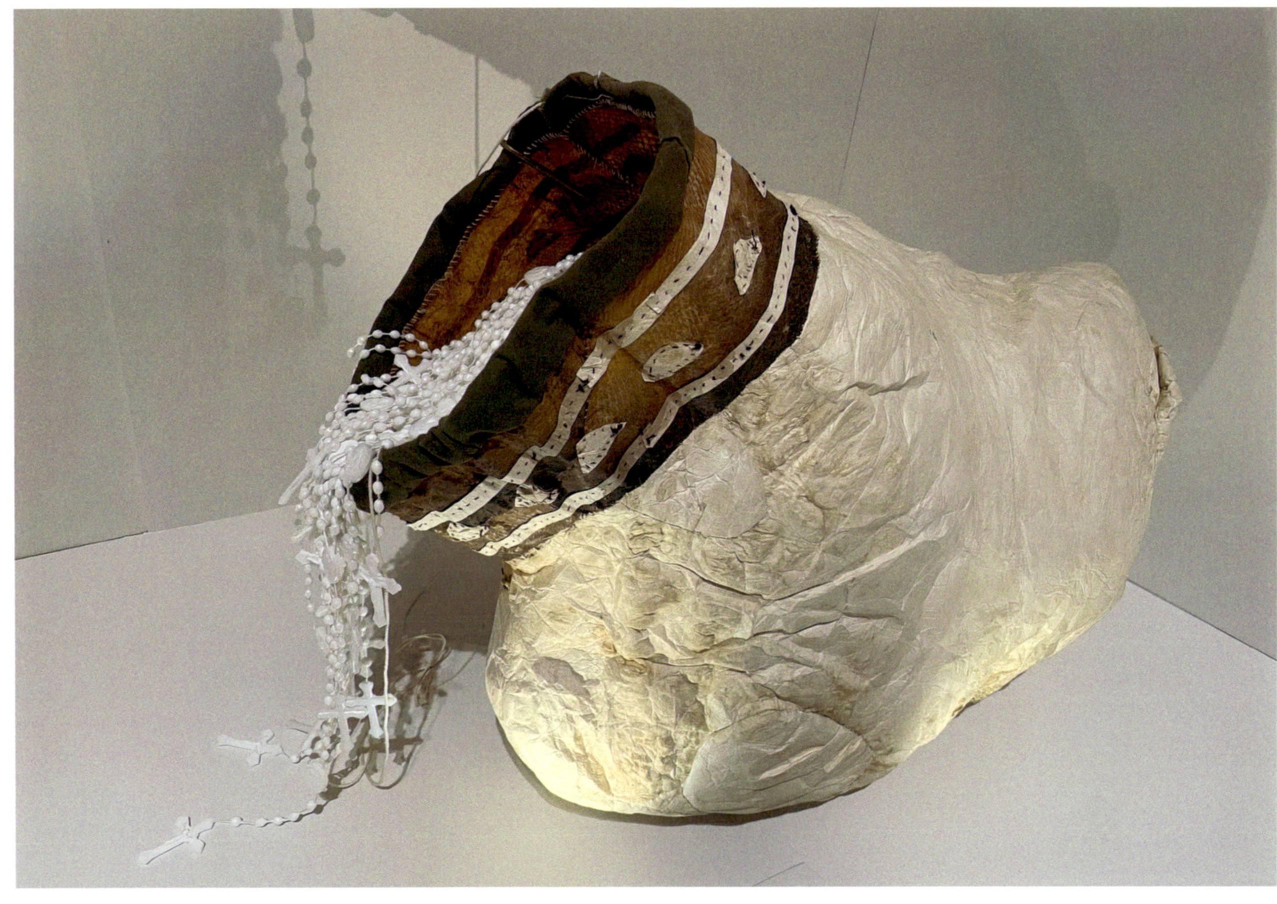

the best. We have so much to learn from them. I'm so happy because my work was able to be in conversation with all the amazing gut objects. In Visceral: Verity there was an opening between my work and a room of gut objects. Even though they were in separate rooms connected by an opening, my Credible, Idiot Strings were moving, and they were alive in conversation with the gut parkas. One represented what was missing and what was found. It was a revelation to me.

CH: Sonya, that would be a revelation, because our materials—the things that are our ancestral belongings—are often so divorced from the way that we work now by the way that they're held in collections, by the way they're categorized. I think that we need to break those lines down, because it creates these boundaries between us. Now it's about tethering them together. I think your work does that.

**Legacy: Resilience* focuses on gut vessels historically used in the gathering, preparation, and storage of foods and materials. In some of the vessels, the sustenance has been replaced by plastic rosaries. This installation builds upon Kelliher-Combs' series *Forgive You, Father, For You Have Sinned*. Contemporary Alaska Native people have experienced both positive and negative exposure to religion and have lived with historical trauma and loss of identity. The vacancies are often replaced by negative life patterns, including addiction, suicide, violence, and mental illness.

WORKS

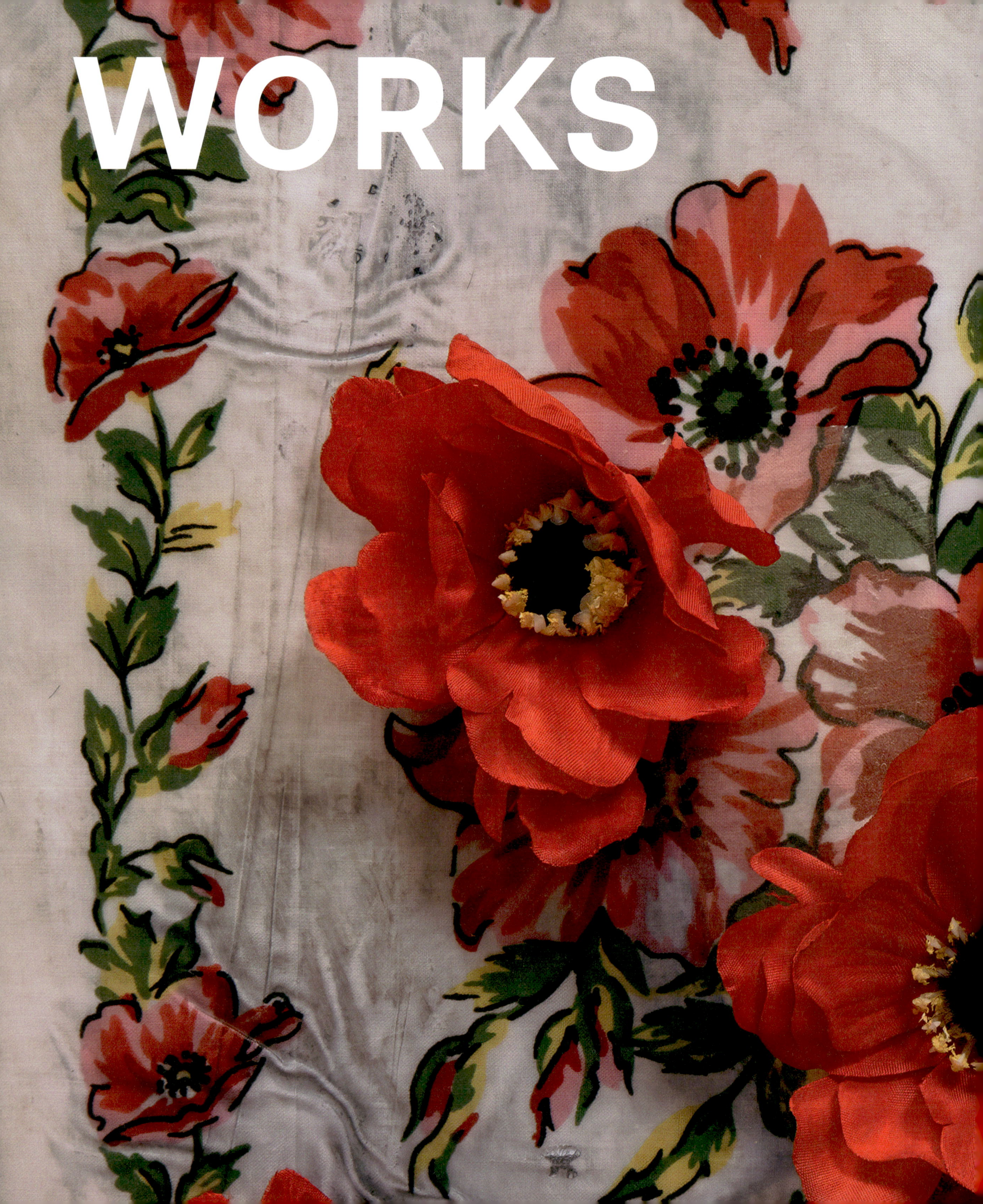

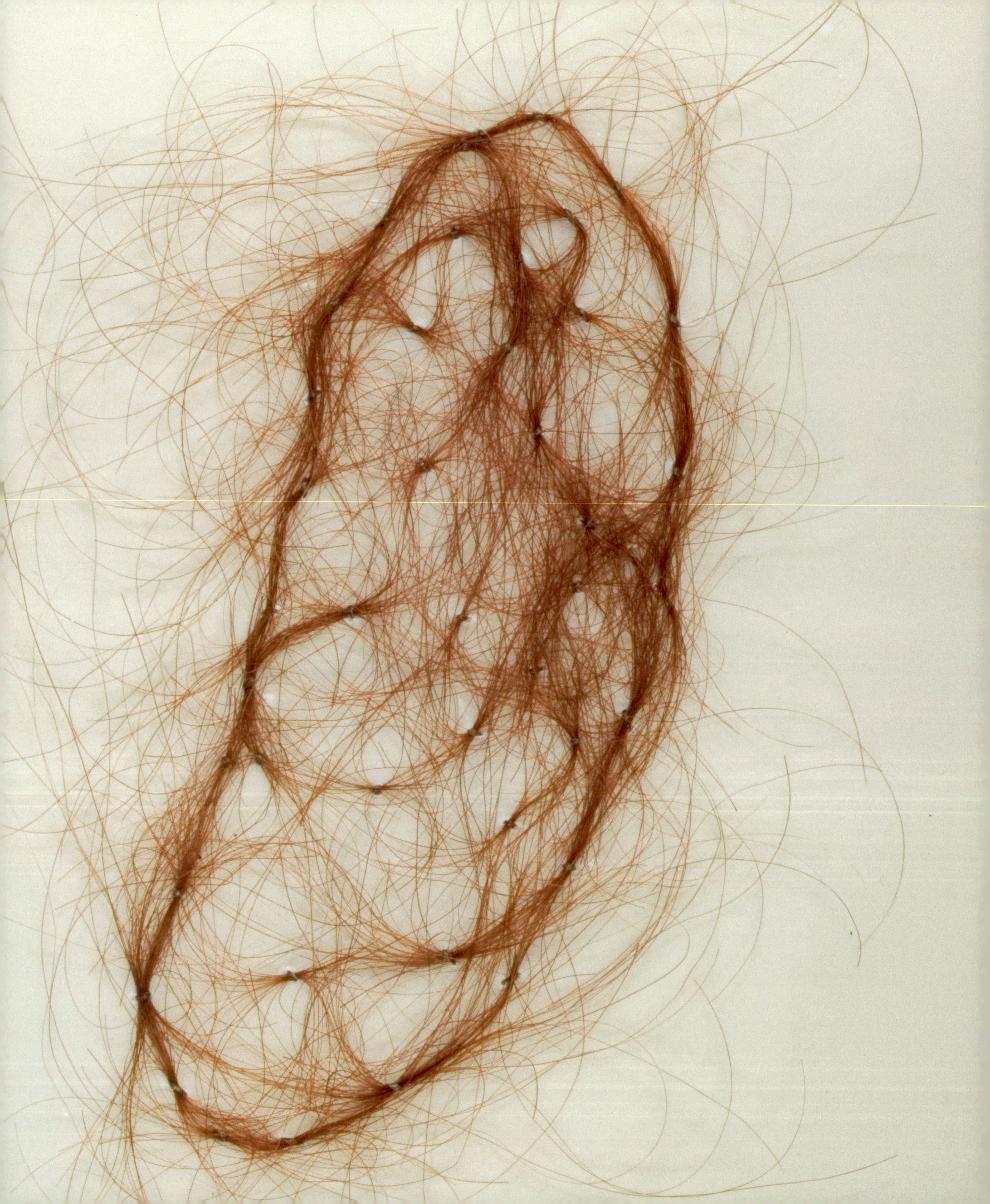

DRAWINGS

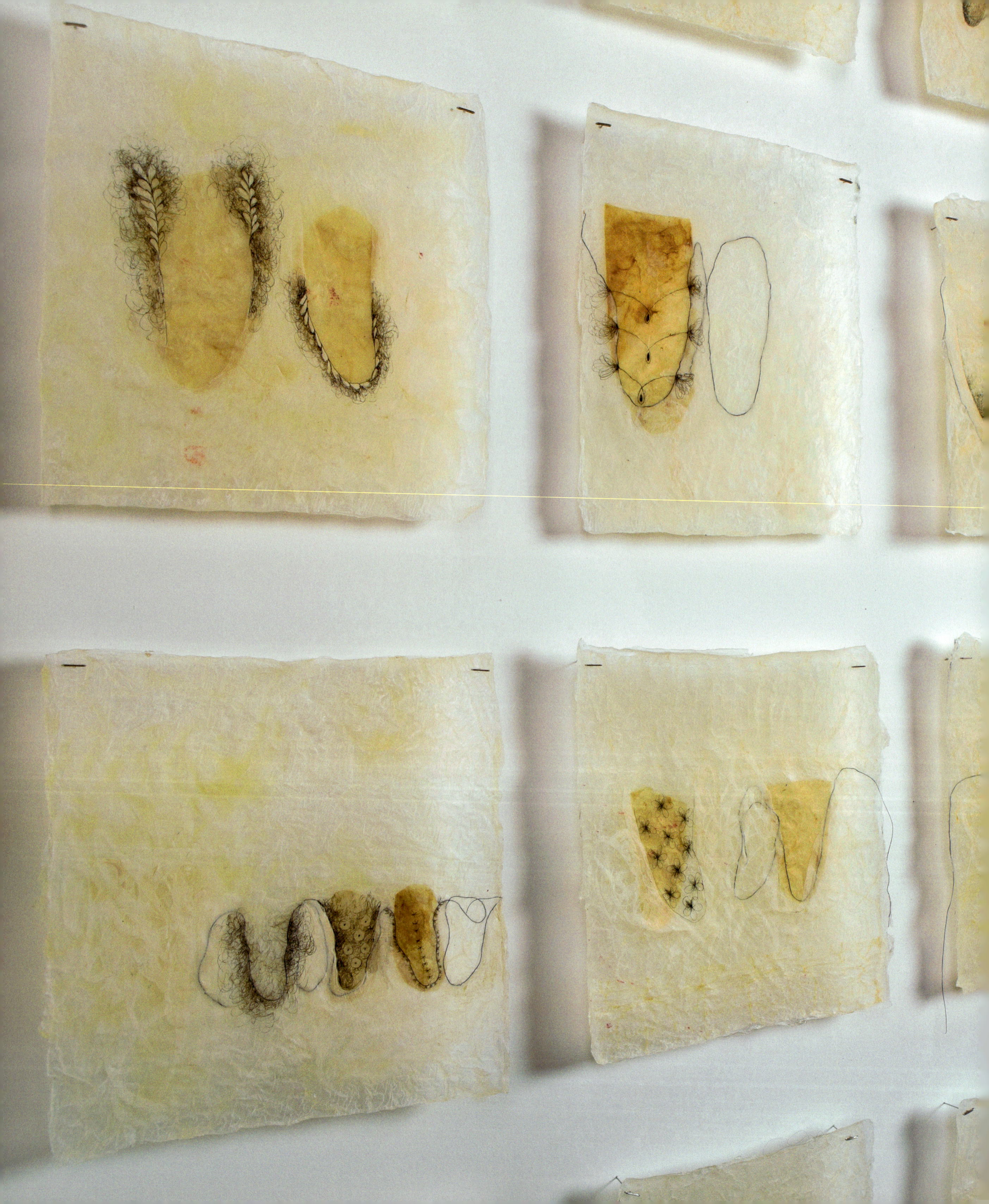

Buried Secrets

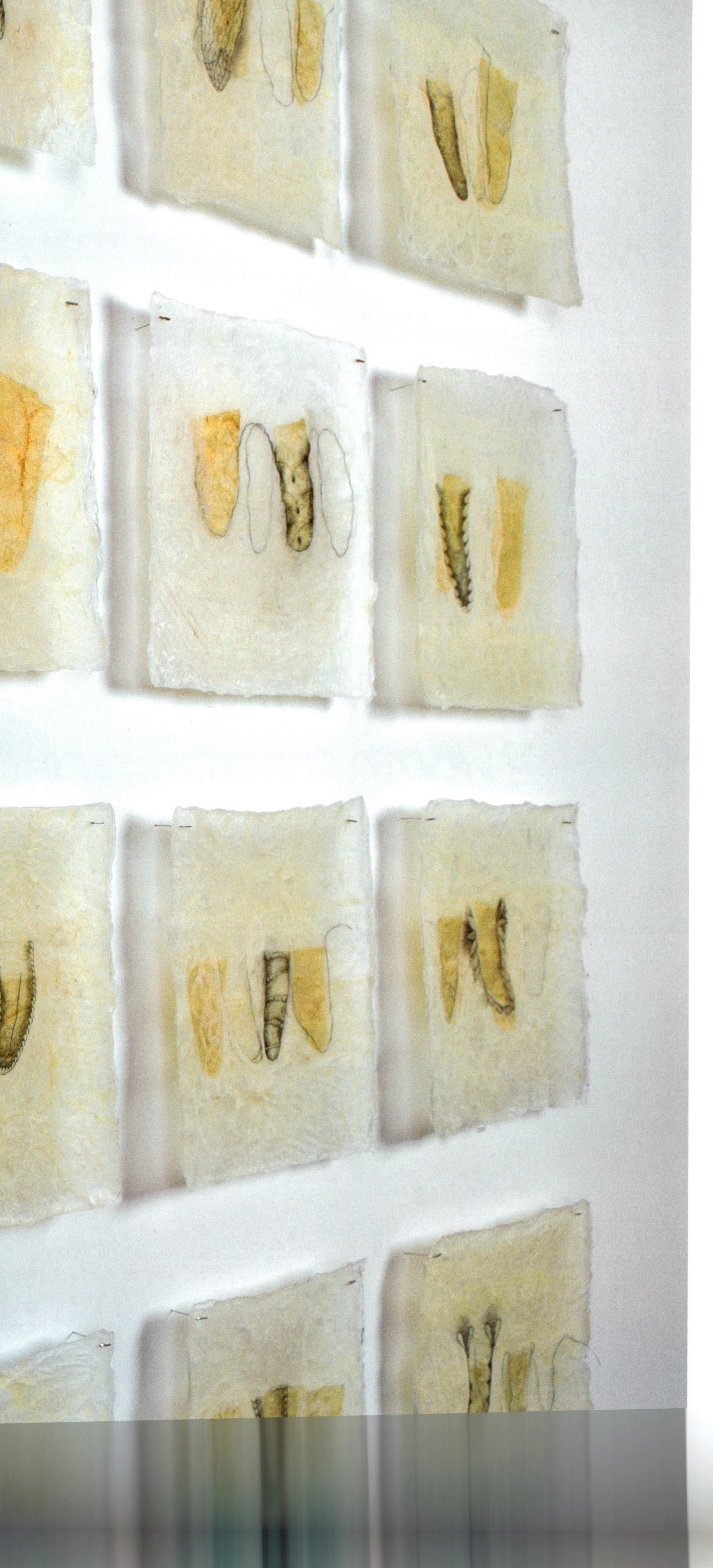

Buried Secrets, 2014. Acrylic polymer, walrus stomach, hog intestine, archival ink, thread, steel pins, dimensions variable. Collection of the Nordamerika Native Museum, Zurich, Switzerland. Photograph by Chris Arend

Buried Secrets

Buried Secrets, 2014. Acrylic polymer, walrus stomach, hog intestine, archival ink, thread, steel pins, dimensions variable. Collection of the Nordamerika Native Museum, Zurich, Switzerland. Photograph by Chris Arend.

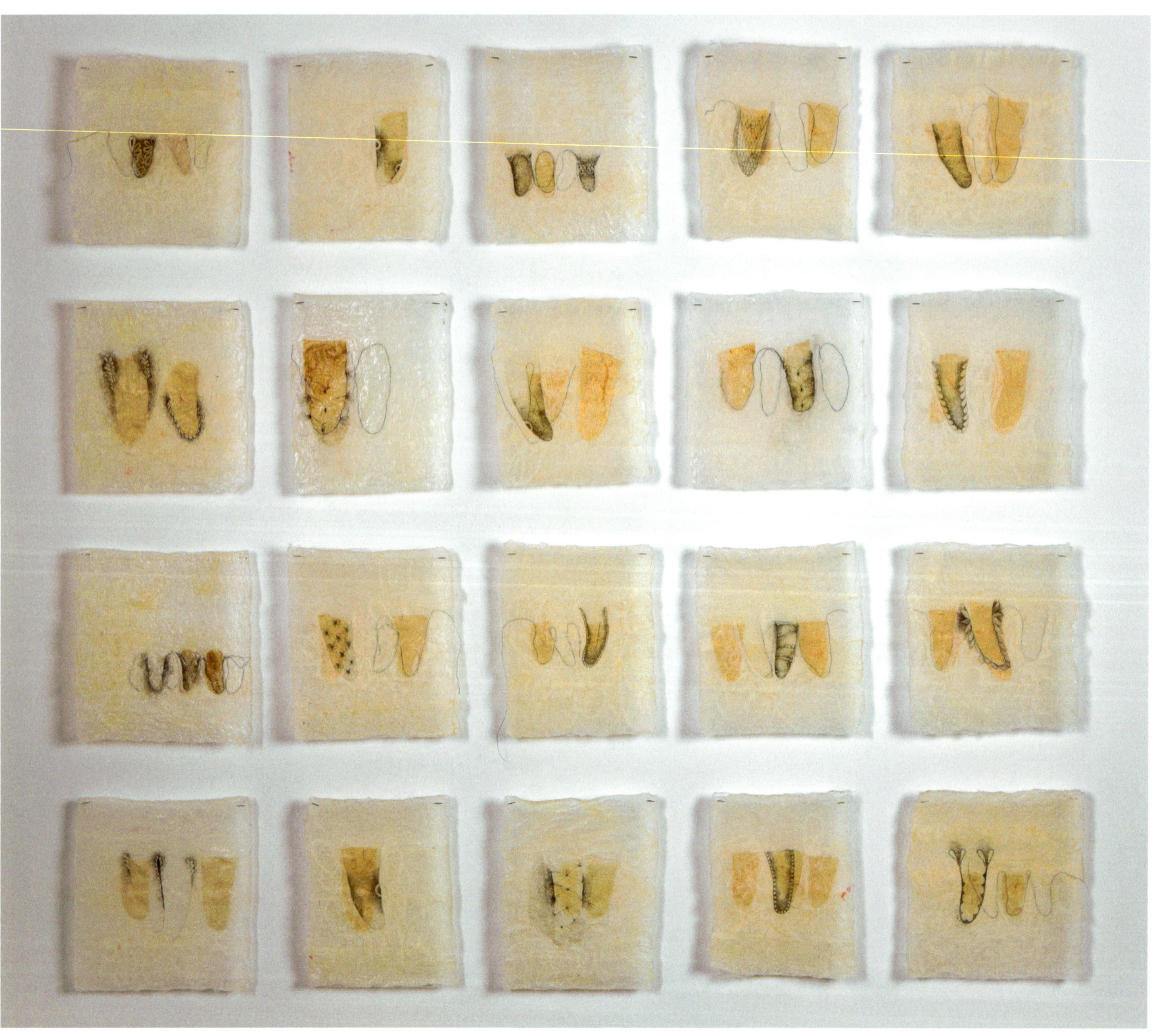

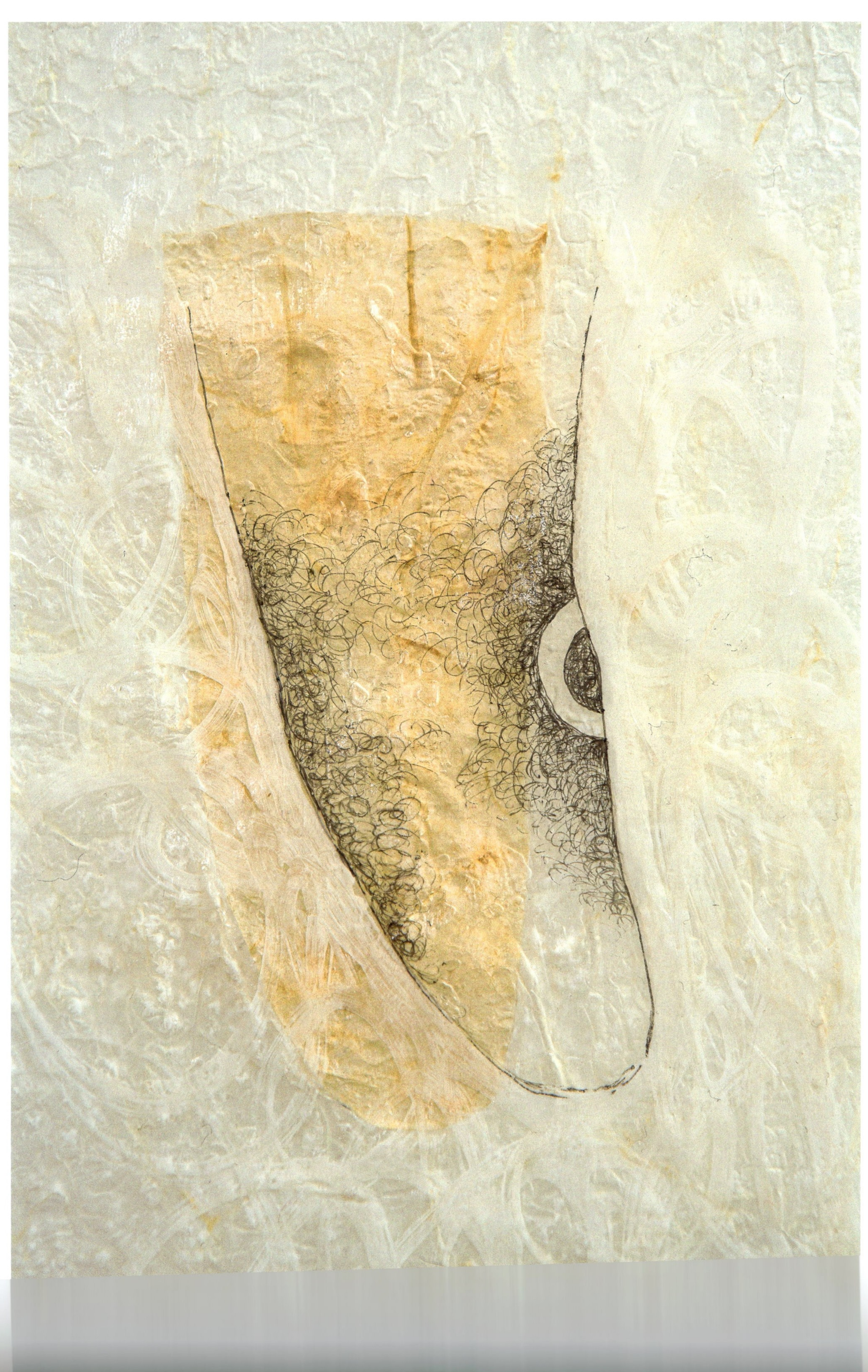

From the Body

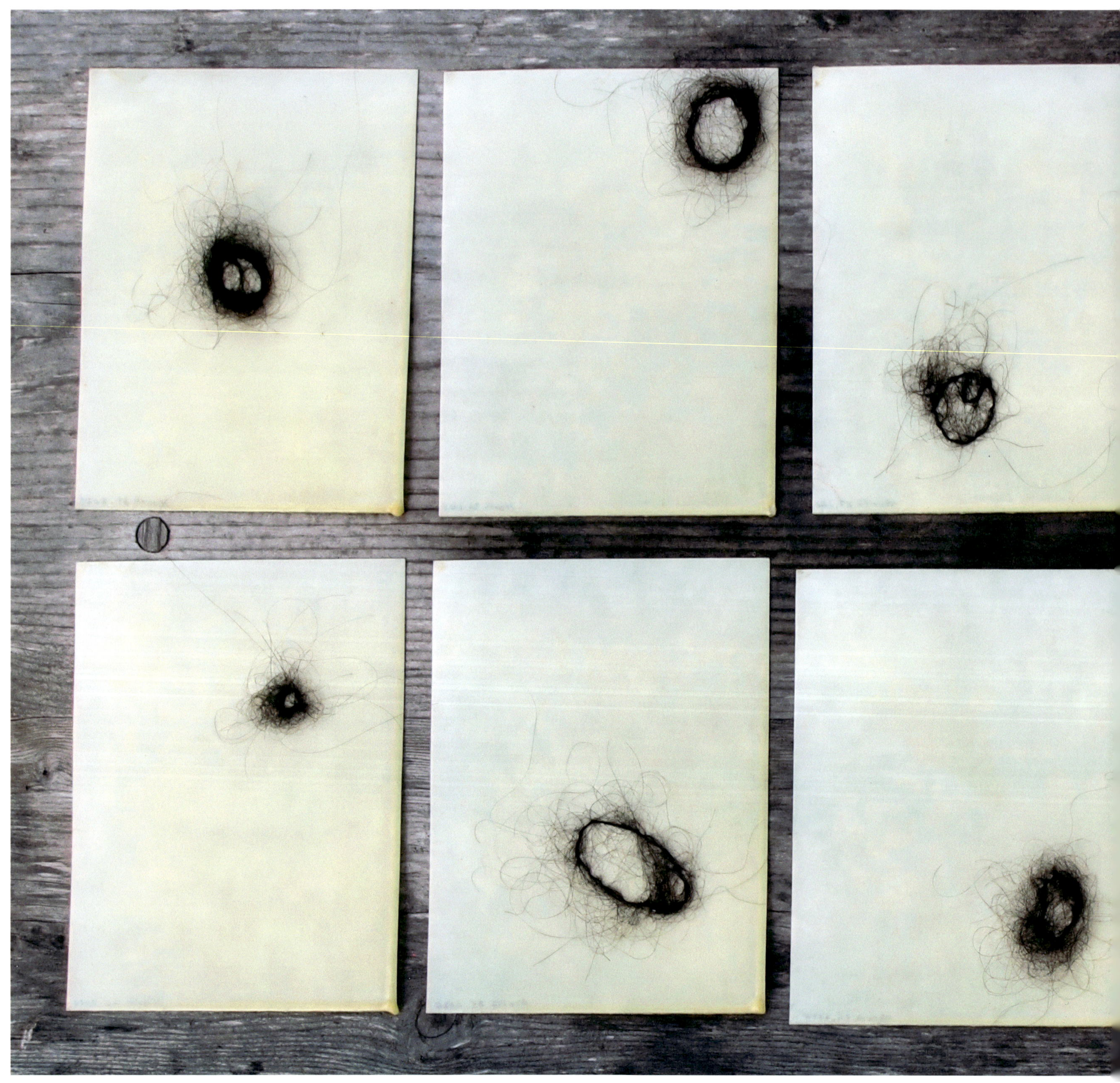

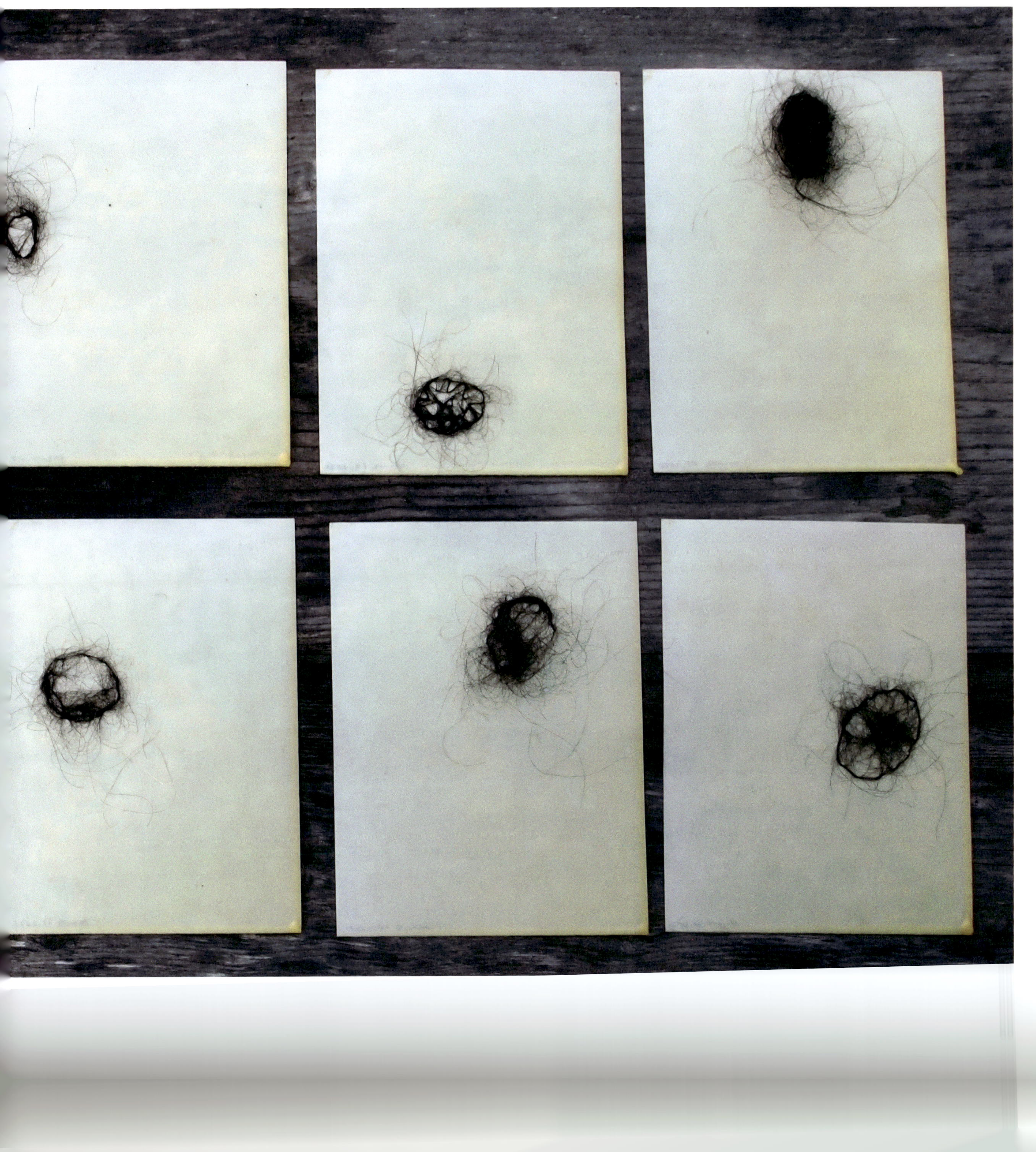

From The Body, 2020. Human hair, nylon thread, paper, beeswax, dimensions variable. Collection of the Carrie McLain Memorial Museum, Nome, Alaska. Photograph by the artist.

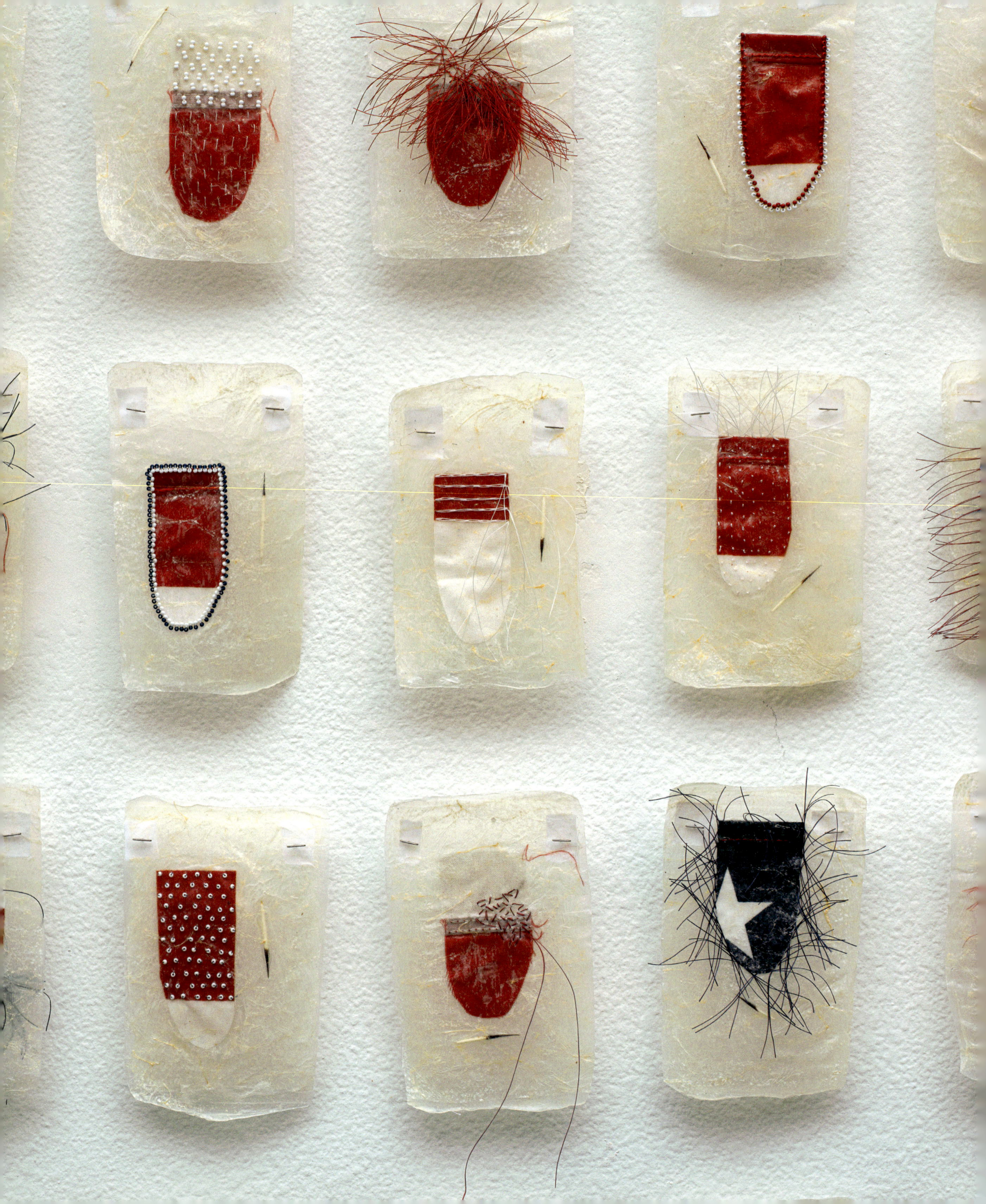

Red, White and Blue Buried Secrets Portraits

Red, White and Blue Buried Secret Portraits, 2023. Acrylic polymer, hog gut, nylon thread, glass beads, porcupine quills, nylon/cotton fabric, steel pins, dimensions variable. Tia Collection, Santa Fe, NM. Photograph by Paul Salveson.

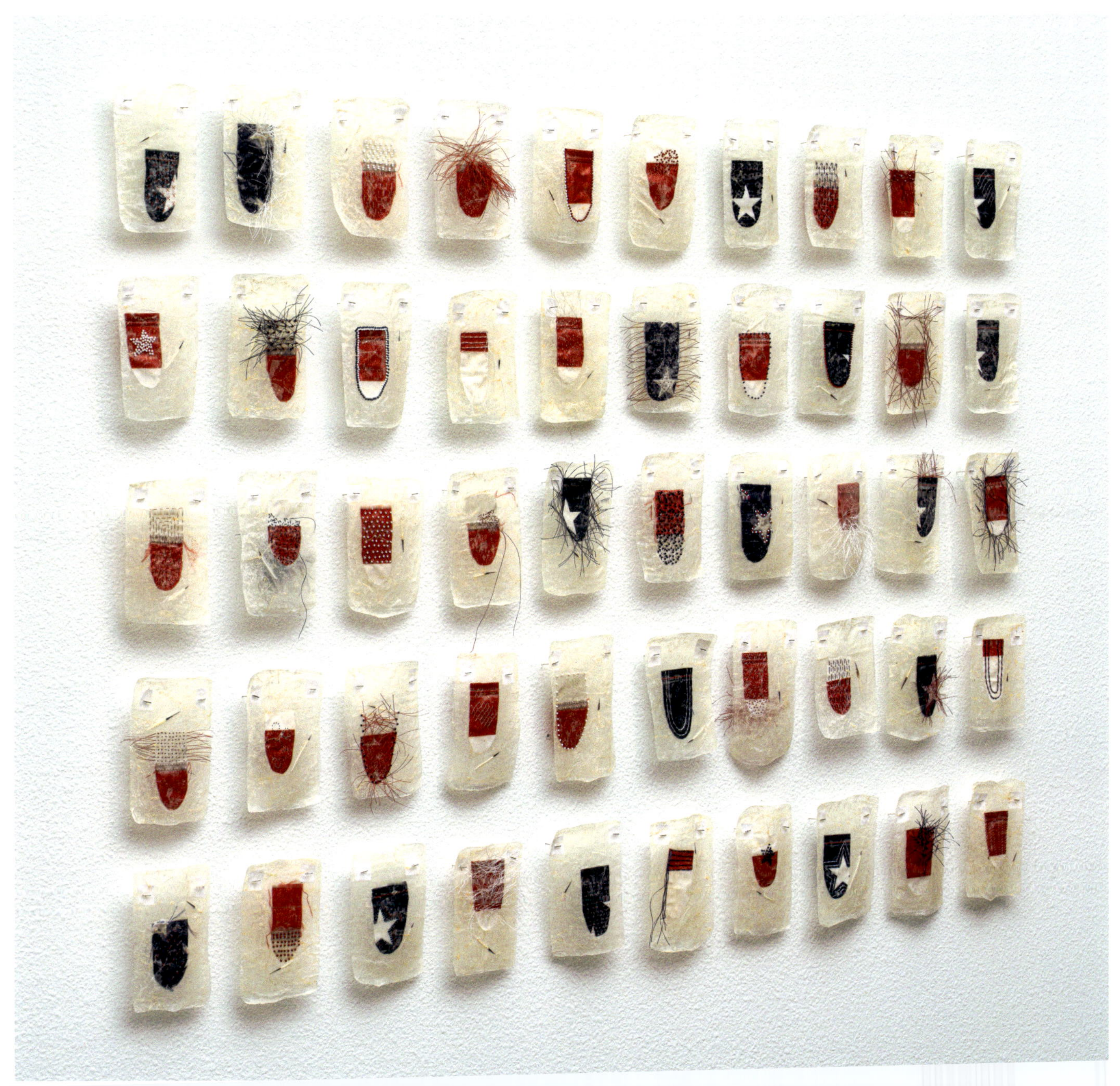

Secret Portraits

Secret Portraits are small, intimate drawings based on the art of scrimshaw: the practice of carving or incising intricate designs on whalebone, baleen, or walrus ivory. Pigment is added to the engraved lines to highlight the drawing. In reference to this practice, each Secret Portrait is inked on both sides of the paper and then dipped in beeswax. This makes the paper translucent enough to see the fine line work on the back of the drawing and gives the paper the feeling of hide vellum.

Secret Portraits, 2005. Mixed media, dimensions variable. Private collection. Photograph by Kevin G. Smith.

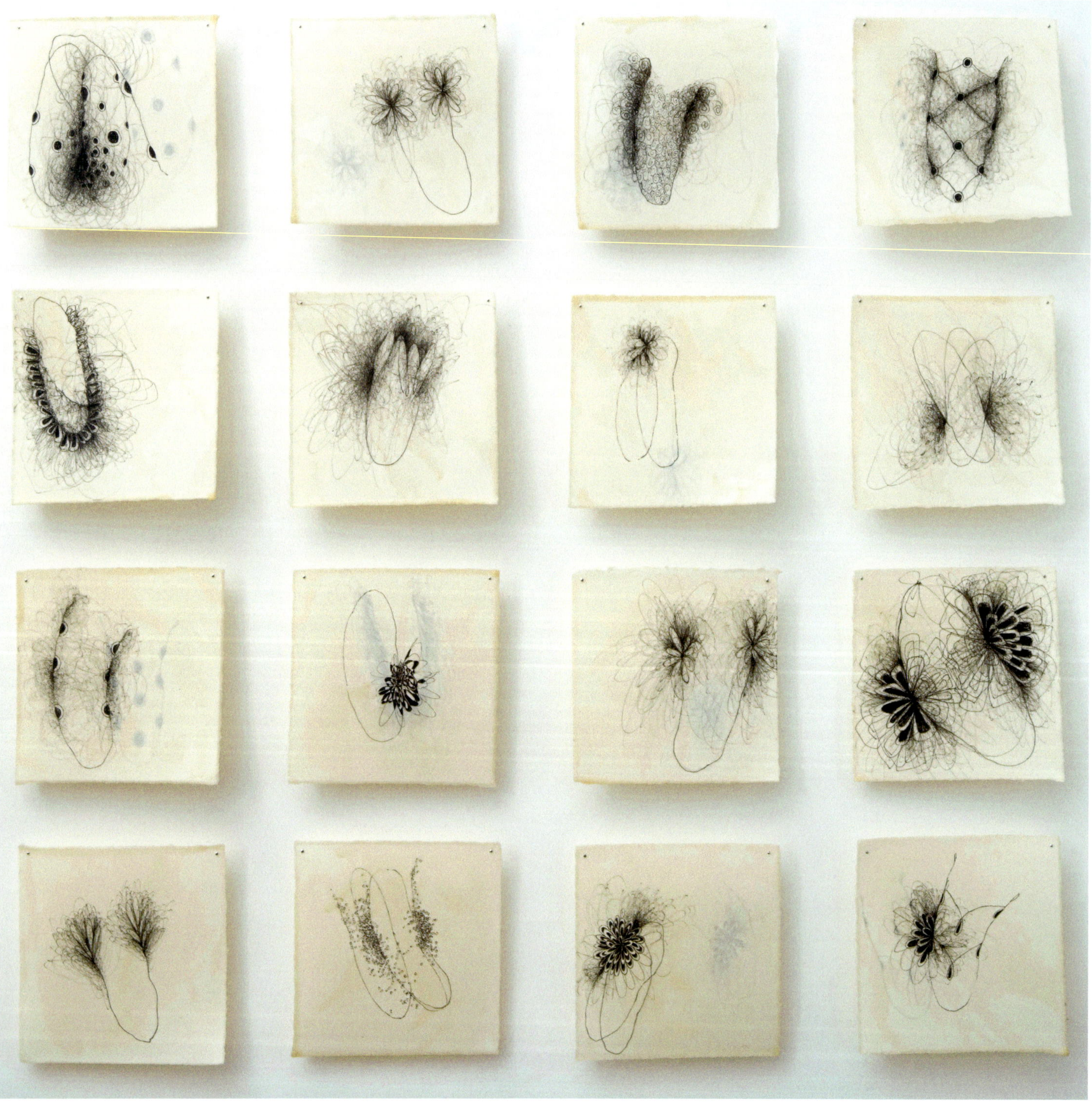

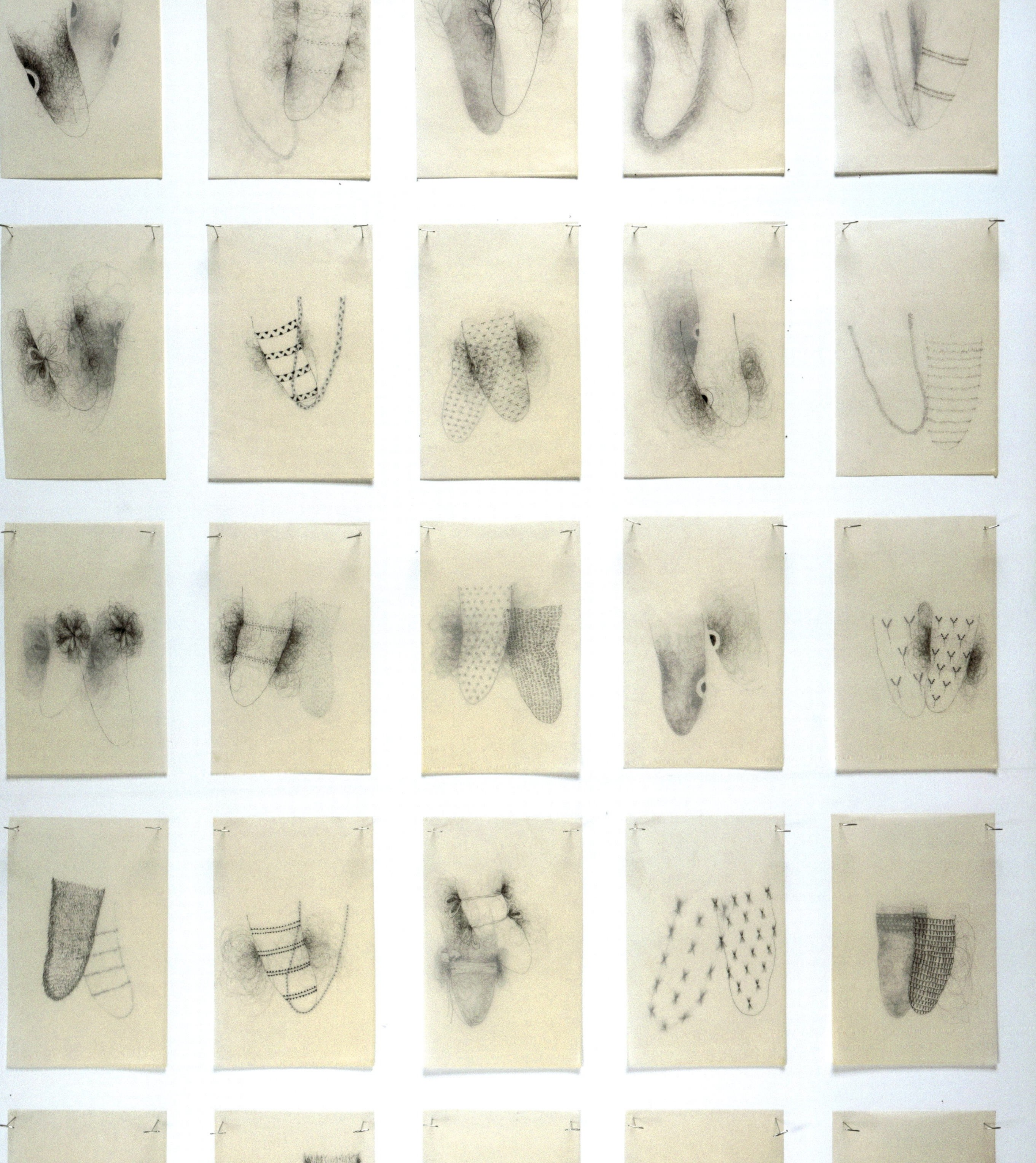

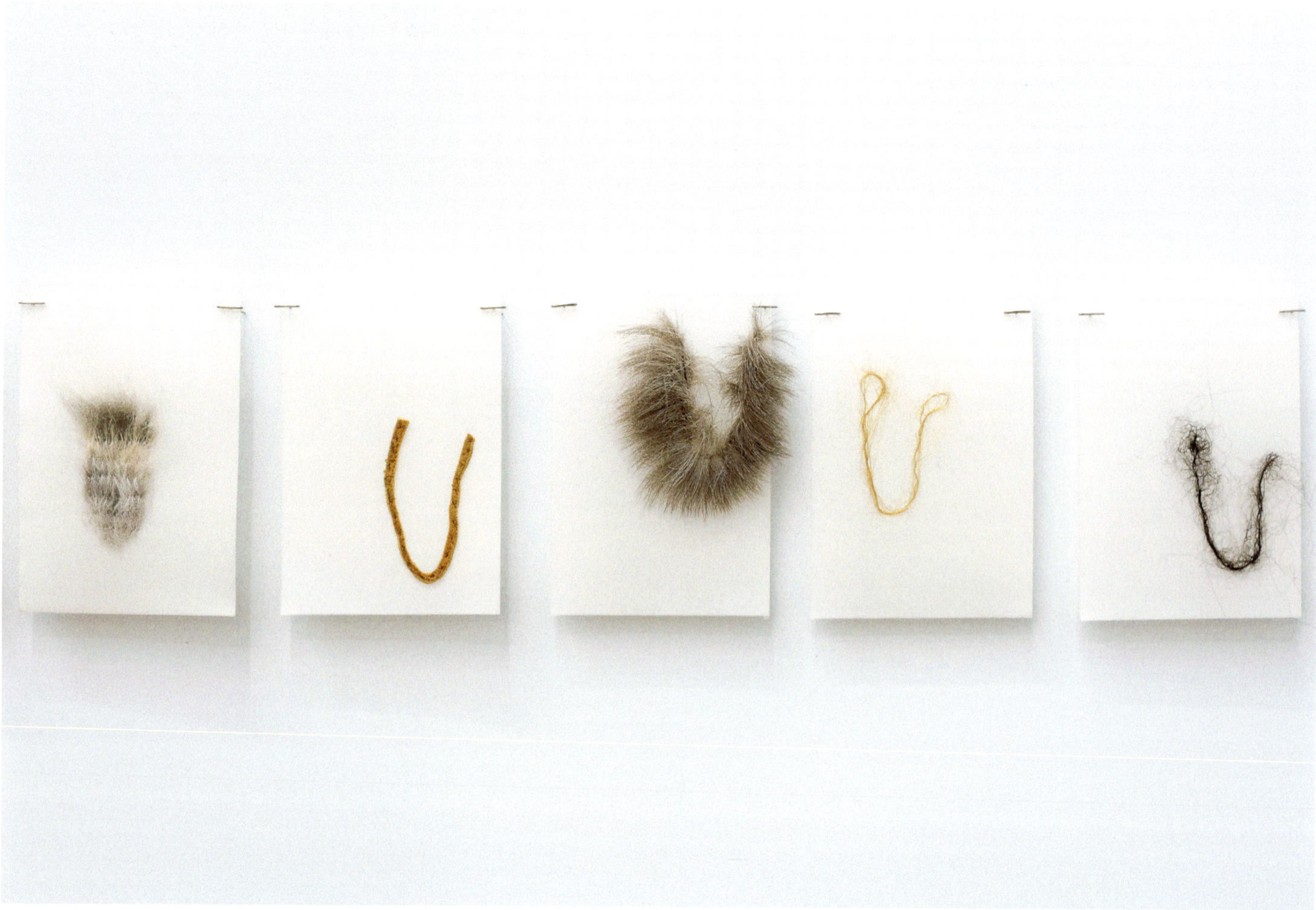

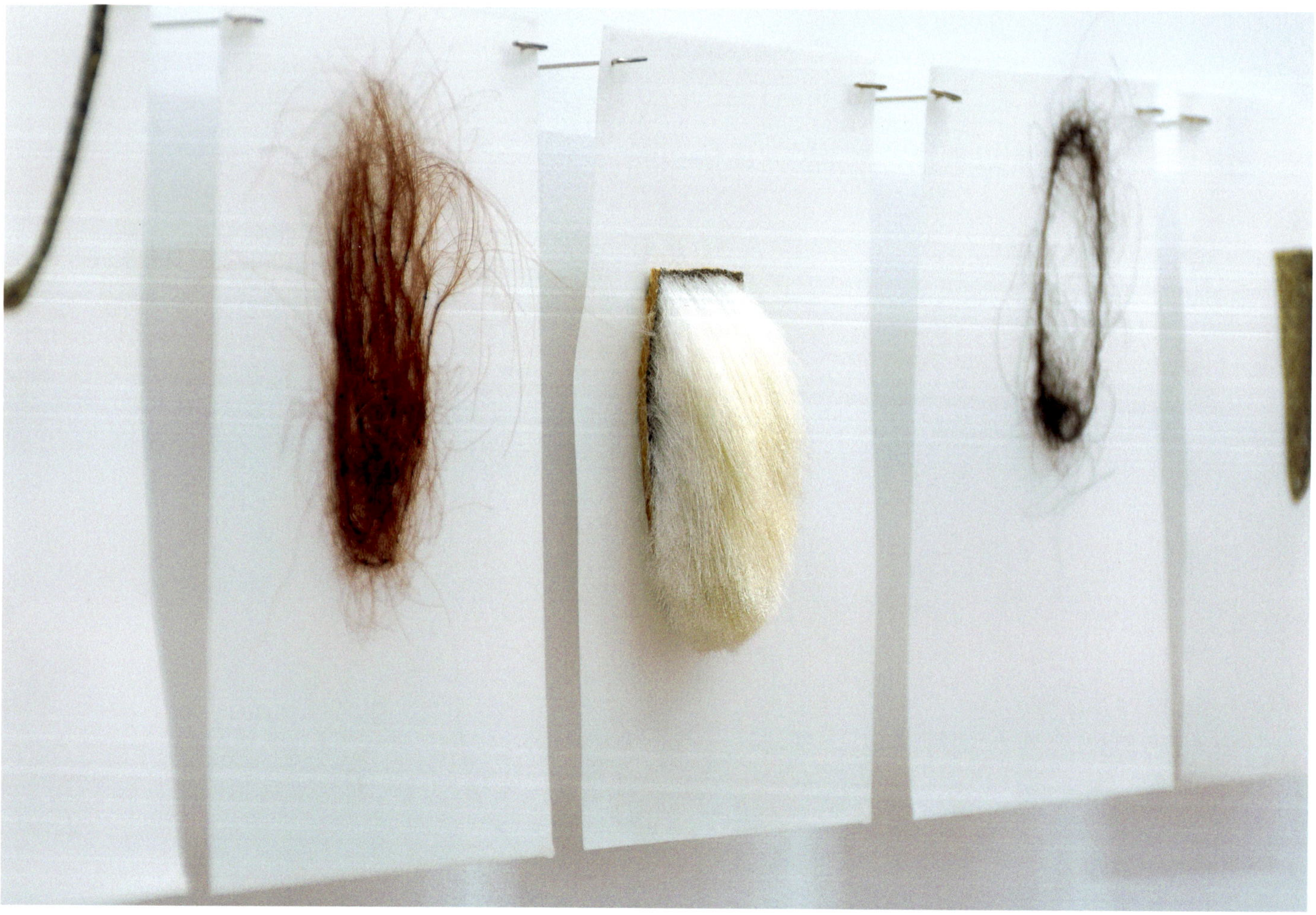

Hair and Fur Secret Portraits

Hair and Fur Secret Portraits, 2023.
Drawing and mixed media, dimensions variable. Private collection.
Photographs by Kunning Huang.

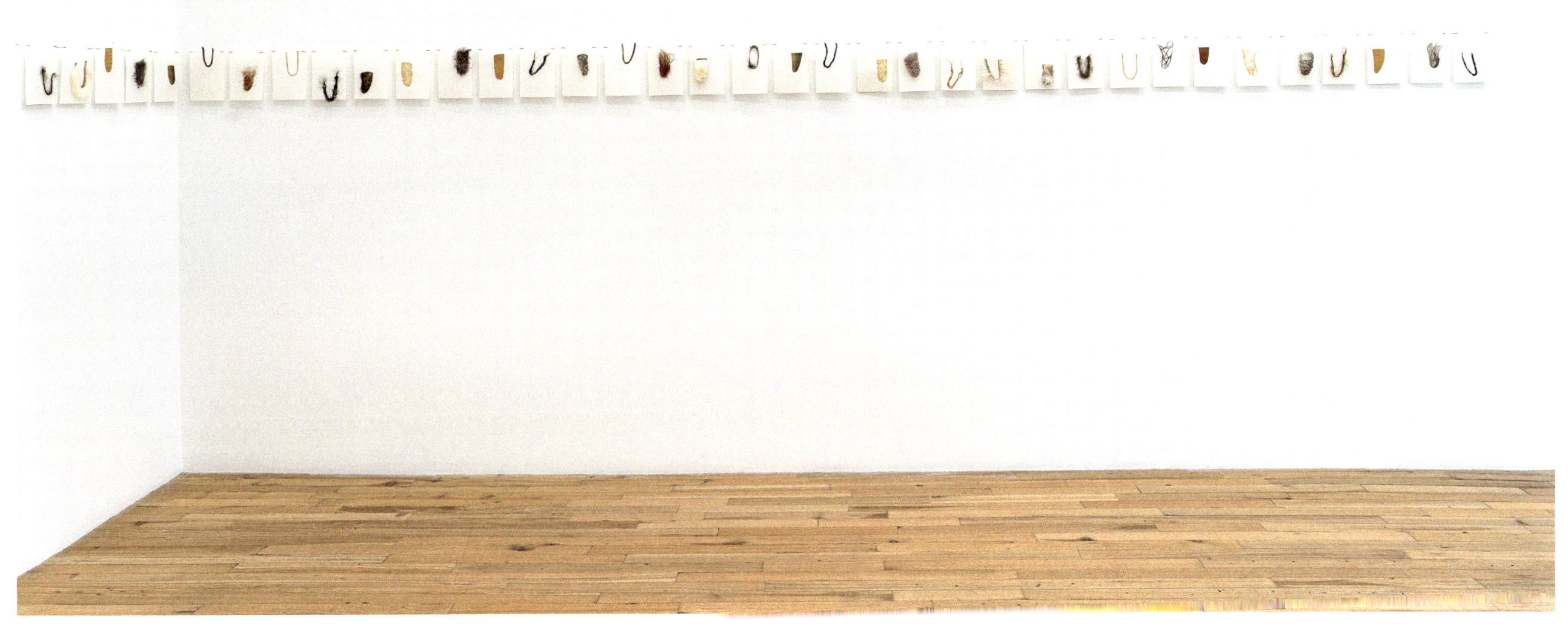

Secret Portraits

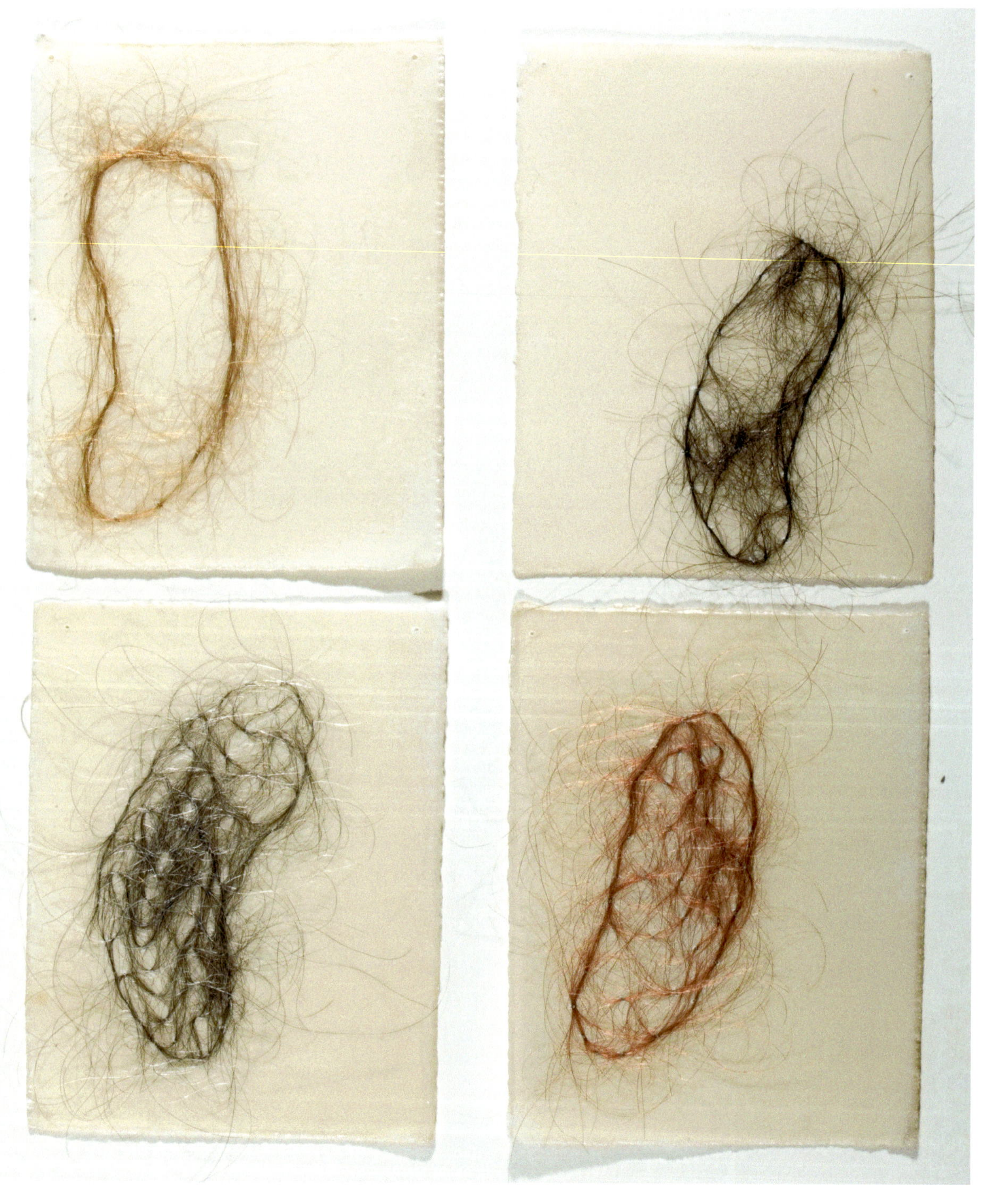

Secret Portraits, 2005. Mixed media, dimensions variable. Private collection. Photograph by Kevin G. Smith.

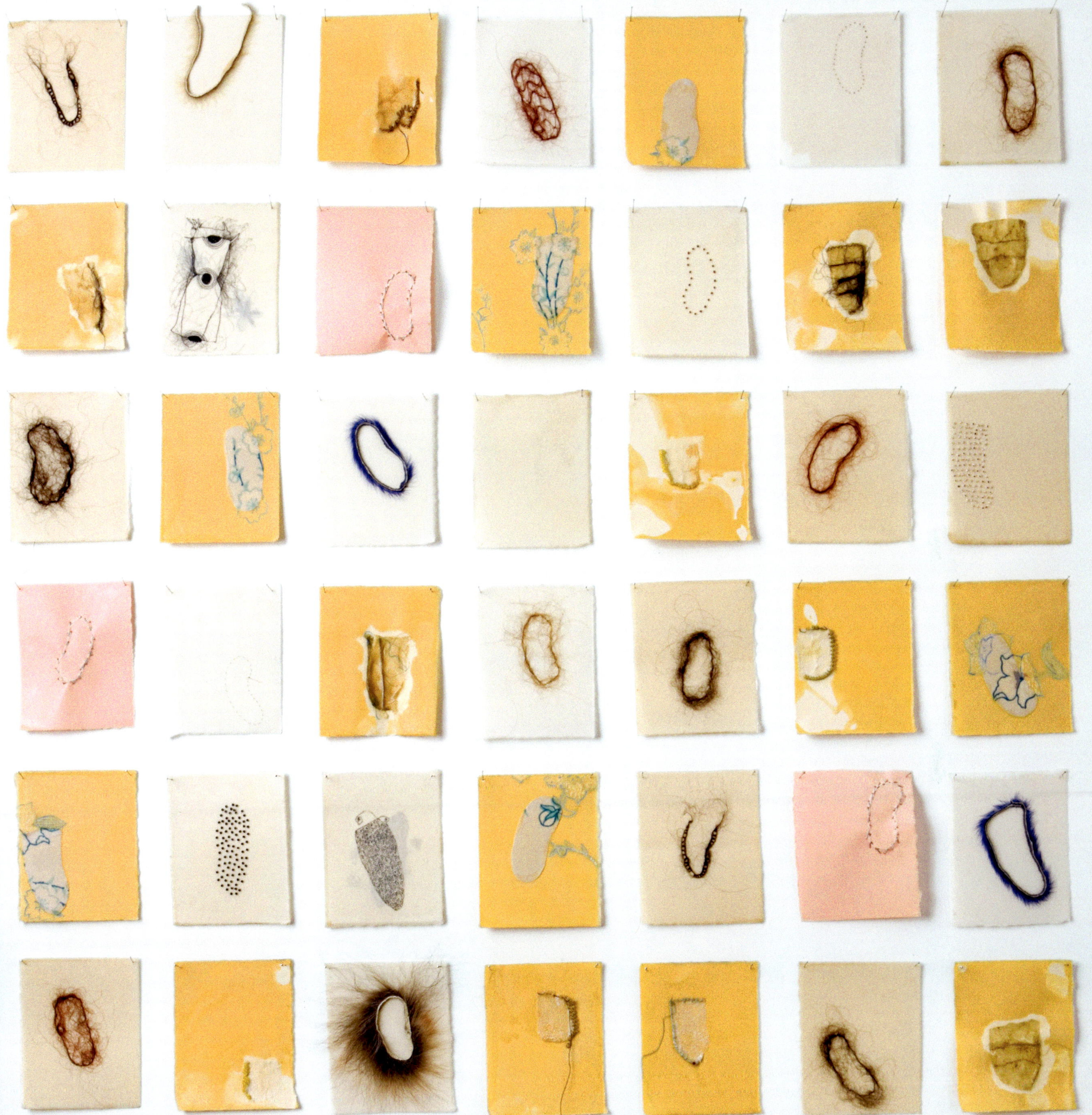

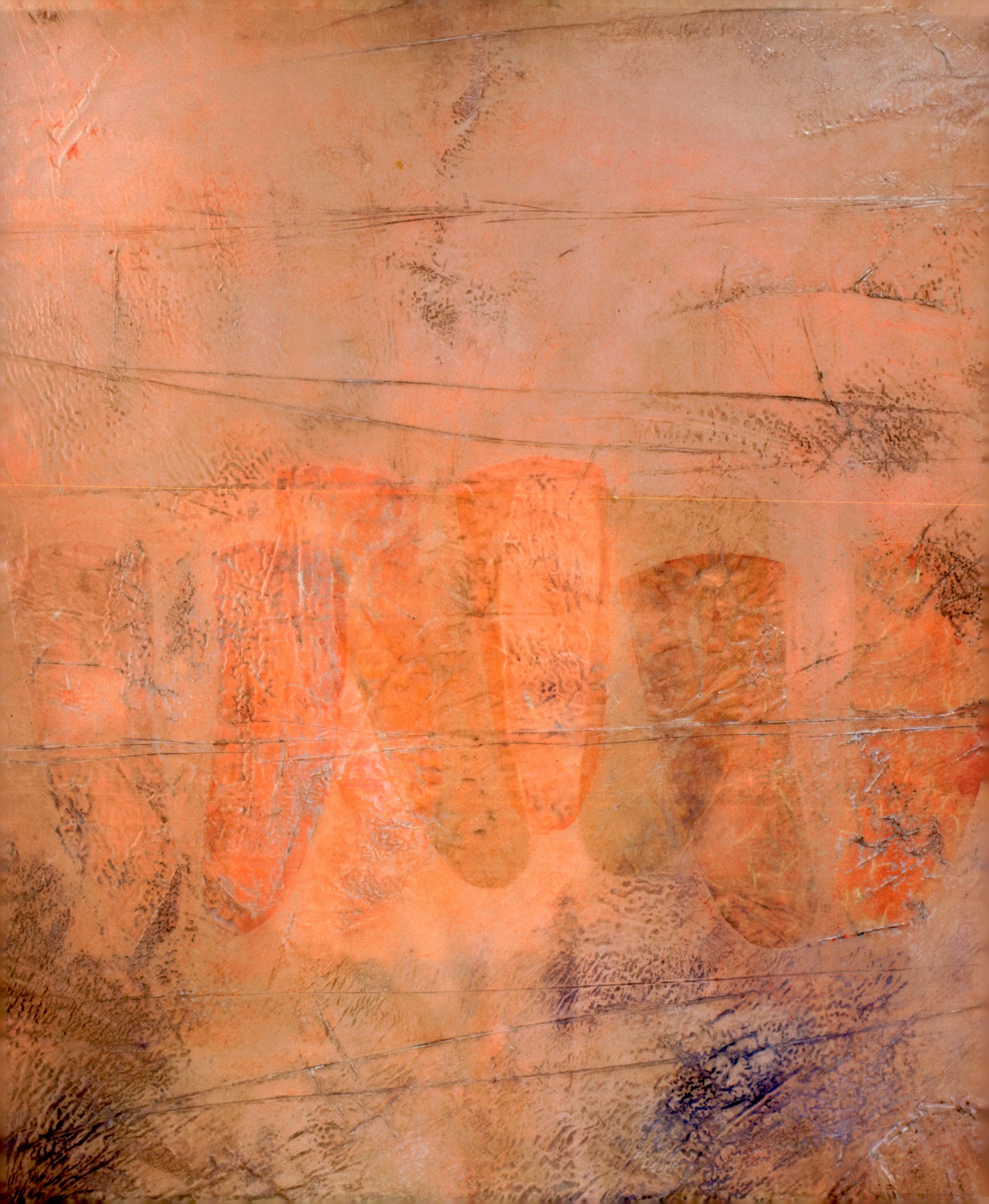

PAINTINGS

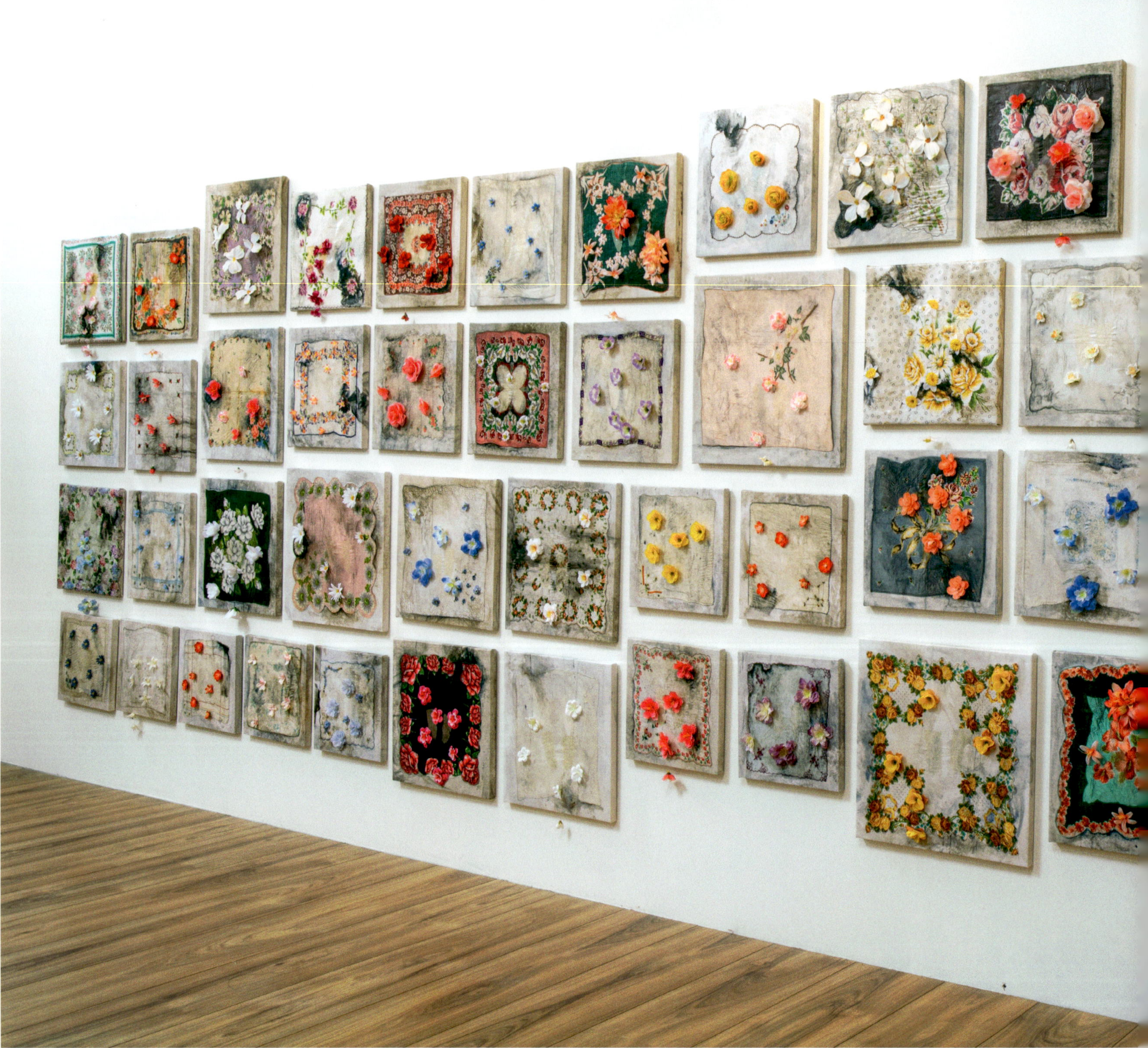

A Million Tears

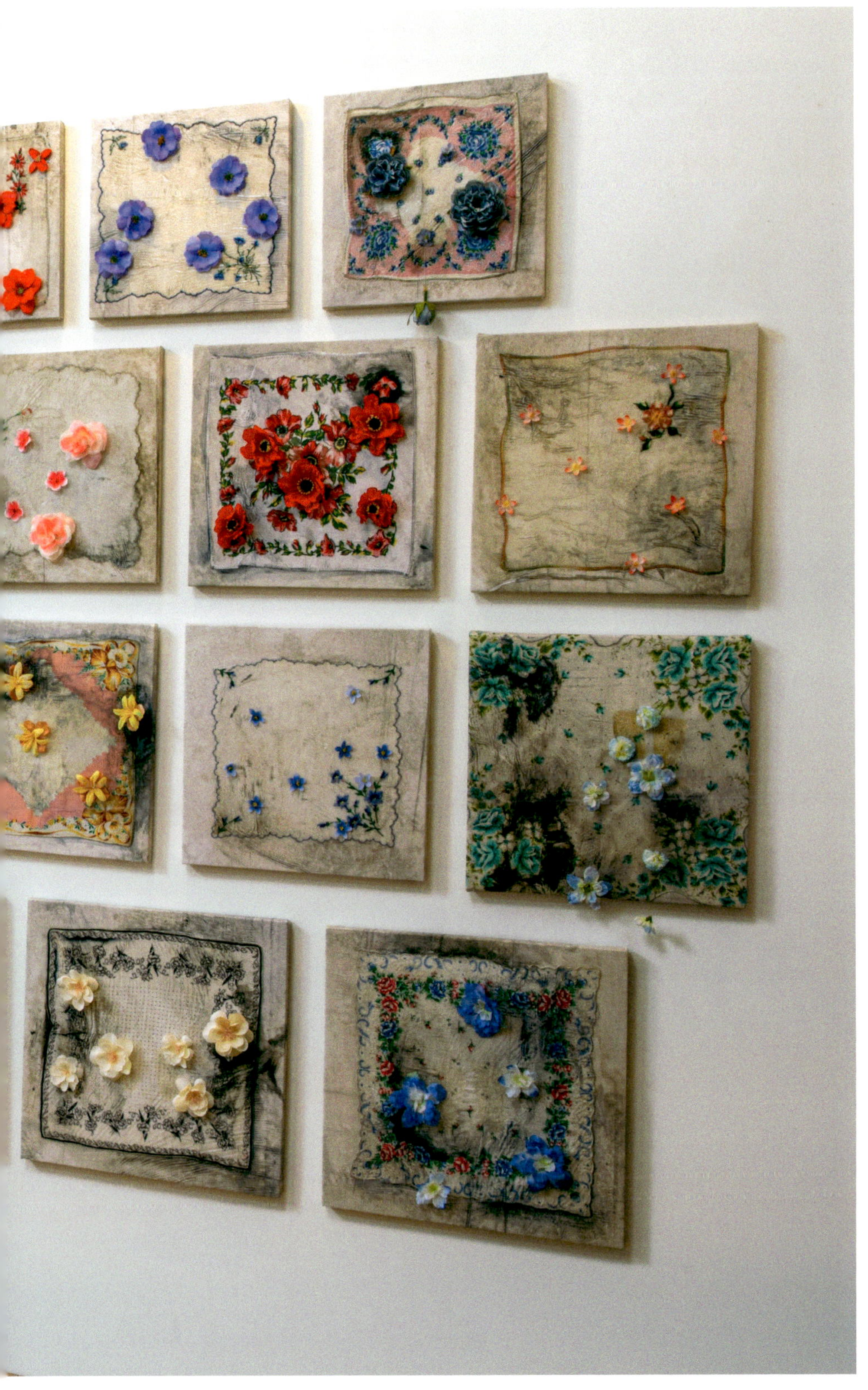

A Million Tears, 2021. Acrylic polymer, found handkerchief, plastic flower, nylon thread, cotton fabric, dimensions variable. Photograph by Chris Arend.

A Million Tears

A Million Tears is a series of works in response to the many painful accounts Sonya Kelliher-Combs has heard of abuse. In Alaska and across the globe, Indigenous communities experience extreme, disproportionate levels of abuse. The delicately embroidered handkerchiefs are repositories for decades of sorrow and grief, and the plastic flowers call to mind the mourning of individuals, families, and communities that have endured things no one should have to experience.

A Million Tears (detail), 2021. Acrylic polymer, found handkerchief, plastic flower, nylon thread, cotton fabric, dimensions variable. Photographs by Chris Arend.

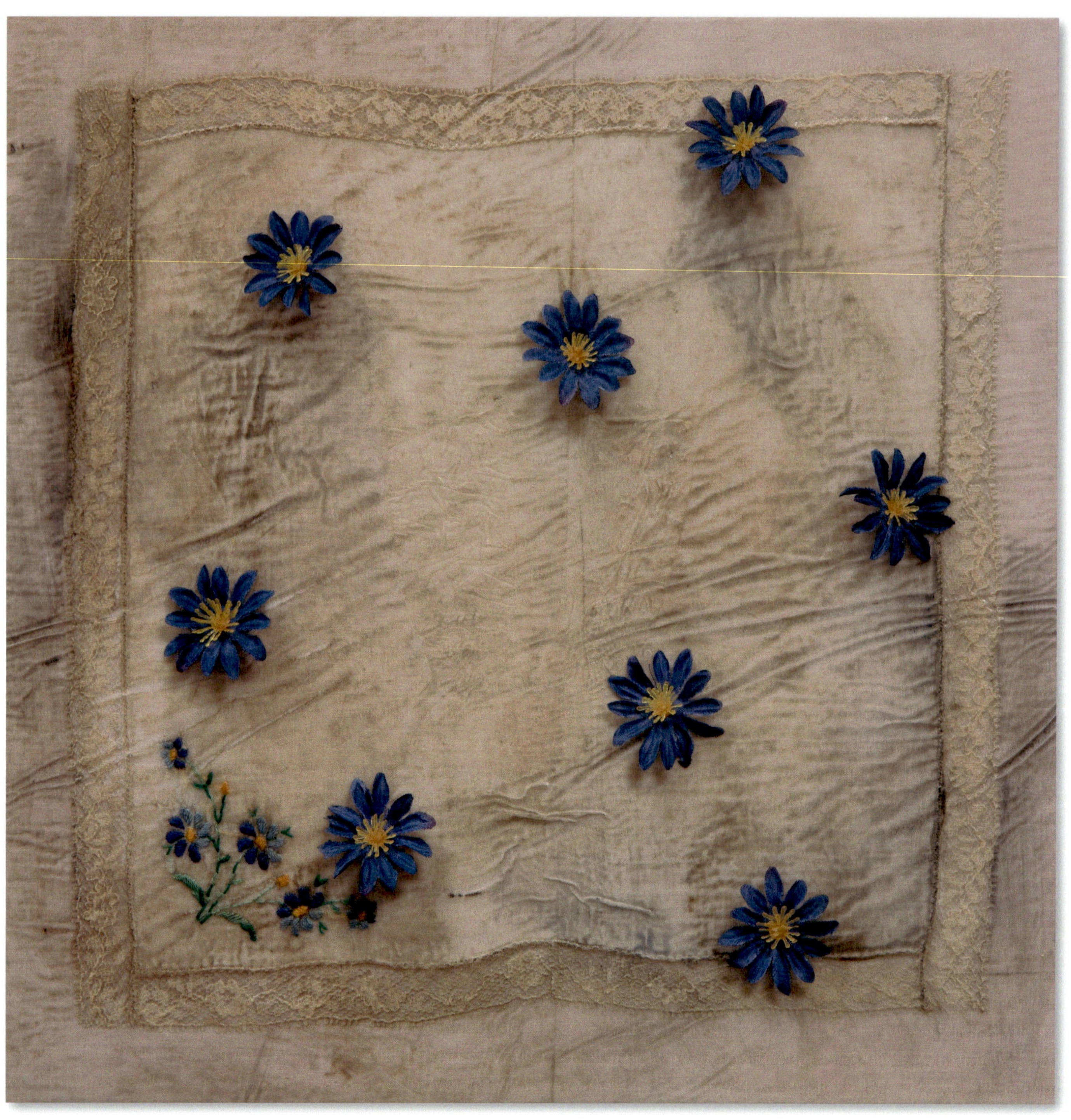

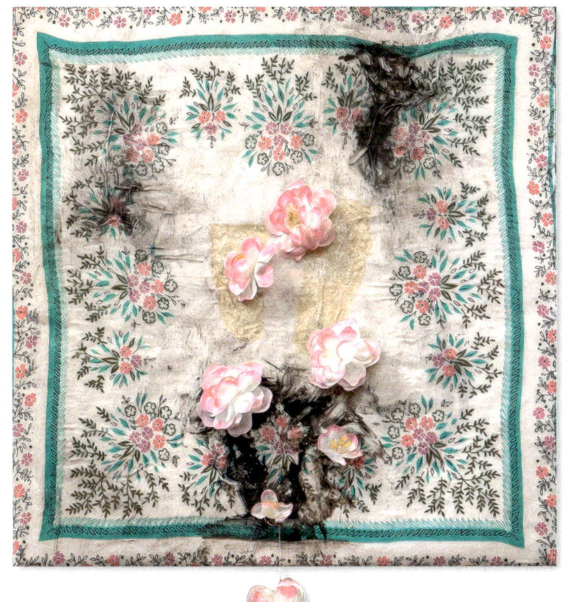
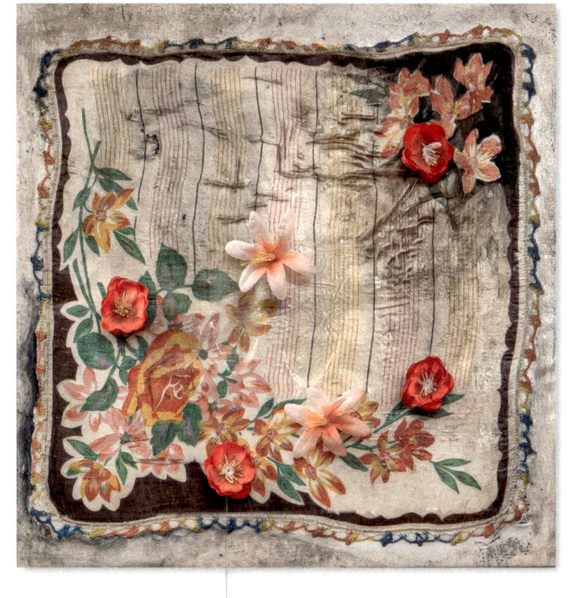
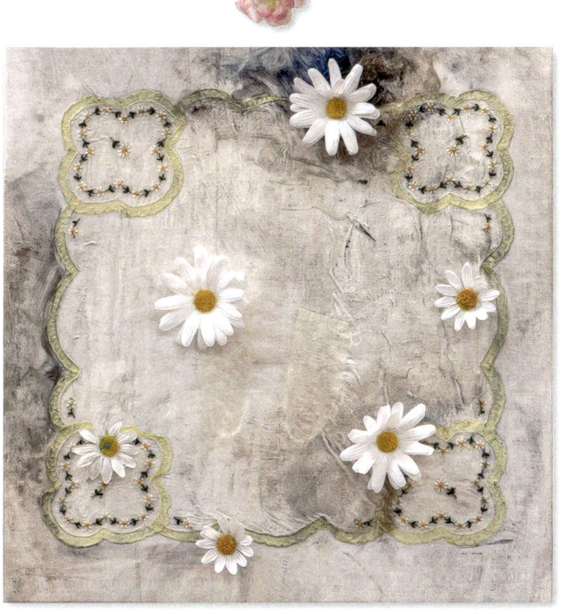
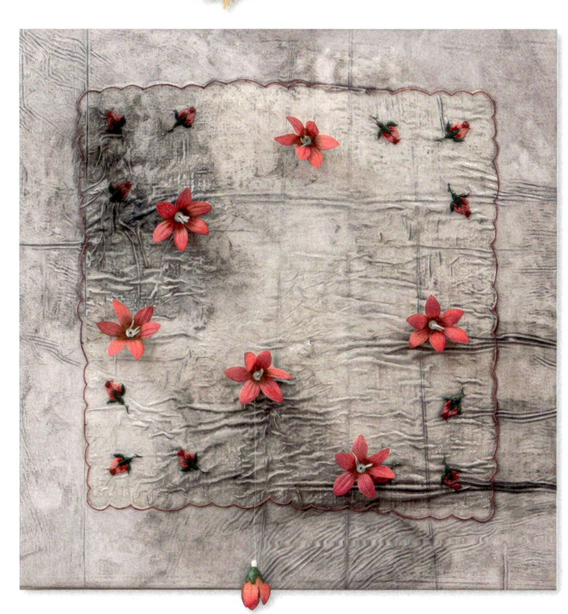
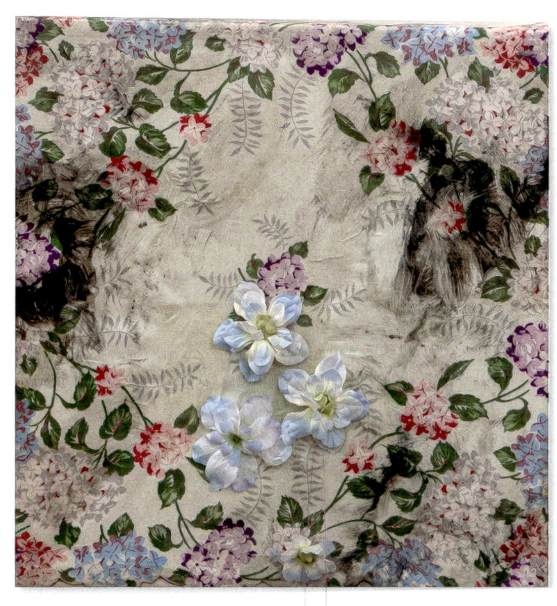
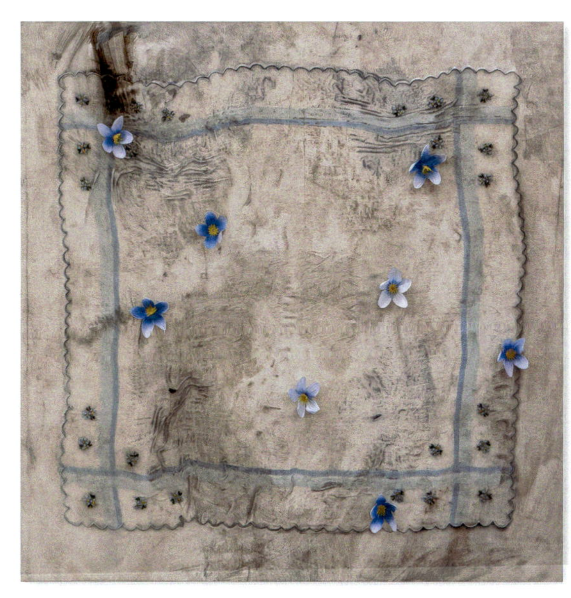
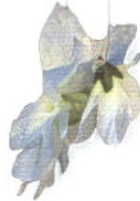

Inlet

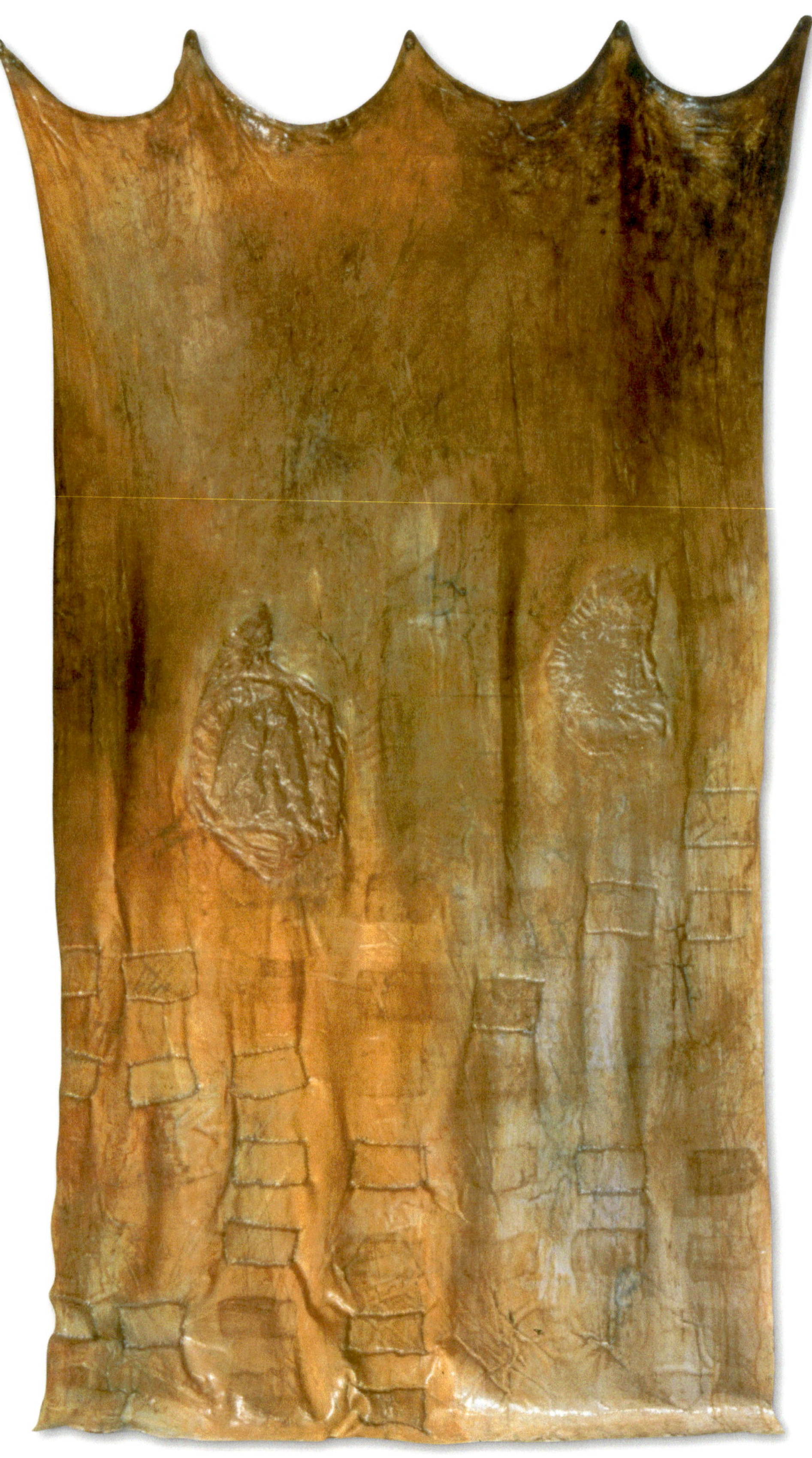

Inlet. 1997. Mixed media, 48 × 82 in. Private collection. Photograph by the artist.

Burgundy Walrus Family Portrait

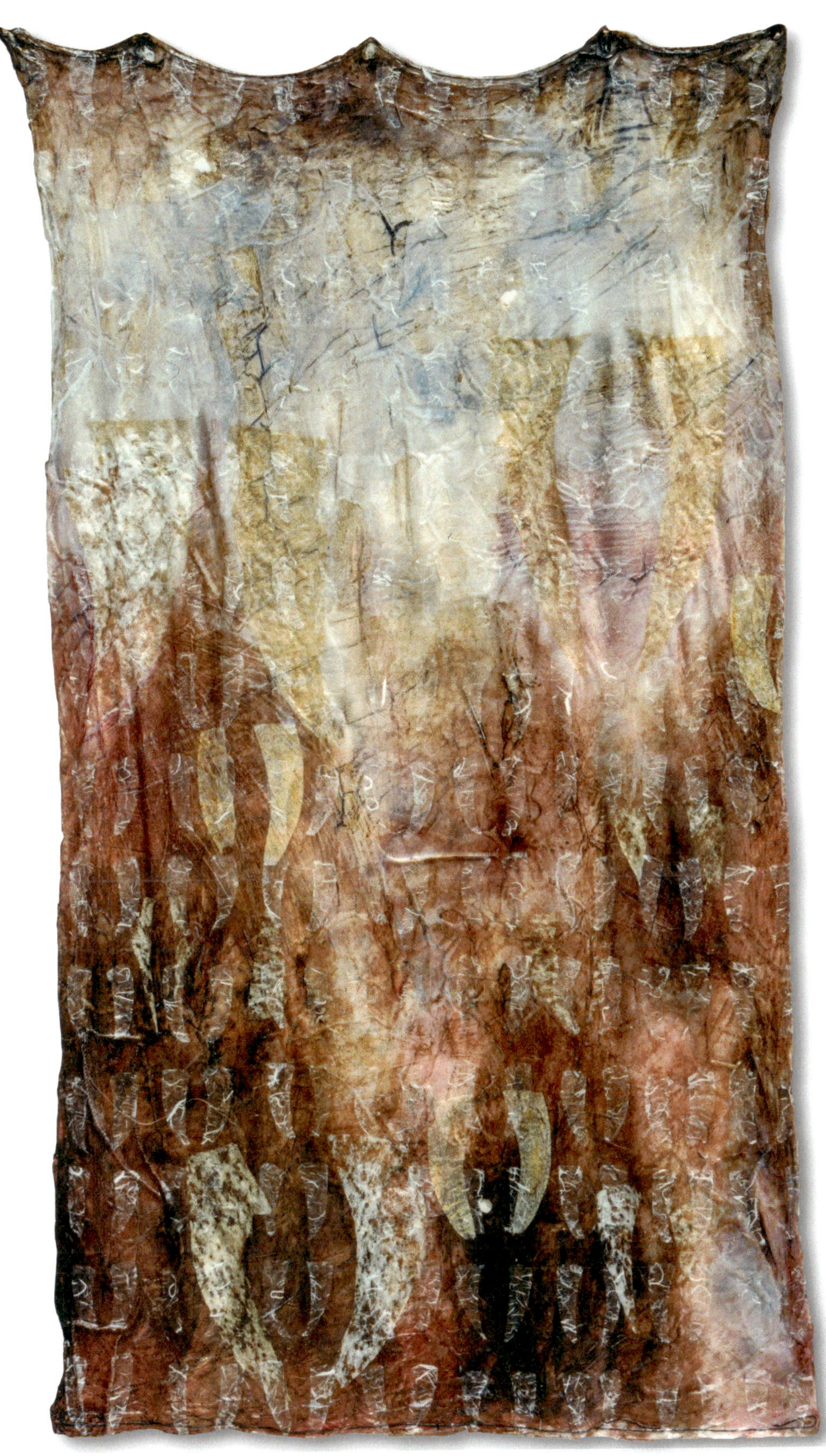

Burgundy Walrus Family Portrait, 1998.
Paint and mixed media, 48 × 82 in.
Private collection. Photograph by the artist.

Three Sisters

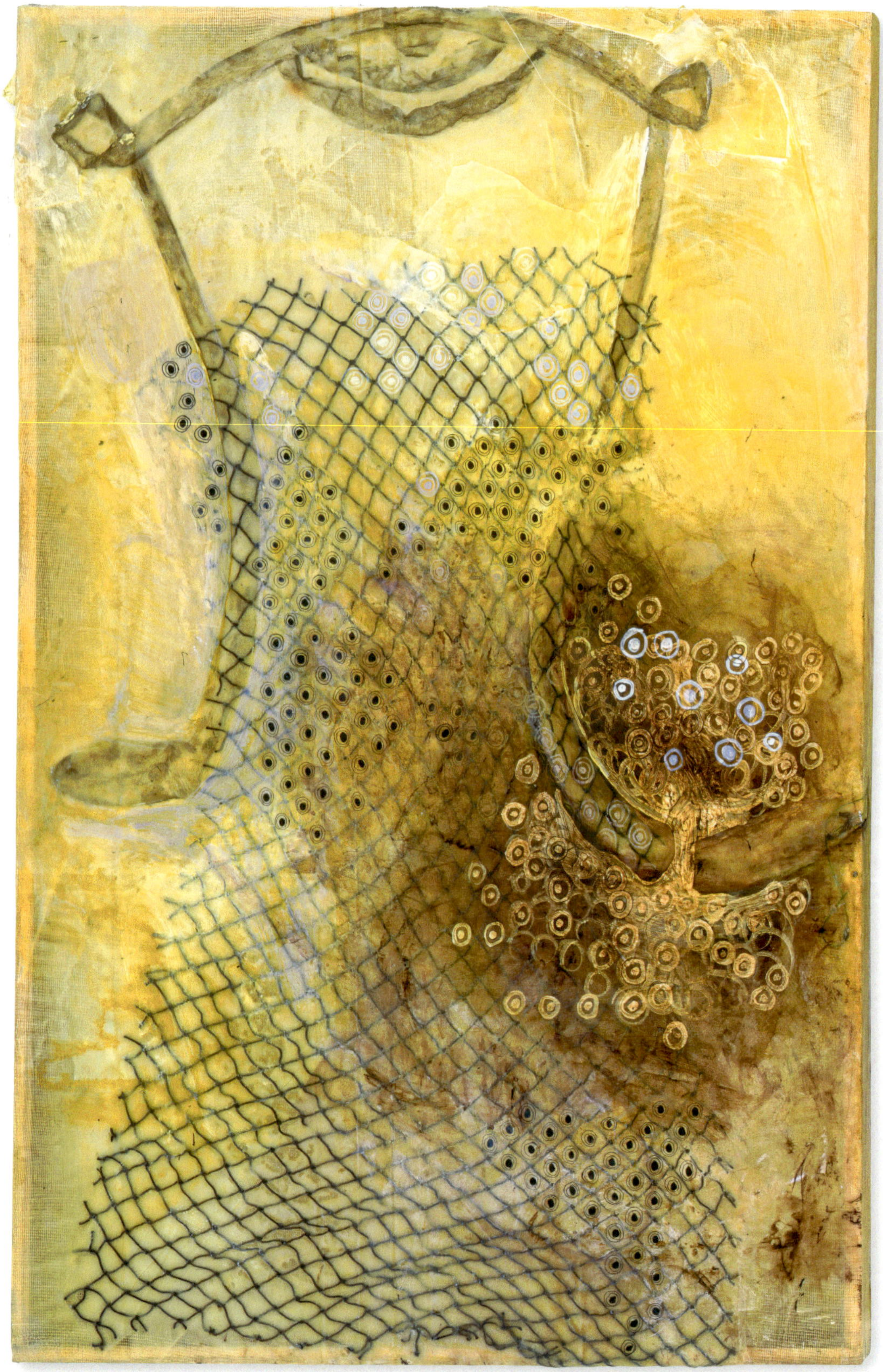

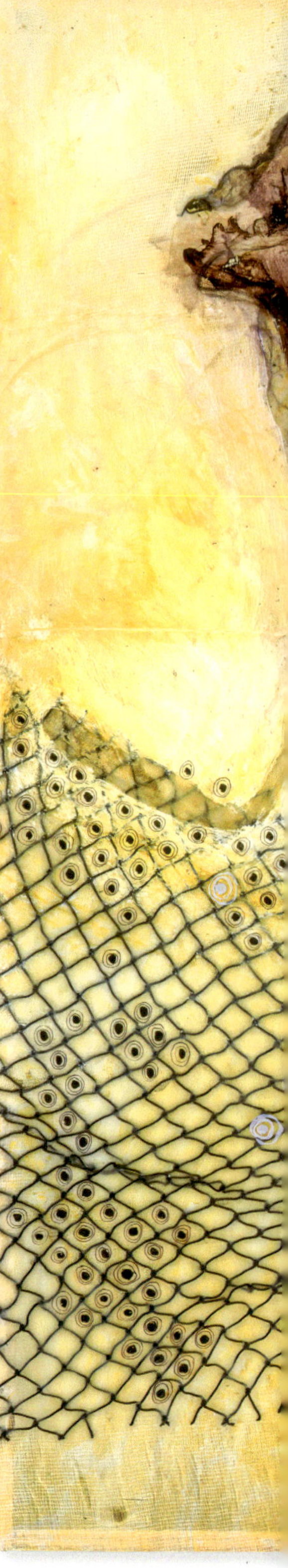

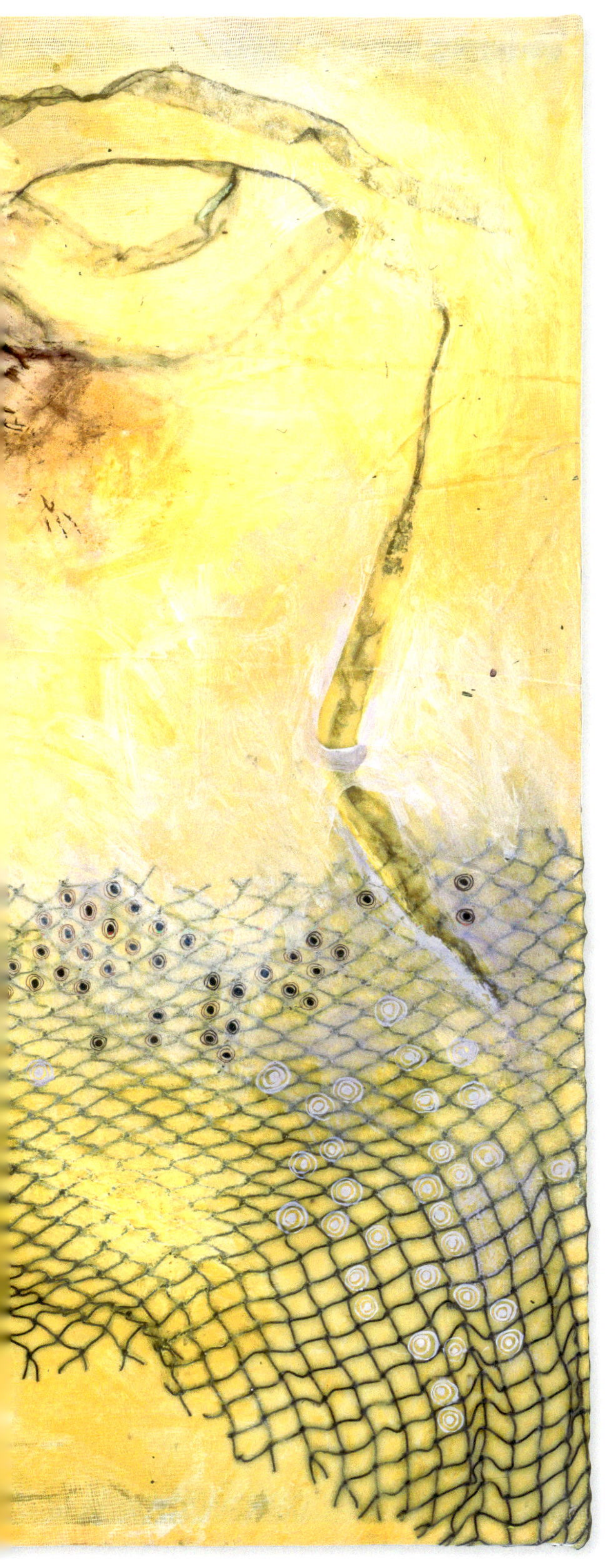

Three Sisters, 1998. Mixed media, 64 × 34 in. Collection of the artist. Photograph by the artist.

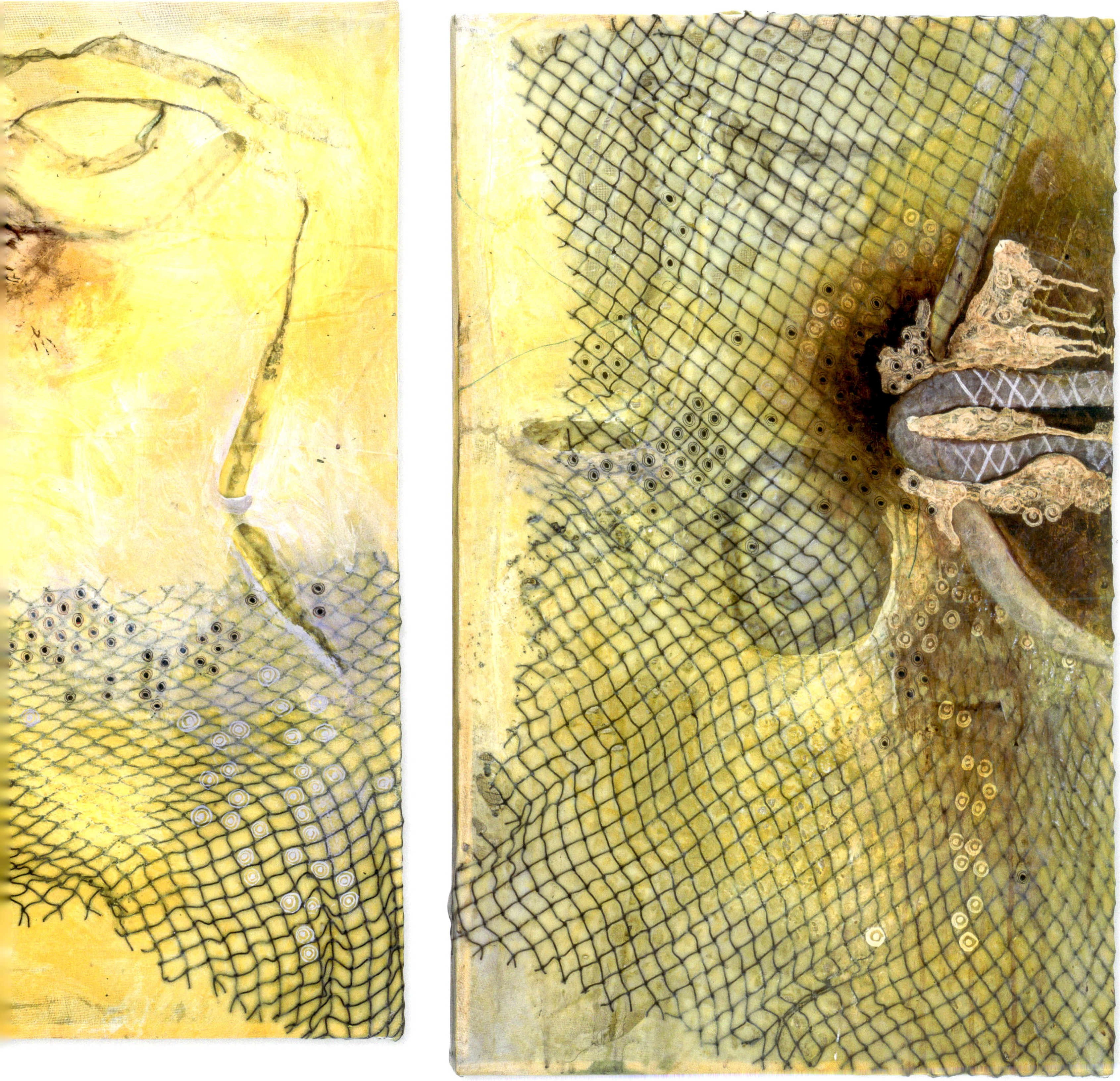

Black and White Secrets

Black and White Secrets 1–3, 2002. Paint and mixed media, 12 × 12 in. Private collection. Photographs by the artist.

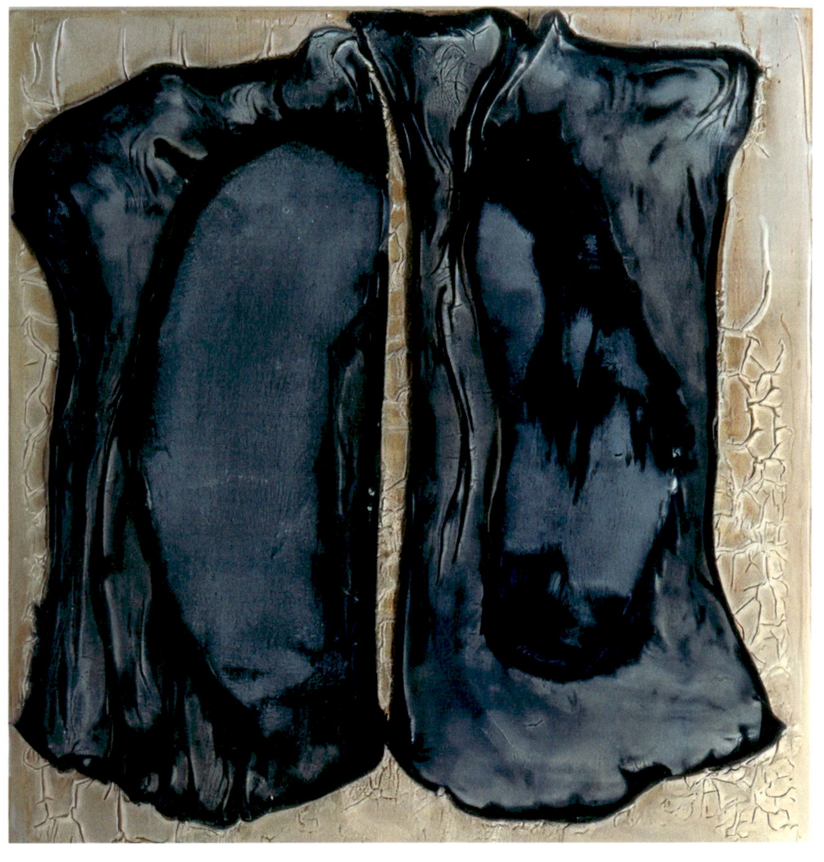

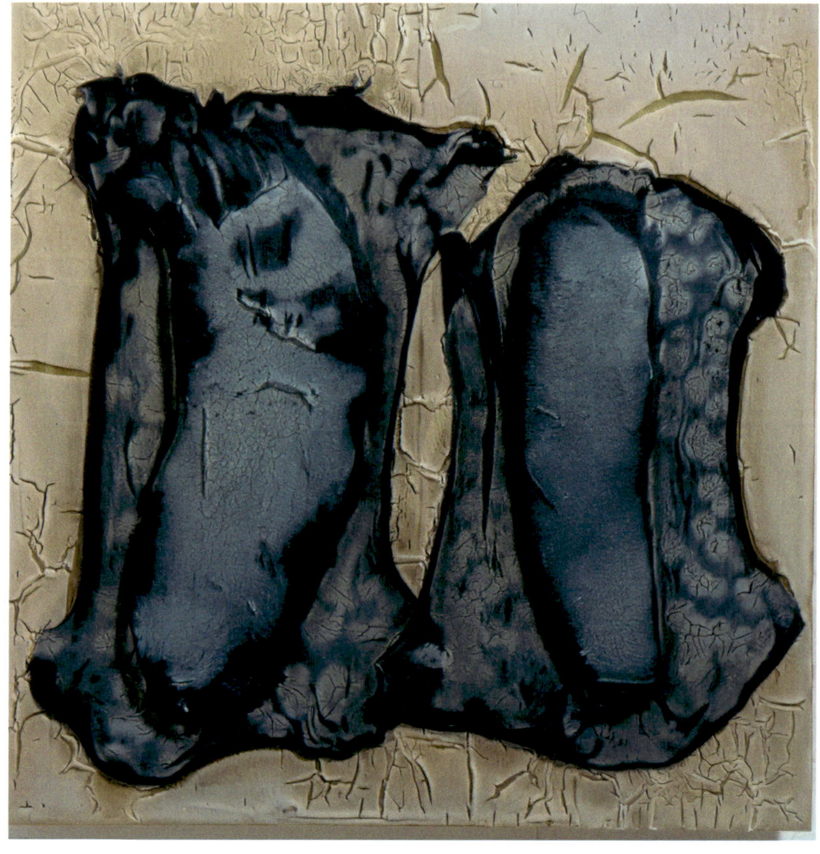

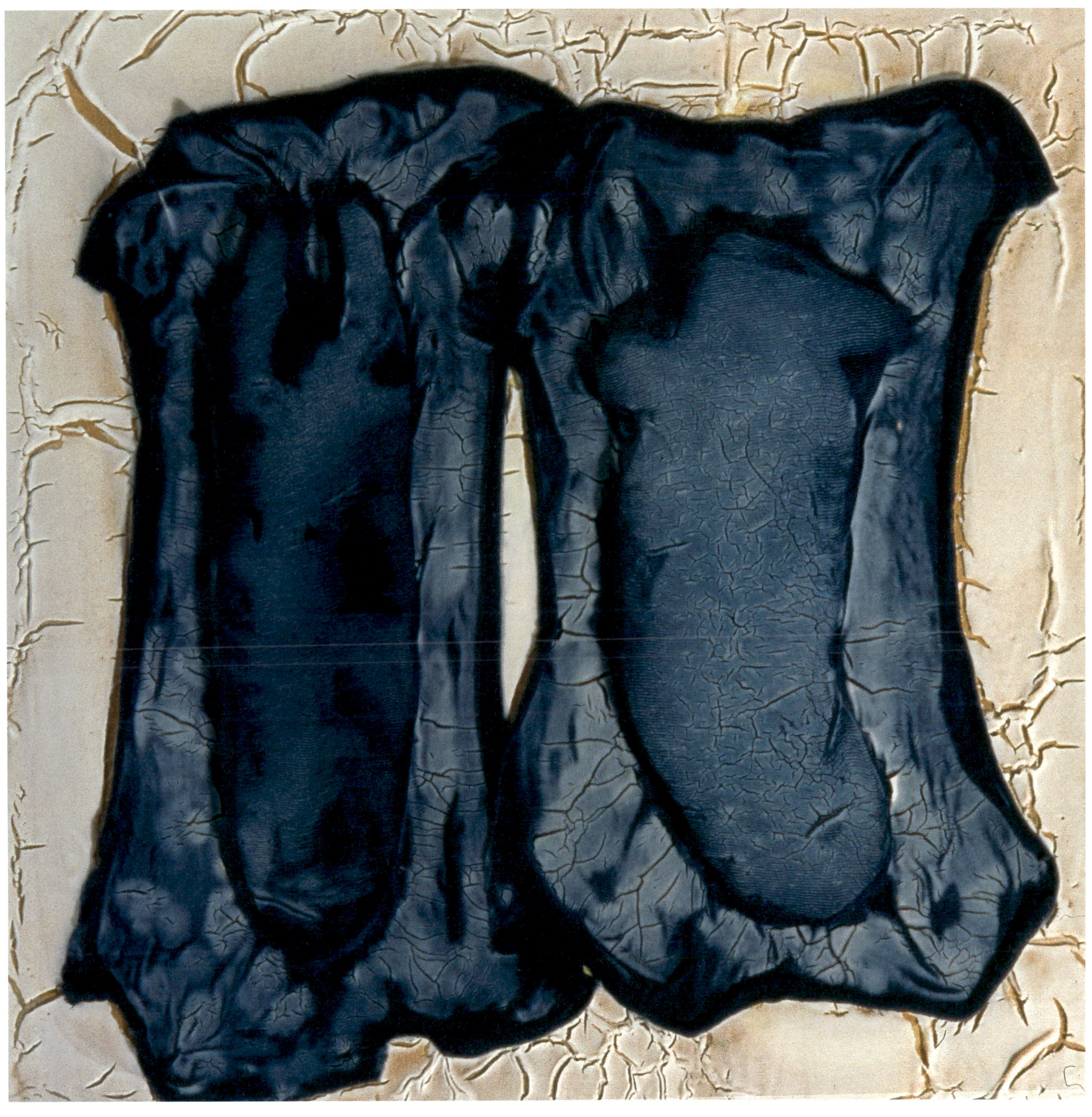

Brand

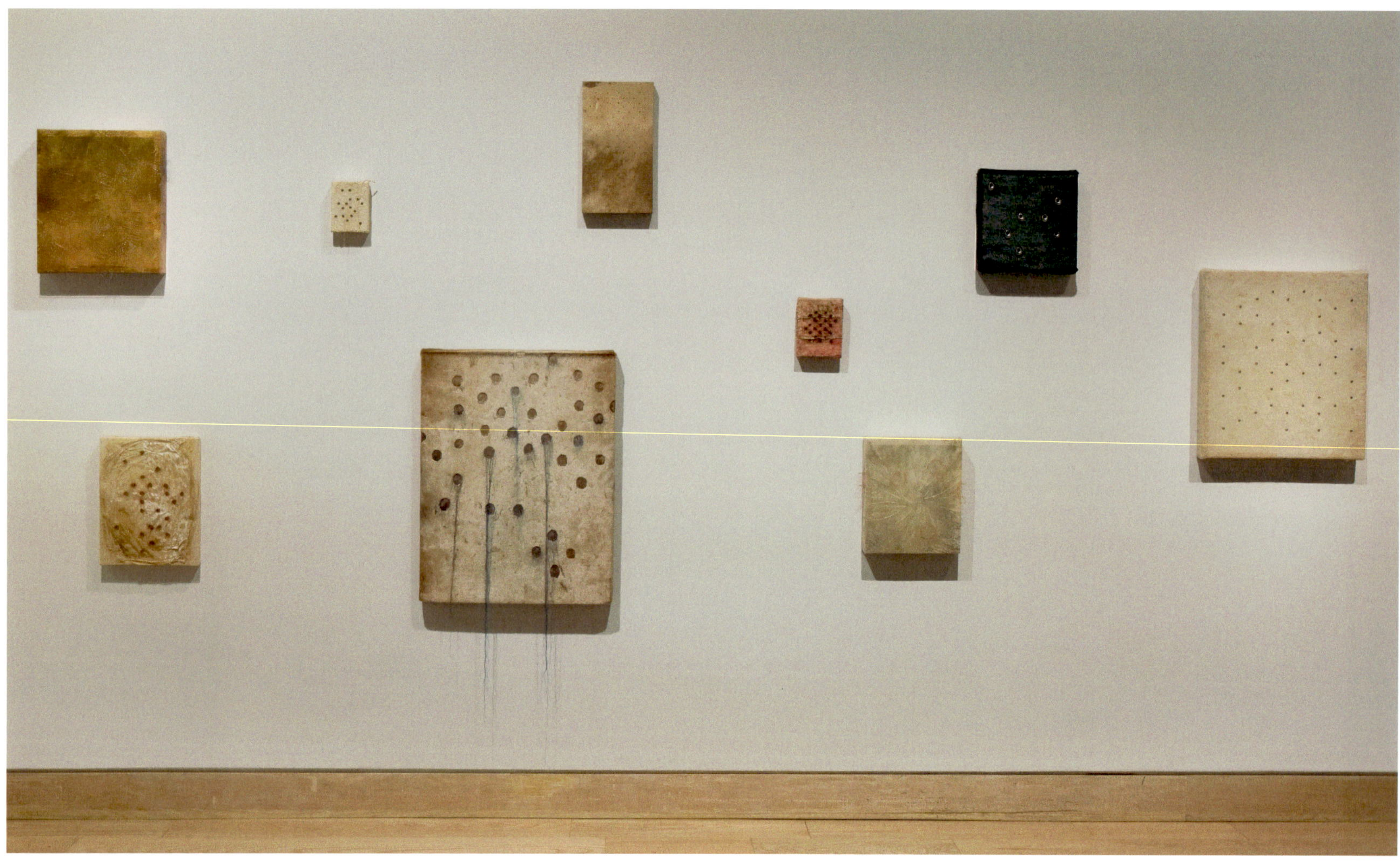

Brand, 2010. Paint and mixed media, dimensions variable. Private collection. Photograph courtesy of the National Museum of the American Indian.

Raven Brand

Raven Brand, 2010. Paint and mixed media, 12 × 14 in. Private collection. Photograph courtesy of the National Museum of the American Indian.

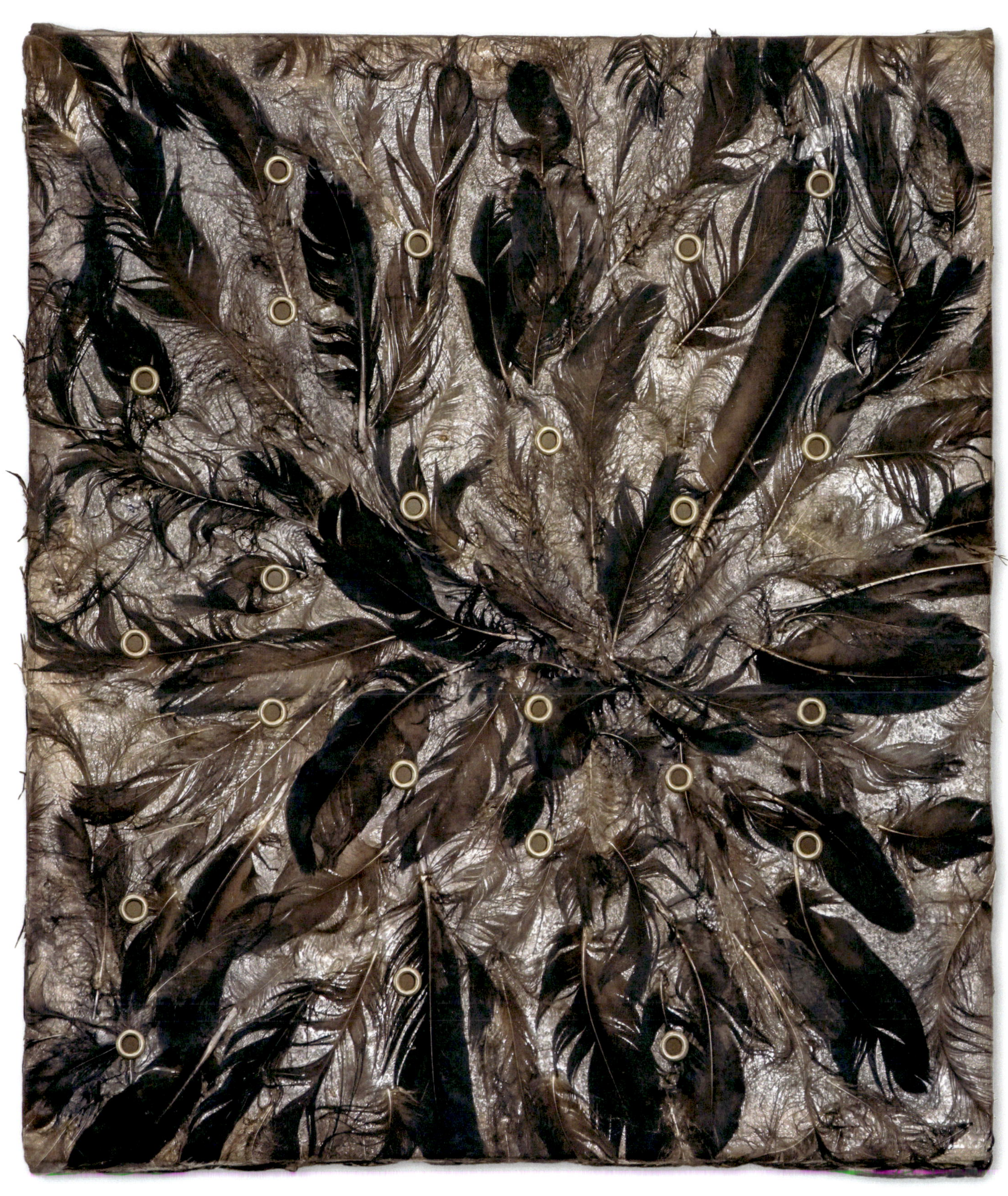

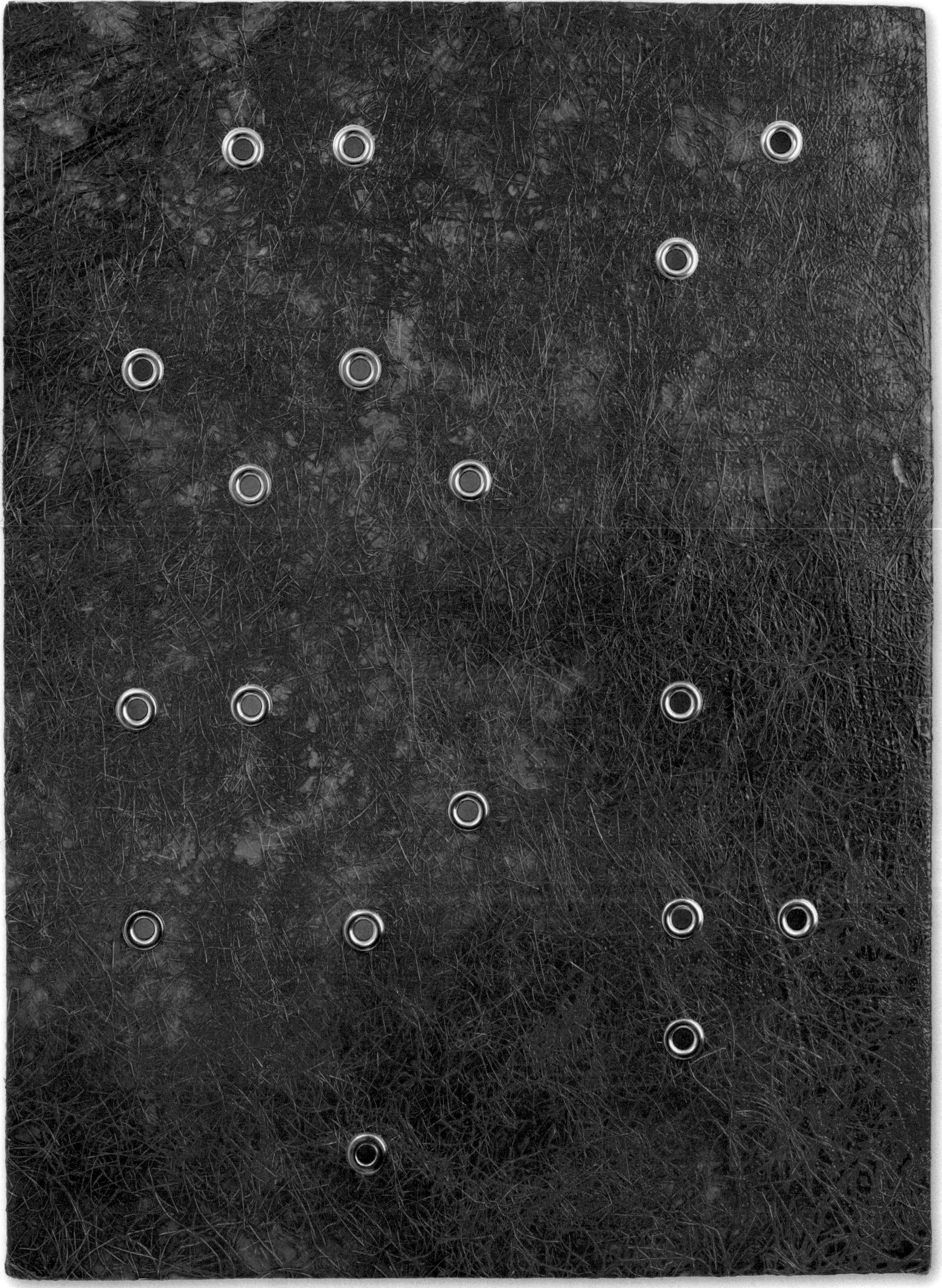

Red Reindeer Brand

This work from the *Brand* series was exhibited in *HIDE: Skin as Material Metaphor* at the National Museum of the American Indian, New York, in 2010. *Brand* is a series created from natural materials: hides, fur, gut, and feathers scarred with circular marks and punctuated with synthetic objects. Historically, circular marks were made on Iñupiaq tools to allow the spirit of a harvested animal to return to the land. The opening was a passageway to the spirit world, and it demonstrated the hunter's respect for the animal hunted. In another context, a brand is an identifying mark used to claim ownership. This body of work is a comment on Western culture's need for consumption and control, which have often placed it at odds with Indigenous value systems.

Red Reindeer Brand, 2010. Paint and mixed media, 24 × 18 in. Collection of the British Museum, London. Photograph by Kevin G. Smith.

Grey Qupak

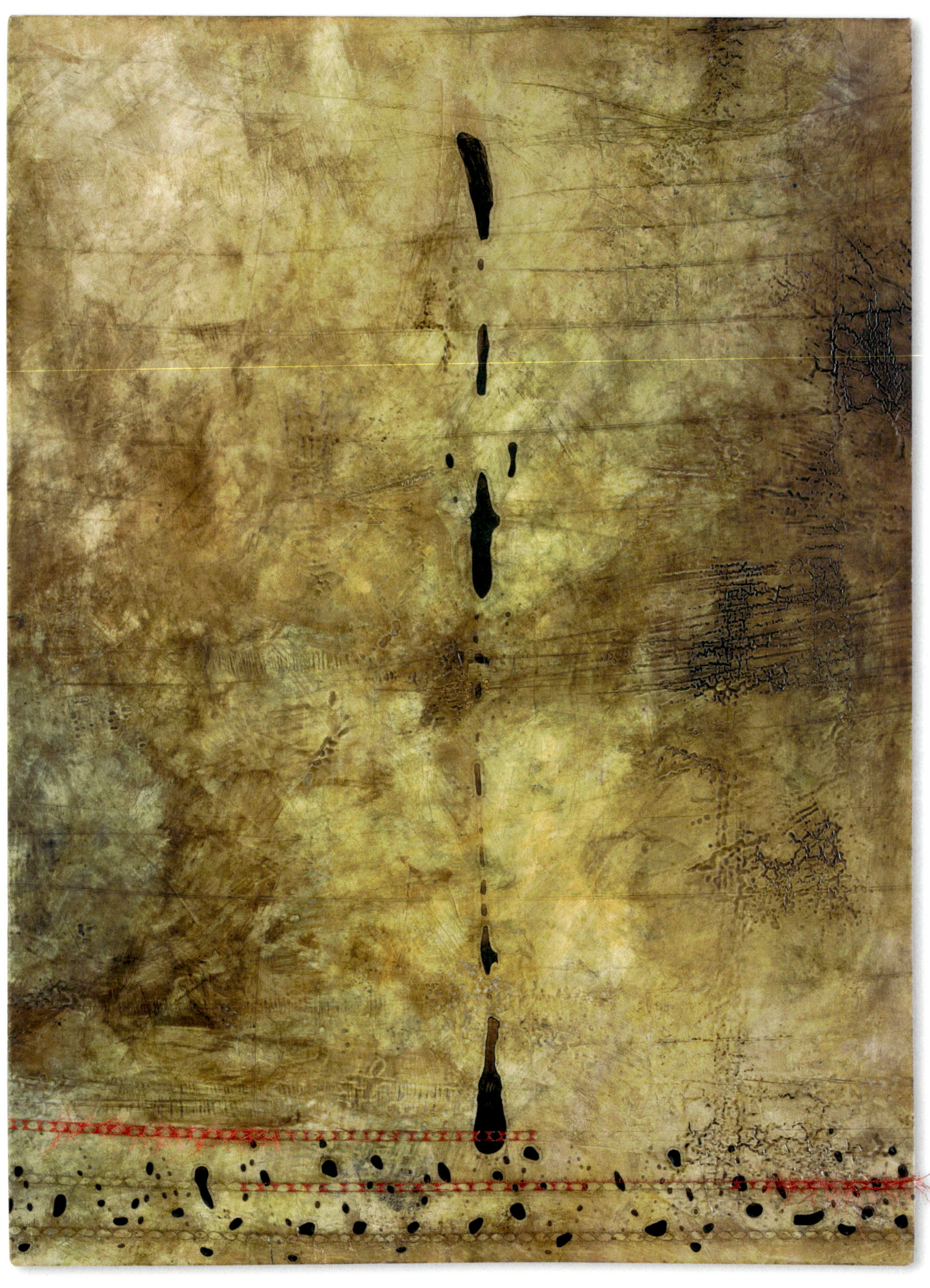

Grey Qupak with Red, 2013. Paint and mixed media, 30 × 40 in. Private collection. Photograph by Chris Arend.

Pink Qupak

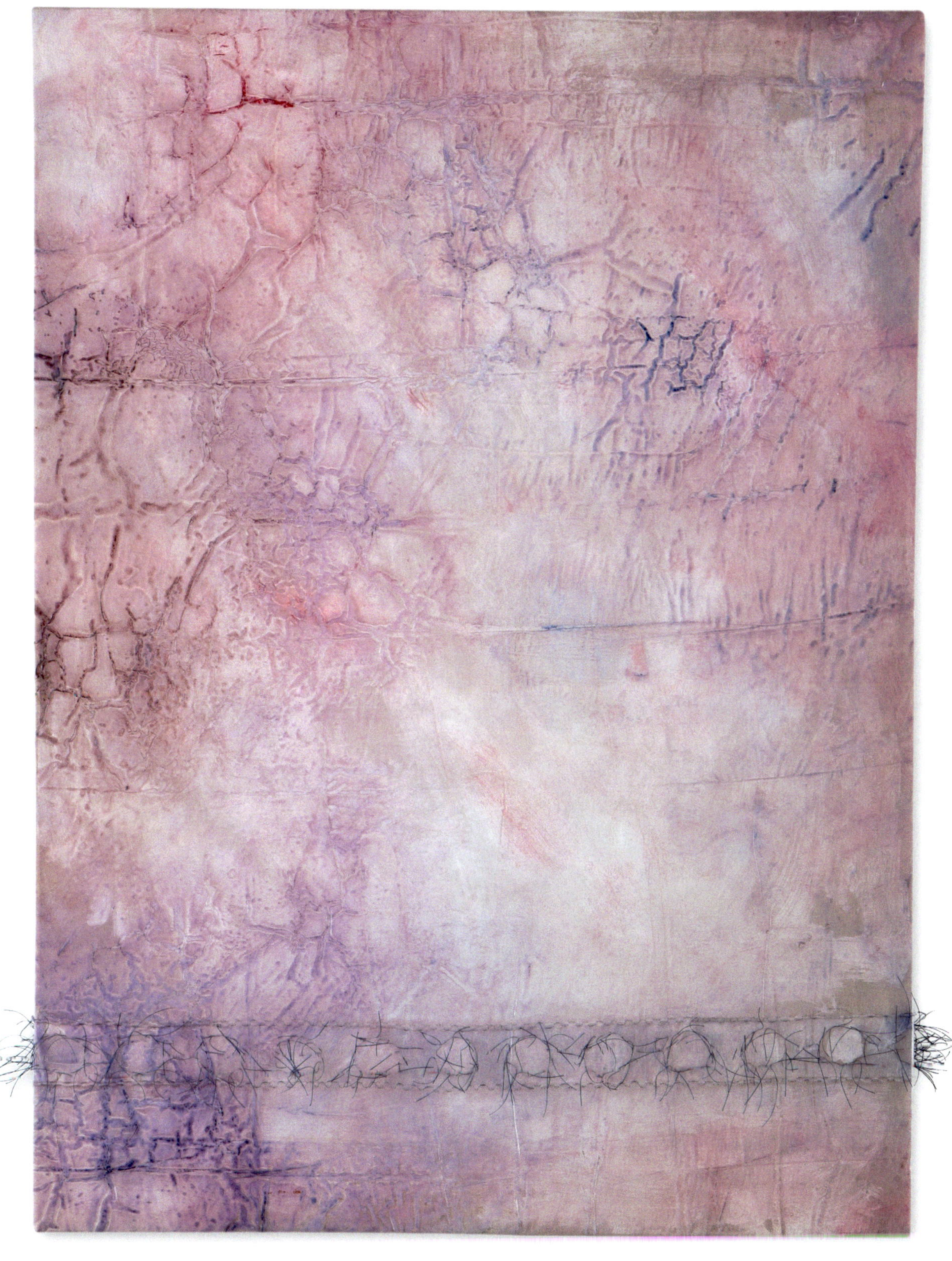

Pink Qupak, 2013. Paint and mixed media, 24 × 16 in. Private collection. Photograph by Chris Arend.

Credible

Credible
1. capable of being believed; convincing
2. worthy of belief; trustworthy

Credible is a series addressing the overwhelming abuse of Indigenous peoples by members of the Catholic Church in the state of Alaska. It continues a series Kelliher-Combs has been exploring since 2007. These paintings represent the 35 villages that have credible claims of abuse by the hand of those sent to "save" them. Below each work is a list of those accused. This information was generously shared by Kyle Hopkins of the *Anchorage Daily News*. His research was obtained from Jesuits West and supplemented by a report from the Catholic Diocese of Fairbanks that lists "all known individuals, including priests, religious and lay employees, and volunteers against whom a complaint of sexual abuse has been filed by one or more individuals" and against whom the abuse has been proven, admitted, or "credibly accused."

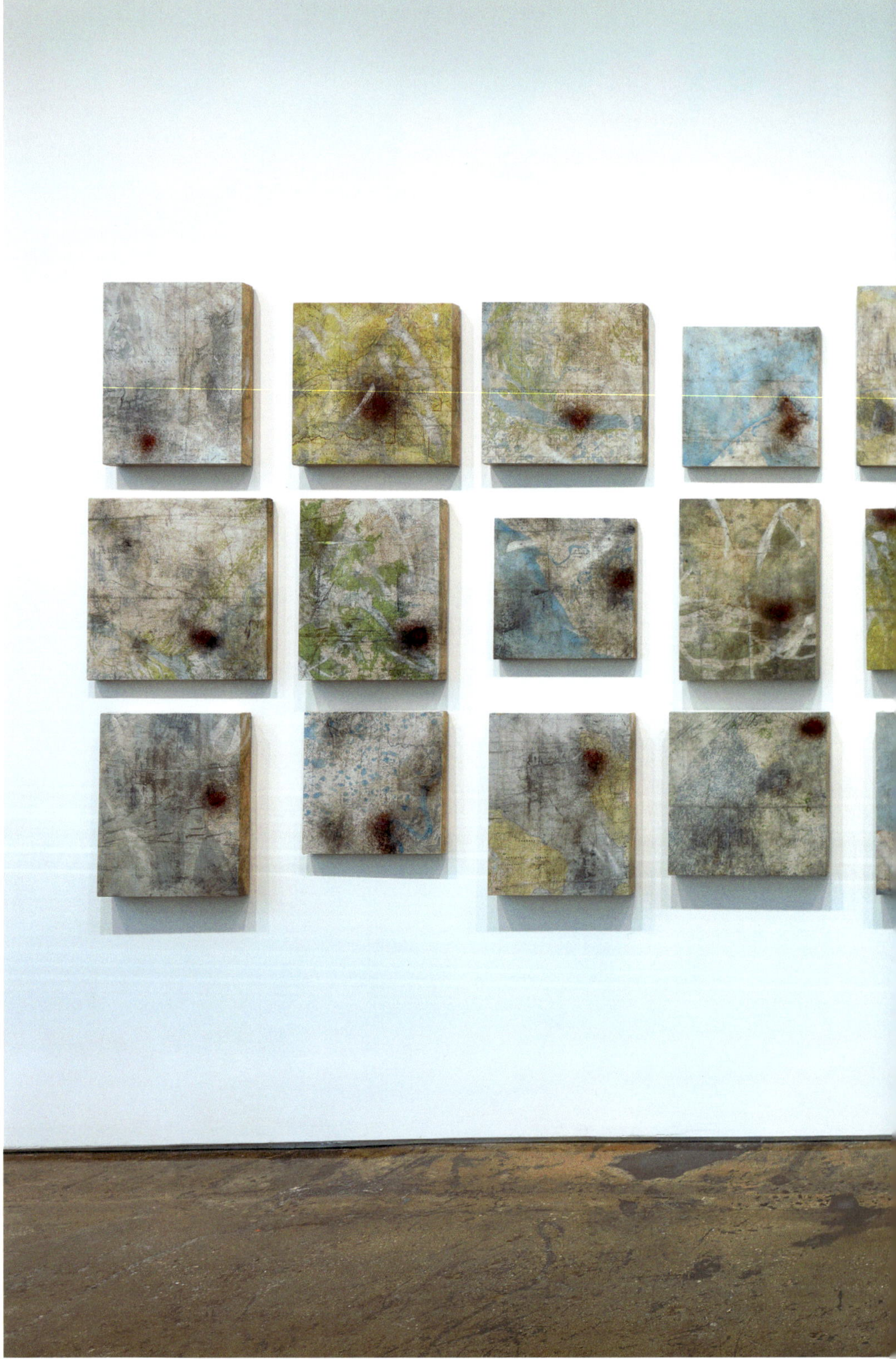

Credible, 2019. Mixed-media installation.
Collection of the Denver Art Museum.
Photograph courtesy of Minus Space.

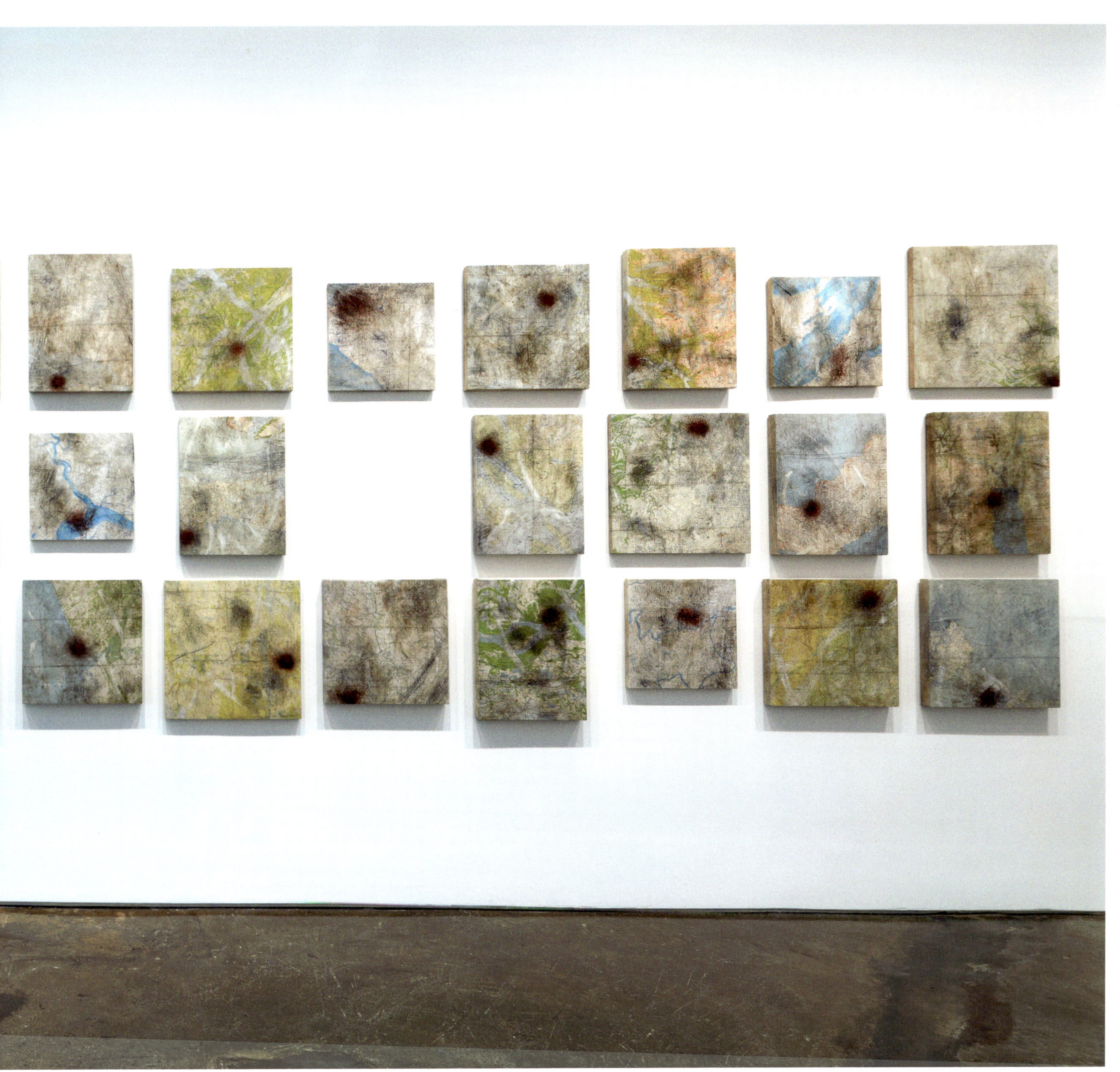

Credible

Labels for each village with corresponding "credible" claims against agents of the Church and dates of their assignments:

Credible, Tununak
Rev. Henry G. Hargreaves ('97–98)
Rev. Richard L. McCaffery ('78–79)
Rev. Bernard F. McMeel ('77–78)
Rev. Norman E. Donohue ('74–75)
Rev. Francis J. Fallert ('65–74)
Rev. James E. Jacobson ('61–62)
Rev. Paul Linssen ('56–60)

Credible, Hooper Bay
Rev. Richard L. McCaffery ('79–81)
Rev. James E. Jacobson ('70–76)
Joseph Lundowski ('65–75)
Rev. George S. Endal ('64–68)
Rev. Bernard F. McMeel ('58–59, '76–77)
Rev. Norman E. Donohue ('57–64)
Rev. Henry G. Hargreaves ('49–52, '53–56)
Rev. Paul C. O'Connor ('46–53)
Rev. Jules M. Convert ('42–45)
Rev. John P. Fox ('31–46)

Credible, Pilot Station
Rev. Paul C. O'Connor ('31–33)

Credible, Sitka
Patrick J. O'Reilly ('42–46)

Credible, Seward
Arnold L. Cluster ('52–61)

Credible, Nunam Iqua
Rev. Segundo Llorente ('56)

Credible, Teller
Rev. Jules M. Convert ('68–69)

Credible, Ketchikan
Frederick Simoneau ('67–69)

Credible, Wrangell
Patrick J. O'Reilly ('40–42)

Credible, Juneau
Rev. William T. McIntyre ('45–46)
Gabriel M. Menager ('28–30)

Credible, Tanana
Rev. Charles A. Saalfeld ('66–73)

Credible, Kotzebue
Rev. Andras Eordogh ('67–68)
Rev. William T. McIntyre ('54–59)
Rev. Paul C. O'Connor ('41–46)
Rev. Segundo Llorente ('38–41)

Credible, Toksook Bay
Rev. Henry G. Hargreaves ('87–88, '94–97)
Rev. Francis J. Fallert ('74–75, '86–90)

Credible, Chefornak
Rev. Norman E. Donohue ('75–83)
Rev. James E. Jacobson ('62–66)

Credible, Cordova
Rev. Segundo Llorente ('67–70)

Credible, Anchorage
Rev. George S. Endal ('87–96)
Rev. William T. McIntyre ('80–81)
Brother Robert L. Benish ('75–76)
Rev. Robert F. Corrigal ('74–78, '84–88)
Rev. Segundo Llorente at Holy Family Church ('70–76)
Rev. Henry G. Hargreaves ('69–72)
Rev. John P. Fox ('68–77)
Rev. Paul C. O'Connor at Providence Hospital ('66–76)
Arnold L. Cluster at St. Anthony's Church ('61–62)

Credible, Utqiaġvik
Rev. James E. Poole at St. Patrick's Mission ('65–66)

Credible, Dillingham
Rev. Norman E. Donohue ('64–66)
Rev. George S. Endal ('48–62)
Rev. Harold J. Greif ('52–57)

Credible, Bethel
Rev. Richard L. McCaffery ('87–98)
Rev. Charles Bartles ('86–88)
Rev. Robert F. Corrigal ('63–65, '66–70, '81–84)
Rev. William T. McIntyre ('62–63)
Rev. Henry G. Hargreaves ('56–64, '80–87, '98–03)
Rev. Cornelius K. Murphy ('56–68)
Rev. Norman E. Donohue ('50–57)
Rev. Segundo Llorente ('48–50)

Credible, Chevak
Rev. William T. McIntyre ('68–70)
Rev. Francis X. Nawn ('64–68)
Rev. Bernard F. McMeel ('59–64)
Rev. Jules M. Convert ('45–49)
Rev. John P. Fox at Kashunuk ('28–30)

Credible, Kotlik
Rev. Henry G. Hargreaves ('72–80)

Credible, St. Mary's
Vincent P. Scott ('99–00)
Brother Ignatius J. Jakes ('72–95)
Rev. Jules M. Convert ('70–79)
Rev. Robert F. Corrigal ('61–63, '70–79)
Rev. James E. Poole ('59–64)
Brother Robert L. Benish ('46–75, '76–87)
Rev. Norman E. Donohue ('42–50)
Rev. Segundo Llorente ('35–37, '41–48, '50–51)
Rev. Paul C. O'Connor ('34–41, '53–59)
Rev. John P. Fox ('27–28, '63–65)

Credible, Emmonak
Rev. Henry G. Hargreaves ('88–94)

Credible, Glennallen
Rev. James E. Jacobson ('67–70)
Rev. Harold J. Greif ('67–69)
Rev. Richard L. McCaffery ('67–69)
Rev. Norman E. Donohue ('66–67)
Rev. Paul C. O'Connor ('65–66)
Rev. Francis J. Fallert ('56–65)

Credible, Holy Cross
Rev. Andras Eordogh ('68–71)
Rev. Bernard F. McMeel ('64–68)
Rev. Francis X. Nawn ('62–64)
Rev. John P. Fox ('56–63)
Rev. James E. Jacobson ('55–56)
Rev. Jules M. Convert ('54–56)
Rev. Paul Linssen ('52–54)
Joseph L. Obersinner ('52–54)
Brother Ignatius J. Jakes ('51–62)
Rev. Harold J. Greif ('48–52)
James E. Poole ('48–50)
Rev. Francis J. Fallert ('47–49)
Rev. Norman E. Donohue ('41–42)
Rev. Cornelius K. Murphy ('40–42)
Rev. William T. McIntyre ('38–40, '46–54)
Rev. George S. Endal ('36–38)
Rev. Paul C. O'Connor ('30–31)

Credible, Fairbanks
Brother Robert L. Benish ('87–89)
Rev. Francis J. Fallert ('76–82, '87–88)
Rev. Richard L. McCaffery ('73–77, '81–87, '98–05)
Rev. Robert F. Corrigal ('73–74)
Brother Francis Fox at Monroe High School ('69–86)
Rev. Jules M. Convert ('67–68)
Rev. Segundo Llorente ('63–67)
Brother Ignatius J. Jakes ('62–66, '95–99)
Rev. William T. McIntyre ('59–60)
Rev. Charles A. Saalfeld at Monroe Catholic High School ('57–66)
Rev. Cornelius K. Murphy ('56–65, '68–82)
Rev. Bernard F. McMeel at Monroe High School ('55–57) and Jesuit Residence ('68–73)
Rev. Henry G. Hargreaves ('52–53, '64–65)
Patrick J. O'Reilly ('26–28)

Credible, Galena
Rev. Charles Bartles ('82–86)
Rev. Bernard F. McMeel at St. John Berchmans' Church ('73–76)

Credible, Kaltag
Rev. Robert F. Corrigal ('69–70)
Rev. Norman E. Donohue ('67–69)
Rev. Jules M. Convert ('56–67)

Credible, Nome
Rev. Harold J. Greif ('69–83)
Rev. James E. Poole ('66–88)
Rev. Andras Eordogh ('66–67)
Rev. Segundo Llorente ('64–65)
Gabriel M. Menager ('33–34)
Patrick F. Savage ('27–30)

Credible, Unalakleet
Rev. George S. Endal ('82–87)

Credible, Alakanuk
Rev. Francis X. Nawn at St. Ignatius Church ('68–80, '81–83)
Rev. William T. McIntyre ('63–68)
Rev. Segundo Llorente ('51–63)
Rev. George S. Endal ('46–48)

Credible, Nulato
Rev. Charles Bartles ('78–82)
Rev. Charles A. Saalfeld ('74–78)
Rev. Norman E. Donohue ('69–74)
Rev. Henry G. Hargreaves ('66–69)
Brother Francis Fox ('65–69)
Rev. George S. Endal ('62–64)
Rev. Cornelius K. Murphy ('47–48)
Patrick F. Savage ('30–31)

Credible, Mountain Village
Rev. Francis J. Fallert ('82–86)
Rev. William T. McIntyre ('60–62, '70–80)
Rev. James E. Poole ('55–59)
Rev. John P. Fox ('46–56, '65–68)
Rev. George S. Endal ('38–46)

Credible, St. Michael
Rev. Francis X. Nawn ('83–87)
Rev. George S. Endal ('68–82)
Rev. James E. Jacobson ('67)
Rev. Henry G. Hargreaves ('65–66)
Joseph Lundowski – layperson ('65)
Rev. Francis J. Fallert ('54–56)
Rev. Jules M. Convert ('49–54)

Credible, Stebbins
Joseph Lundowski – layperson ('65–75)

Credible, Hamilton
Rev. Paul Linssen ('54–55)

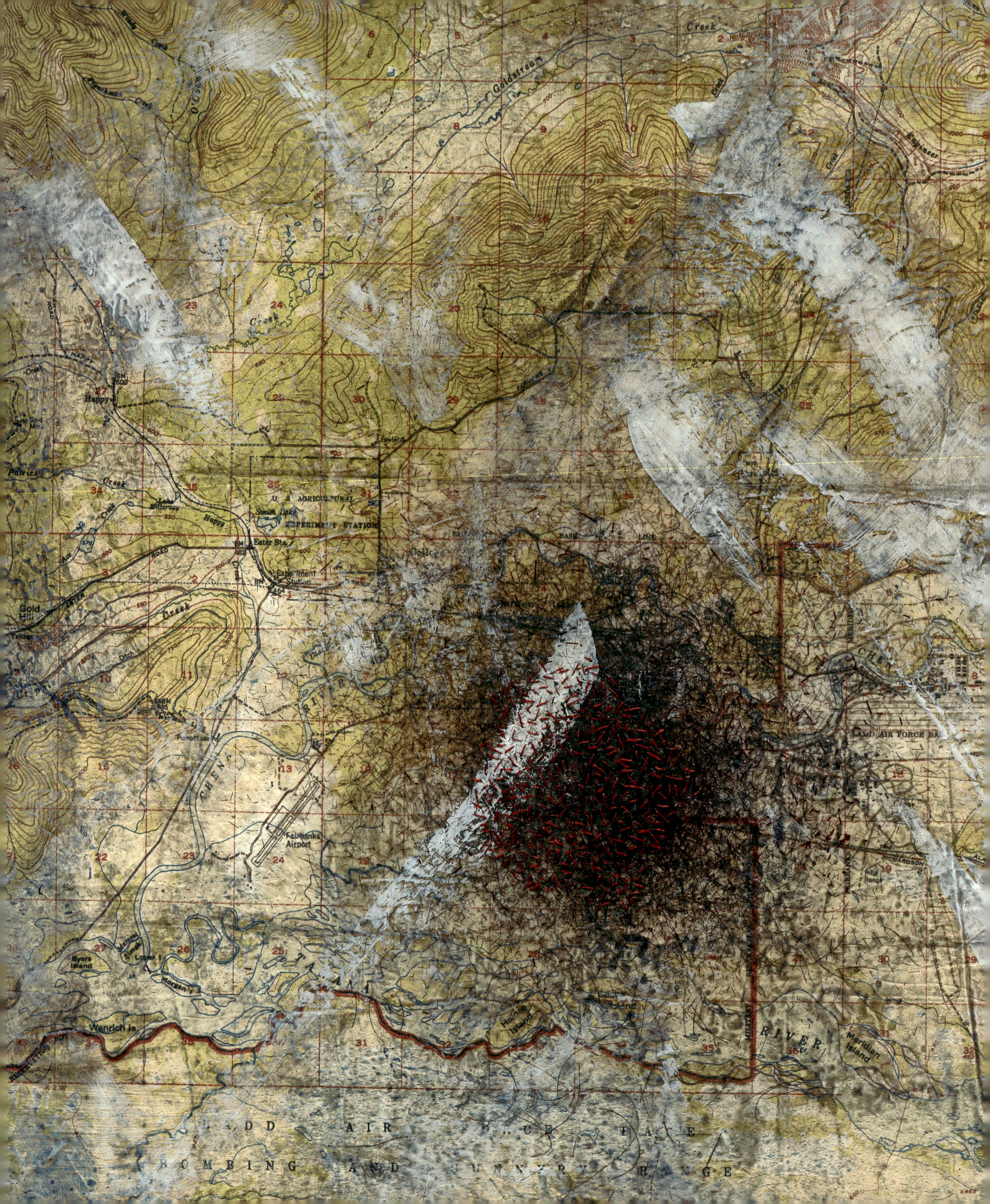

Goldstream
Creek
Happy
Patrick
U S AGRICULTURAL
EXPERIMENT STATION
Ester Sta
Experiment Station
Gold Hill
Fairbanks Airport
Byers Island
Wenrich Is
Meridian Island
RIVER

Credible, Fairbanks, 2019. Paint and mixed media, 16 × 16 in. Collection of the Denver Art Museum. Photograph courtesy of Minus Space.

Credible

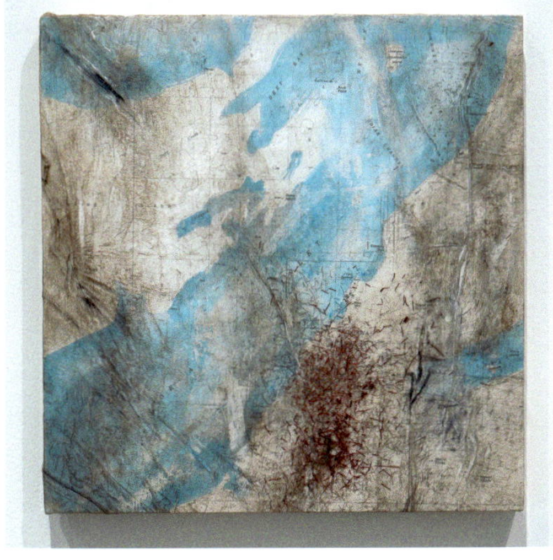
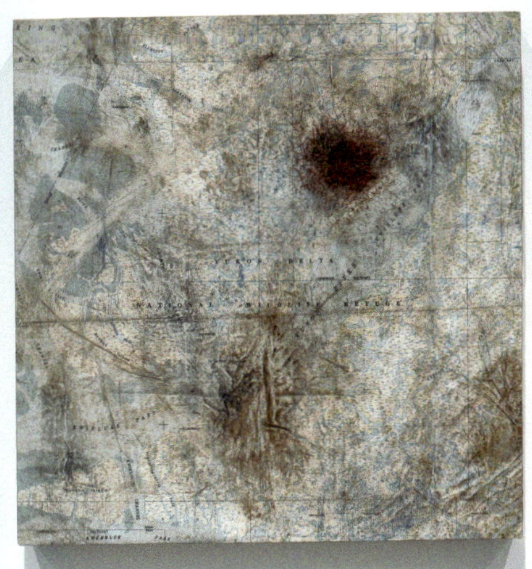
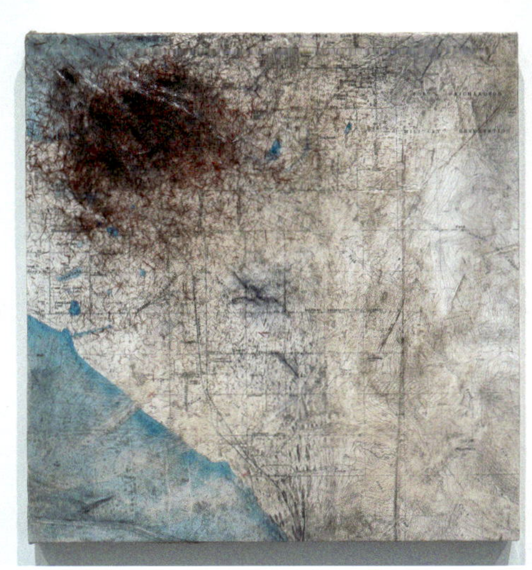
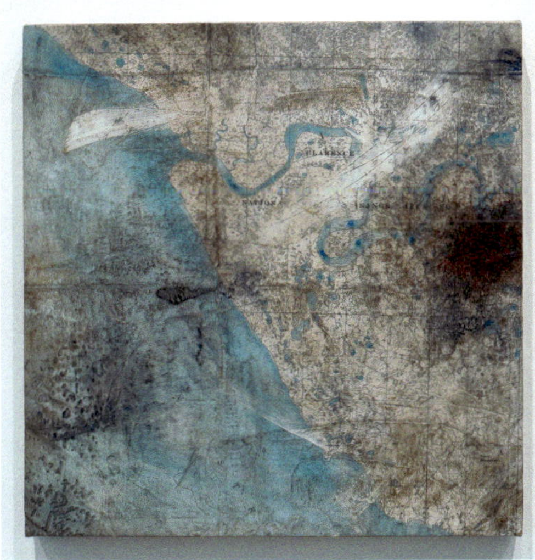
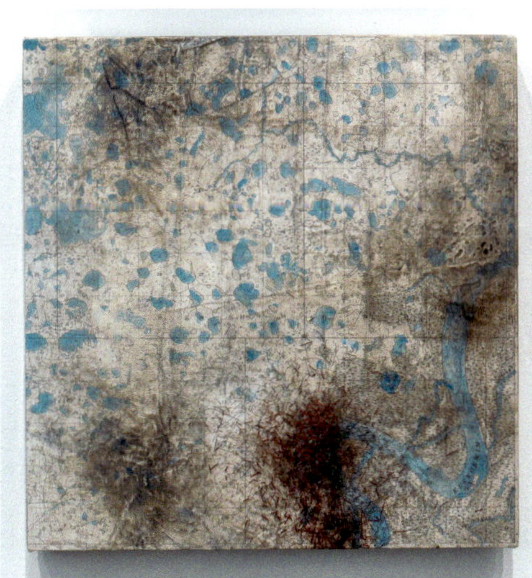
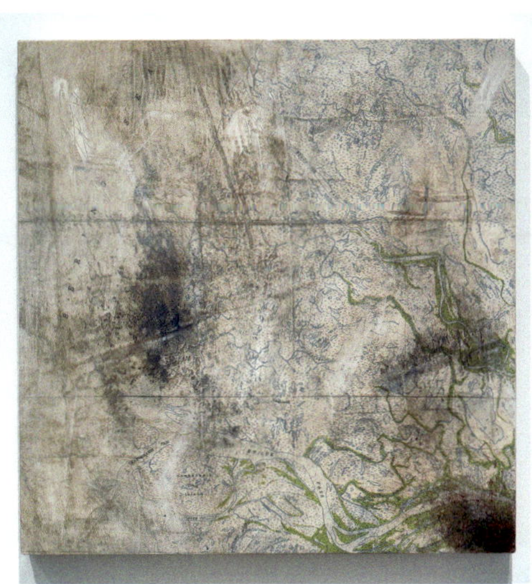

Left to right, top to bottom:
Credible, Cordova
Credible, Alakanuk
Credible, Anchorage
Credible, Chefornak
Credible, Bethel
Credible, Emmonak.
2019. Paint and mixed media, 18 × 18 in. each. Collection of Denver Art Museum. Photographs courtesy of Minus Space.

Credible Alaska

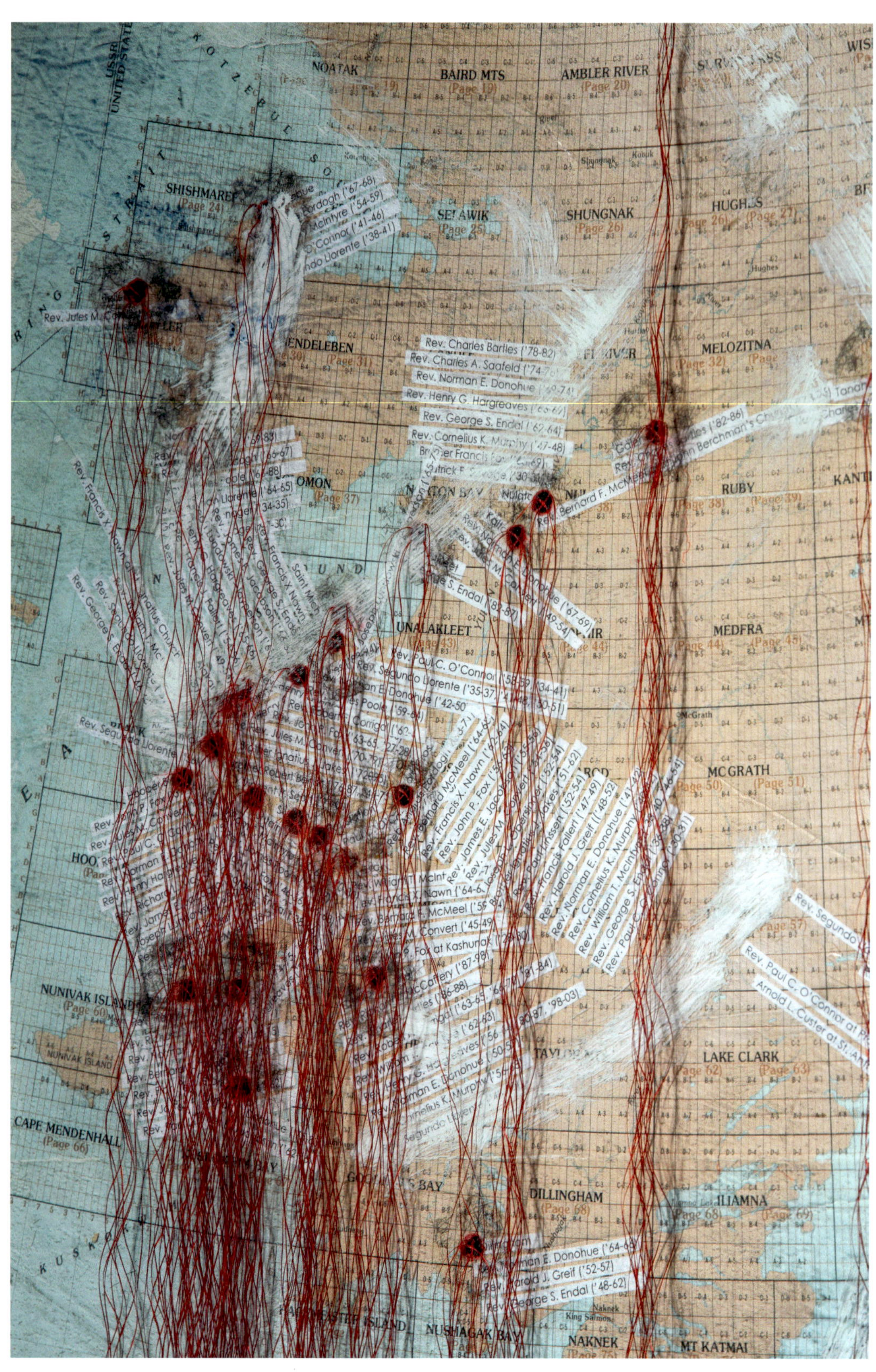

Credible Alaska, 2021. Paint and mixed media, 36 × 36 in. Collection of the Alaska Heritage Center, Anchorage, Alaska. Photographs by Chris Arend.

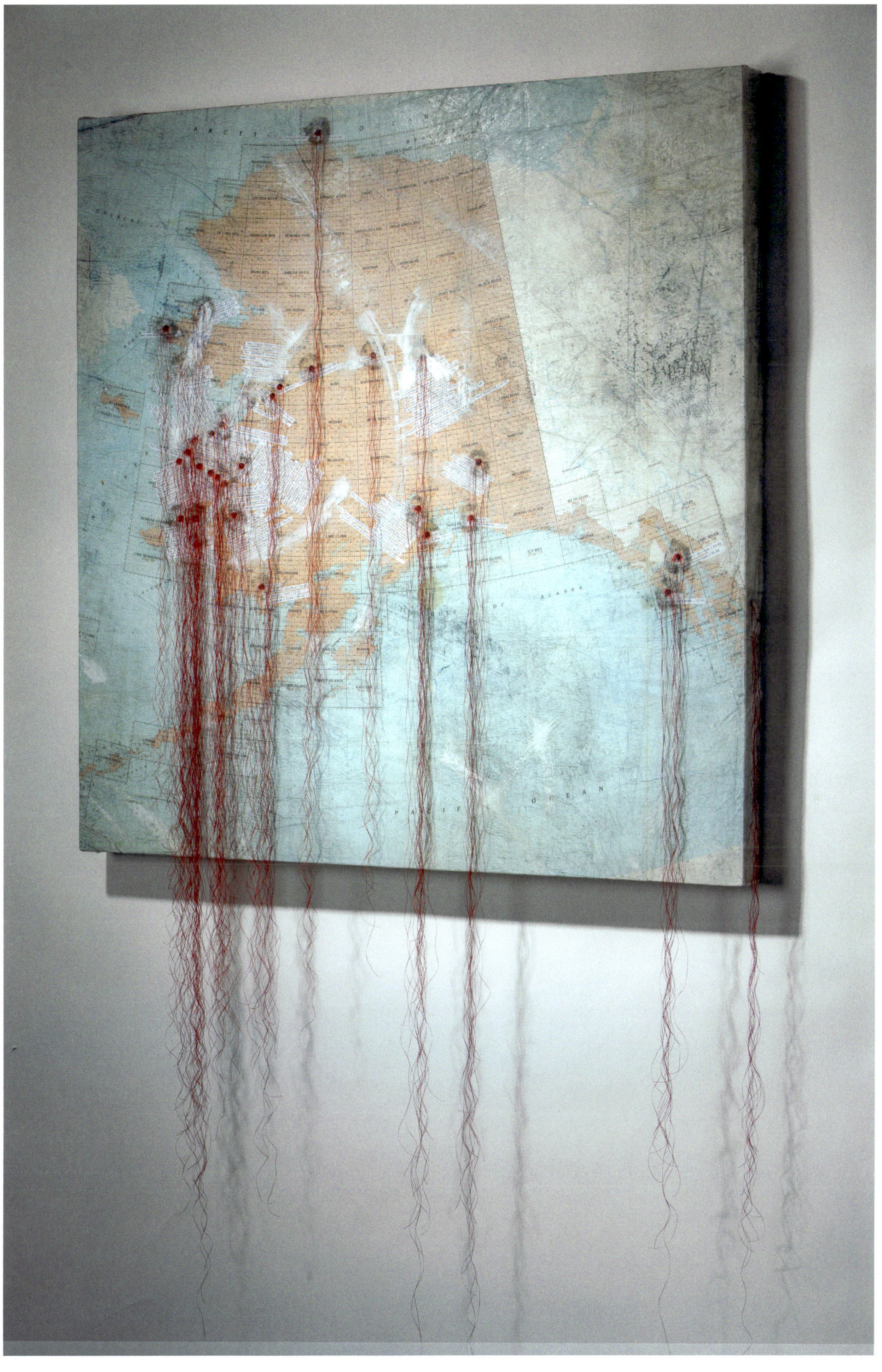

Credible II

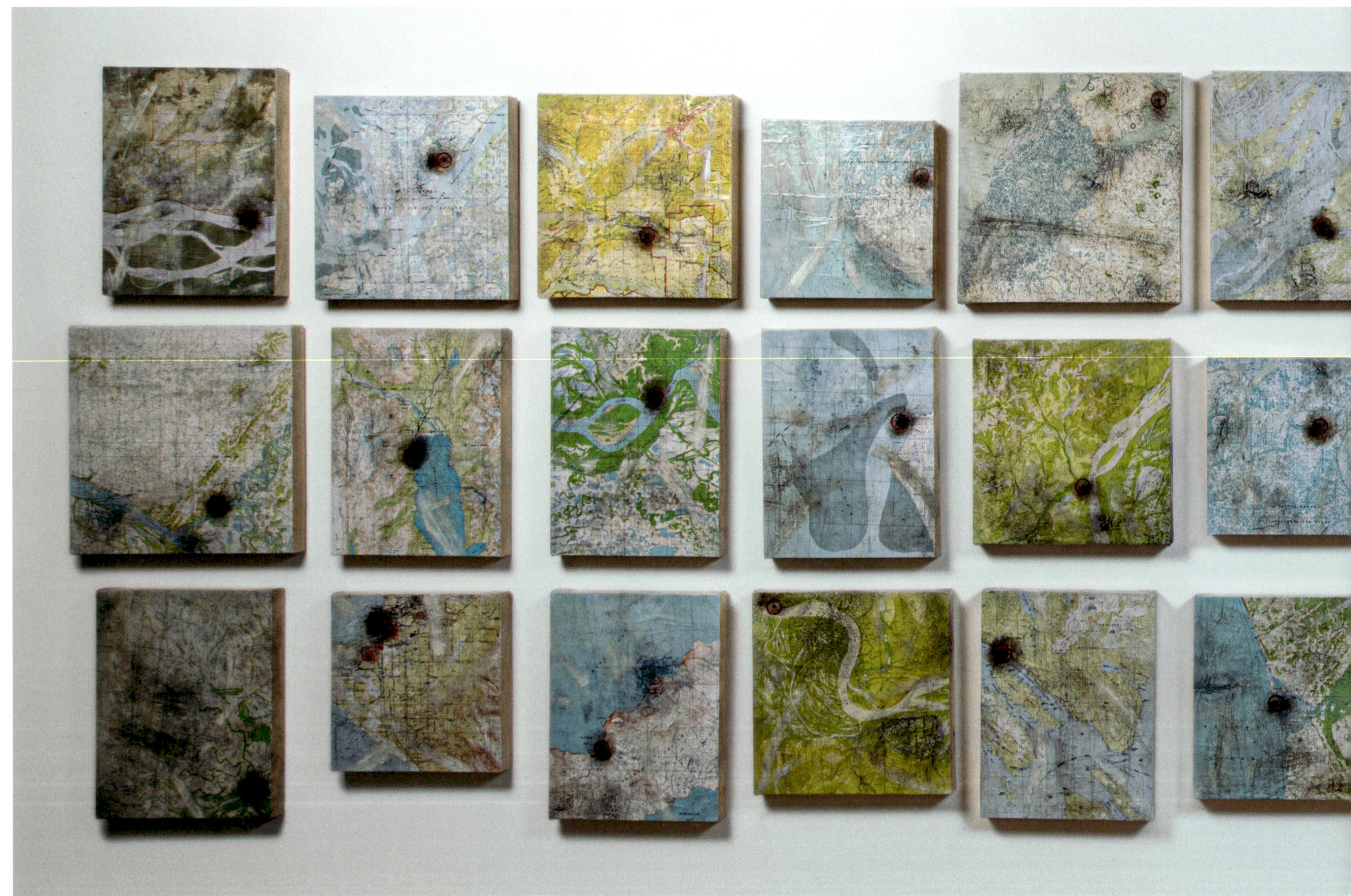

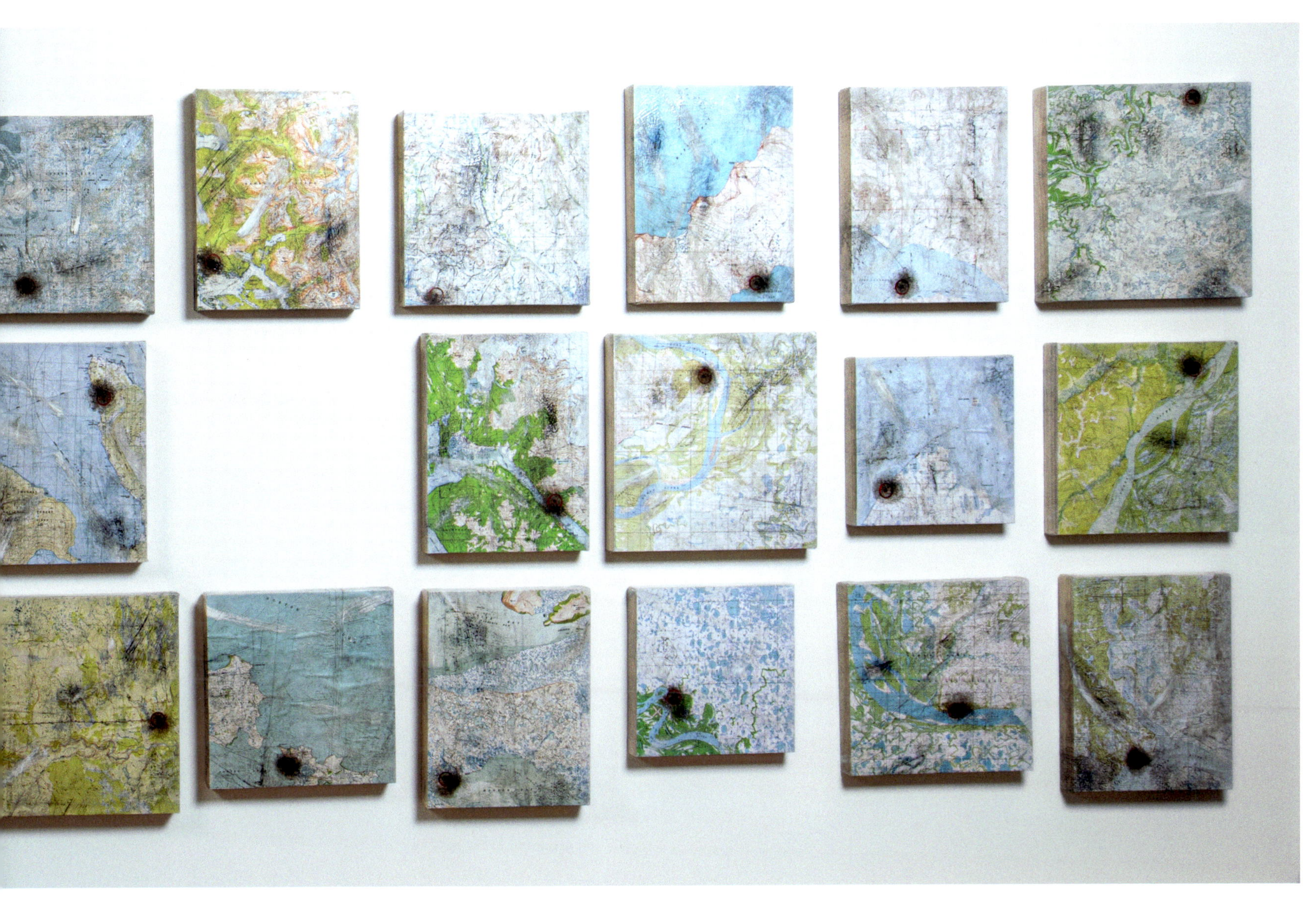

Credible II, 2022. Mixed media, dimensions variable. Collection of the Anchorage Museum. Photograph courtesy of the Mattress Factory.

Eddy

Natural Eddy on White, 2000. Acrylic polymer, walrus stomach, 30 × 30 in. Private collection. Photograph by Kevin G. Smith.

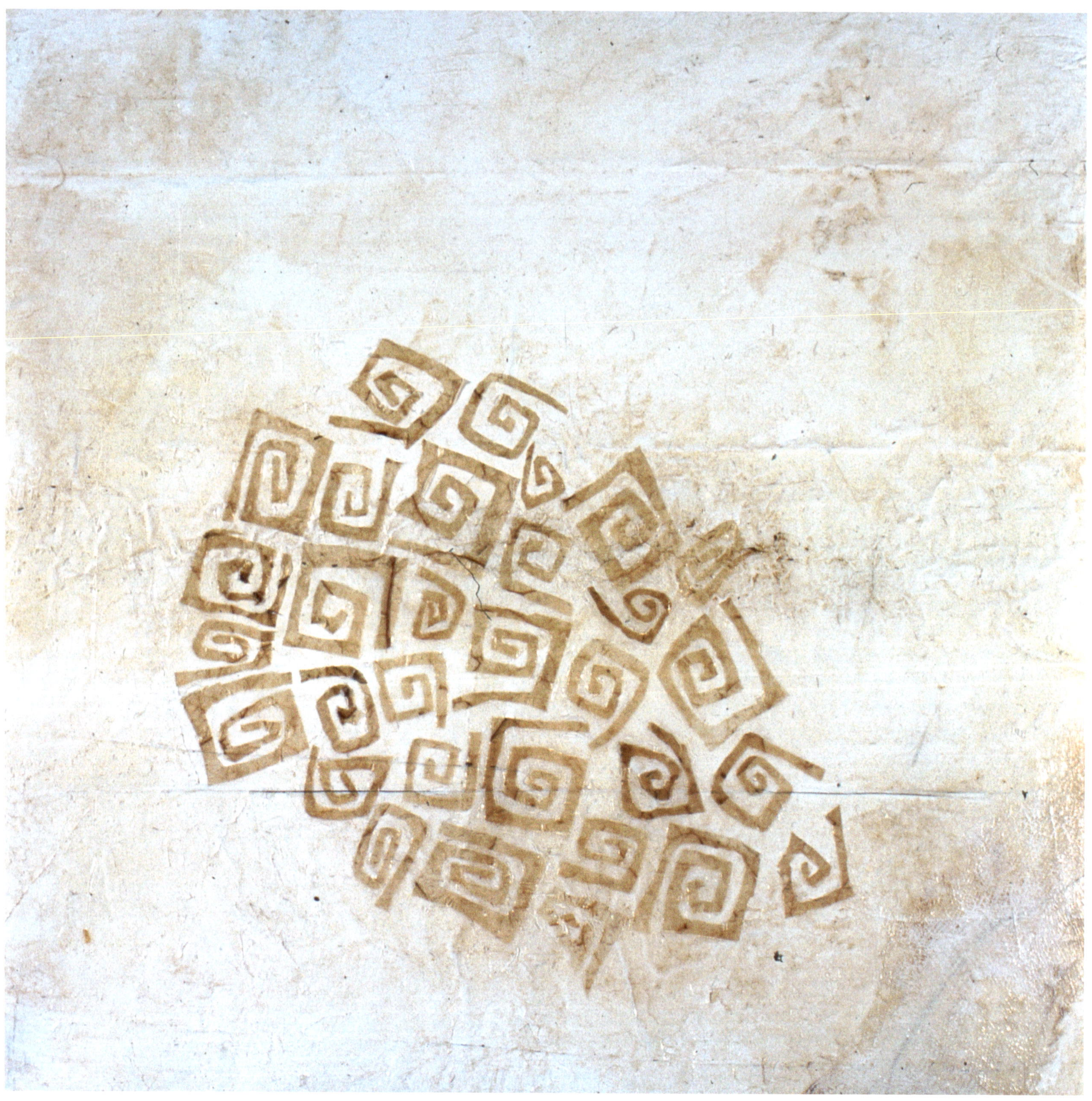

Green Eddy, 2005. Paint and mixed media, 36 × 36 in. Private collection. Photograph by Kevin G. Smith.

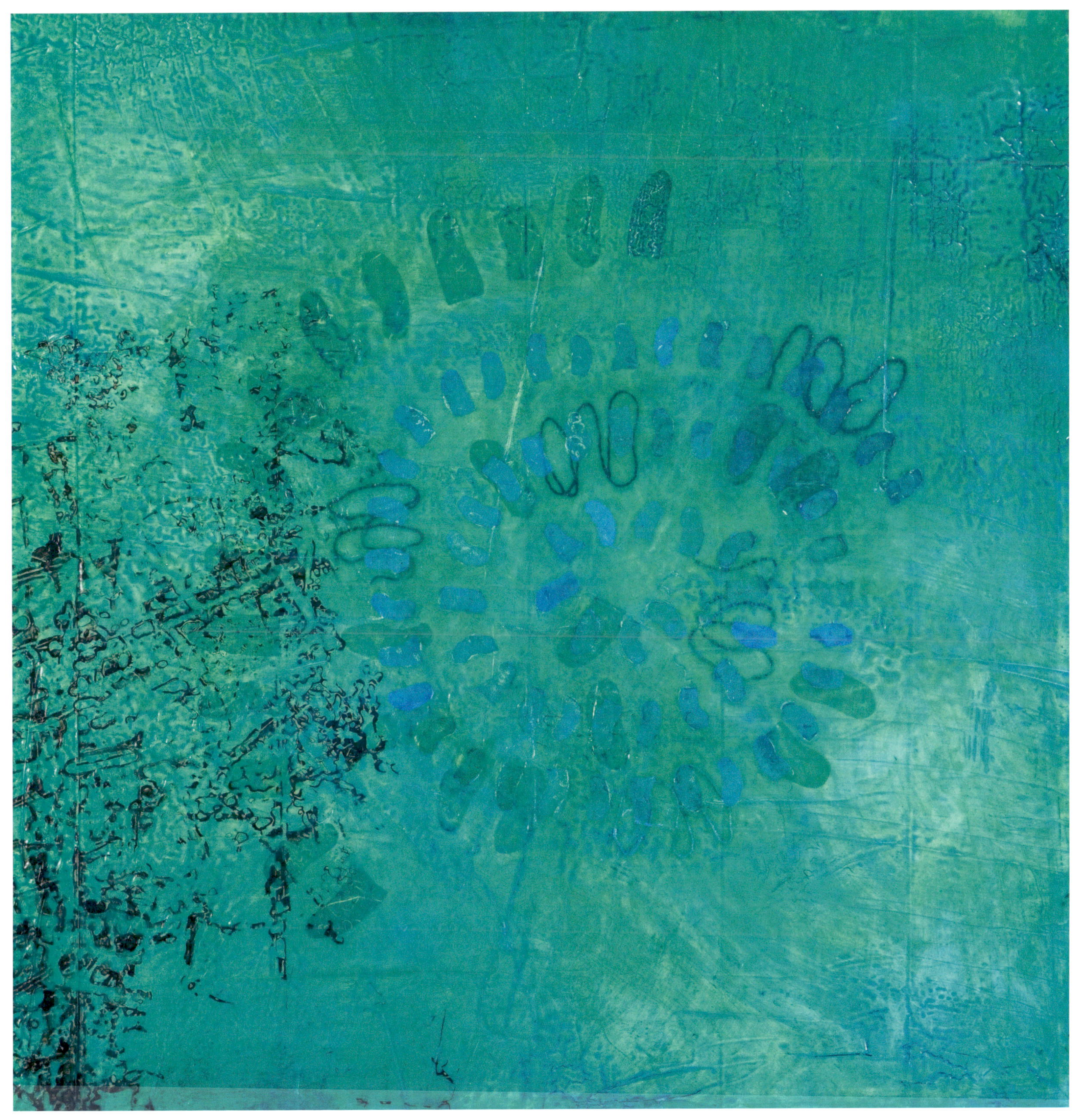

Untitled for Aunti Evi Jo

When she was a young girl, Kelliher-Combs was given a beautiful atikluk (customary summer garment) as a birthday gift. At the time, she had no idea the memories and deep feelings it would hold for her. This childhood atikluk was lost in the many shuffles from youth to adulthood, but she can still

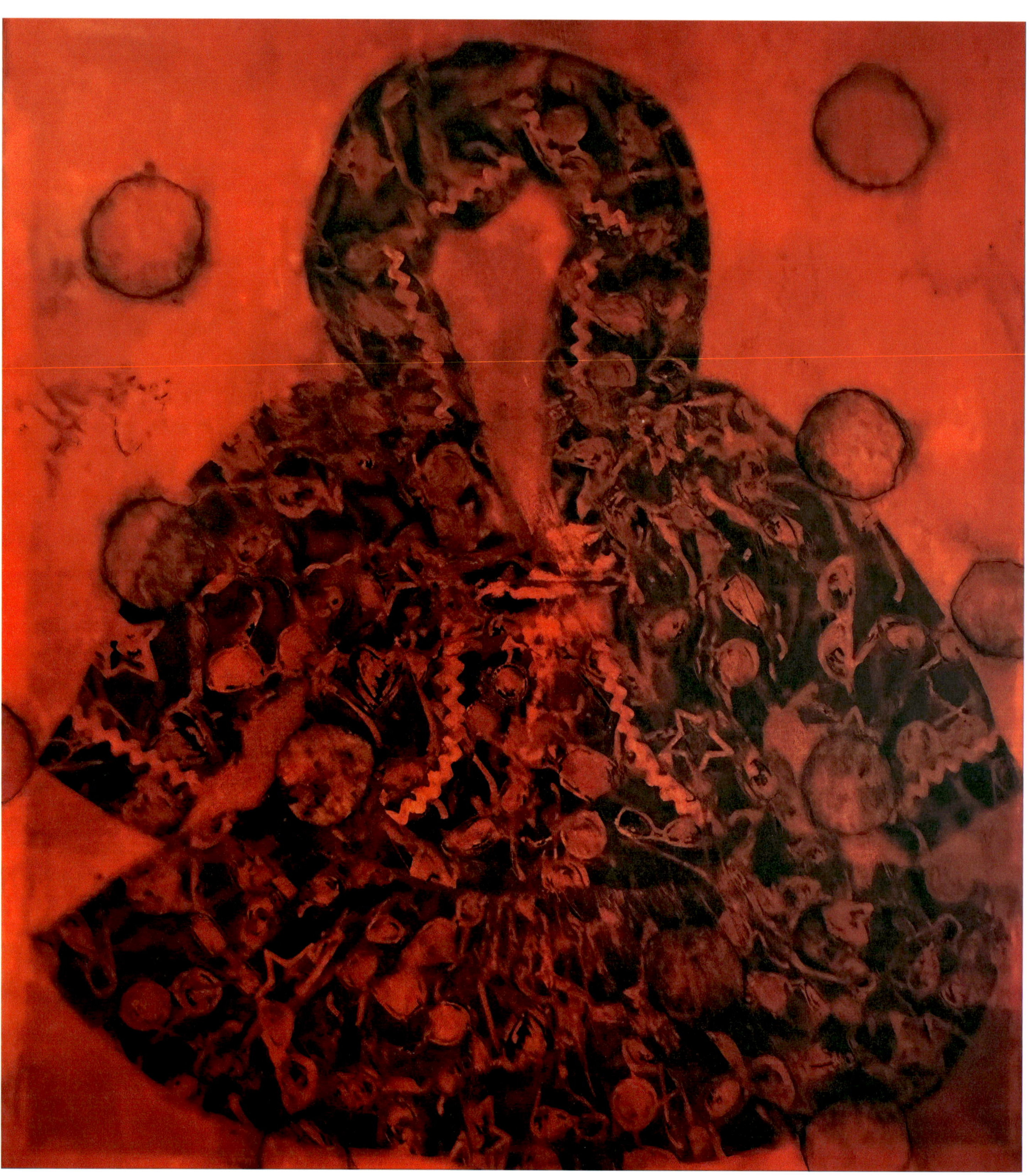

picture in her mind its bright blue form. Certain objects remind us of loved ones who have passed on. The empty atikluk has become a metaphor for those who have made this journey. *Untitled for Auntie Avi Jo* was a memorial to a loved one whose life was tragically cut short.

Untitled for Aunti Evi Jo (her favorite color was red), 2000. Paint and mixed media, 25.5 × 50 in. Private collection. Photographs by Photo Wright Laboratories.

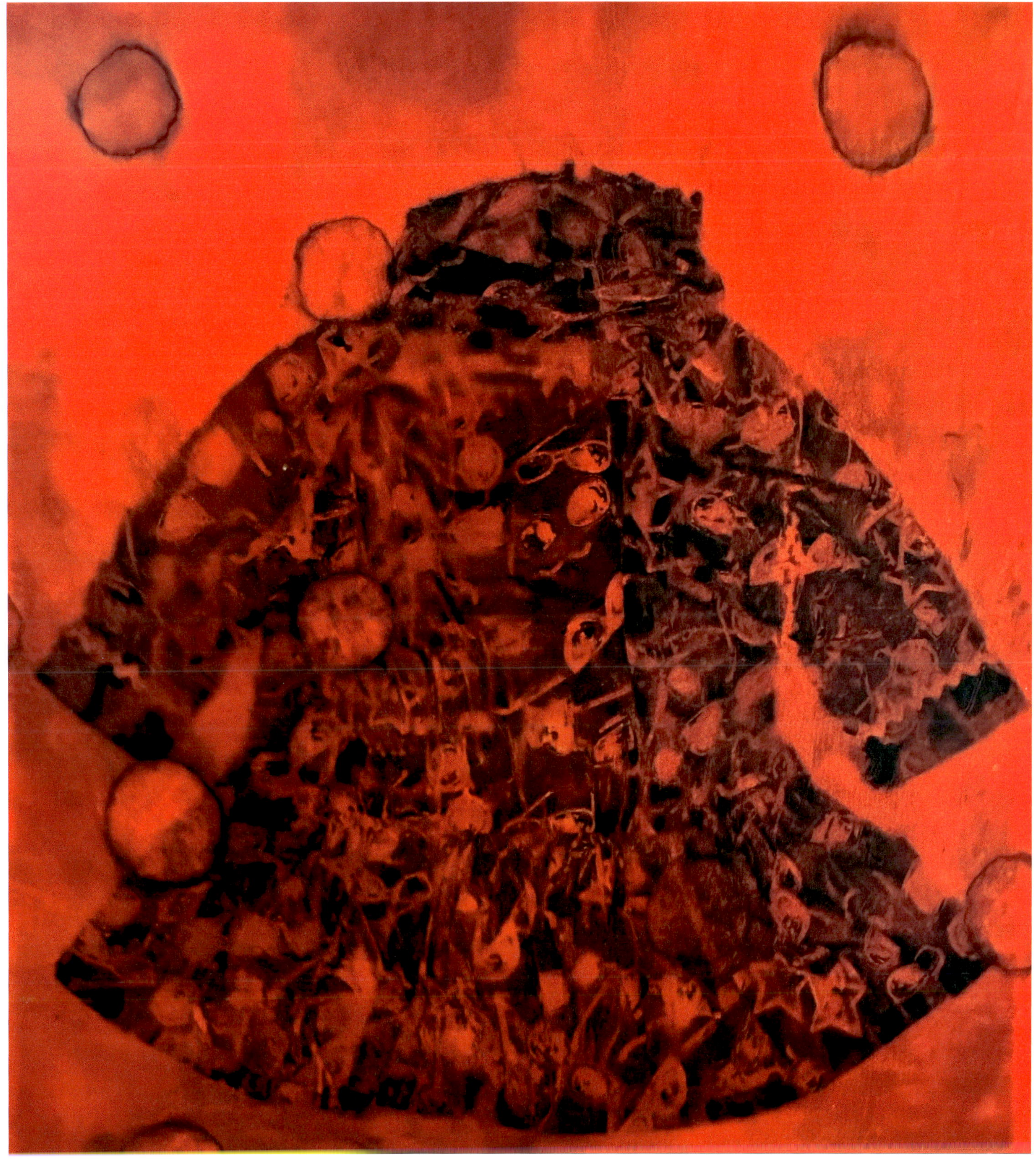

Her Favorite Color was

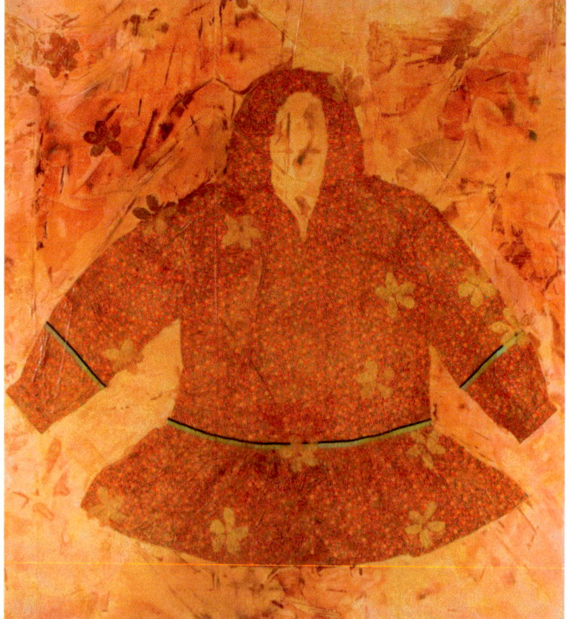

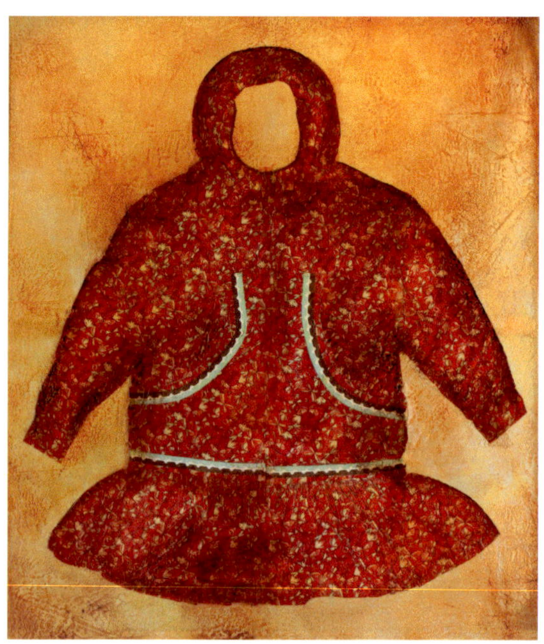

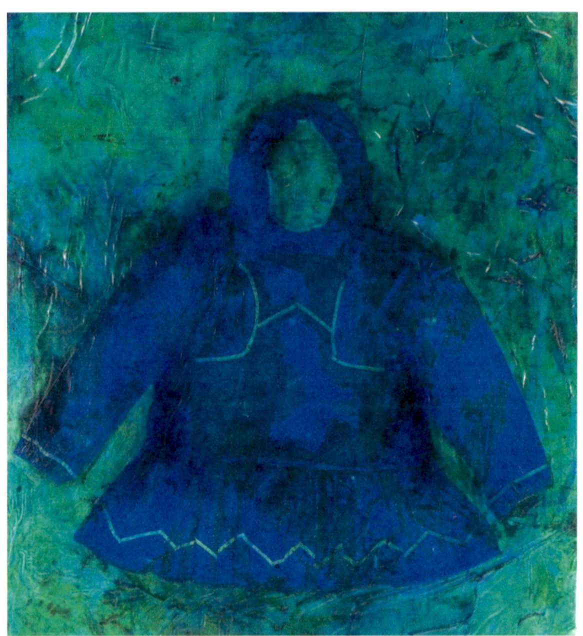

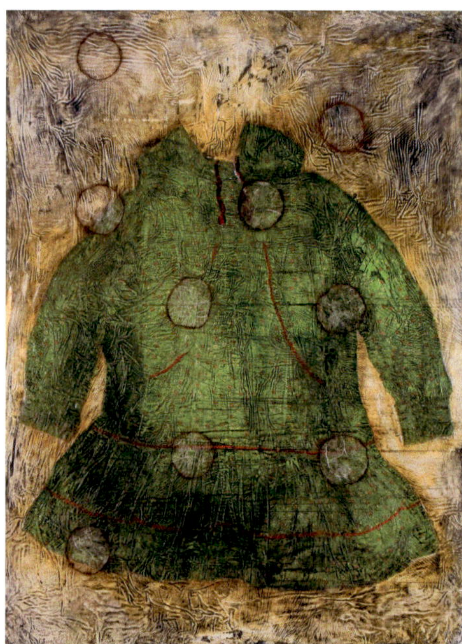

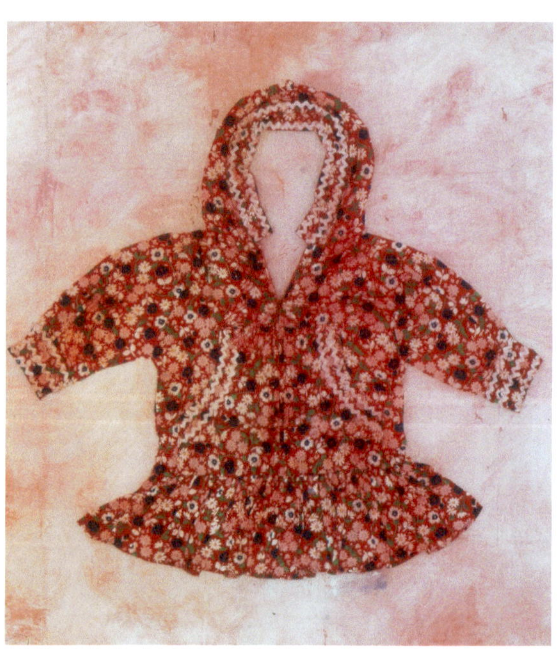

Her Favorite Color Was Orange, 2006. Paint and mixed media, 42 × 48 in. Private collection. Photograph by Chris Arend.
Her Favorite Color Was Red with Butterflies, 2008. Paint and mixed media, 42 × 52 in. Private collection. Photograph by Chris Arend.
Her Favorite Color Was Blue, 2006. Paint and mixed media, 42 × 48 in. Private collection. Photograph by Chris Arend.
Her Favorite Color Was Green, 2008. Paint and mixed media, 42 × 52 in. Private collection. Photograph by Chris Arend.
Her Favorite Color Was Red, 2017. Paint and mixed media, 28 × 32 in. Private collection. Photograph by Chris Arend.

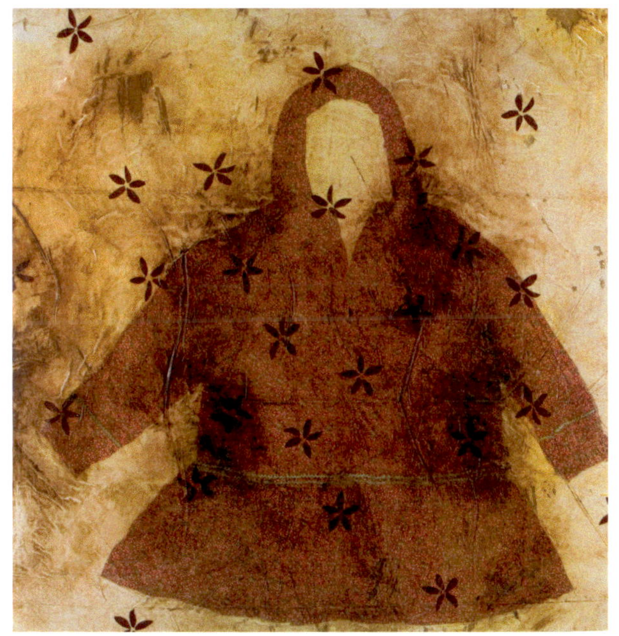
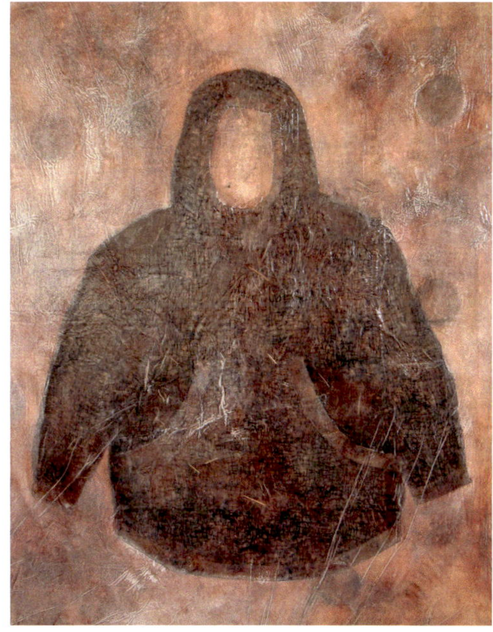
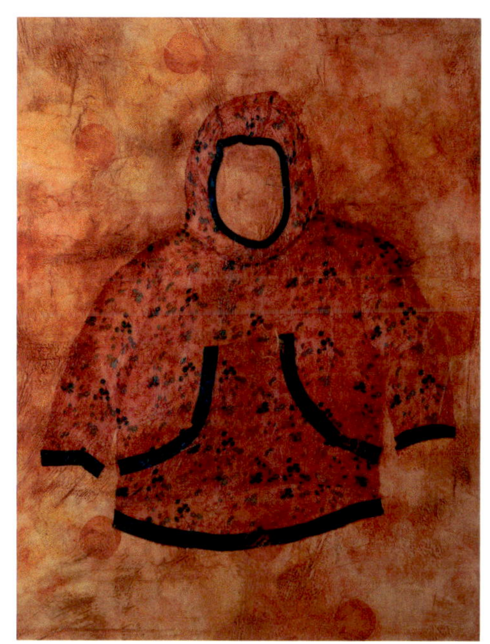
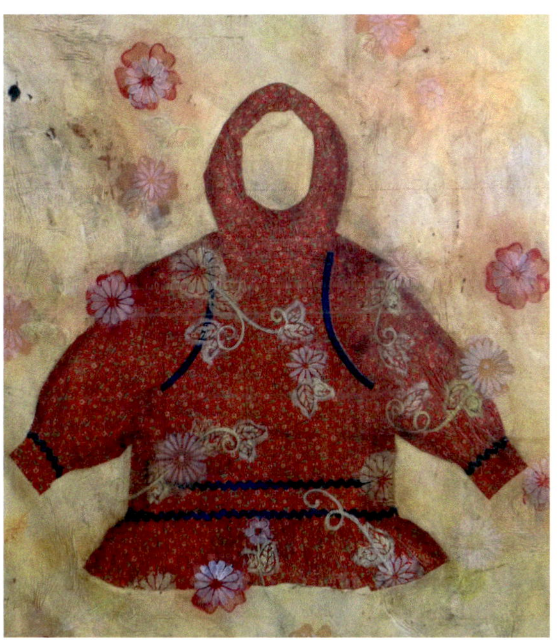
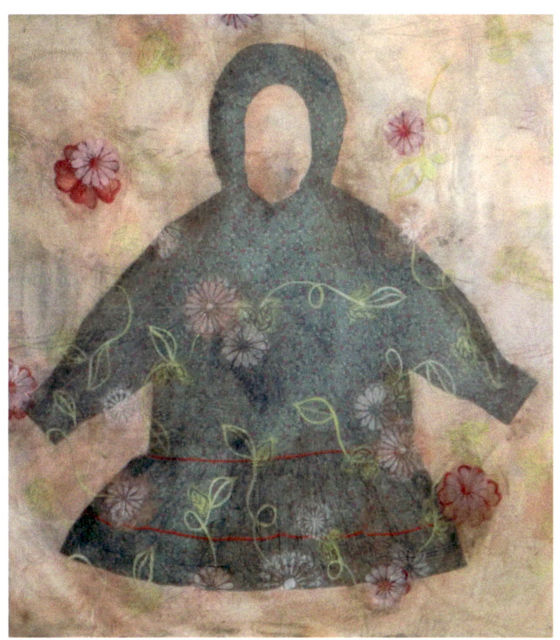
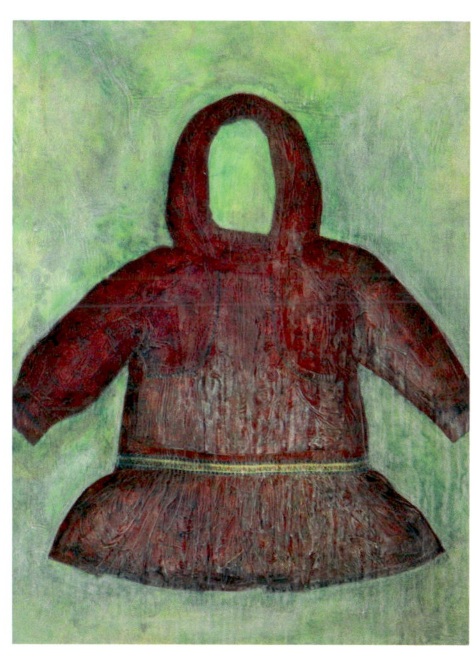

Her Favorite Color Was Red with Flowers, 2006. Paint and mixed media, 42 × 48 in. Private collection. Photograph by Chris Arend.
Her Favorite Color Was Mauve, 2013. Paint and mixed media, 44 × 52 in. Private collection. Photograph by Chris Arend.
Her Favorite Color Was Salmon, 2019. Paint and mixed media, 42 × 50 in. Private collection. Photograph by Chris Arend.
Her Favorite Color Was Orange with Flowers, 2017. Paint and mixed media, 42 × 52 in. Private collection. Photograph by Chris Arend.
Her Favorite Color Was Green with Flowers, 2017. Paint and mixed media, 42 × 52 in. Private collection. Photograph by Chris Arend.
Her Favorite Color Was Red II, 2013. Paint and mixed media, 28 × 34 in. Private collection. Photograph by Chris Arend.

Idiot Strings

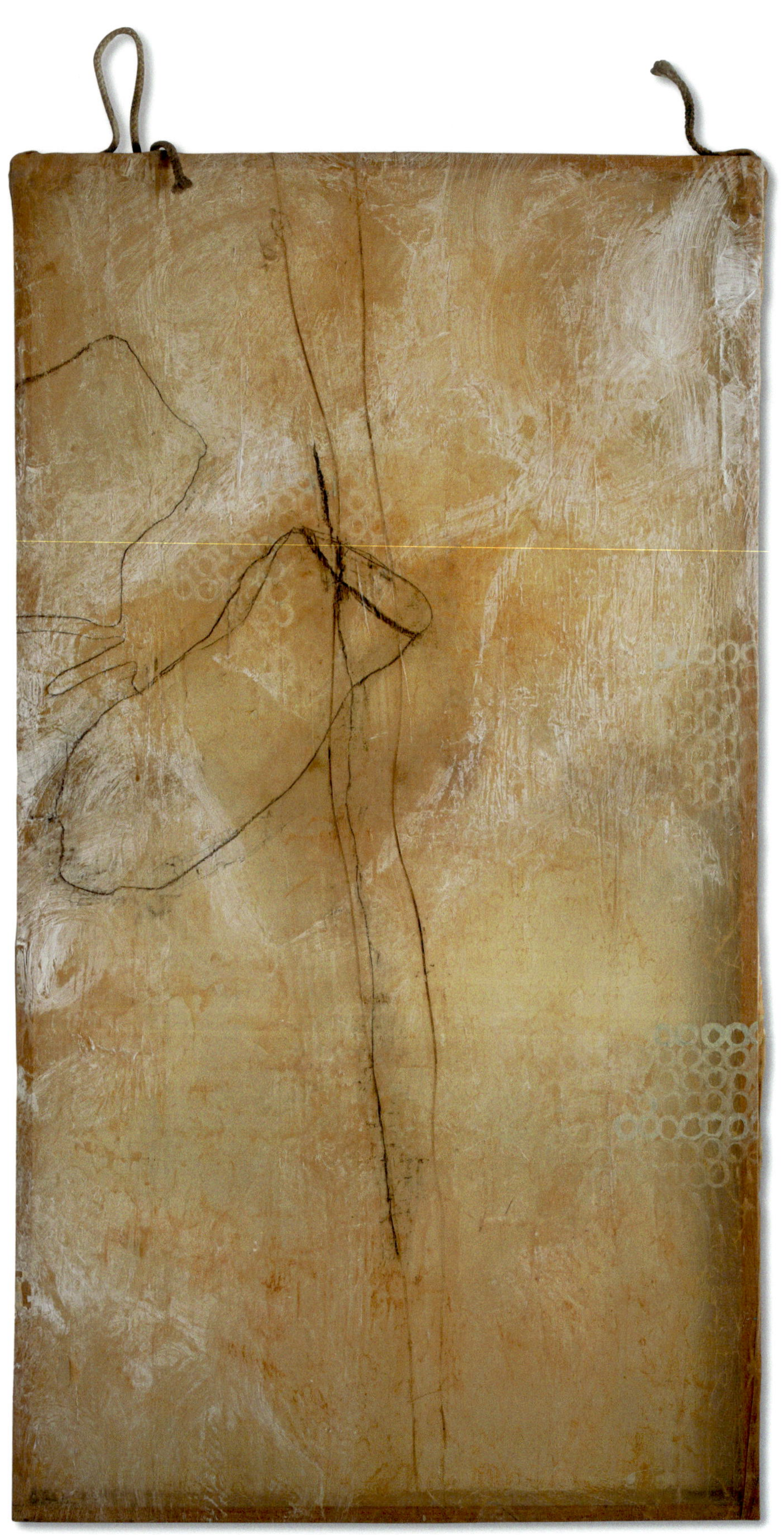

Idiot Strings, 1999. Mixed media, 36 × 60 in. Collection of the artist. Photograph by Chris Arend.

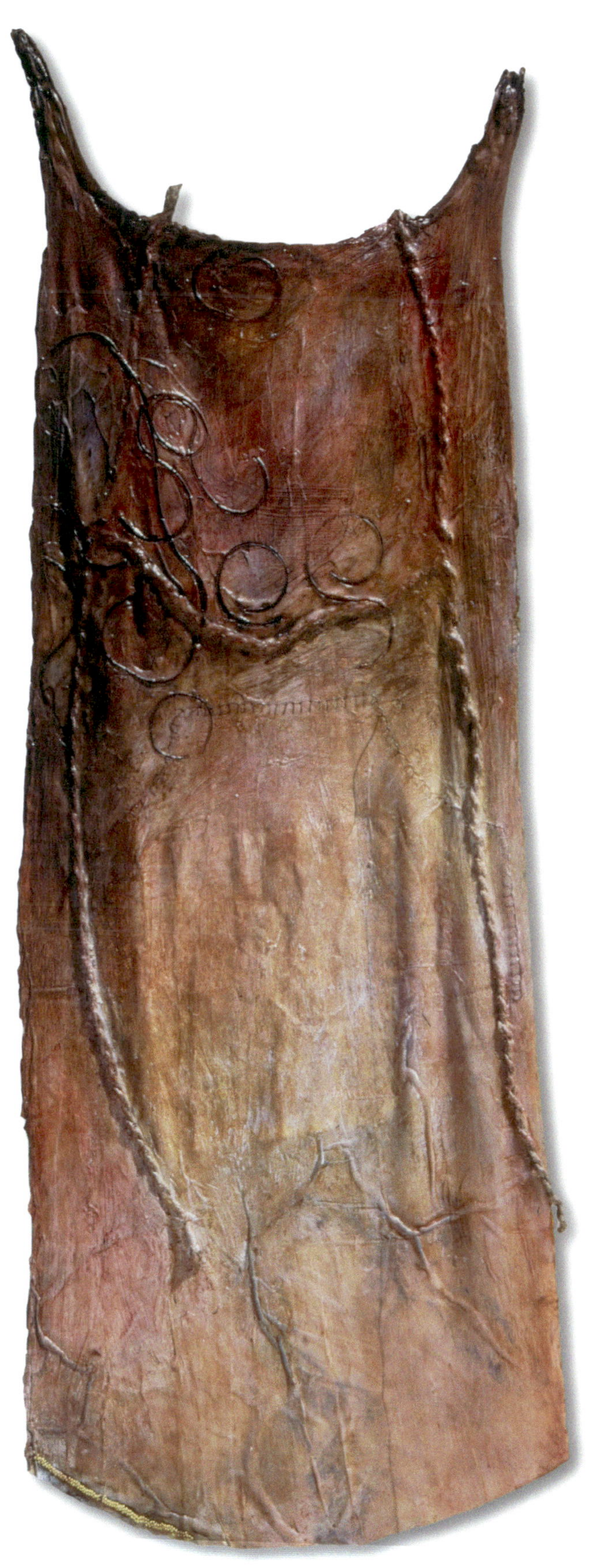

Idiot Strings, Slip, 1998. Paint and mixed media, 20 × 52 in. Private collection. Photograph by Kevin G. Smith.

She Was Only Ten

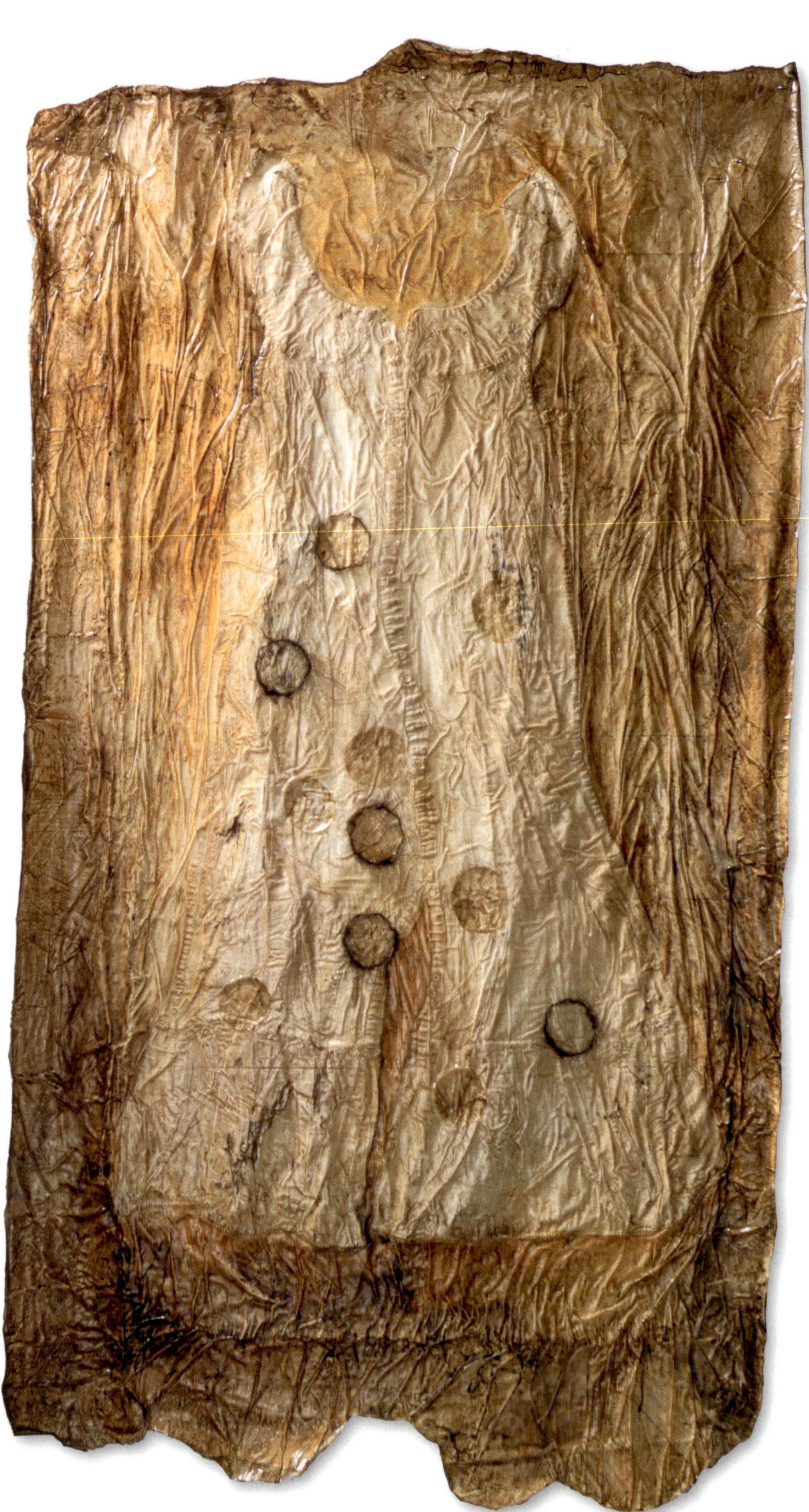

She Was Only Ten, Pore, 2009. Paint and mixed media, 24 × 48 in. Collection of the Anchorage Museum. Photograph by Kevin G. Smith.

She Was Only Ten, White I, 2002. Paint and mixed media, 30 × 30 in. Private collection. Photograph by Kevin G. Smith.

She Was Only Ten, White, 2002. Paint and mixed media, 30 × 30 in. Private collection. Photograph by Kevin G. Smith.

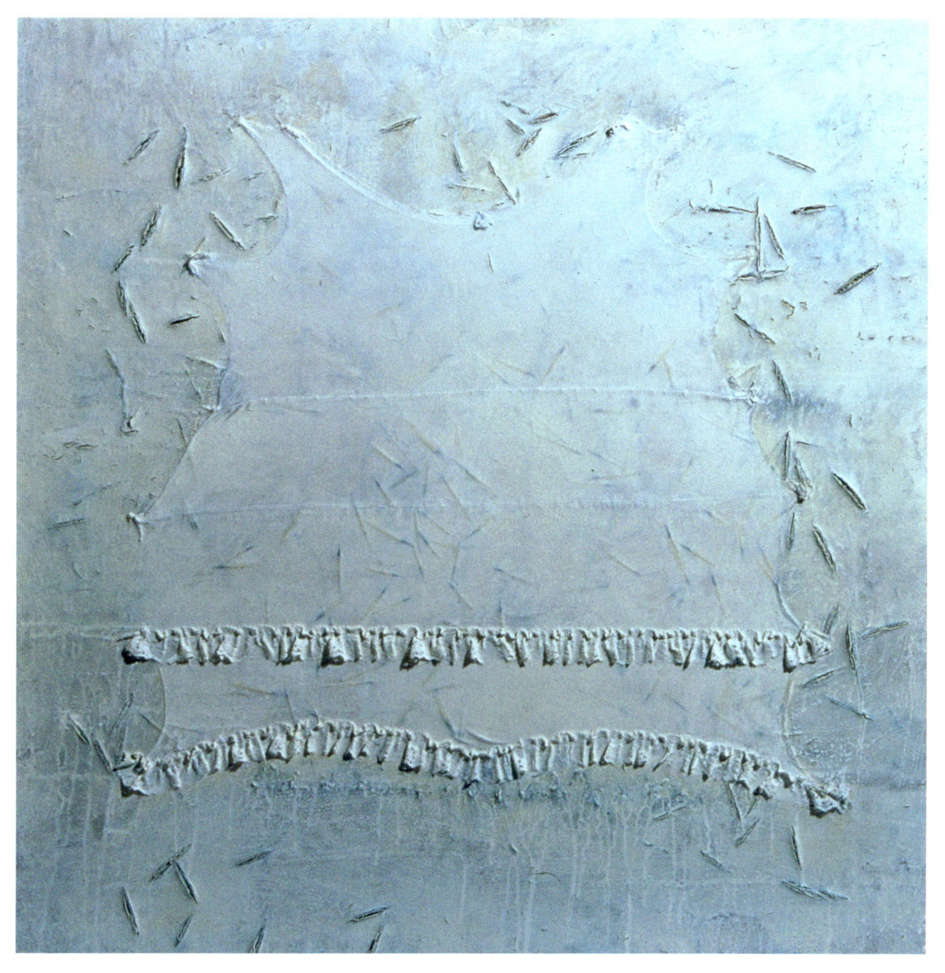

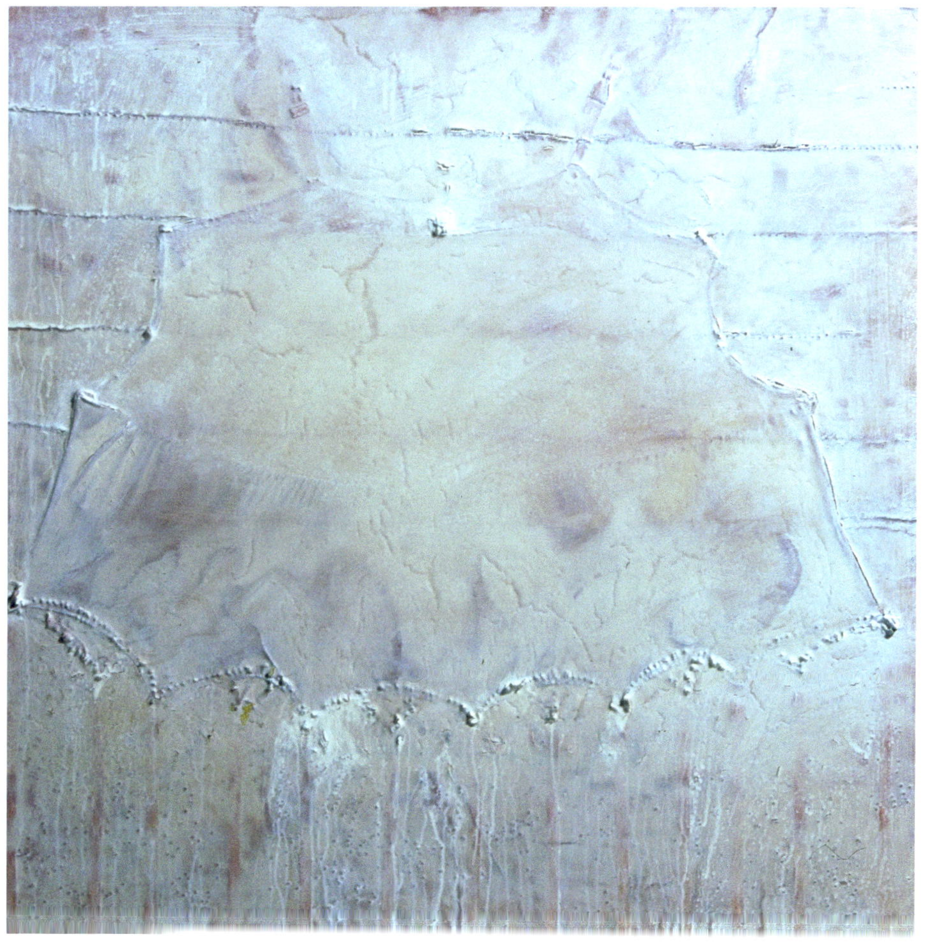

Mark

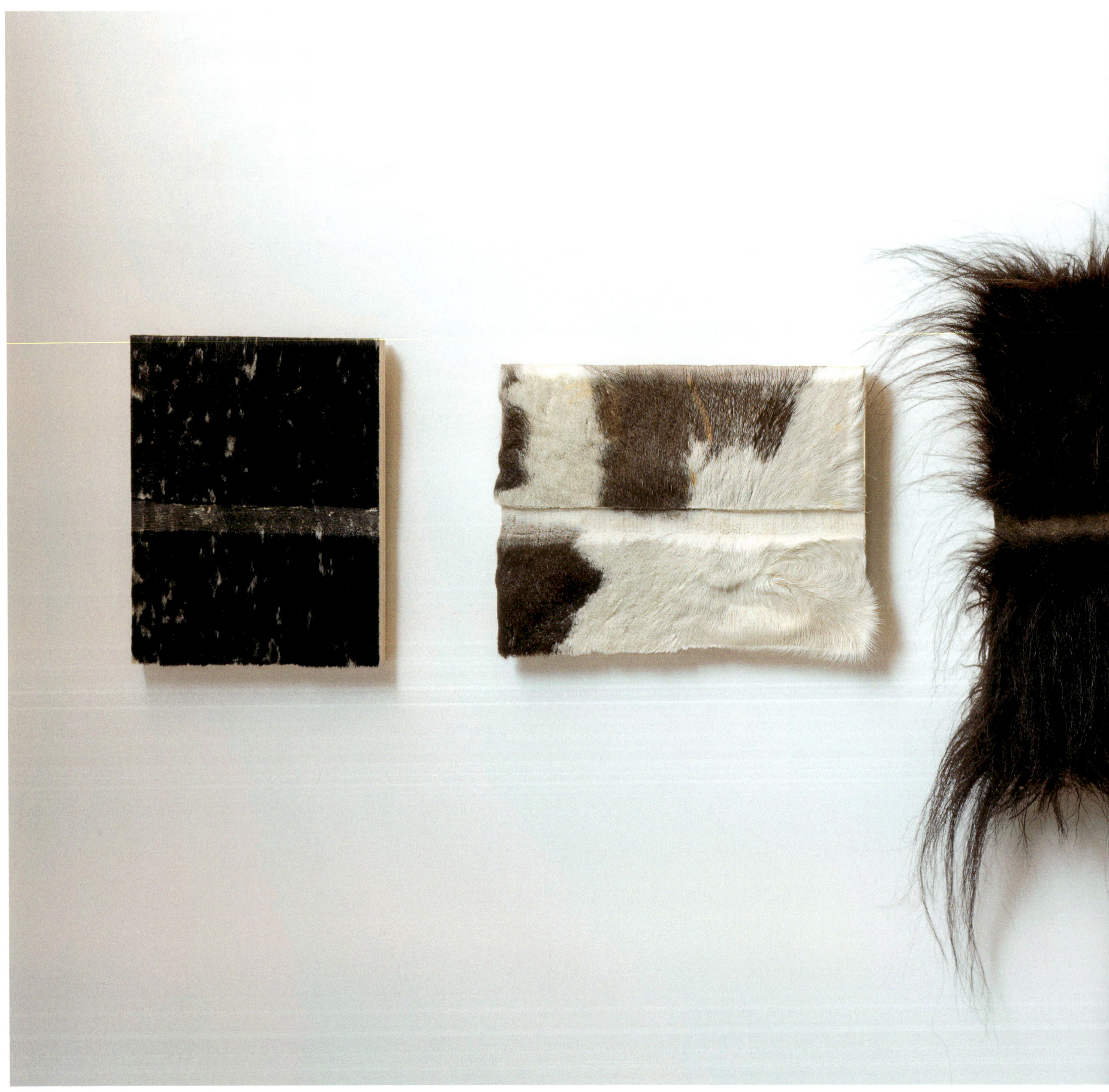

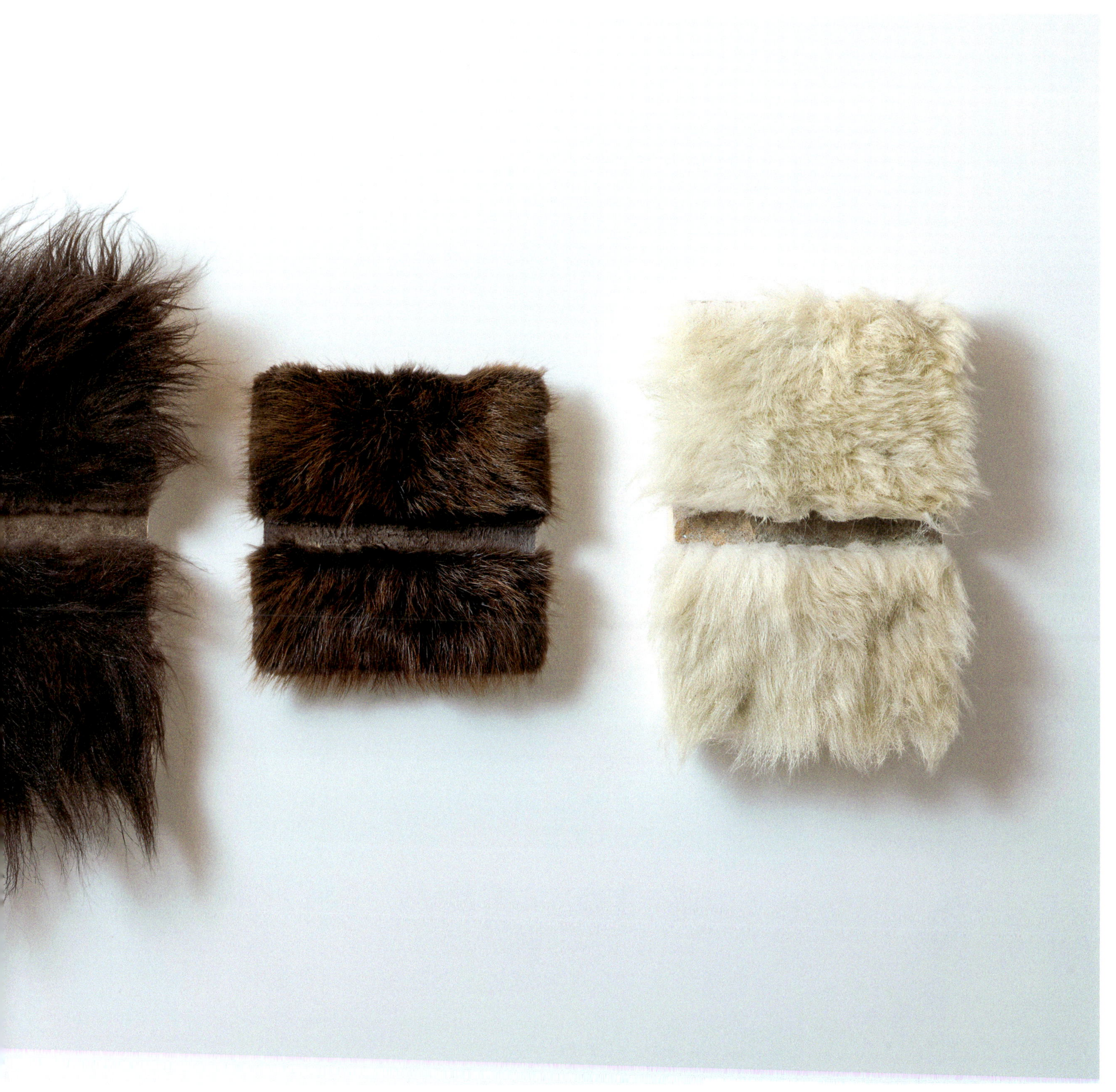

Mark, Seal, Caribou, Musk Ox, Beaver, Polar Bear, 2017. Mixed media, dimensions variable. Collection of the Anchorage Museum. Photograph by Chris Arend.

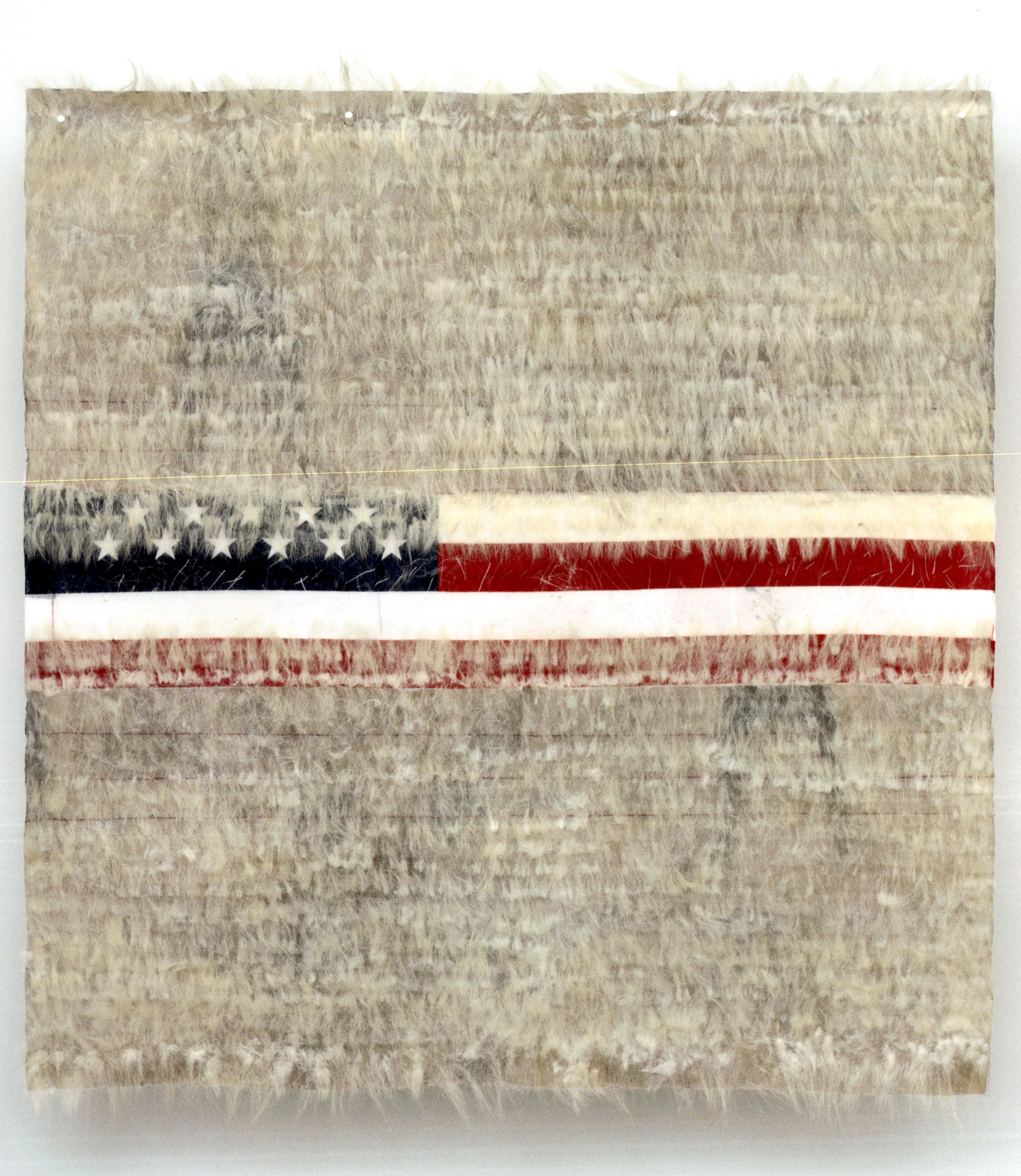

Mark, Nanuq, 2023. Mixed media, 48 × 48 in. Private collection. Photograph courtesy of the Stars Gallery.

Mark, Walrus and Polar Bear, 2018. Mixed media, 42 × 90 in. Collection of the Anchorage Museum. Photograph courtesy of the Anchorage Museum.

Mark

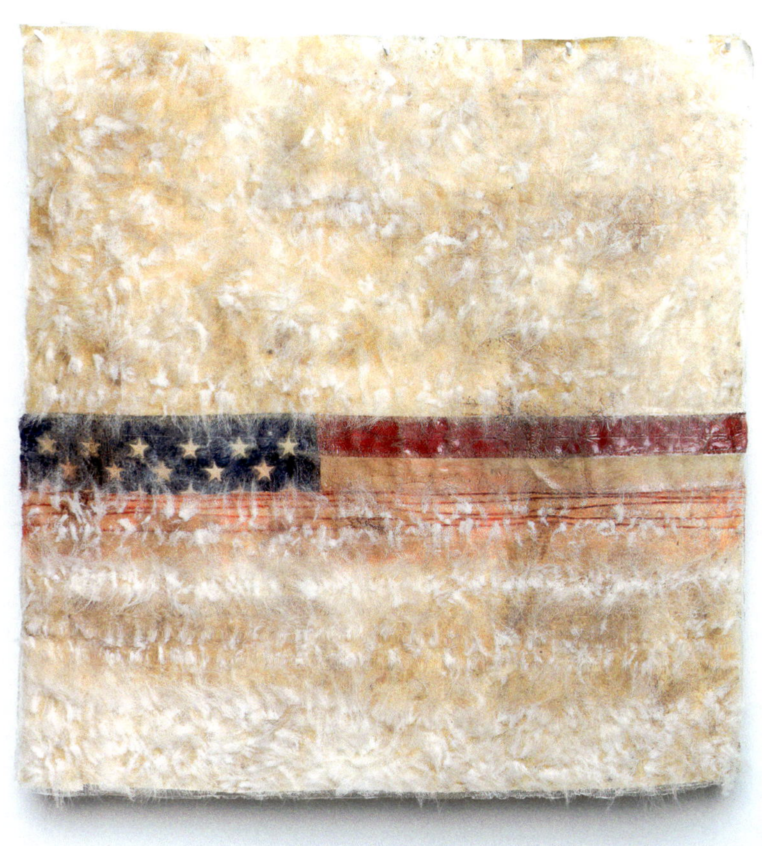

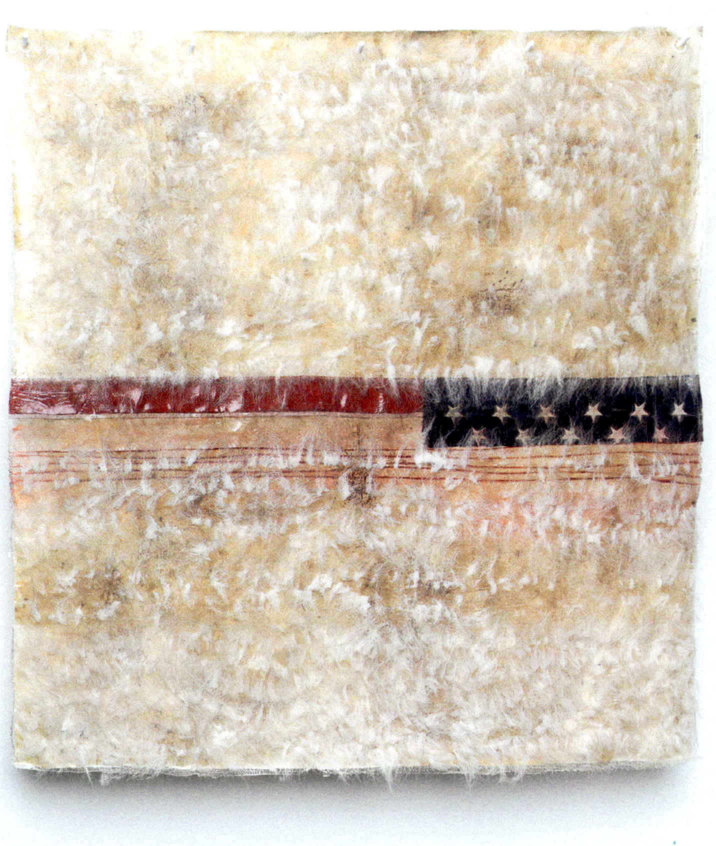

Pore

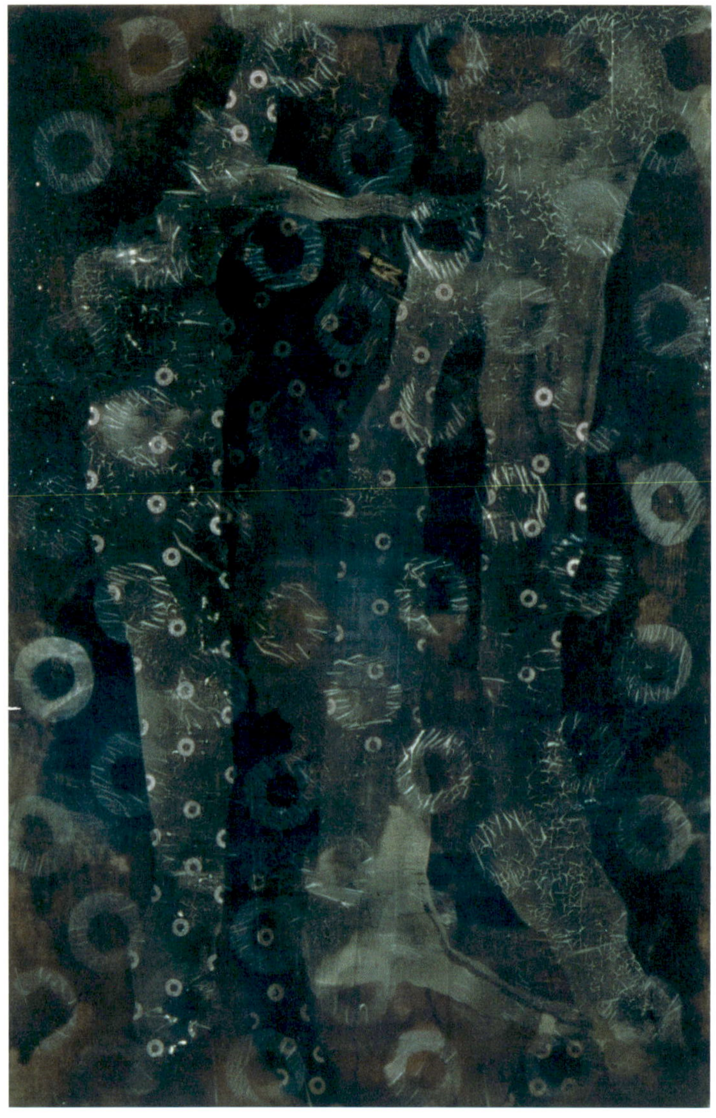

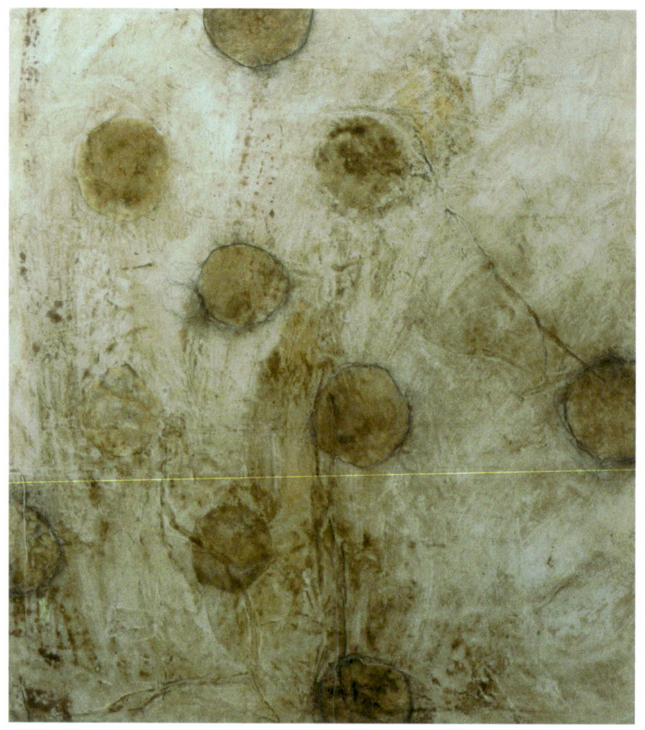

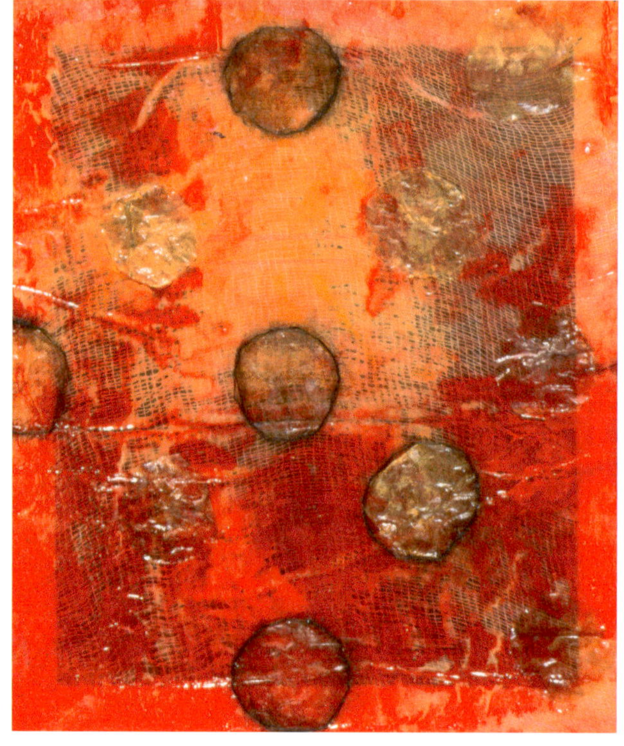

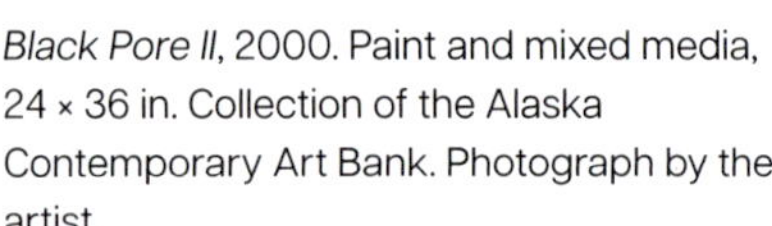

Black Pore II, 2000. Paint and mixed media, 24 × 36 in. Collection of the Alaska Contemporary Art Bank. Photograph by the artist.

Natural Pore with White, 2000. Acrylic polymer, walrus stomach, human hair, nylon thread, 20 × 16 in. Private collection. Photograph by the artist.

Small Red Pore, 1999. Paint and mixed media, 11 × 12 in. Private collection. Photograph by the artist.

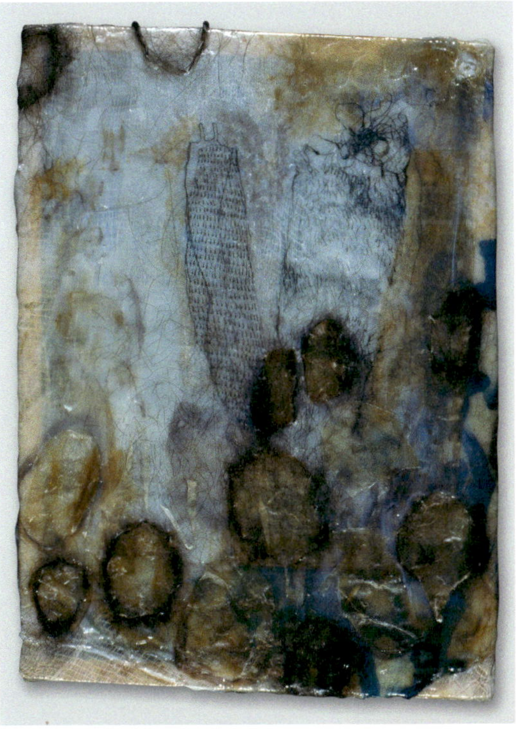

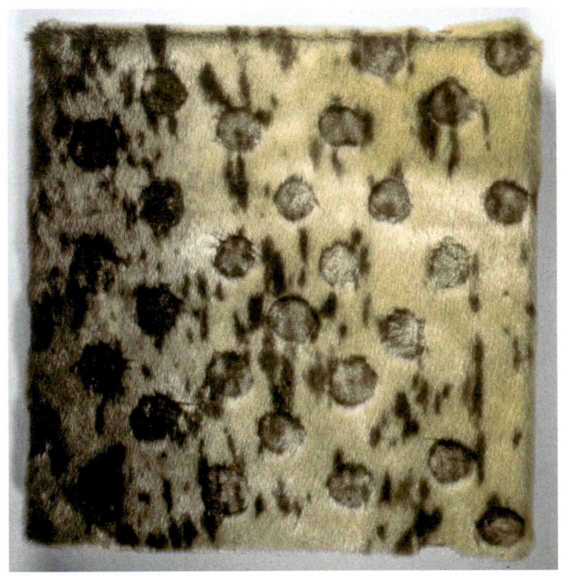

Teal Pore, 1998. Paint and mixed media, 10 × 12 in. Private collection. Photograph by the artist.

Sky Pore, 2009. Paint and mixed media, 24 × 24 in. Private collection. Photograph by Kevin G. Smith.

Seal Skin Pore, 2008. Paint and mixed media, 12 × 12 in. Private collection. Photograph by Kevin G. Smith.

Red Large Pore, 2013. Paint and mixed media, 30 × 40 in. Private collection. Photograph by Chris Arend.

Orange Pore

Orange Pore, 1998. Acrylic polymer, cheesecloth, walrus stomach, paper, human hair, nylon thread, 17 × 46 in. Private collection. Photograph by the artist.

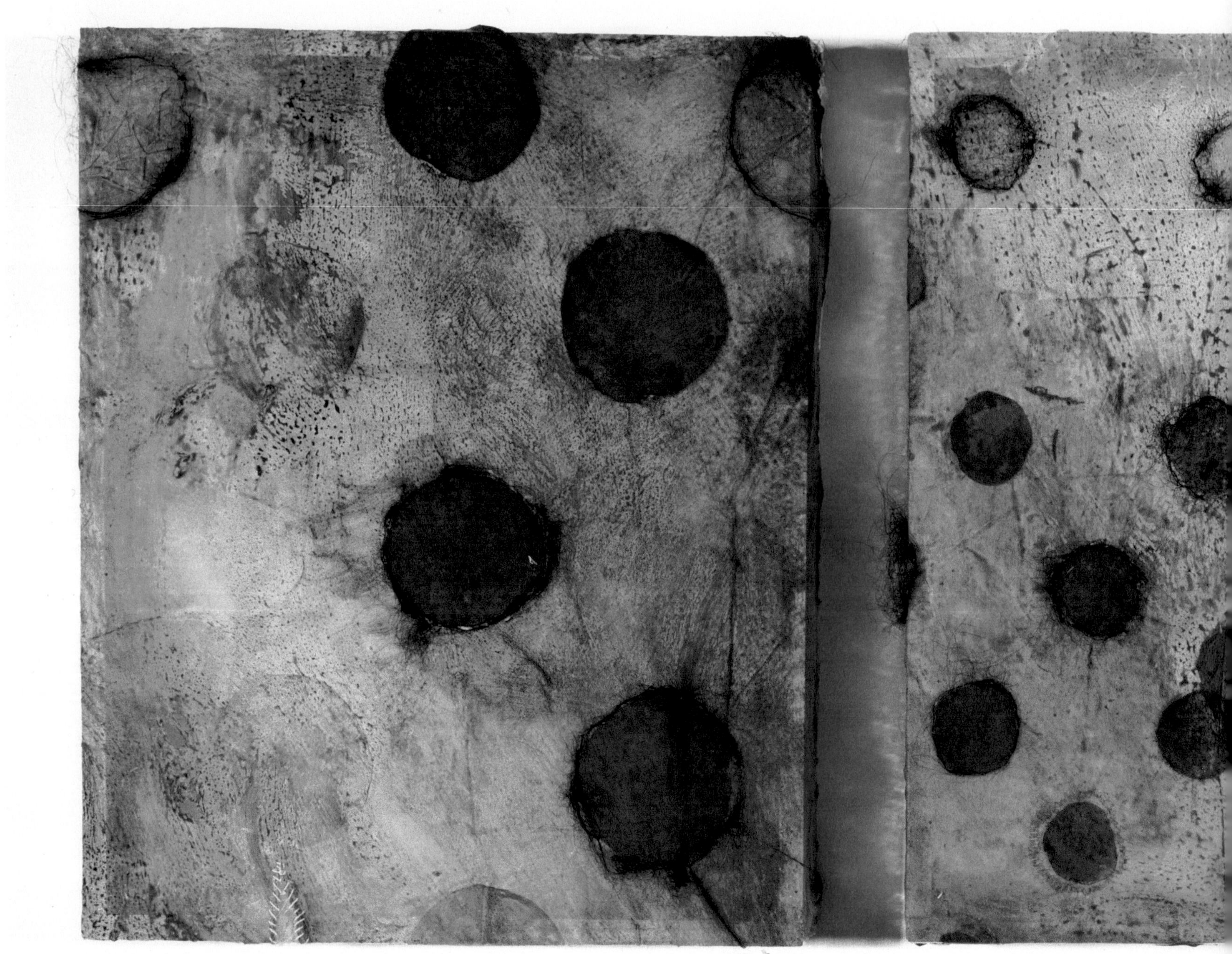

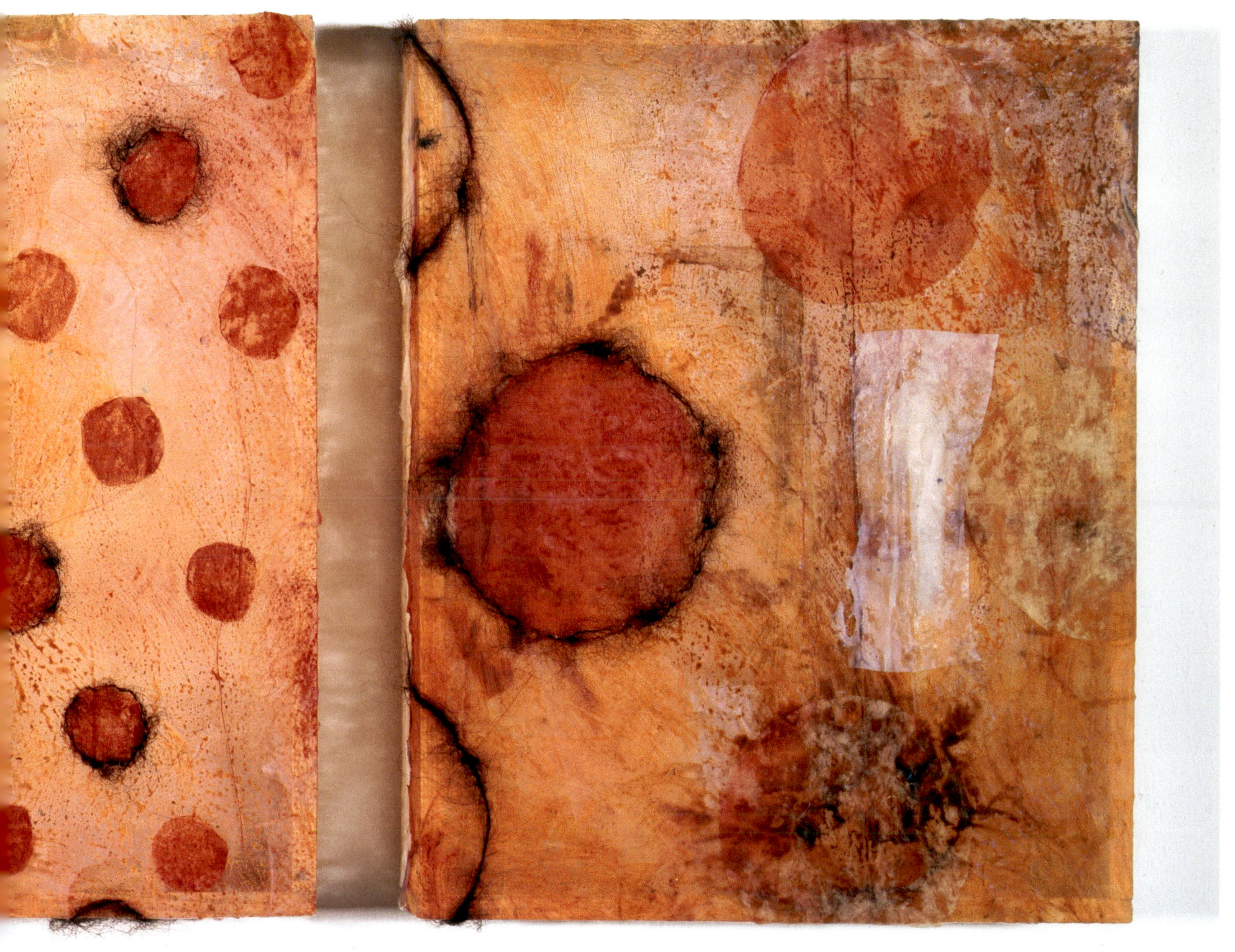

Remnant

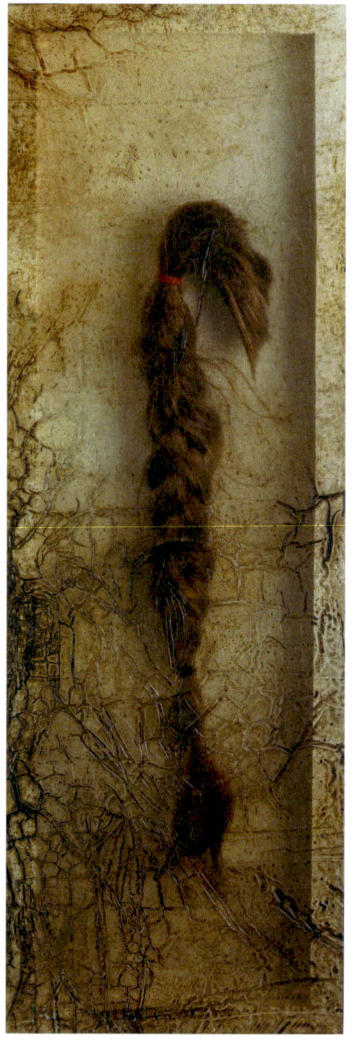

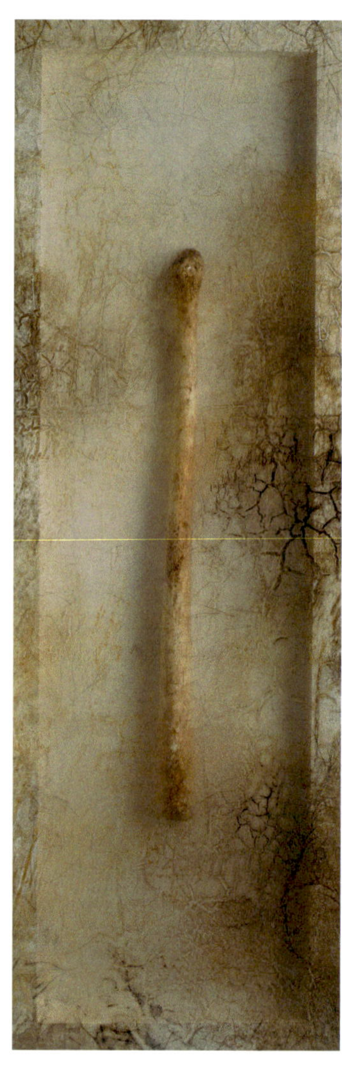

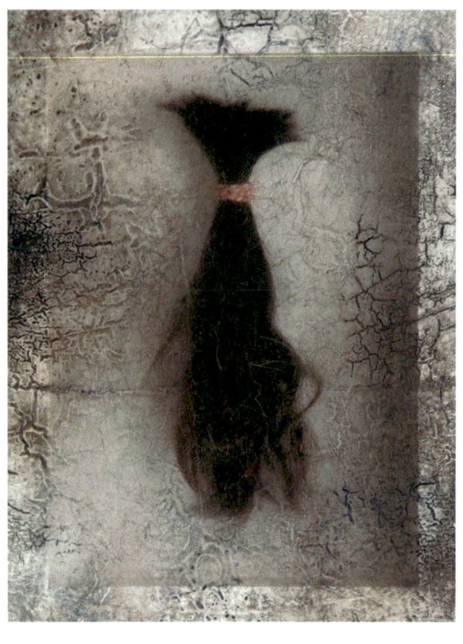

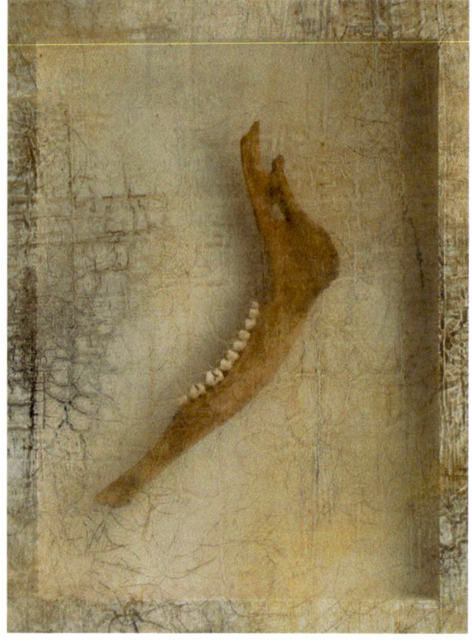

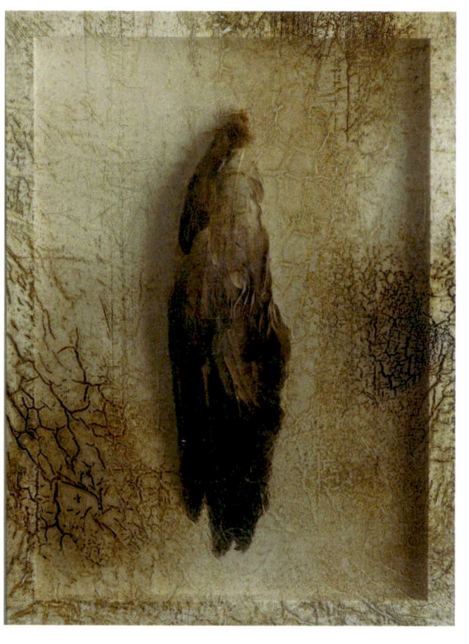

Human Hair, 2016. Paint and mixed media, 36 × 12 in. Private collection. Photograph by Chris Arend.

Walrus Bone, 2016. Paint and mixed media, 12 × 36 in. Private collection. Photograph by Chris Arend.

Human Hair, 2016. Paint and mixed media, 14 × 18 in. Private collection. Photograph by Chris Arend.

Moose Jaw, 2016. Paint and mixed media, 14 × 18 in. Private collection. Photograph by Chris Arend.

Wing, 2016. Paint and mixed media, 24 × 18 in. Private collection. Photograph by Chris Arend.

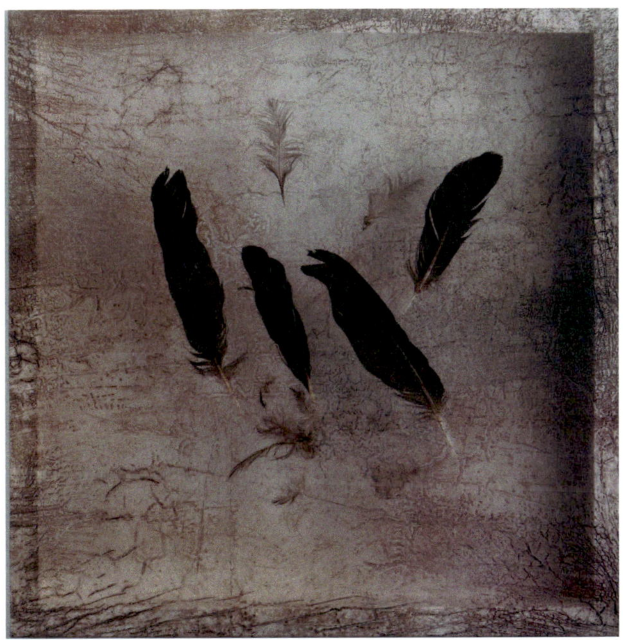

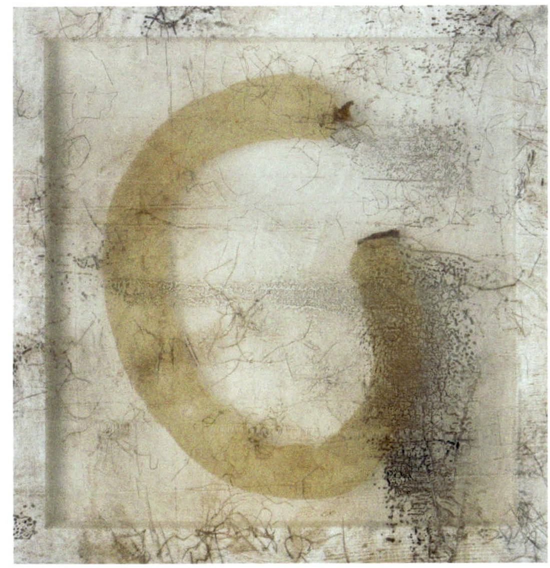

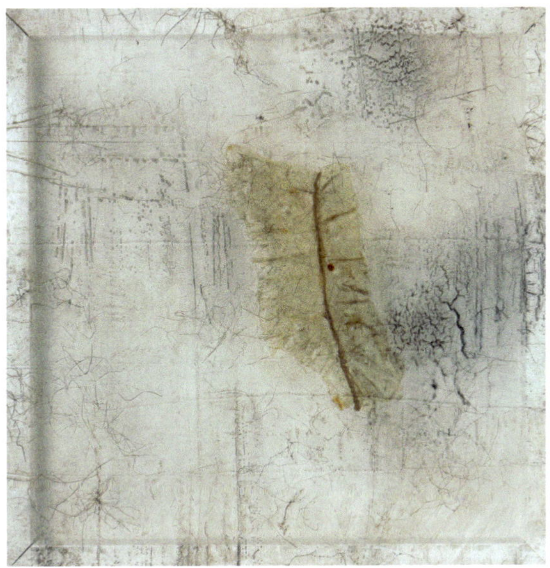

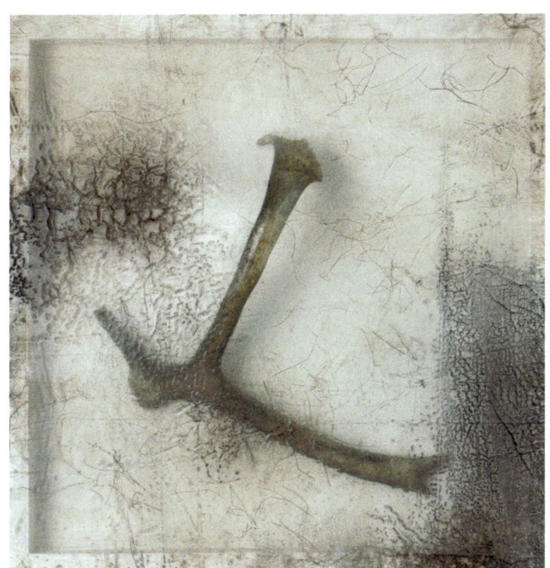

Feather, 2016. Paint and mixed media, 24 × 24 in. Private collection. Photograph by Chris Arend.

Seal Intestine, 2016. Paint and mixed media, 16 × 16 in. Private collection. Photograph by Chris Arend.

Seal Intestine, 2016. Paint and mixed media, 16 × 16 in. Private collection. Photograph by Chris Arend.

Caribou Antler, 2016. Paint and mixed media, 16 × 16 in. Private collection. Photograph by Chris Arend.

Remnant is a series meant to comment on the threatened state of the natural environment in Alaska, a region where the folly of our human-centric approach to industry is achingly clear. These works confront the viewer with fragments and scraps of the world of the North—bits and pieces of animal hide, hair, clothing, and other detritus, submerged in synthetic media like so many specimens from a way of life that no longer exists. *Remnant* invites the viewer into a dialogue that exposes the tenuousness of our own existence. In the end it is really humankind that will be reduced to a mere remnant.

Remnant:
1. a usually small part, member, or trace remaining
2. a small surviving group—often used in the plural
3. an unsold or unused piece of goods
4. what is left of a community after it undergoes a catastrophe (a recurring theme throughout the Hebrew and Christian Bibles)

untitled by Taqralik Partridge

we saw the multitudes
and believed
there were endless hosts
of creatures for our consumption
the birds took flight like
a shoulder of the land
rising into the air
schools of fish turned in the current
and the whole sun in all its glory
shone in the glint of their scales
we had endless land
bottomless wells
clear sweet air to fill
a million million breaths
and never
never would it run out
and how
how today
is it that we can see the edge of this
and how
how today can we not

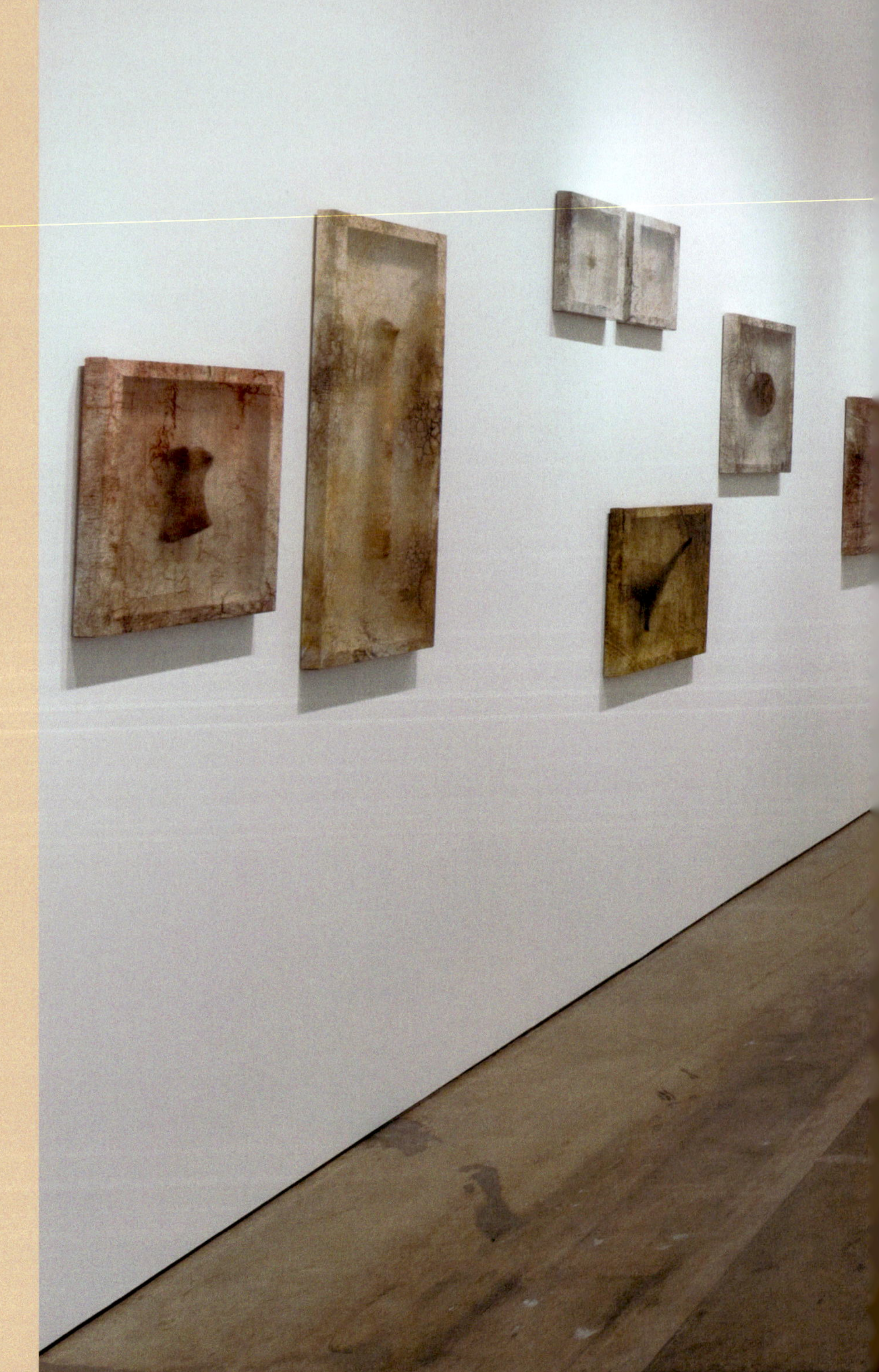

Remnant, 2016. Installation of paintings at Site Santa Fe, NM. Private collection. Photograph courtesy of Site Santa Fe.

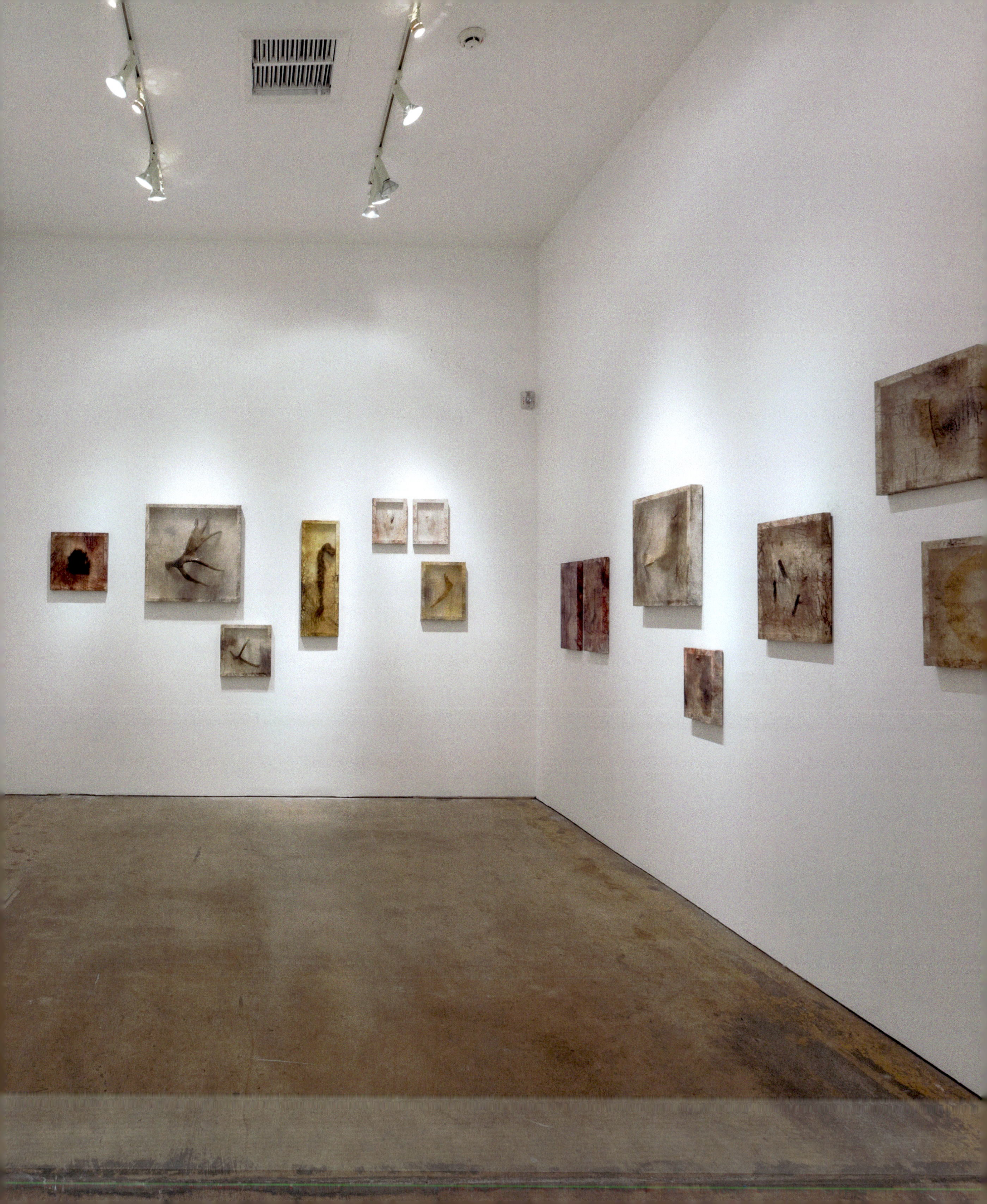

Remnant Clothing

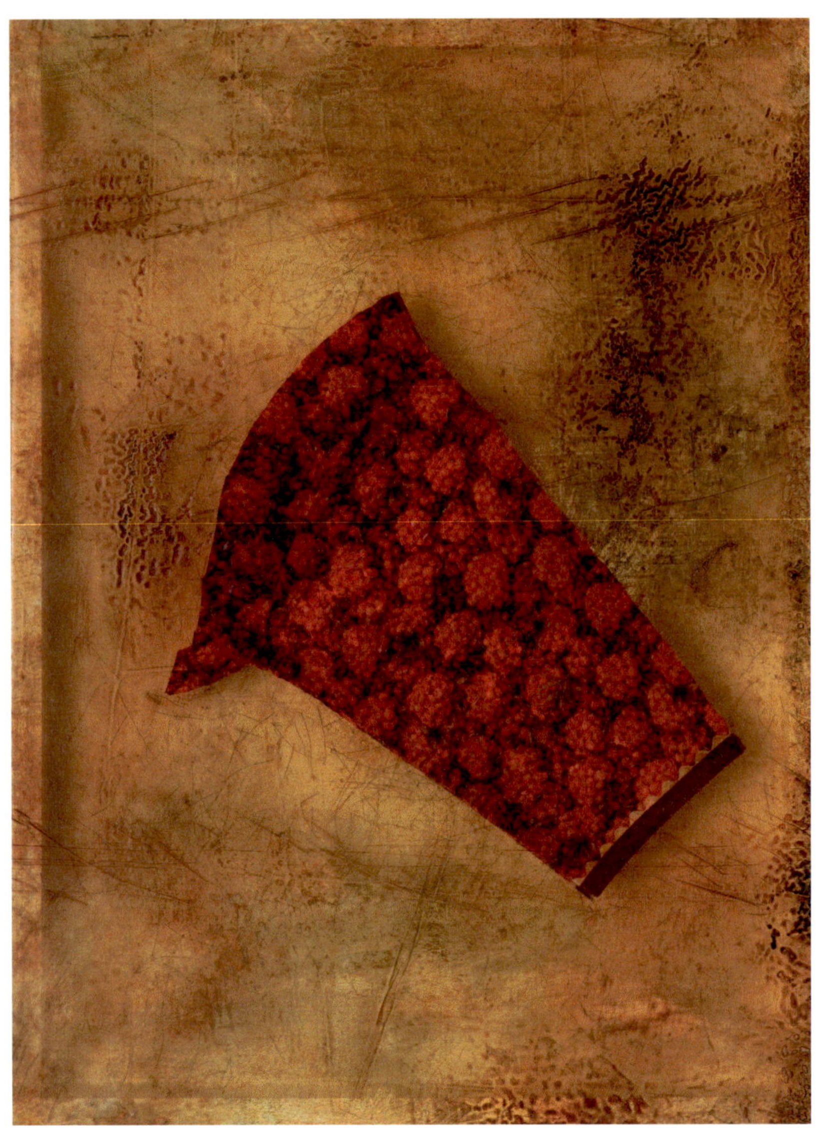

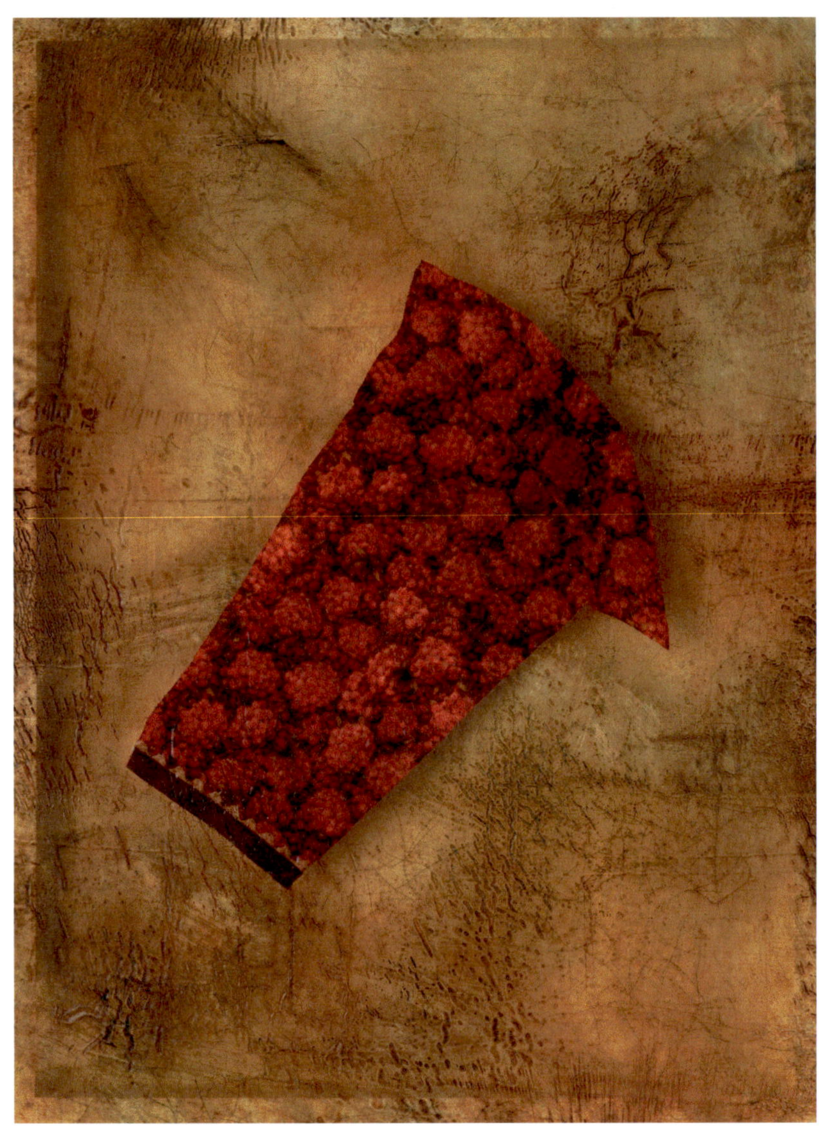

Remnant, Raspberry Sleeve, 2017. Paint and mixed media, 18 × 24 in. Private collection. Photograph by Chris Arend.

Black Pocket, 2017. Paint and mixed media, 18 × 24 in. Private collection. Photograph by Chris Arend.

Orange Ruffle, 2017. Paint and mixed media, 18 × 24 in. Private collection. Photograph by Chris Arend.

Blue Ruffle, 2017. Paint and mixed media, 18 × 24 in. Private collection. Photograph by Chris Arend.

Pink Ruffle, 2016. Paint and mixed media, 24 × 30 in. Private collection. Photograph by Chris Arend.

Pink Sleeve, 2016. Paint and mixed media, 24 × 30 in. Private collection. Photograph by Chris Arend.

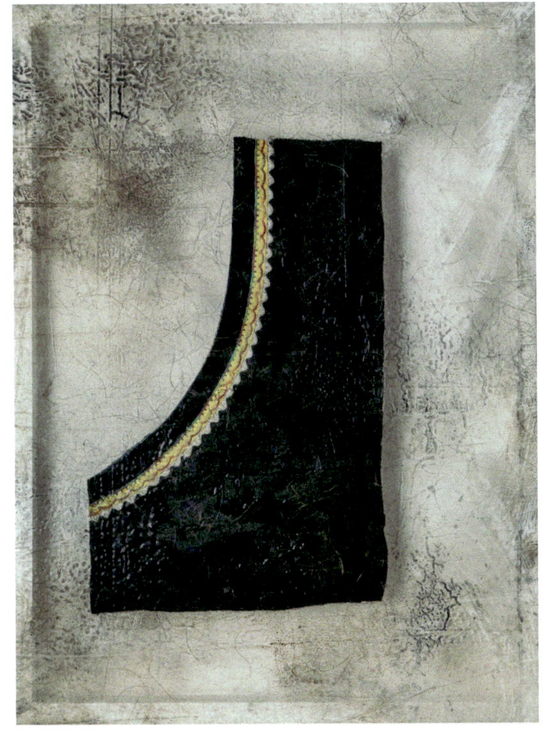
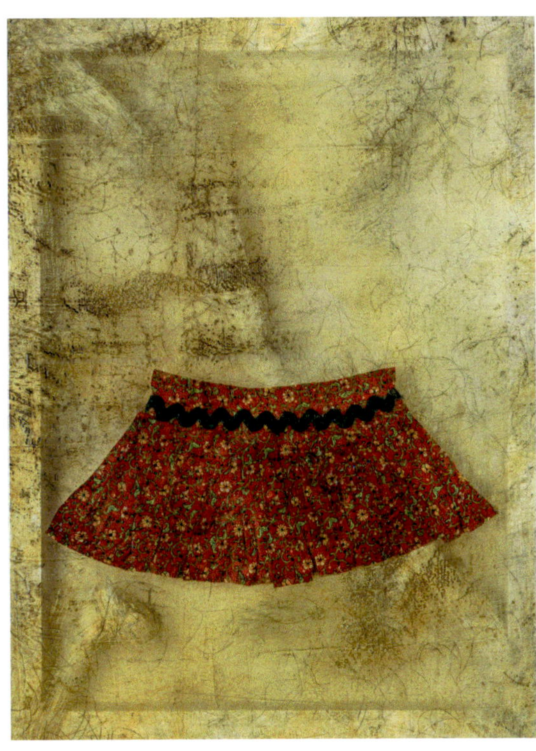
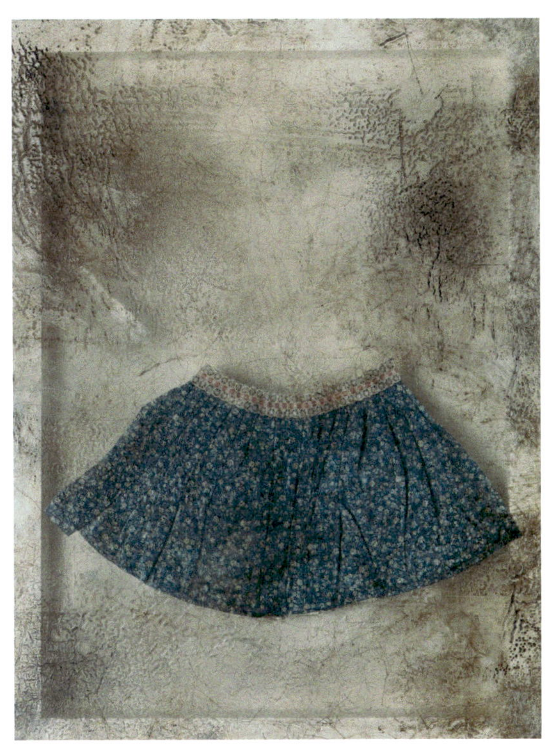
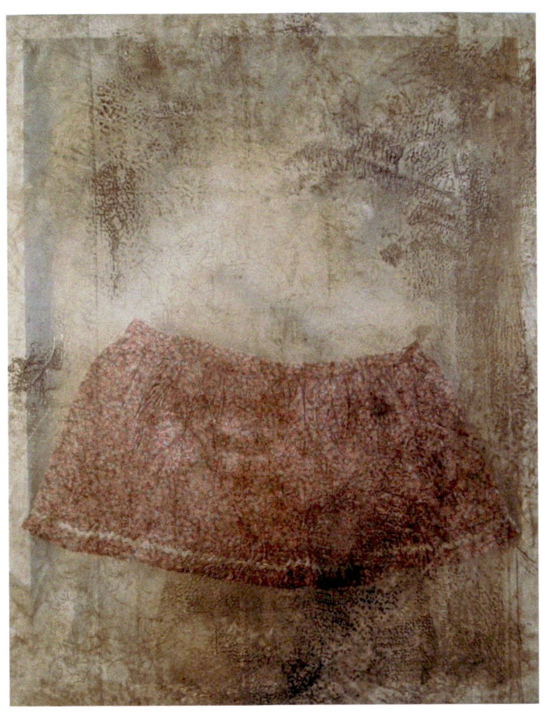
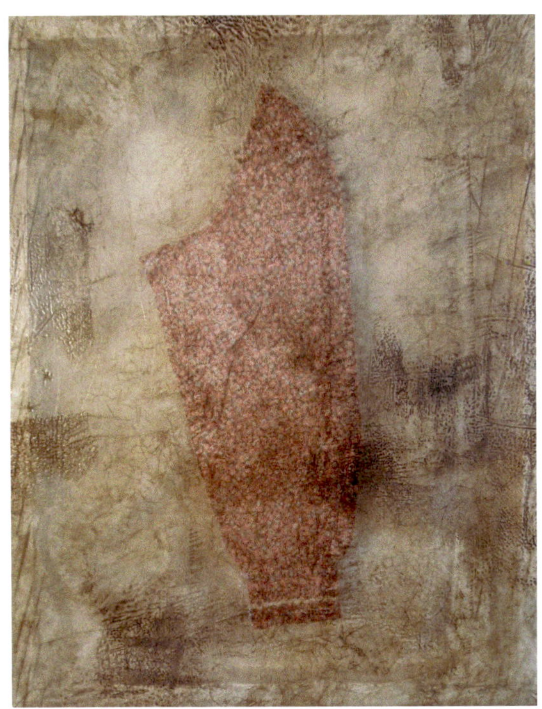

Pink Slip with Red Quill #1–5, 2023. Acrylic polymer, reindeer fur, cotton fabric, plastic knitting counter, steel pins, 44 × 22 × 3 in. – 47 × 16 × 3 in. Photograph by Kevin Todora.

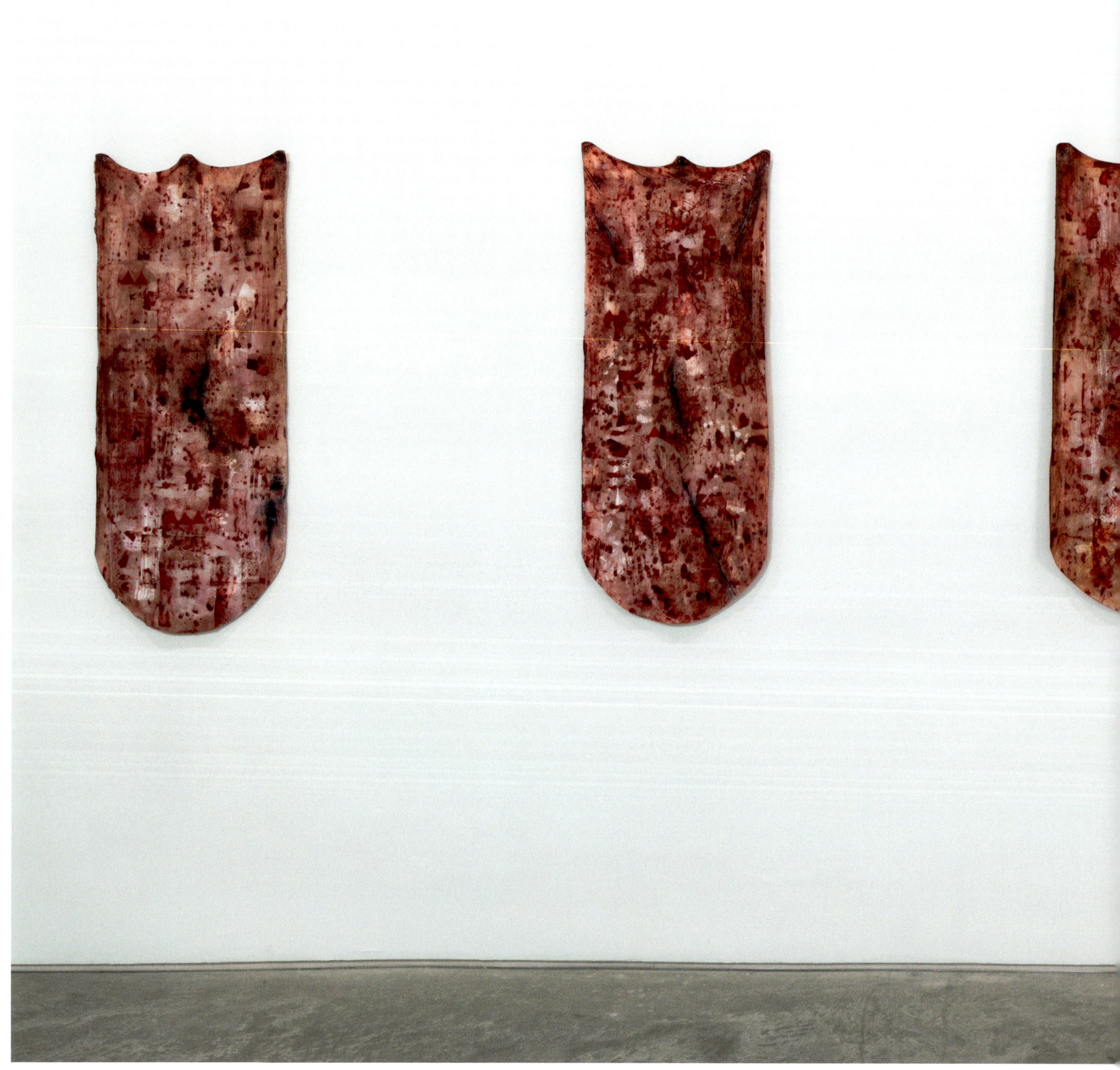

Pink Slip

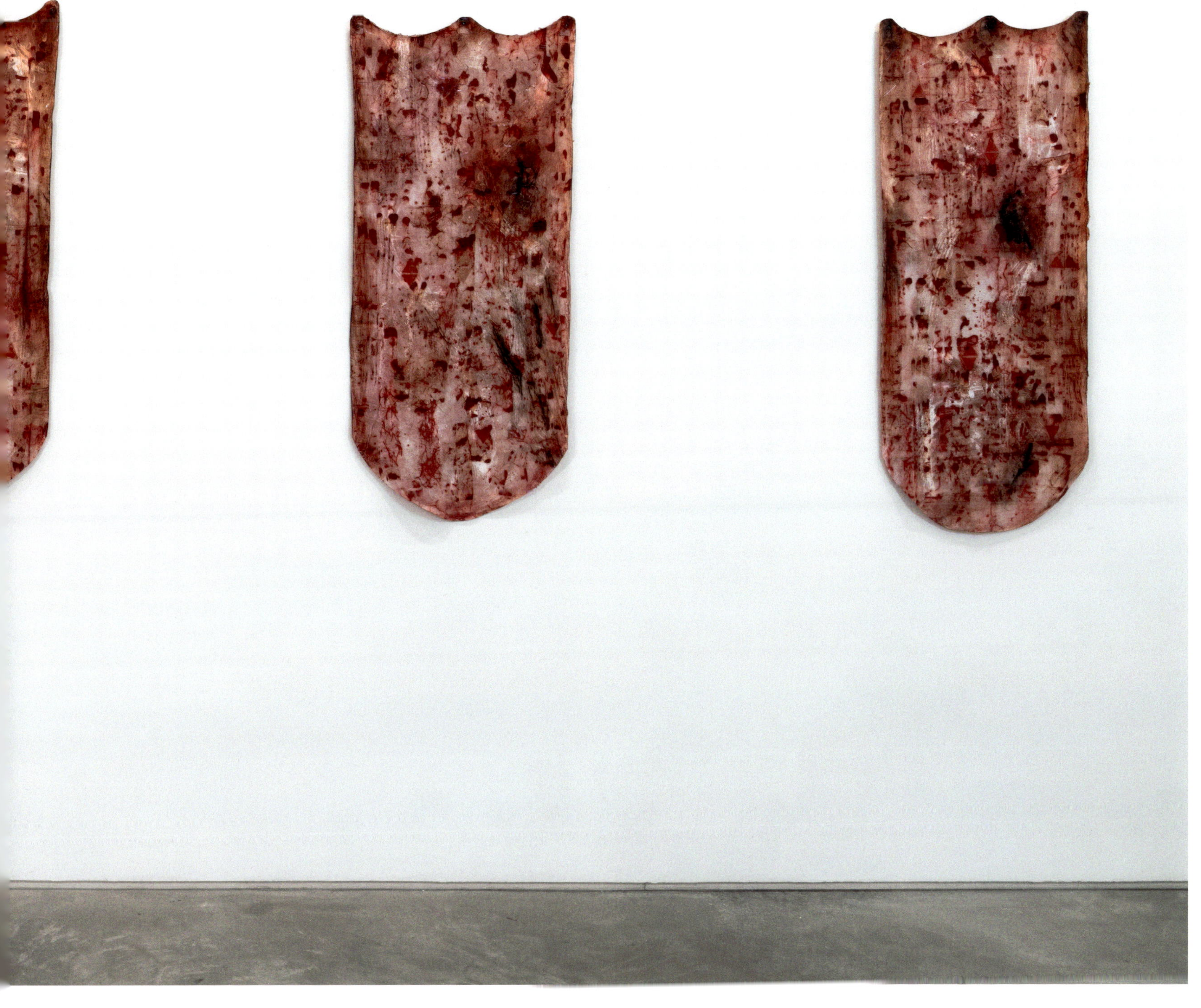

Slip

Burgundy Slip, 2012. Paint and mixed media, 18 × 48 in. Private collection. Photograph by Kevin G. Smith.

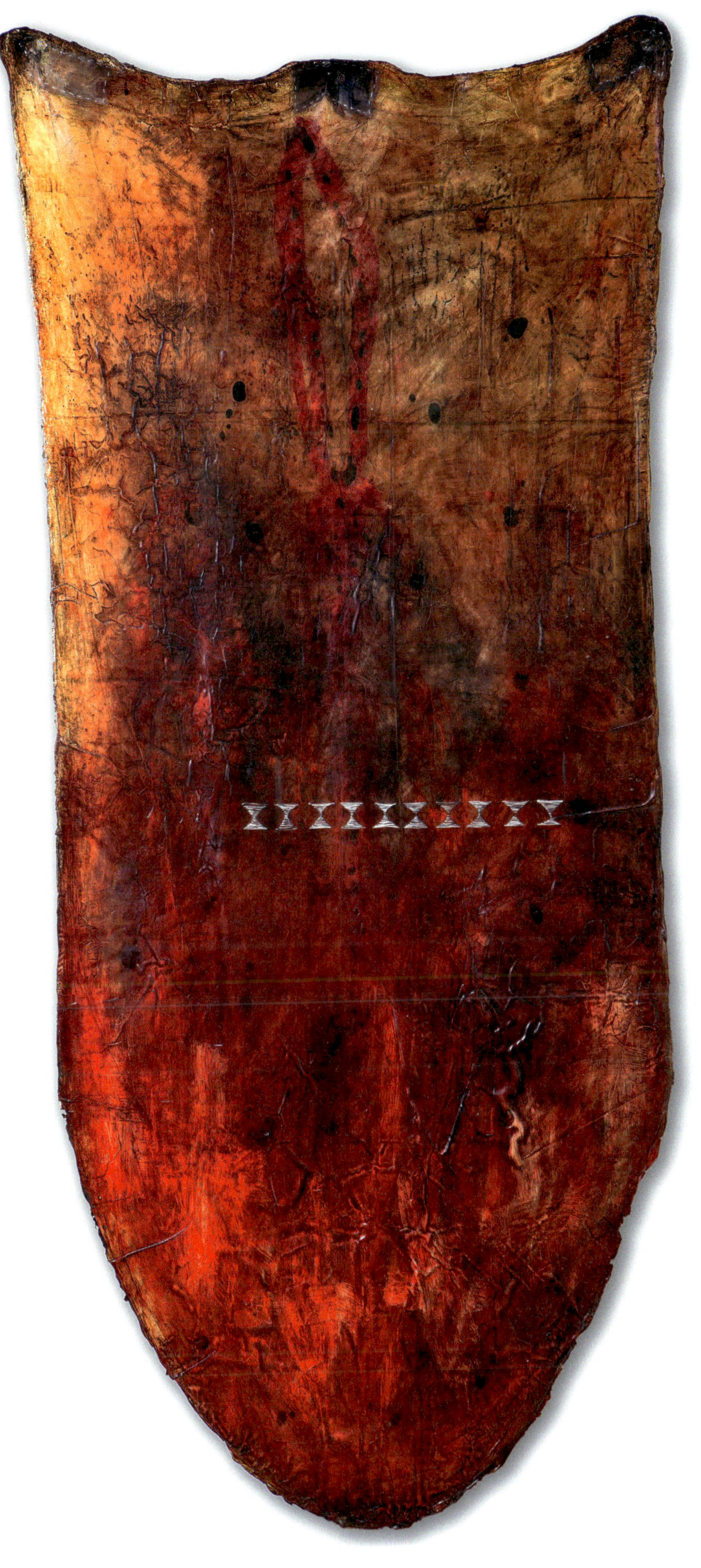

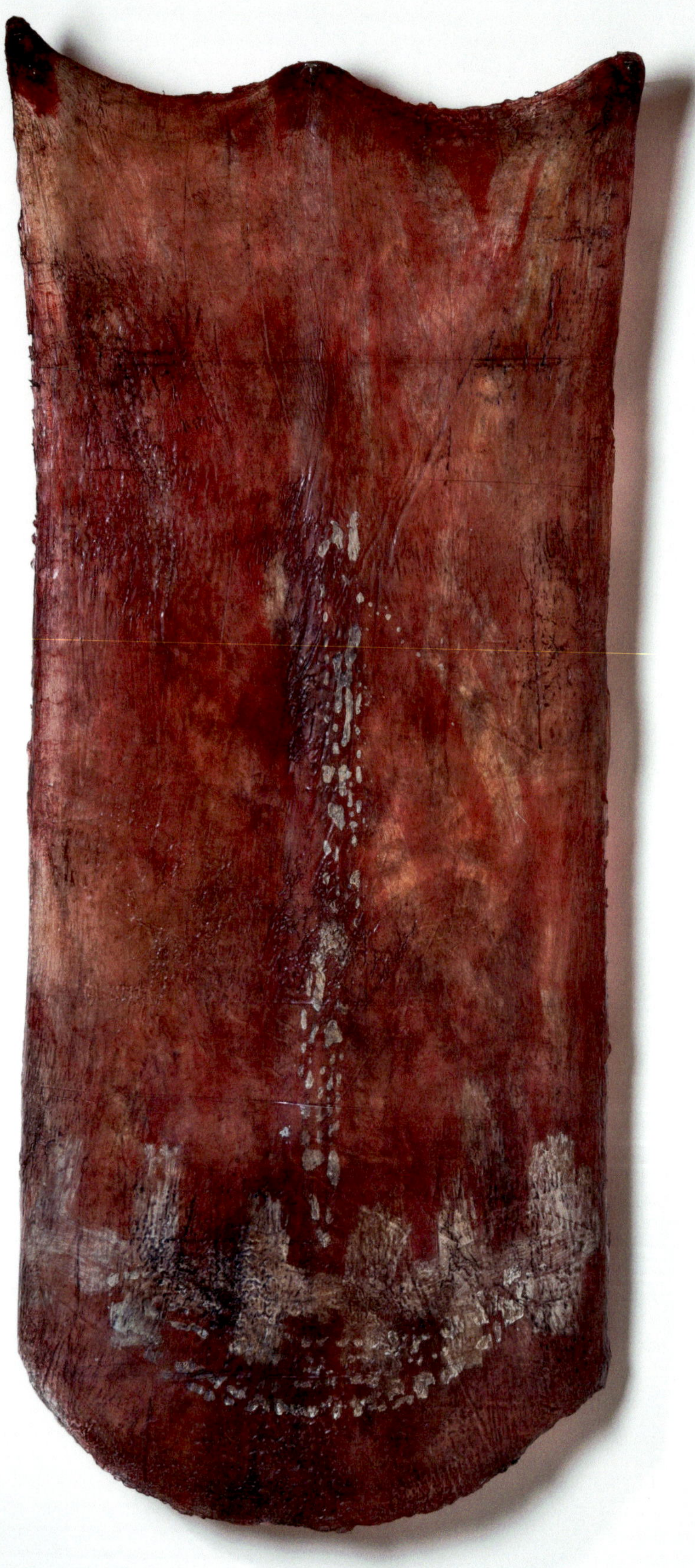

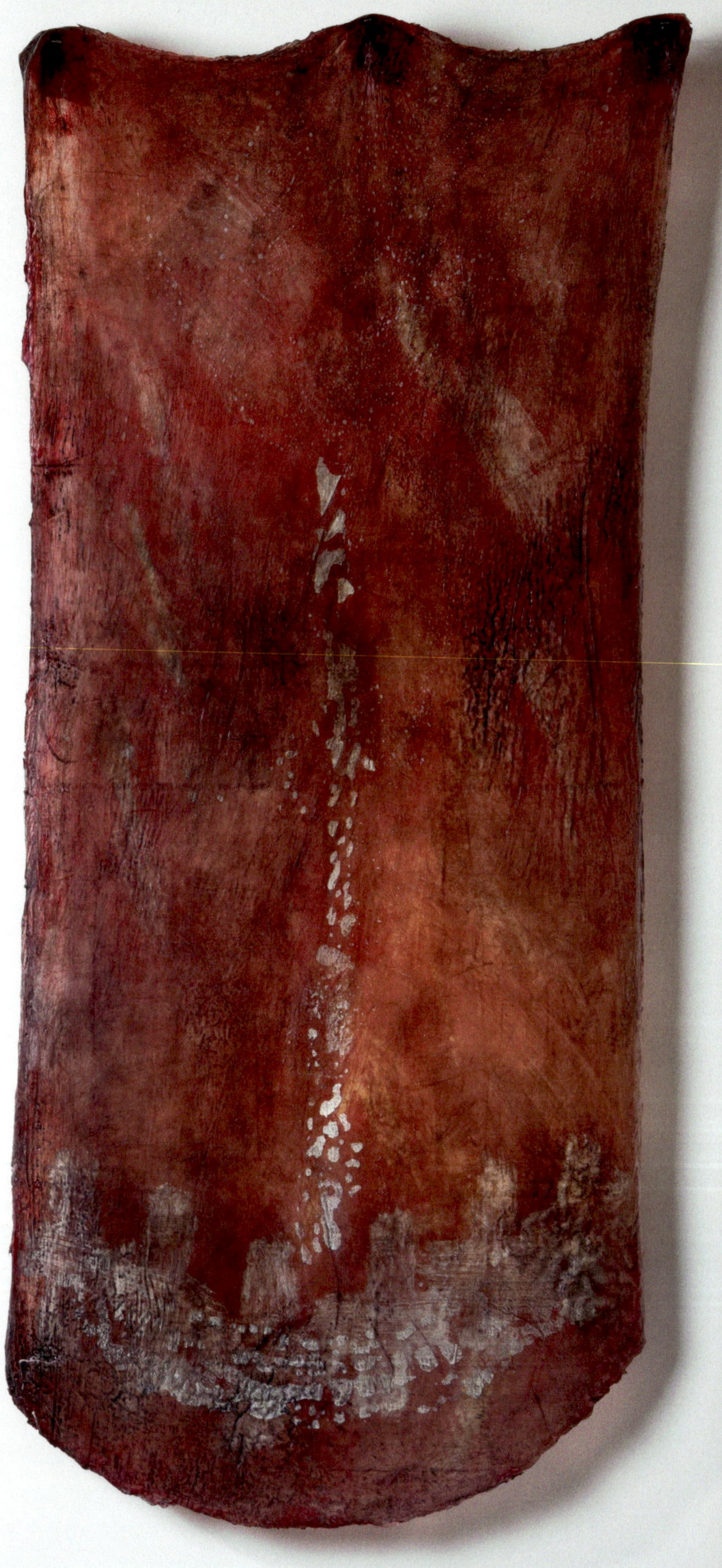

Pink Slip, 2012. Mixed media, 22 × 48 in.
Private collection. Photograph by
Kevin G. Smith.

For Loretta, For Cindy by Taqralik Partridge

don't read it, if you can help it
don't read it, because it's not just another bad article about a bad
thing
it's a true story and it's a stupid story and you will wish
that you could take it back
make it unhappen
you will wish you could switch the sequence of events and remove
the part
where she gets killed
you will wish for a miracle
and not even a miracle but just a small edit in the paragraph that
will take away the words that describe how she died
because it was just a stupid, stupid, stupid way to end her life
and how could anyone go on
after that—in words
or in steps or breaths that are not screams
how can we go on
when our sisters are murdered and their deaths are just murmurs
on the news
if we are lucky if we are lucky there will be an outcry on social media and an
article in the paper about the outcry
and if we are lucky they will only go into the details of her life like
they have to
and if we are lucky no one will revel in her shortcomings or tsk tsk
about her lifestyle

and if we are lucky there will be some time between this death and
the next where we can sigh and rail and deal with just the day to
day shit that makes native women worth less on insurance claims
and on city streets, and in bedrooms, and hotel rooms, and court
rooms, and back alleys, and history books, and grocery stores, and
subways, and payrolls, and police stations, and doctor's offices, and
he said she said, and waiting at the teller, and waiting for answers,
and waiting for good news, and waiting for any news, and waiting
for loved ones, and waiting for justice

justice
and did I tell you about the time the police asked me if I was a hooker
because I was crying in the street?

and in that vein
do you remember if they told you in school that the words
prostitute and murder cannot exist in the same sentence?
or at least that the sentence will be commuted, or reduced, or
overturned
and if we are lucky they won't get out and reoffend
repeat repeat repeat

reoffend
and if we are lucky, one day, we won't have to count ourselves lucky
to be counted as human beings

Stain

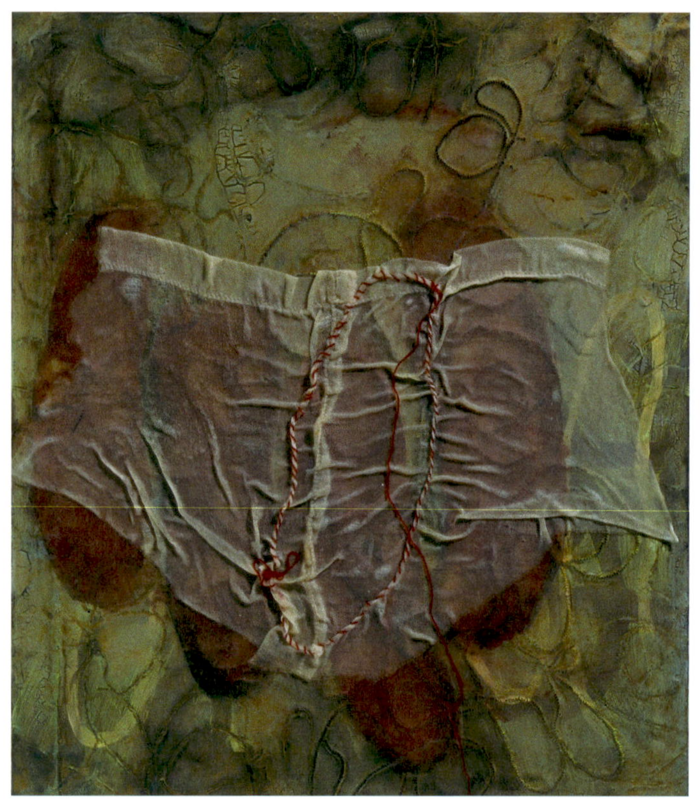

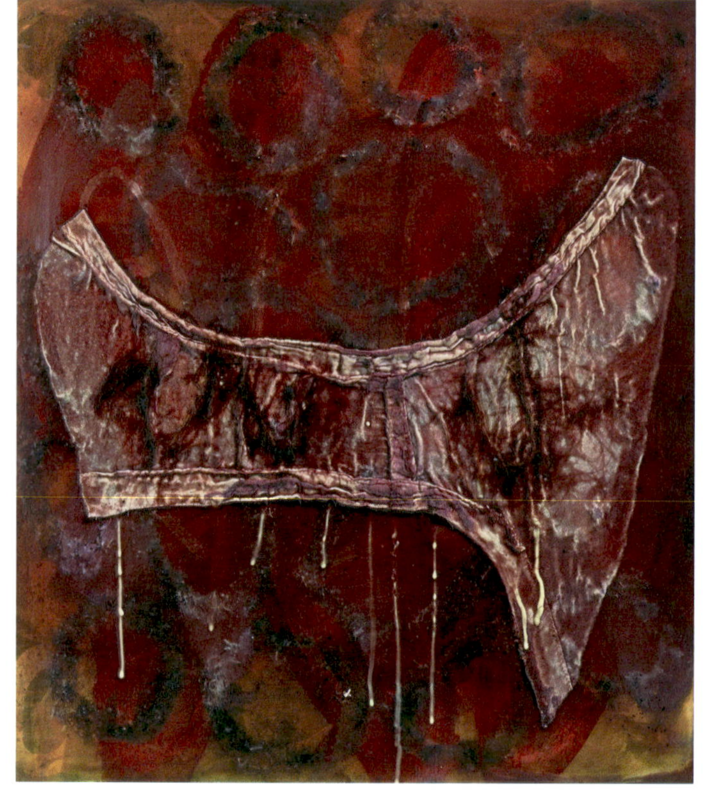

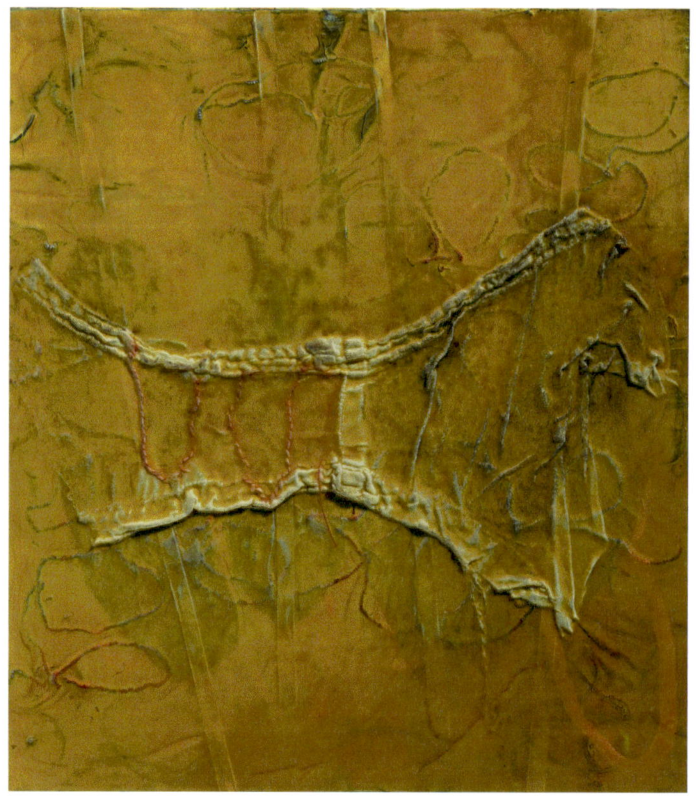

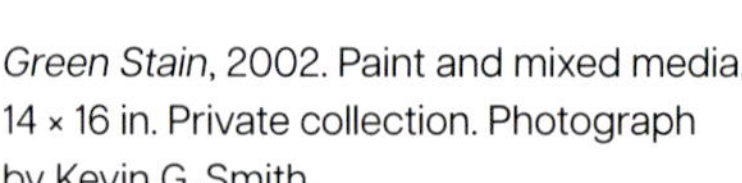

Green Stain, 2002. Paint and mixed media, 14 × 16 in. Private collection. Photograph by Kevin G. Smith.

Purple Stain, 2002. Paint and mixed media, 14 × 16 in. Private collection. Photograph by Kevin G. Smith.

Gold Stain, 2002. Paint and mixed media, 14 × 16 in. Private collection. Photograph by Kevin G. Smith.

Trim

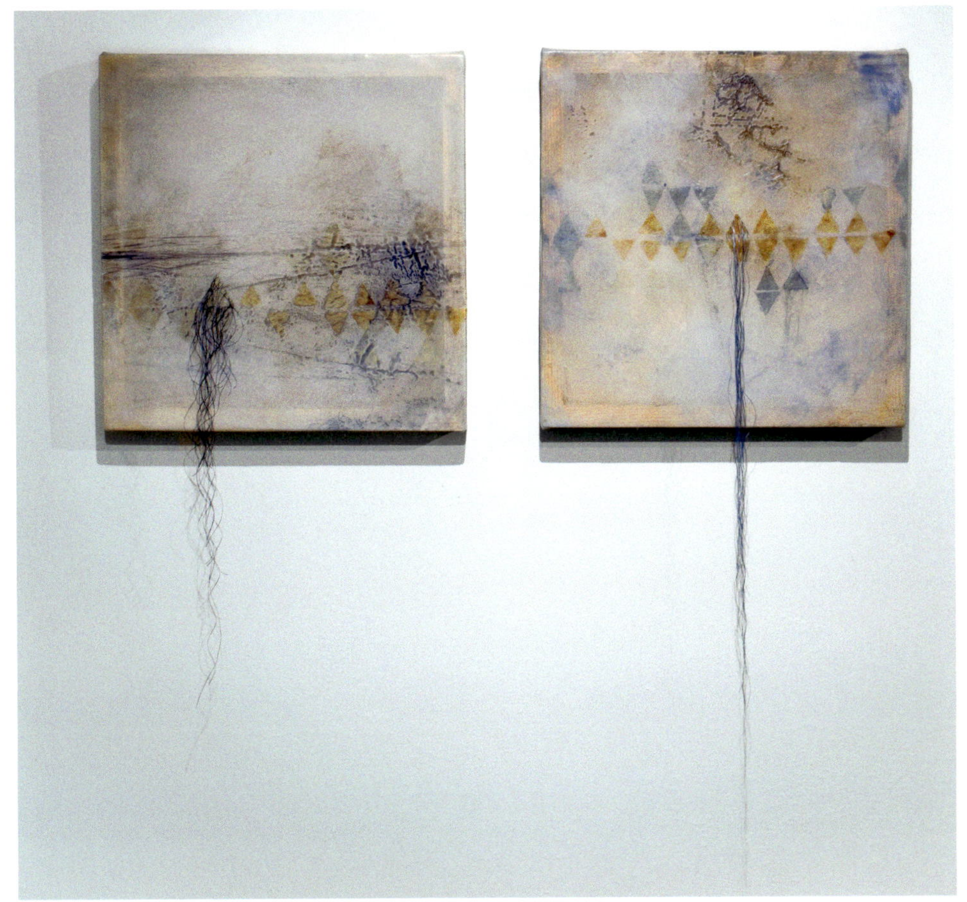

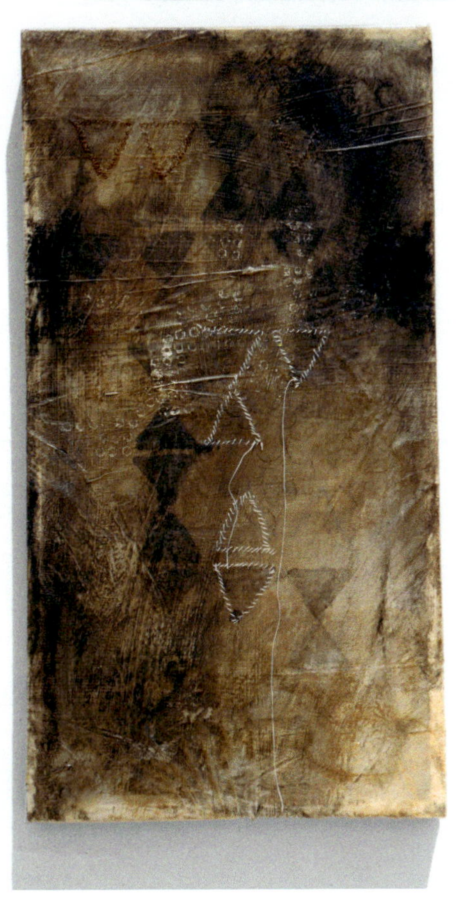

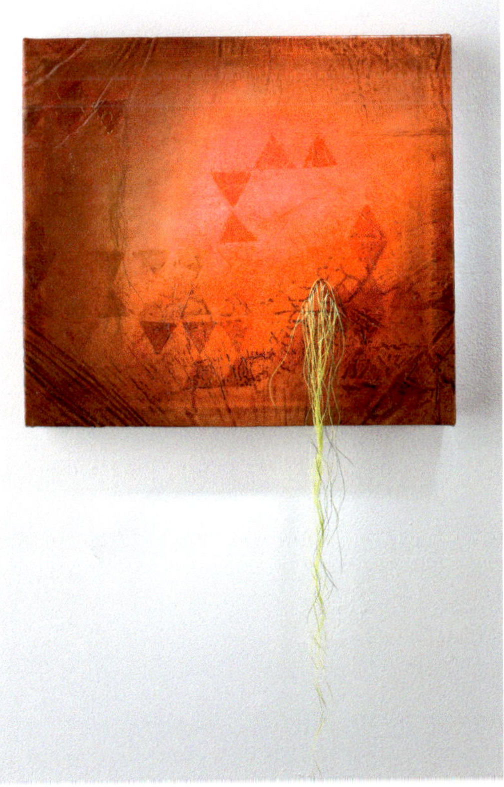

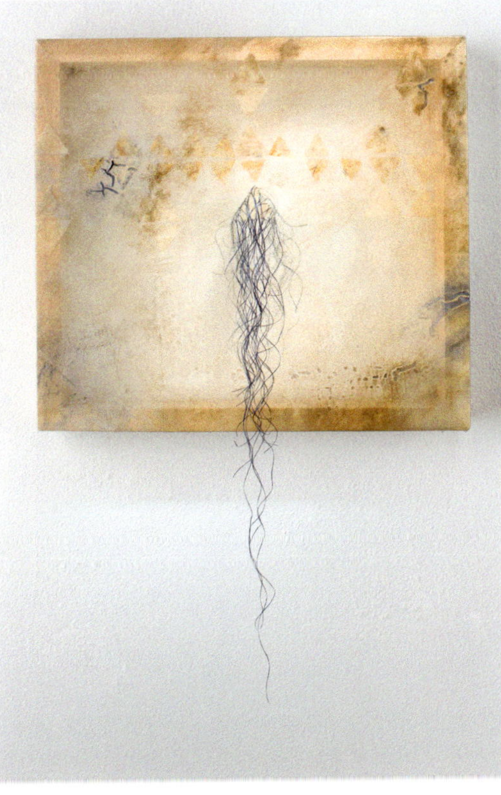

Sky Trim I and II, 2008. Mixed media, 27 × 30 in. Private collection. Photograph by Kevin G. Smith.

Trim II, 1998. Mixed media, 12 × 22 in. Private collection. Photograph by the artist.

Red Trim, 2008. Mixed media, 24 × 12 in. Private collection. Photograph by Kevin G. Smith.

Natural Trim, 2008. Mixed media, 12 × 18 in. Private collection. Photograph by Kevin G. Smith.

Credible Secrets with Red

Credible Secrets with Red, 2023. Acrylic polymer, nylon thread, cotton muslin, paper, printed fabric, 66 × 30 in. Photograph by Paul Salveson.

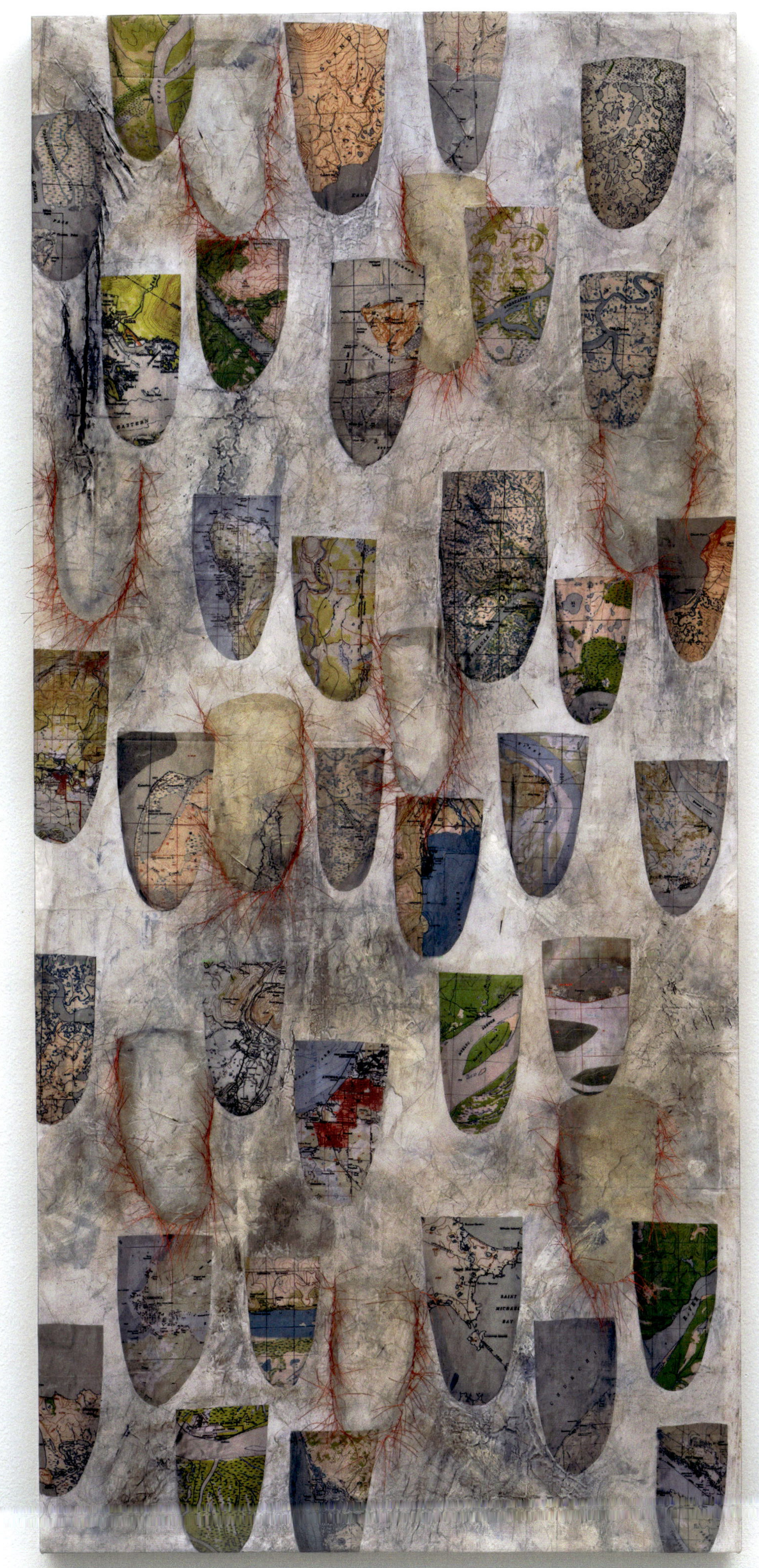

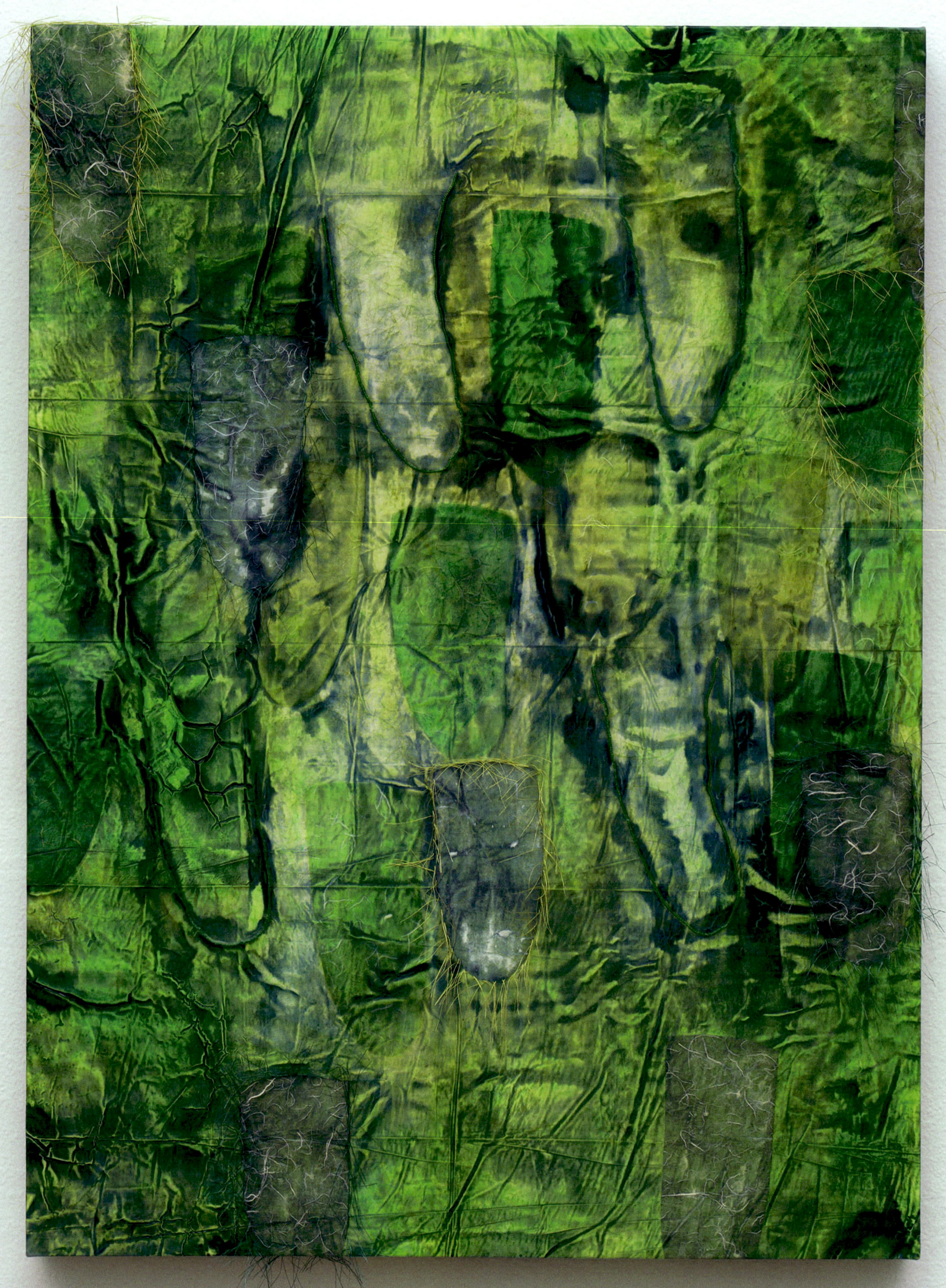

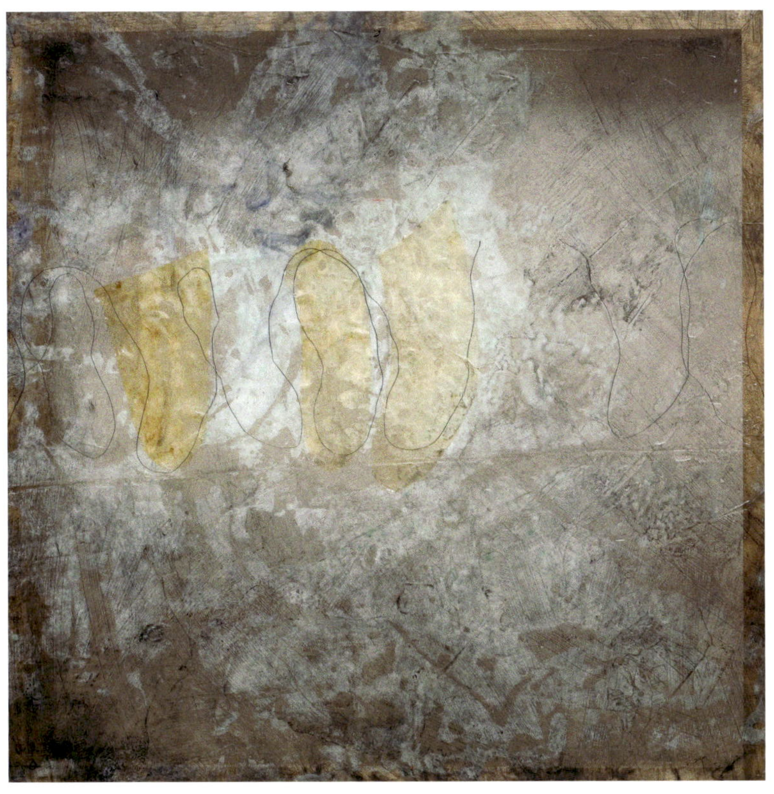

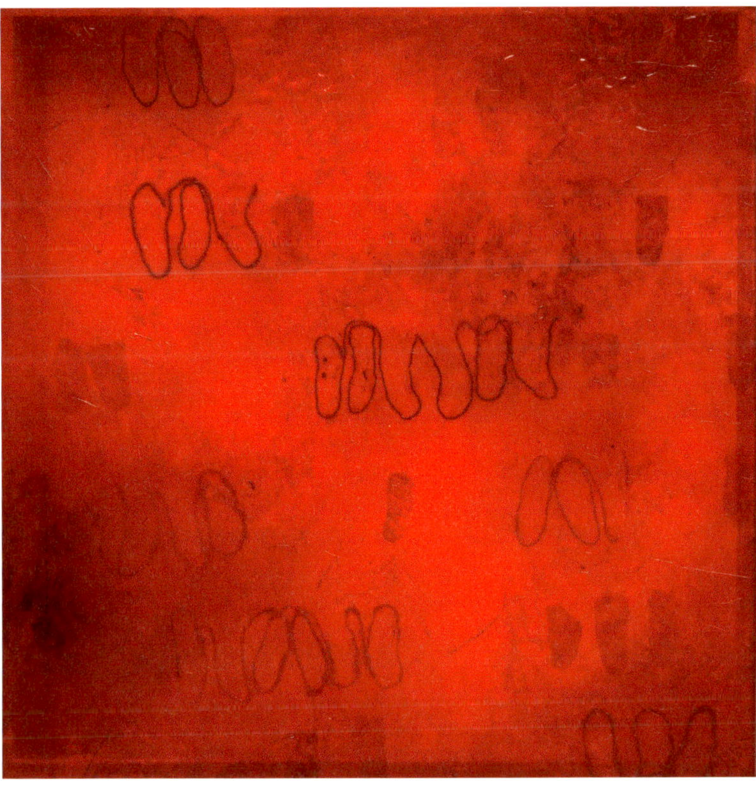

Large Fern Secrets, 2023. Acrylic polymer, glass bead, polyurethane, nylon thread, cotton muslin, paper, 40 × 30 in. Photograph by Paul Salveson.

Unraveled Grey Secret, 2006. Paint and mixed media, 24 × 24 in. Private collection. Photograph by Kevin G. Smith.

Light Blue Secret, 2005. Paint and mixed media, 42 × 72 in. Private collection. Photograph by Kevin G. Smith.

Red Beaded Secrets, 2006. Paint and mixed media, 24 × 24 in. Eiteljorg Museum of American Indians and Western Art, Indianapolis. Photograph by Kevin G. Smith.

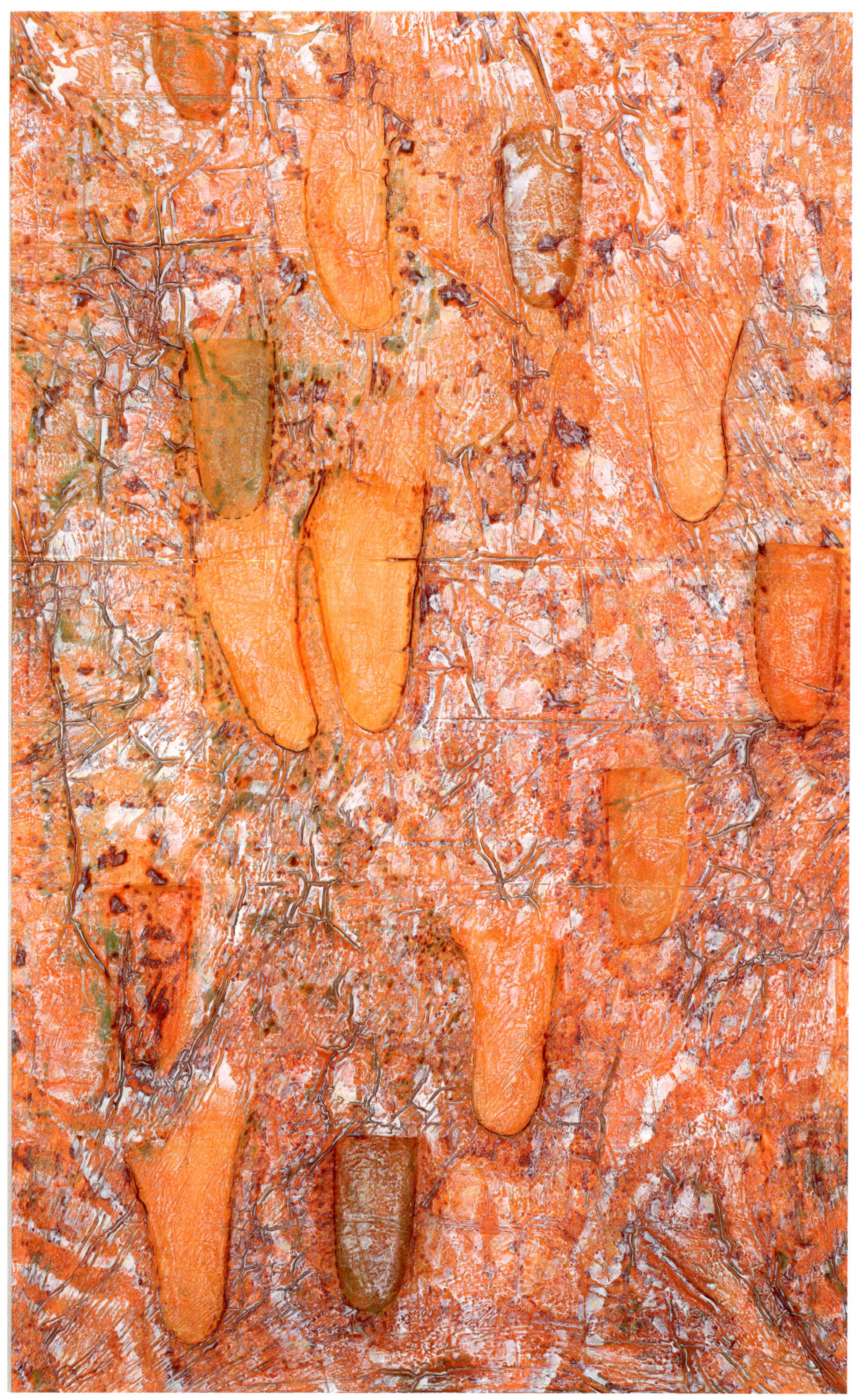

Secrets

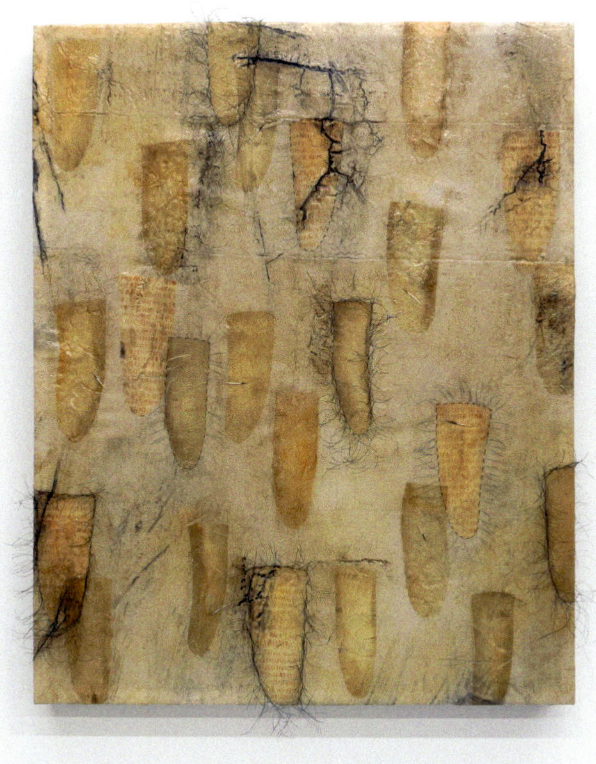

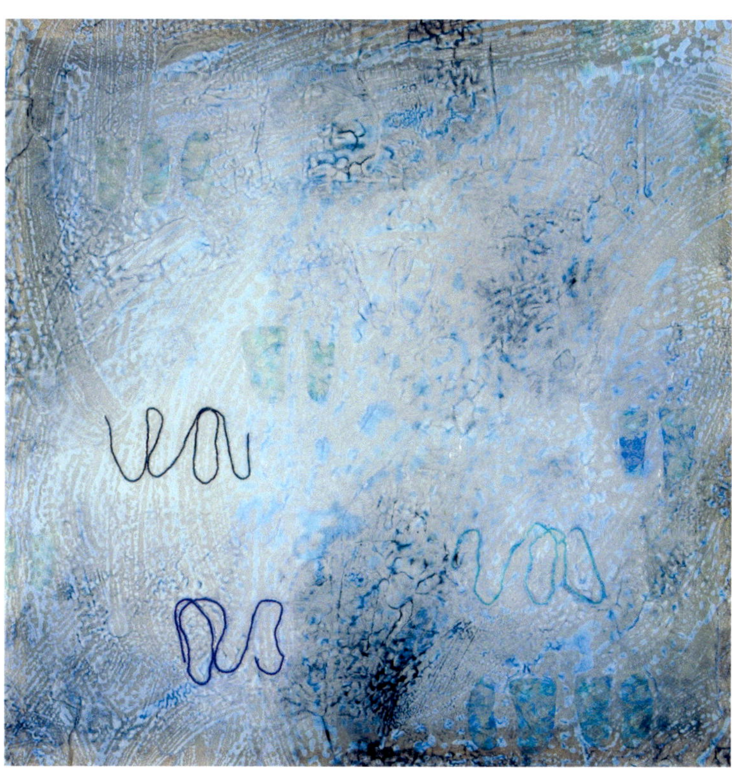

Salmon Buried Secrets, 2023. Acrylic polymer, polyurethane, nylon thread, glass bead, paper, 66 × 40 in. Photograph by Paul Salveson.

Small White Secrets with Neutral, 2023. Acrylic polymer, glass bead, nylon thread, paper, cotton muslin, 40 × 30 in. Photograph by Kevin Todora.

Large Natural Secret with Black, 2023. Acrylic polymer, nylon thread, cotton fabric, reindeer fur, porcupine quill, airplane fabric. 36.25 × 29.75 × 2.5 in. Photograph by Kunning Huang.

Blue Beaded Secrets, 2007. Painting, mixed media, 24 × 24 in. Eiteljorg Museum of American Indians and Western Art, Indianapolis. Photograph by Kevin G. Smith.

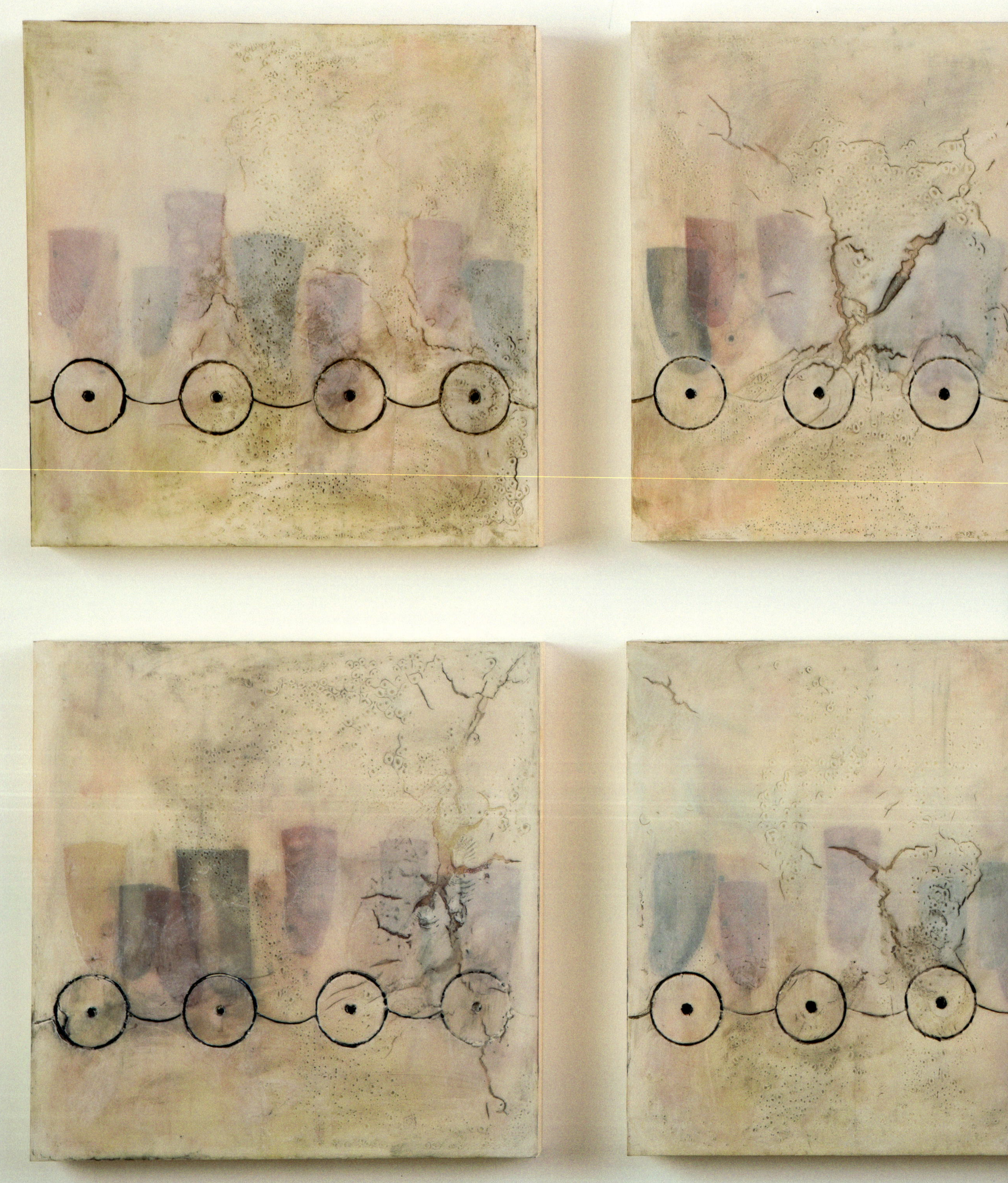

Buried Walrus Family Portrait

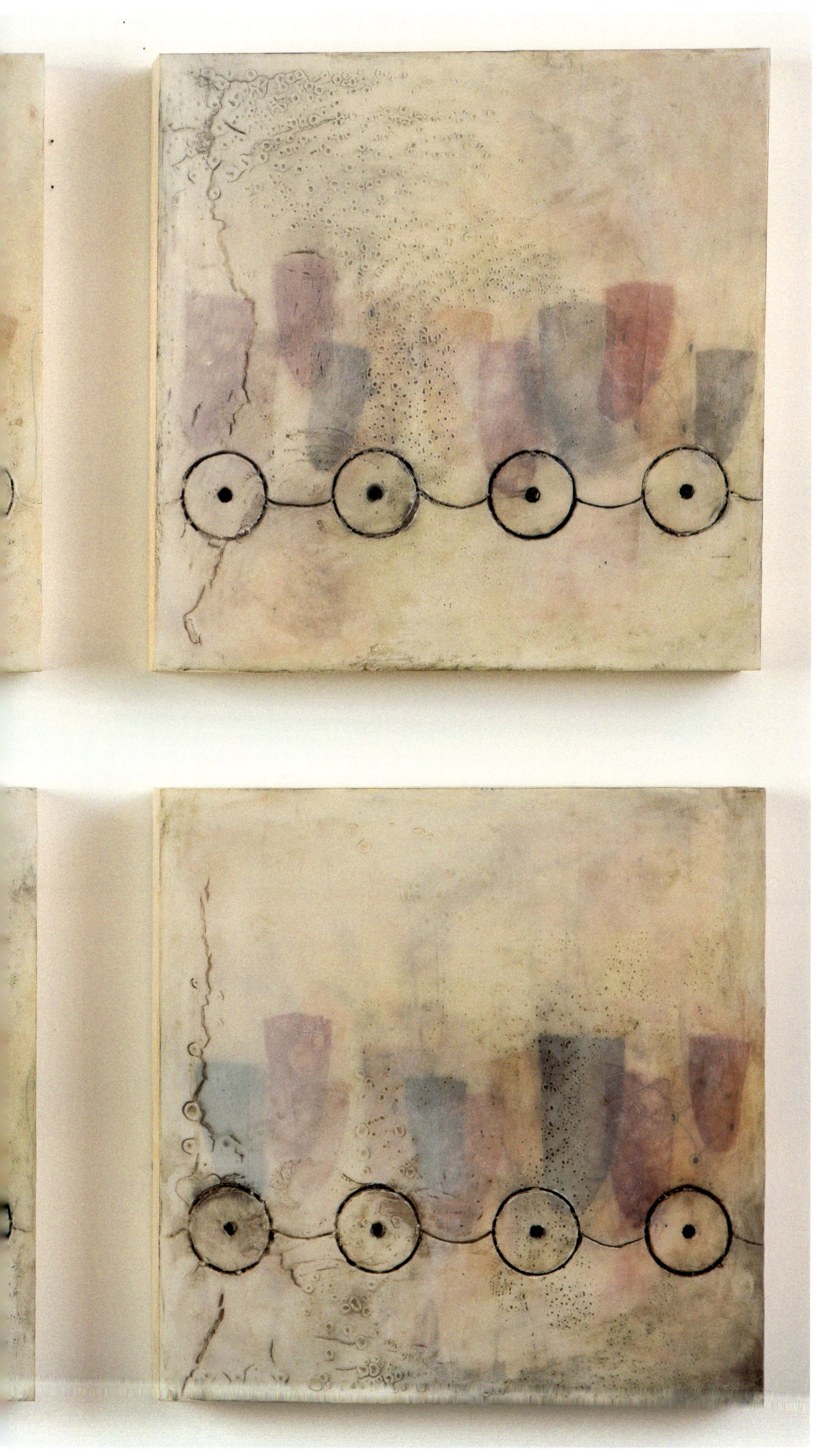

Buried Walrus Family Portrait, Cream 1–6, 2008. Paint and mixed media, 26 × 39 in. Private collection. Photograph by Kevin G. Smith.

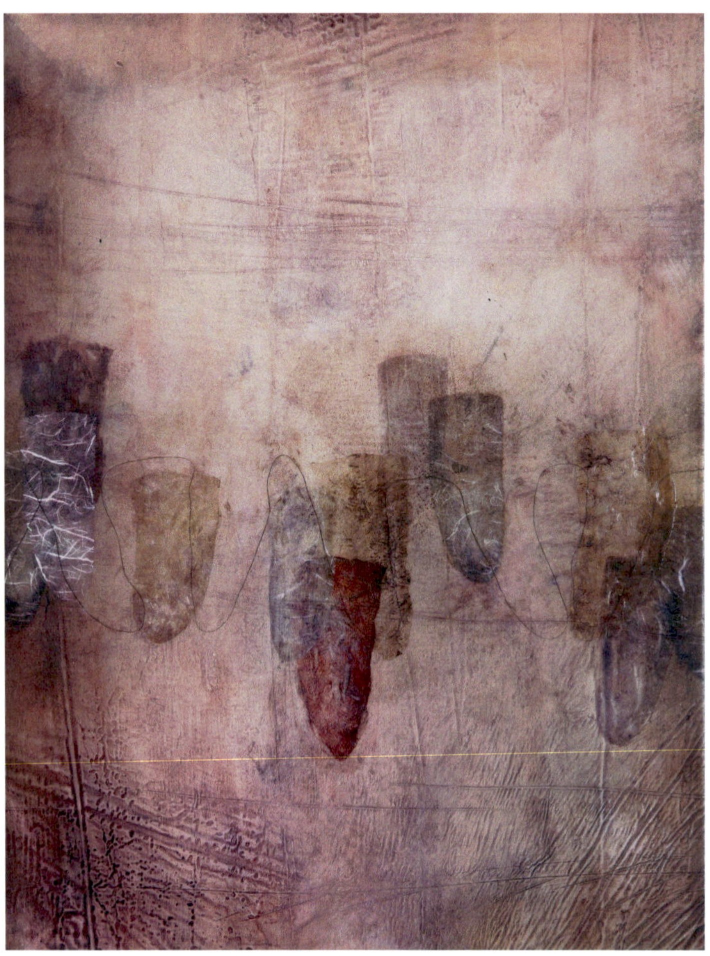

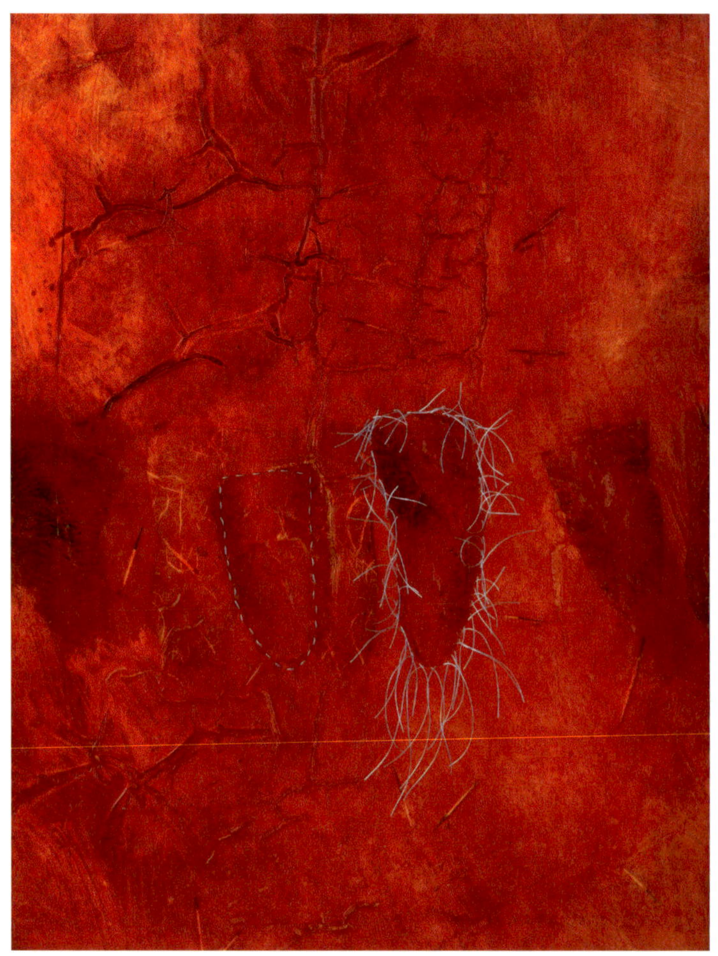

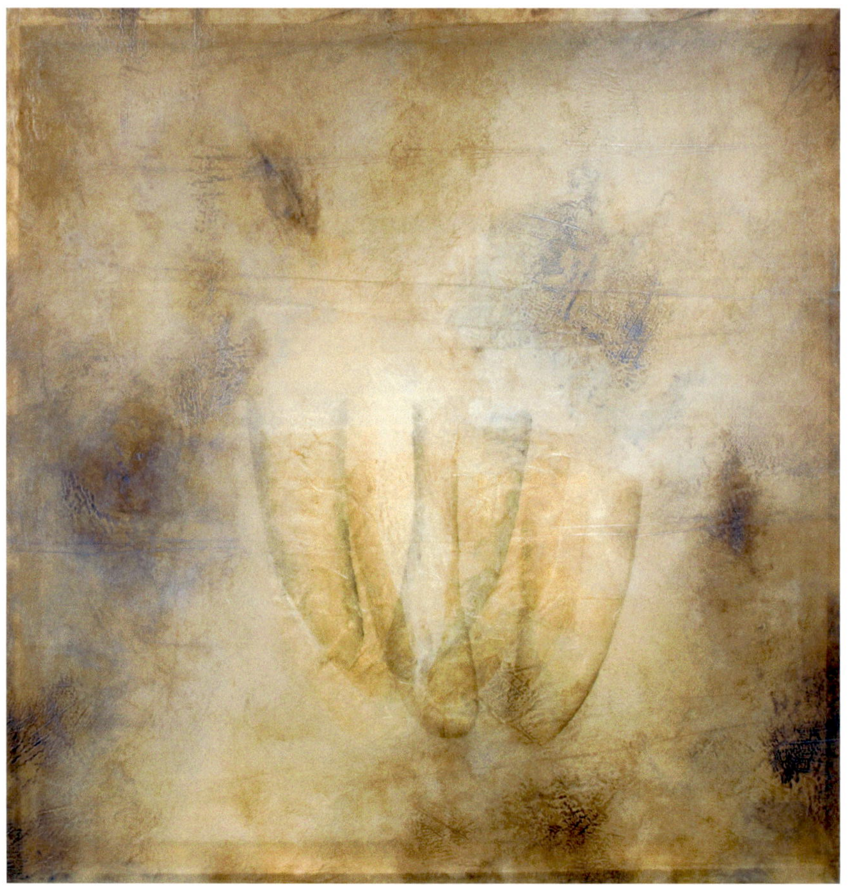

Grape Walrus Family Portrait, 2013.
Paint and mixed media, 18 × 24 in. Private collection. Photograph by Chris Arend.

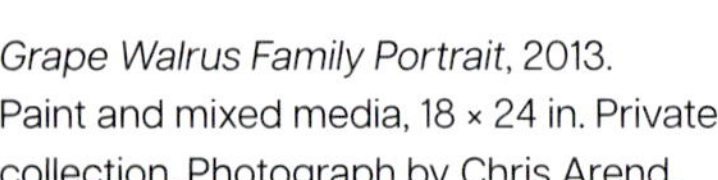

Raspberry Walrus Family Portrait, 2013.
Paint and mixed media, 14 × 18 in. Private collection. Photograph by Chris Arend.

Natural Walrus Family Portrait, 2008.
Paint and mixed media, 42 × 42 in. Private collection. Photograph by Chris Arend.

Walrus Family Portrait

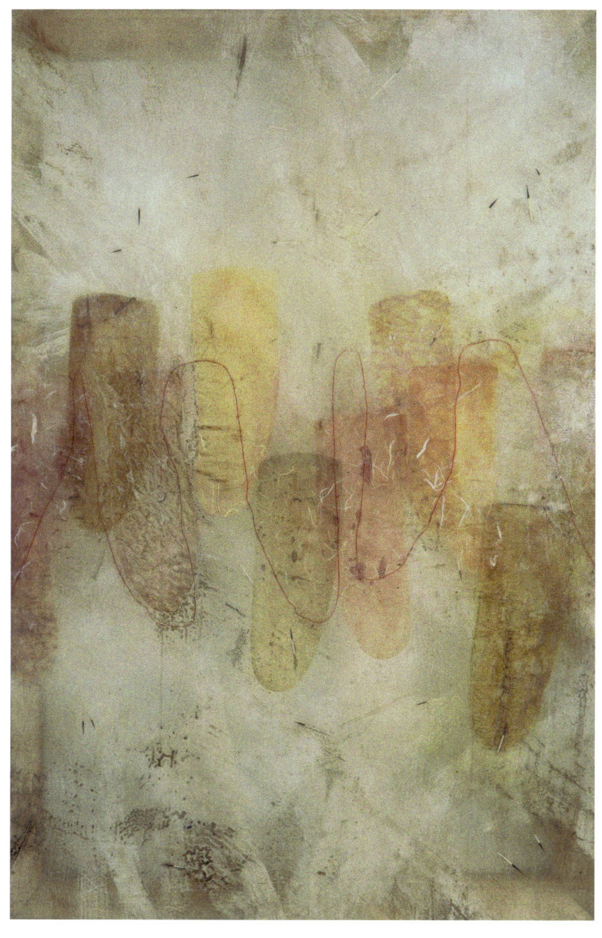

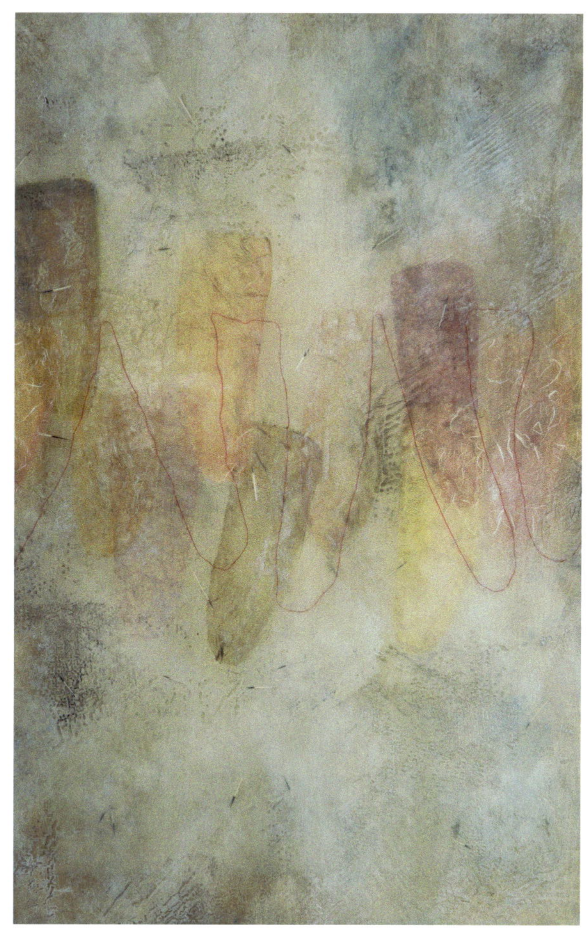

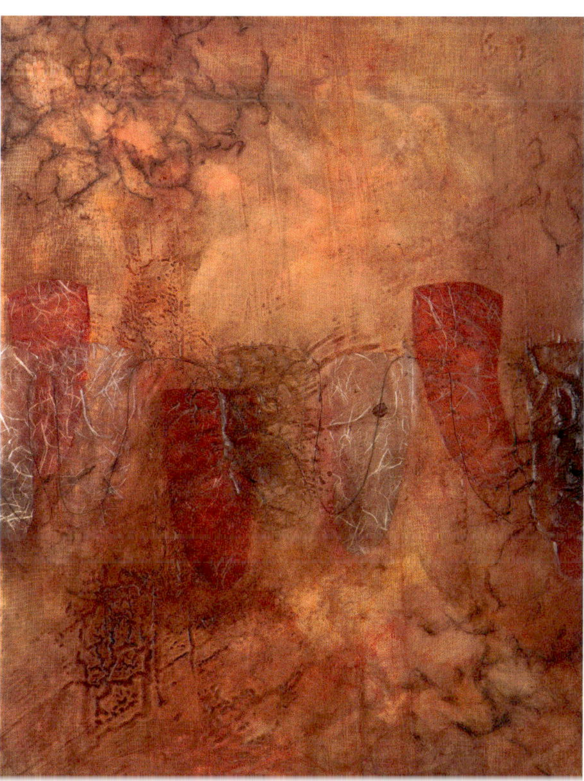

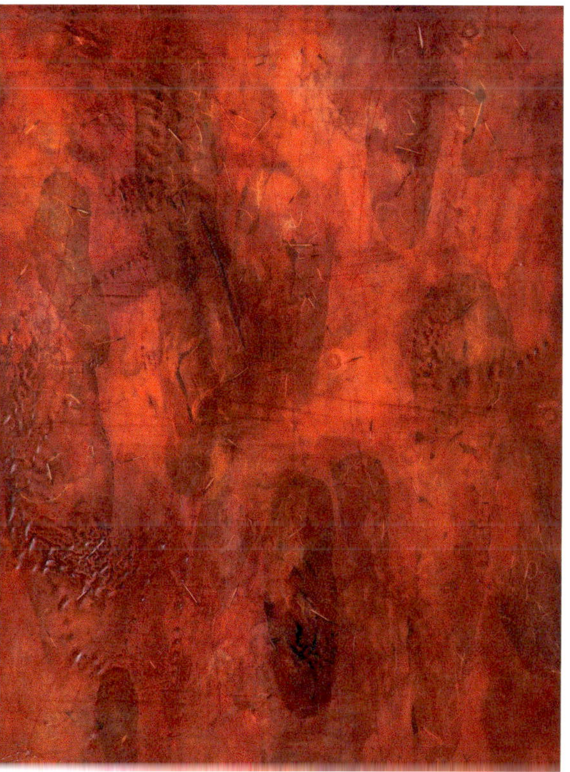

Lemon Walrus Family Portrait I and II, 2013. Paint and mixed media, 20 × 30 in. each. Private collection. Photograph by Chris Arend.

Small Natural Walrus Family Portrait, 2013. Paint and mixed media, 14 × 18 in. Private collection. Photograph by Chris Arend.

Tangerine Walrus Family Portrait, 2013. Paint and mixed media, 30 × 40 in. Private collection. Photograph by Chris Arend.

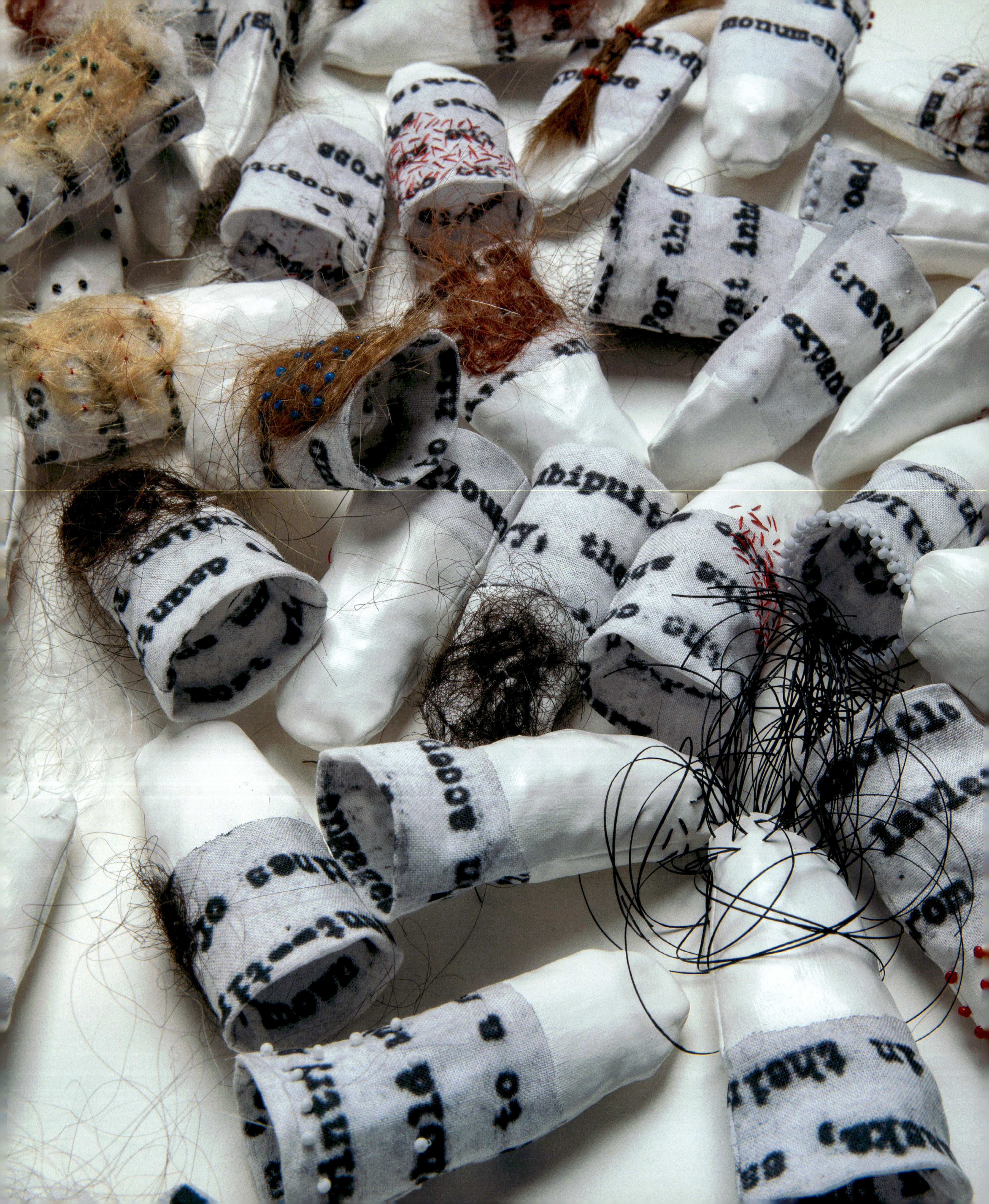

SCULPTURES

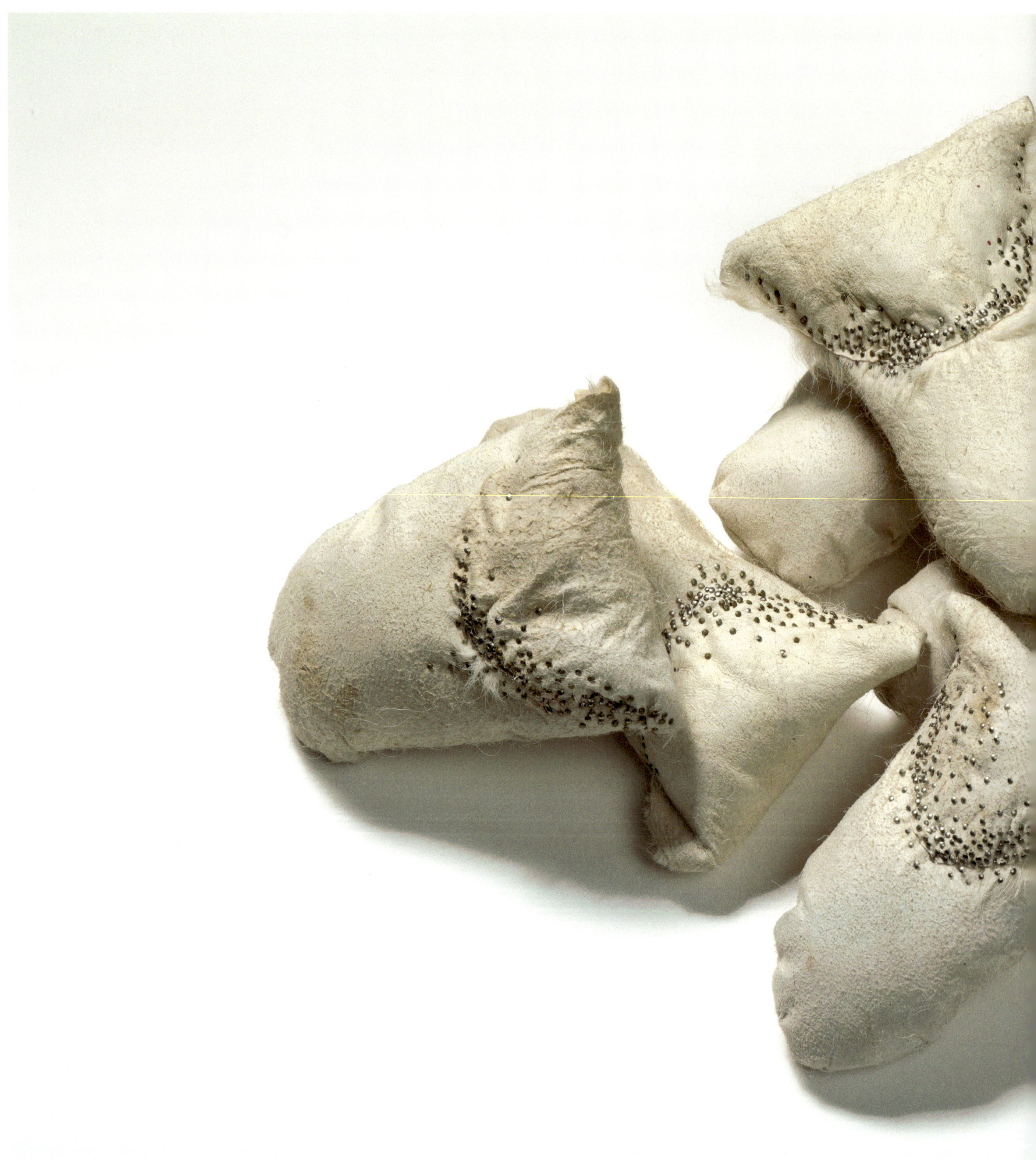

Closed Secrets

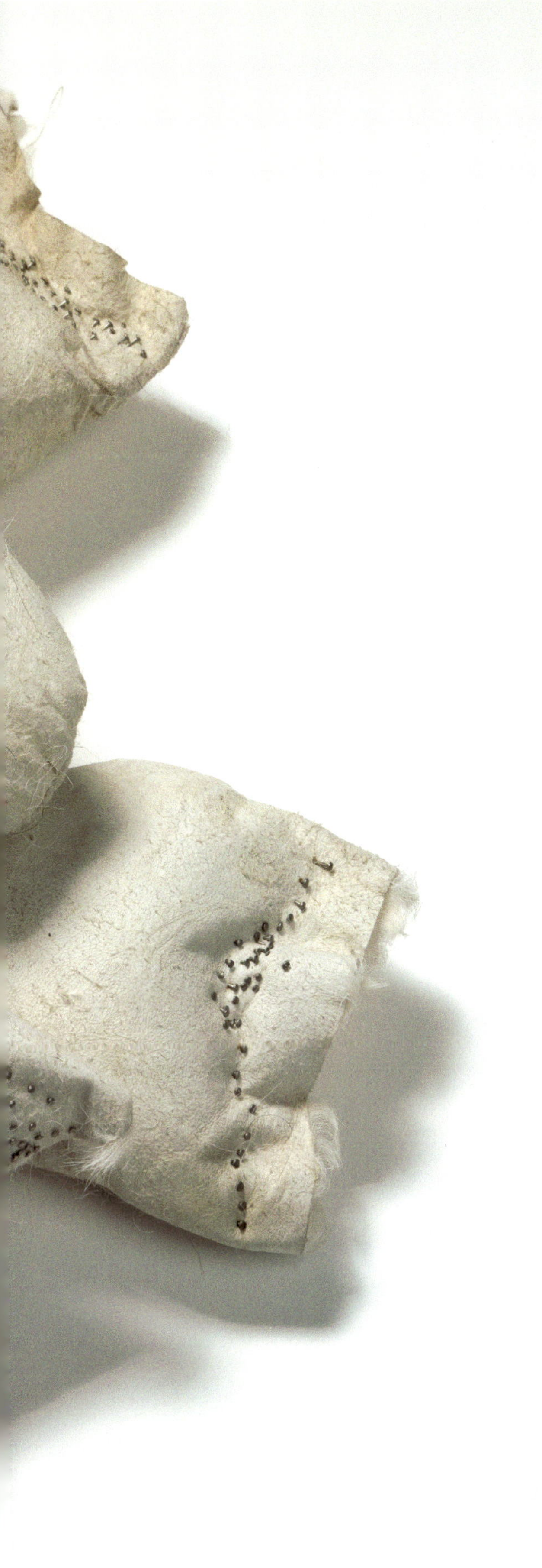

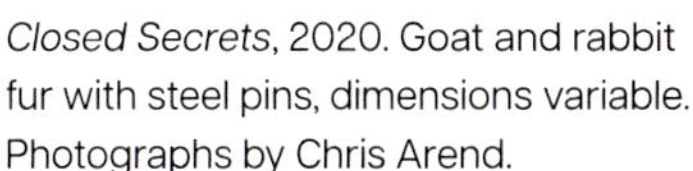

Closed Secrets, 2020. Goat and rabbit fur with steel pins, dimensions variable. Photographs by Chris Arend.

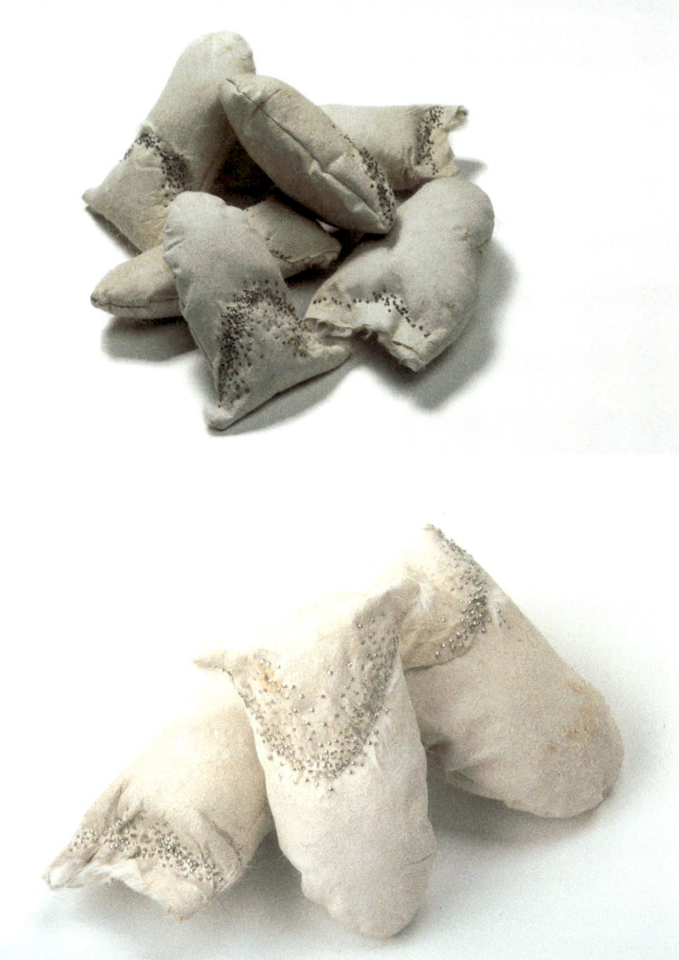

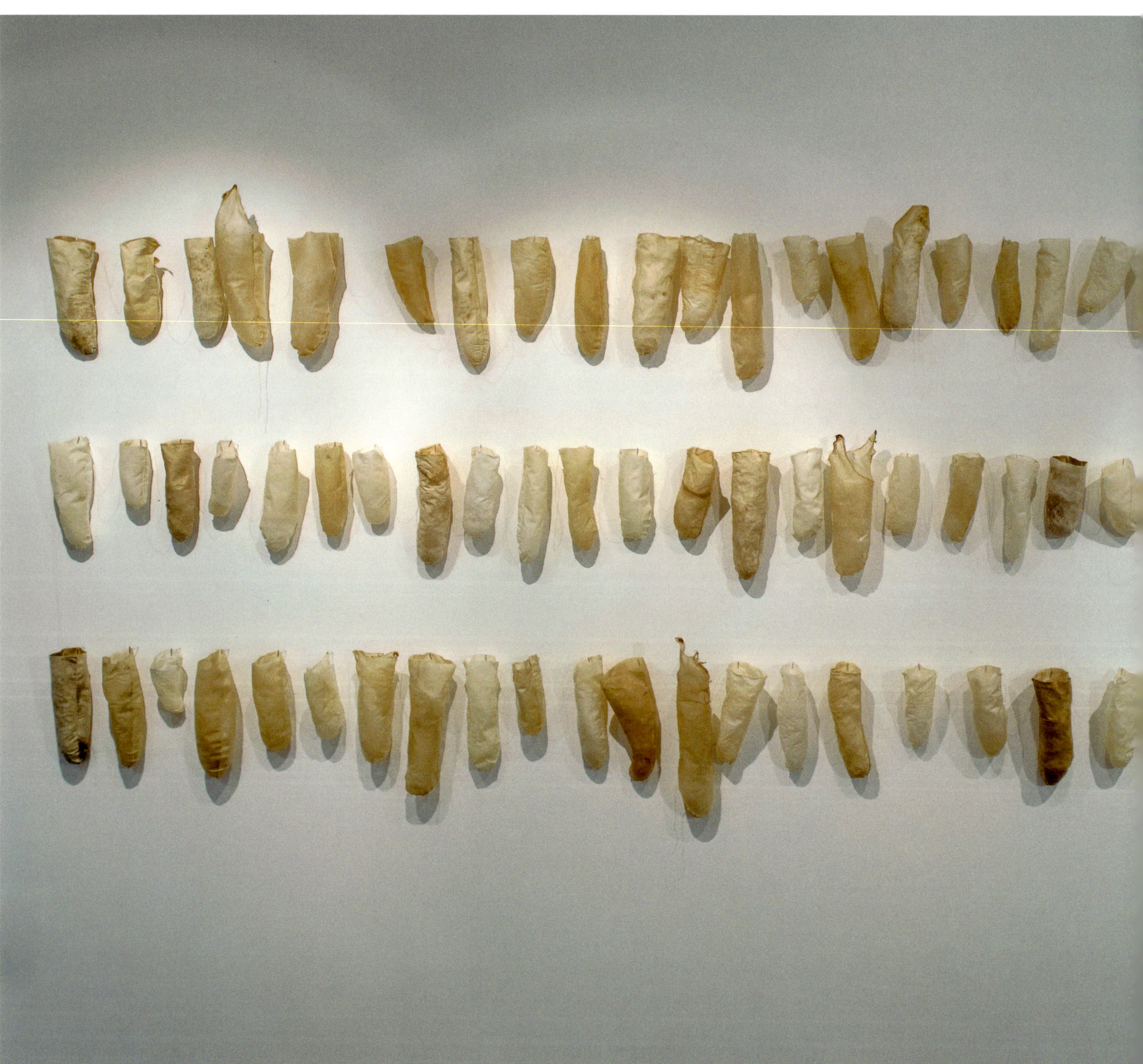

Common Thread

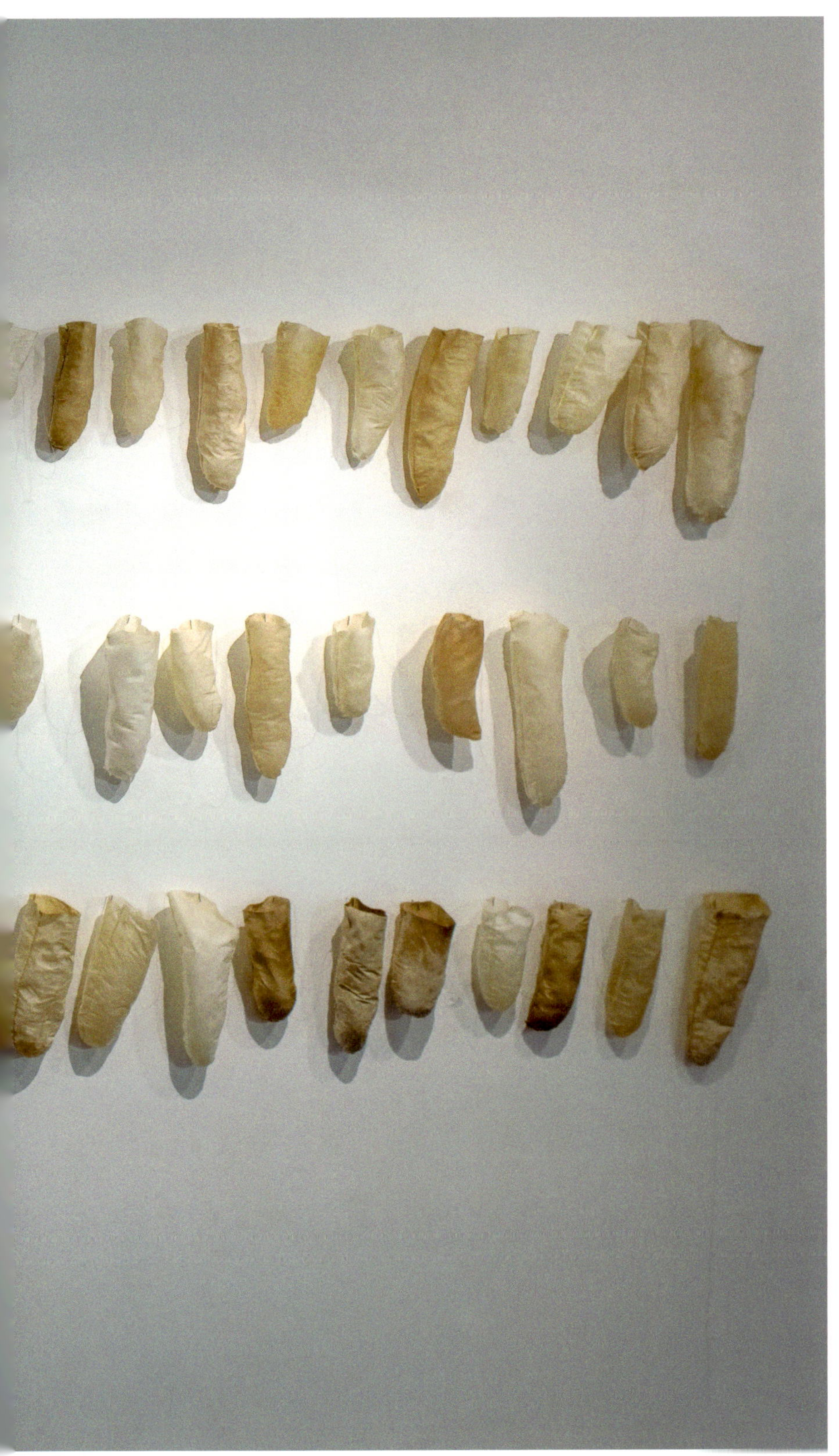

Common Thread speaks to shared heritage and community, to the way that traditions and culture are passed on across generations. A single thread connects these forms. Similar but not the same, they remind us of the individuals that make up the whole. This walrus tusk pouch form is found throughout Kelliher-Combs' work. Part of her Iñupiaq heritage, this pattern is commonly found on parka collars. This piece is made from reindeer and sheep rawhide, which is stitched wet and then stuffed to create the cocoon-like shapes.

Common Thread, 2008–10. Reindeer and sheep rawhide, steel pins, dimensions variable. Private collection. Photograph by Chris Arend

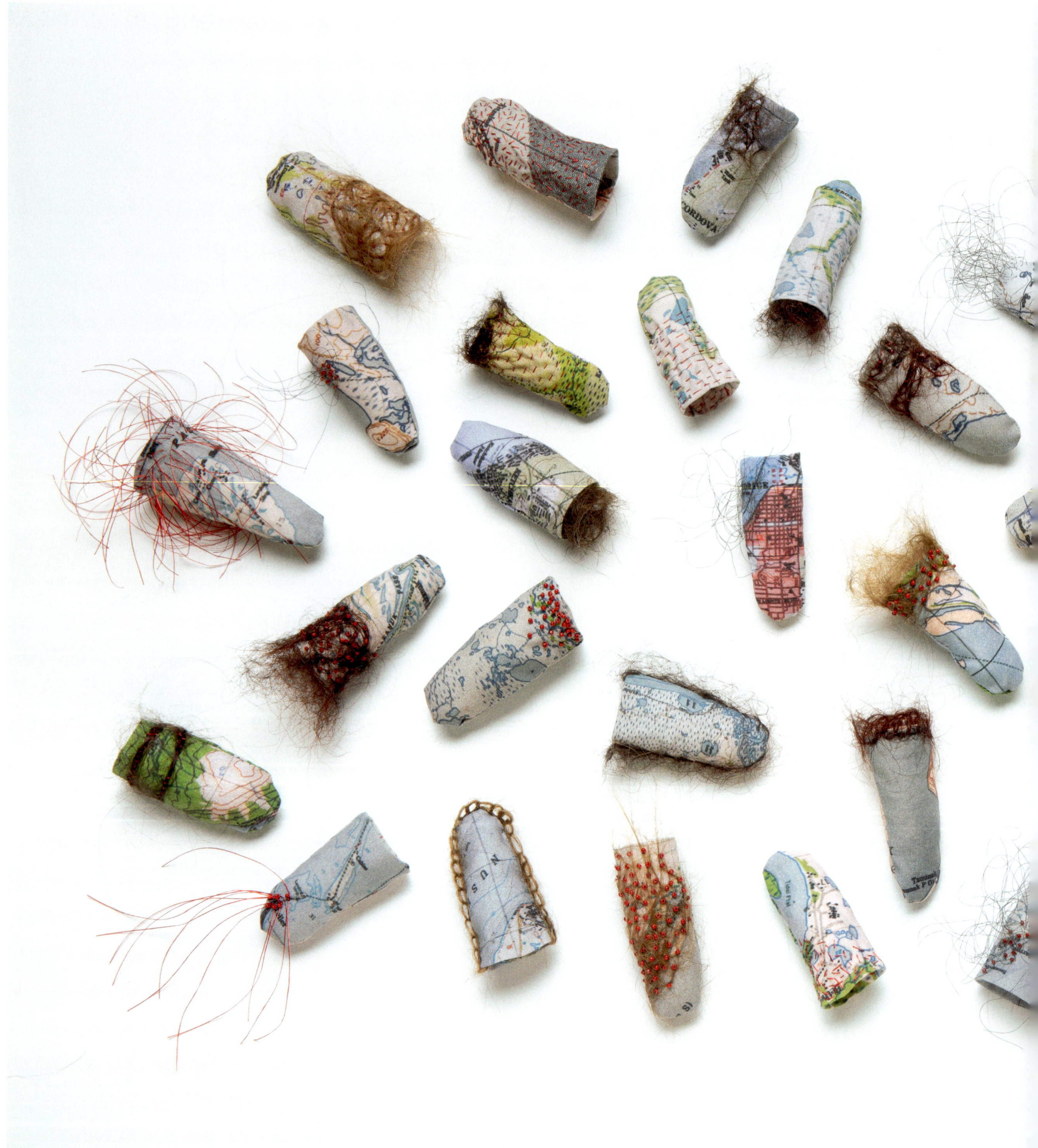
CORDOVA

Credible Small Secrets

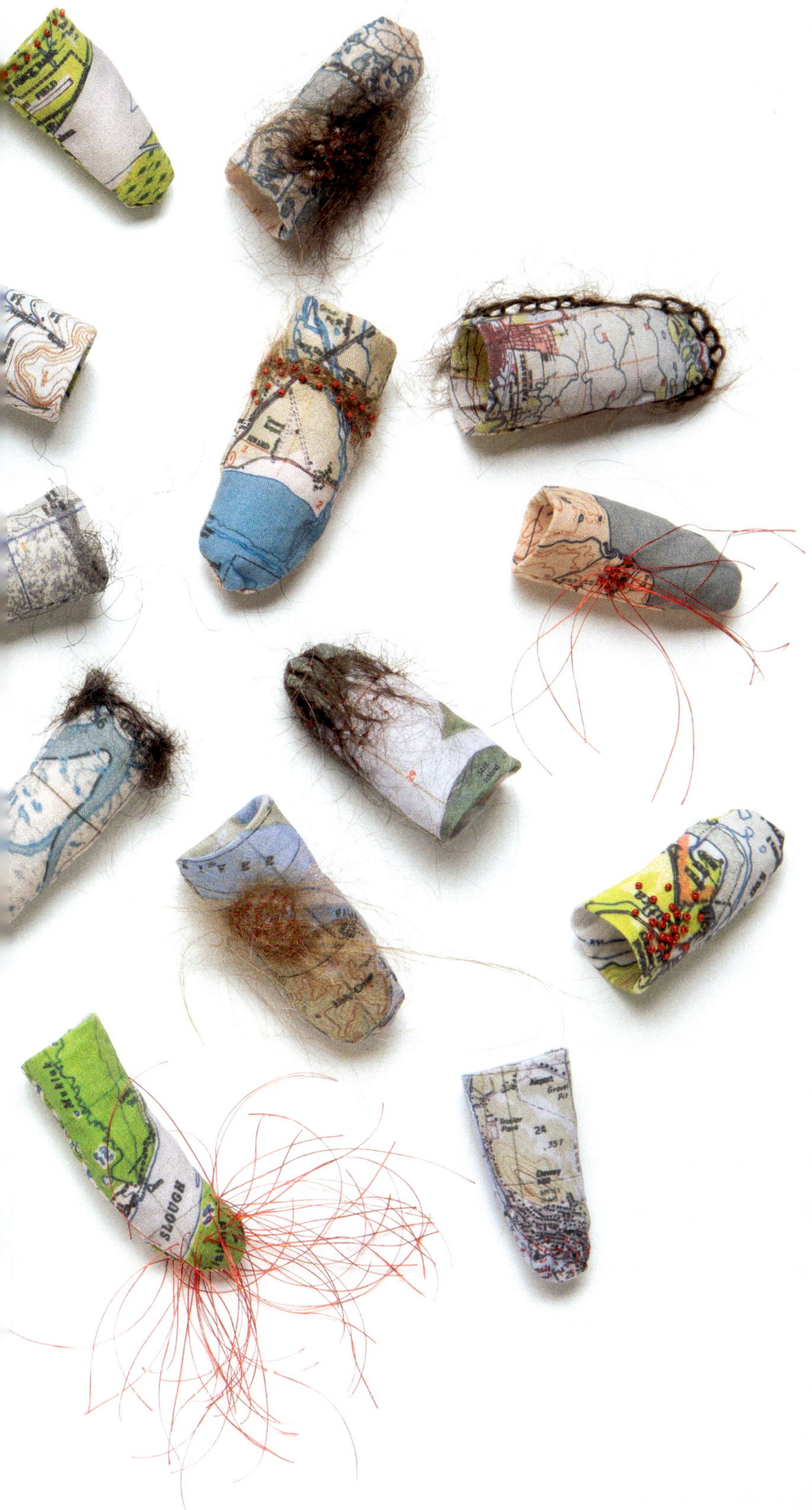

Credible Small Secrets, 2021–present. Printed fabric, human hair, nylon thread, glass bead, steel pins, dimensions variable. Photographs by Chris Arend.

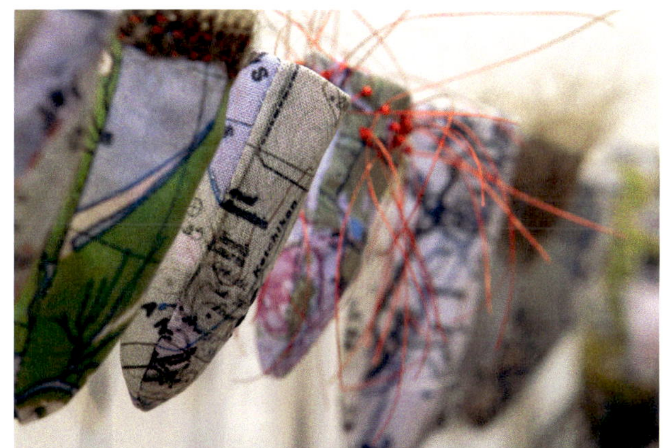

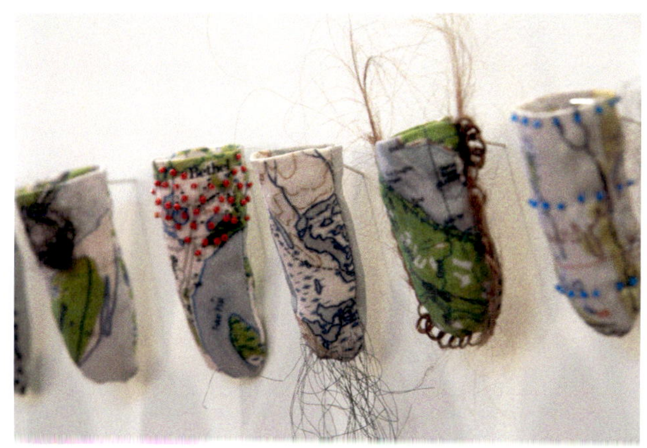

Credible Small Secrets

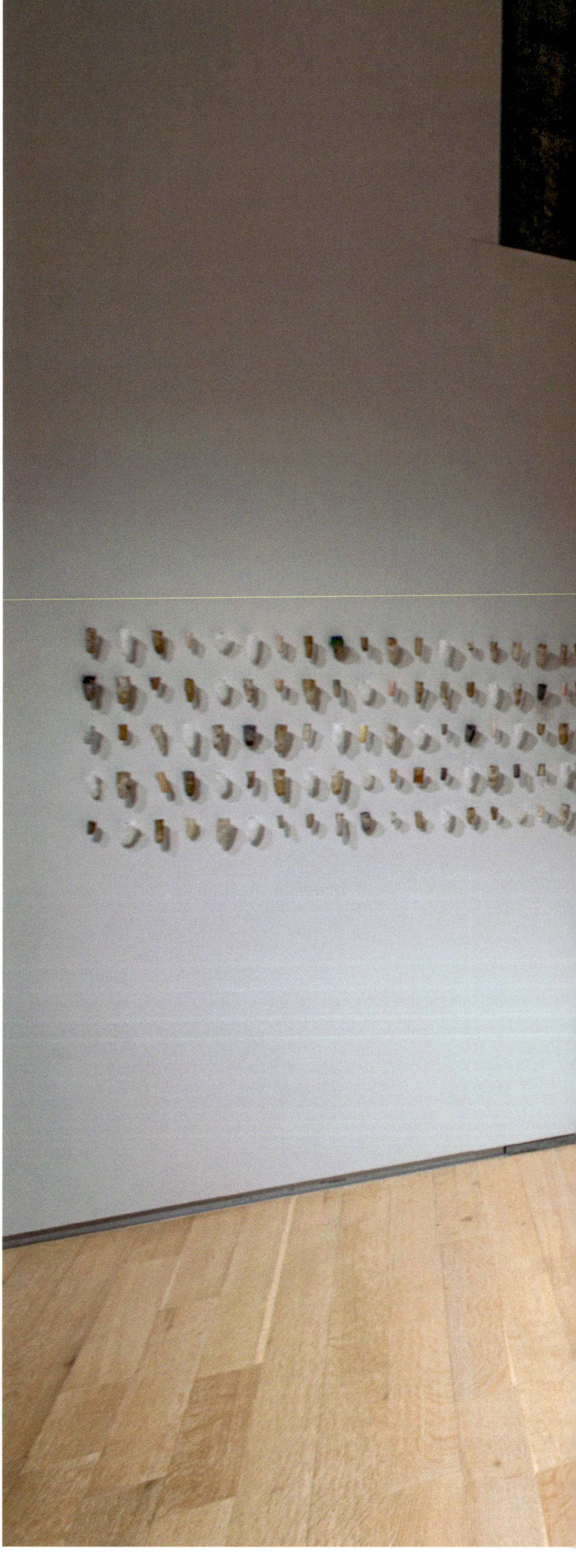

Credible Small Secrets 355, 2023.
Printed fabric, human hair, nylon thread, glass bead, walrus stomach, reindeer and sheep rawhide, acrylic polymer, steel pins, dimensions variable.
Photograph by Brian Wallace.

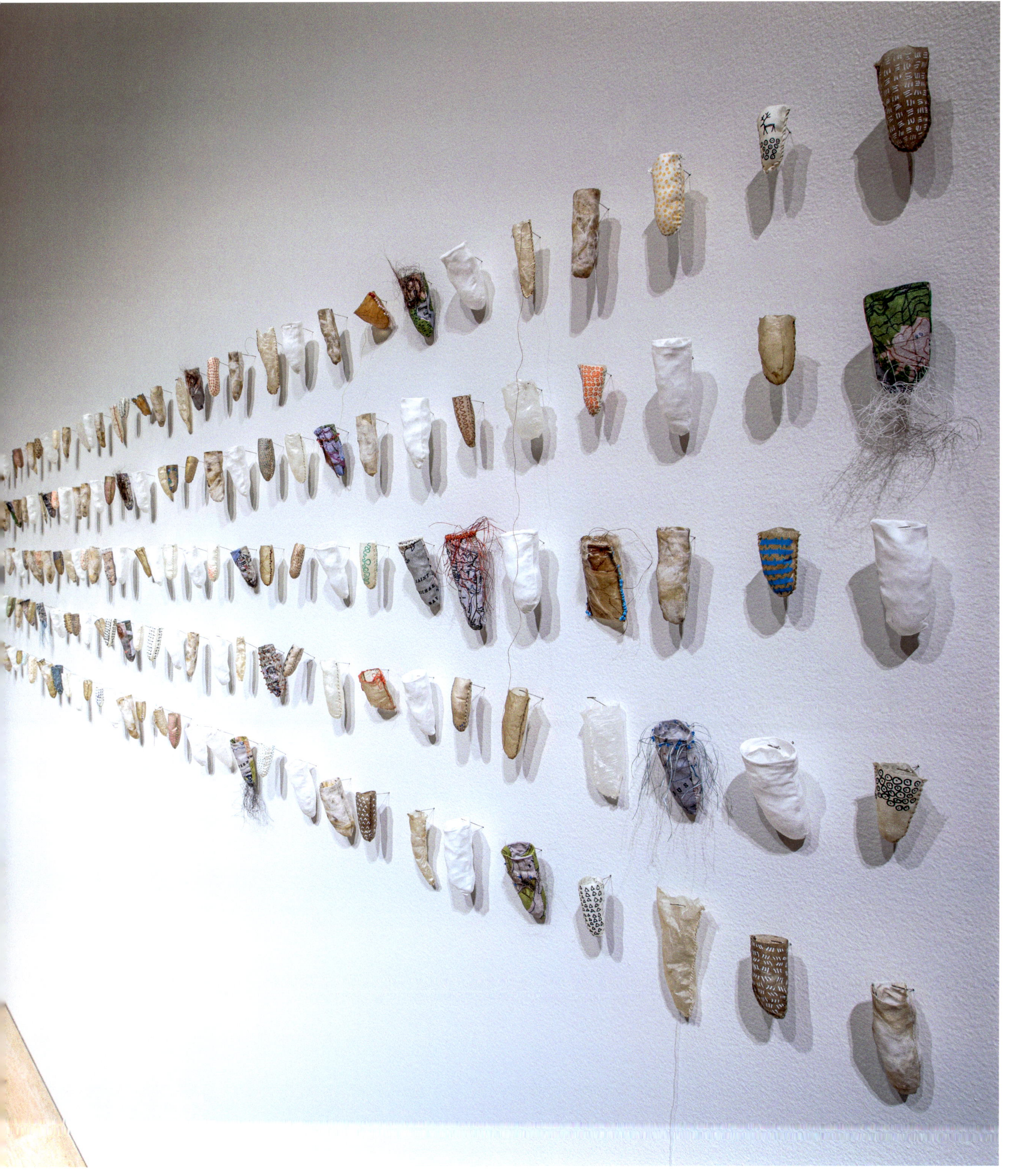

Floral Small Secrets

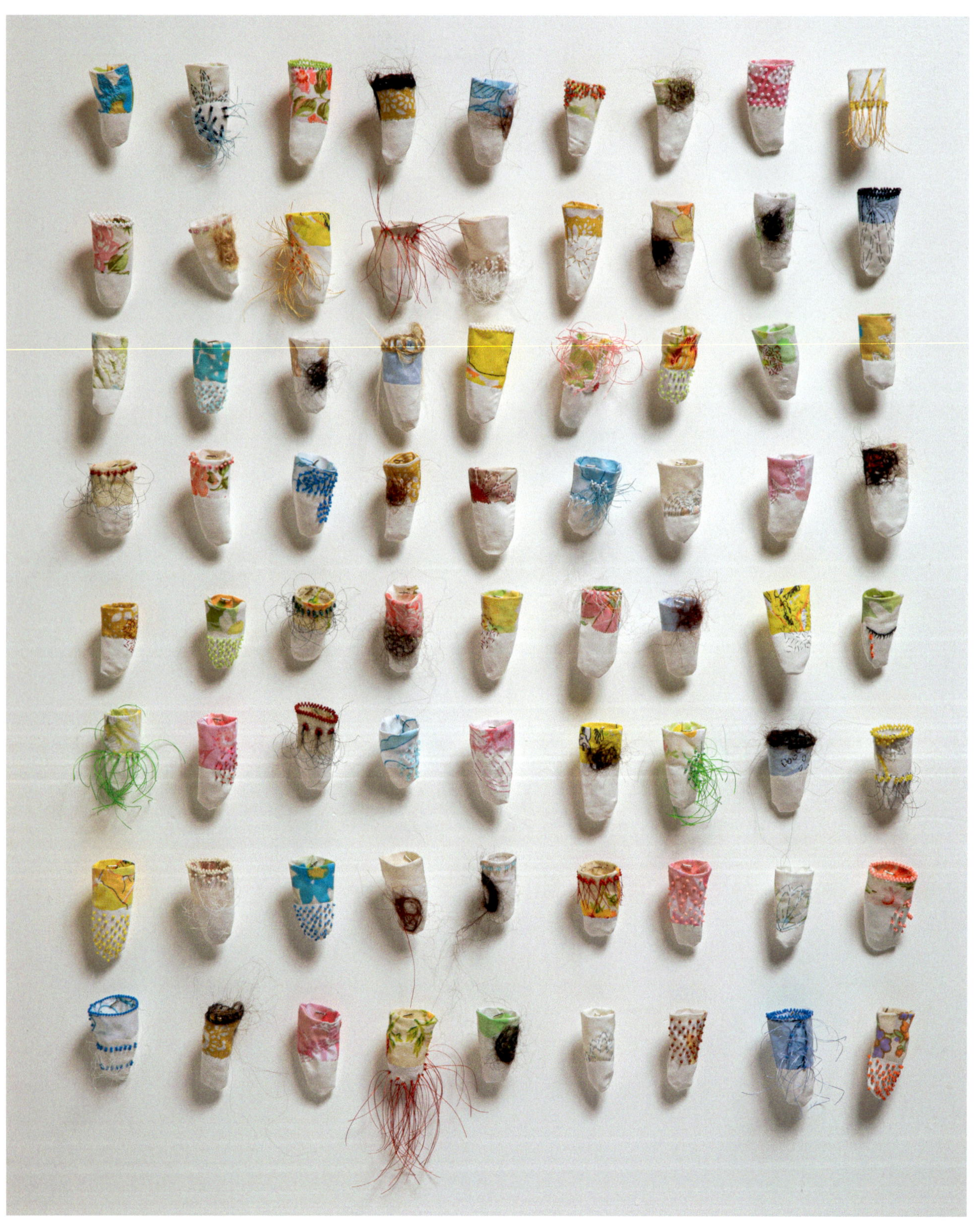

Floral Small Secrets, 2022–present. Acrylic polymer, found fabric, nylon thread, human hair, glass bead, steel pins, dimensions variable. Photographs by Chris Arend.

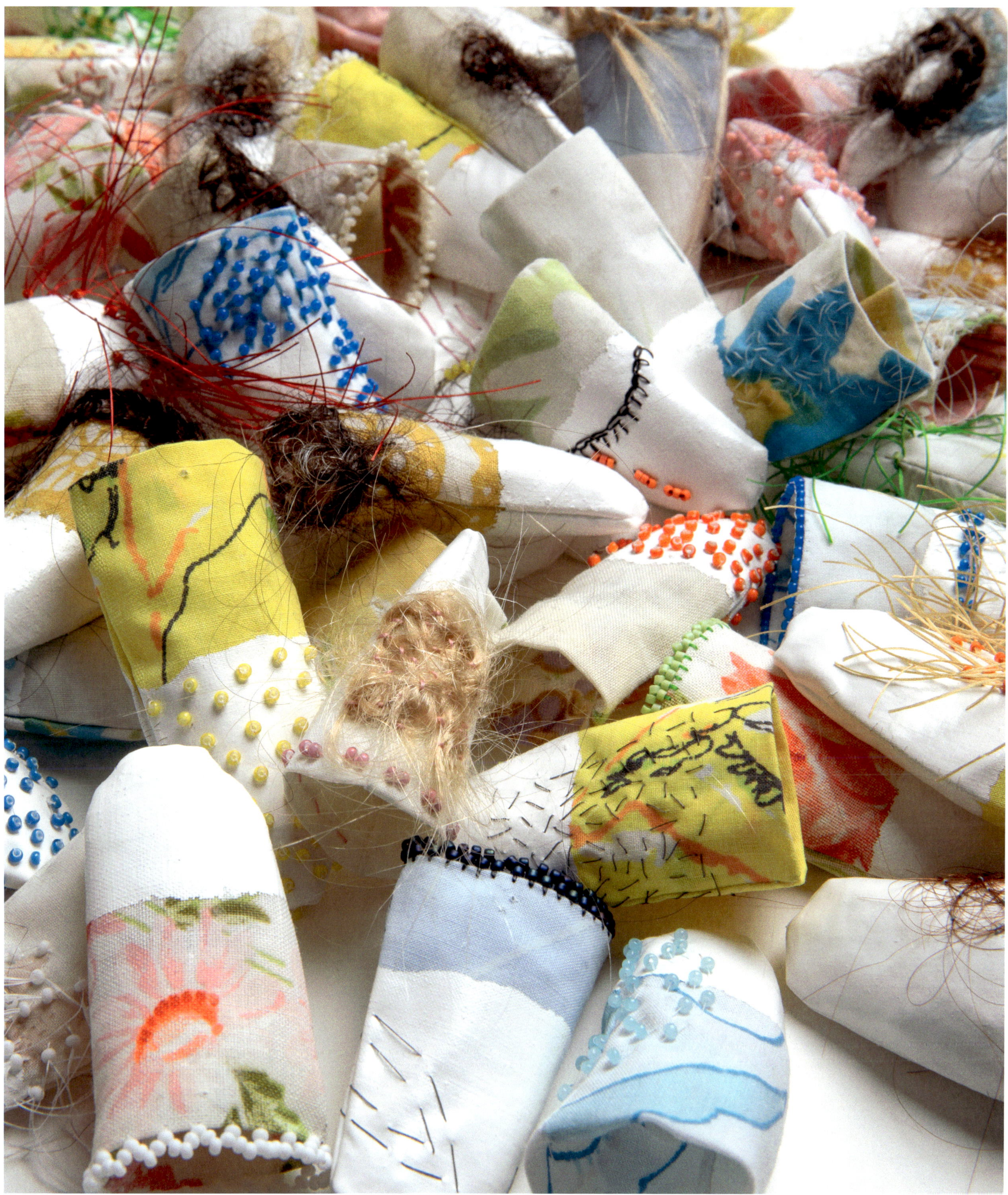

Guarded Secrets

The cocoon-shaped patterns are based on Iñupiaq walrus tusk trim design. These designs were placed on either side of the neck on the front of parkas and were meant to empower the wearer. In this work, the shape is a metaphor for a secret. By definition, a secret is something hidden, unspoken, repressed, and kept unknown. *Guarded Secrets* is a series that reveals the protected secret which is shielded from the outside and fortified from within.

Guarded Secrets, 2004. Walrus stomach, porcupine quill, archival glue, nylon thread, dimensions variable. Collection of the Museum of the North, University of Alaska Fairbanks. Photograph by Kevin G. Smith.

Guarded Secrets, 2013. Reindeer and sheep rawhide, porcupine quill, archival glue, nylon thread, dimensions variable. Collection of the Anchorage Museum. Photograph by Chris Arend.

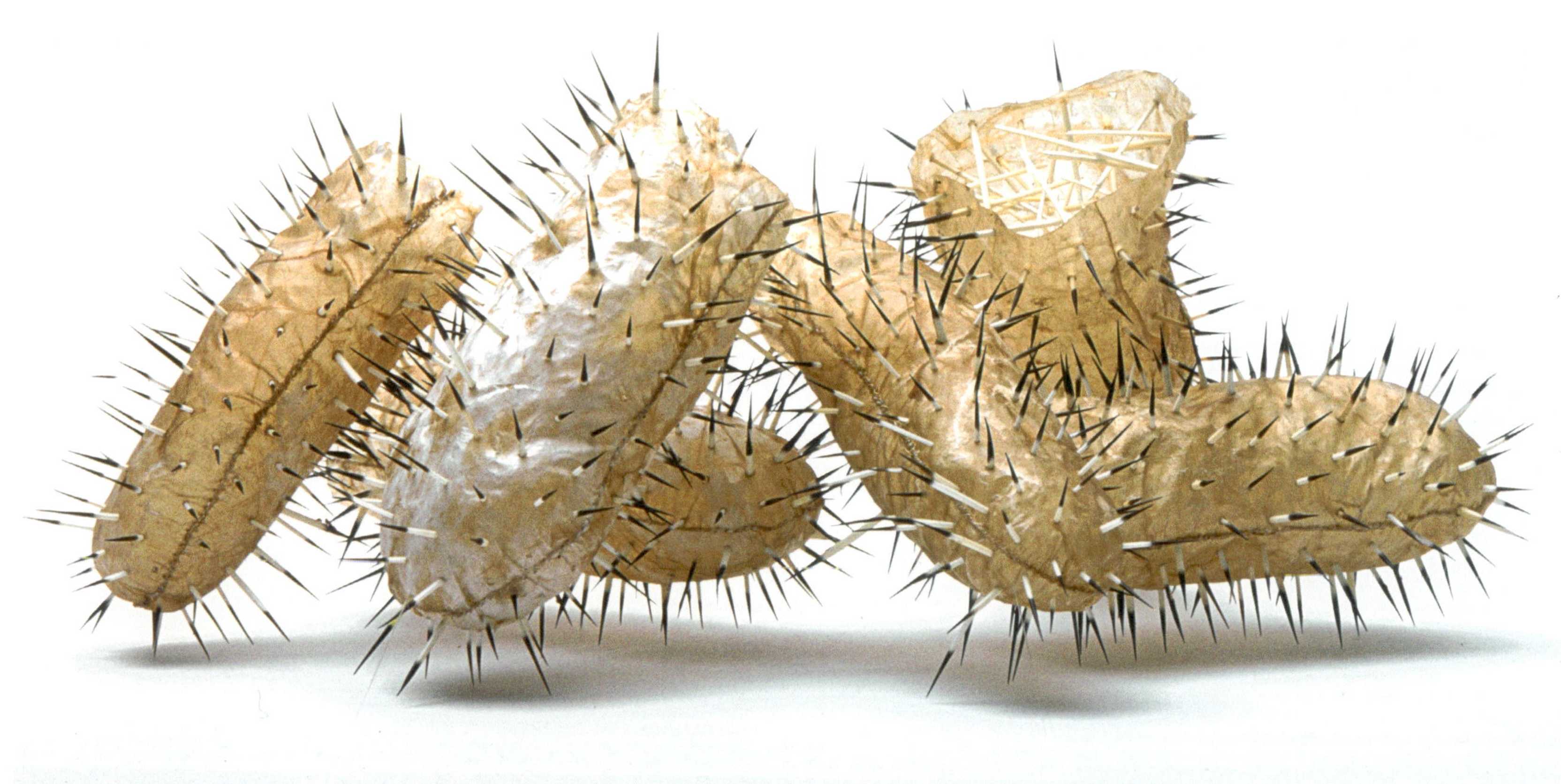

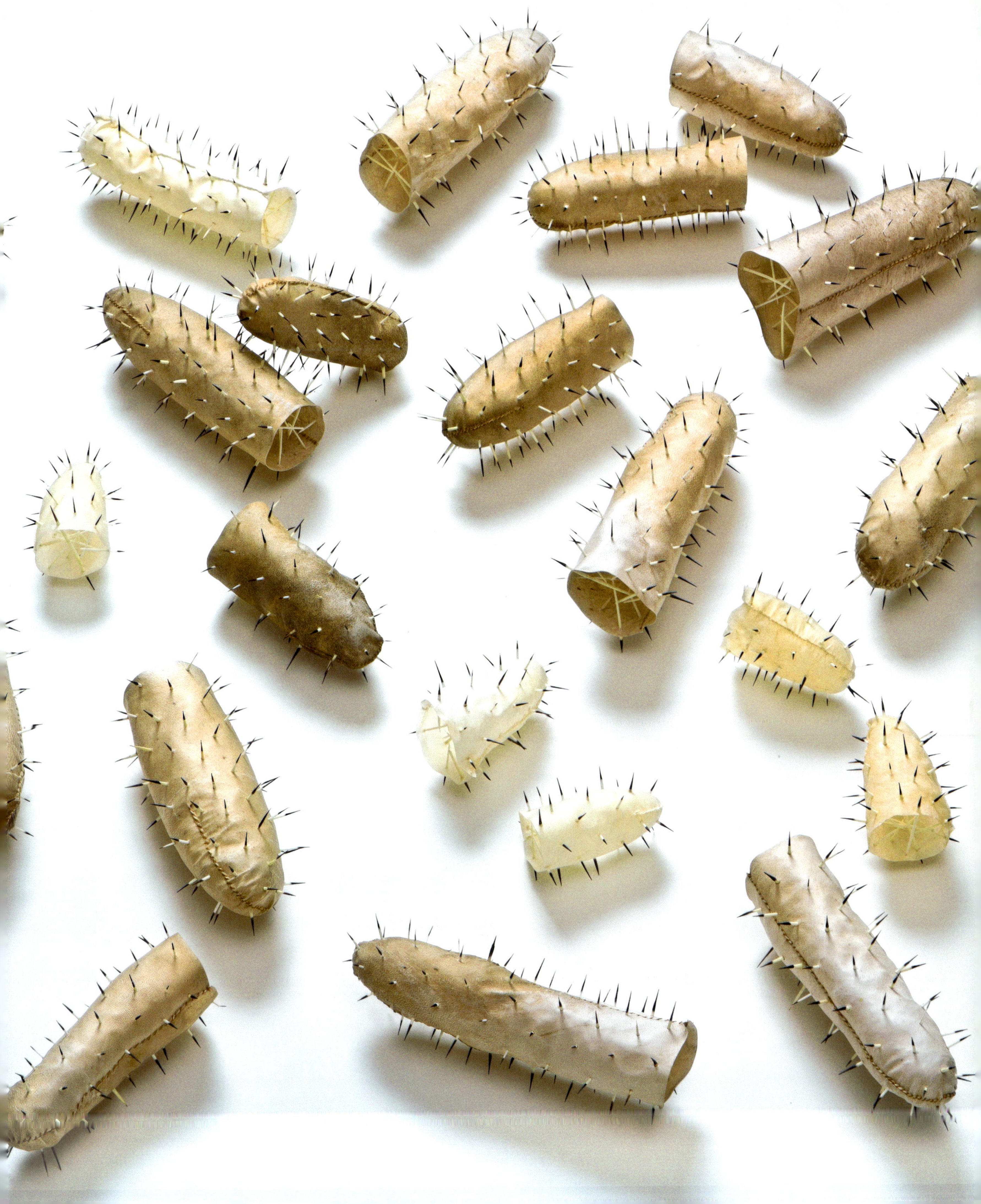

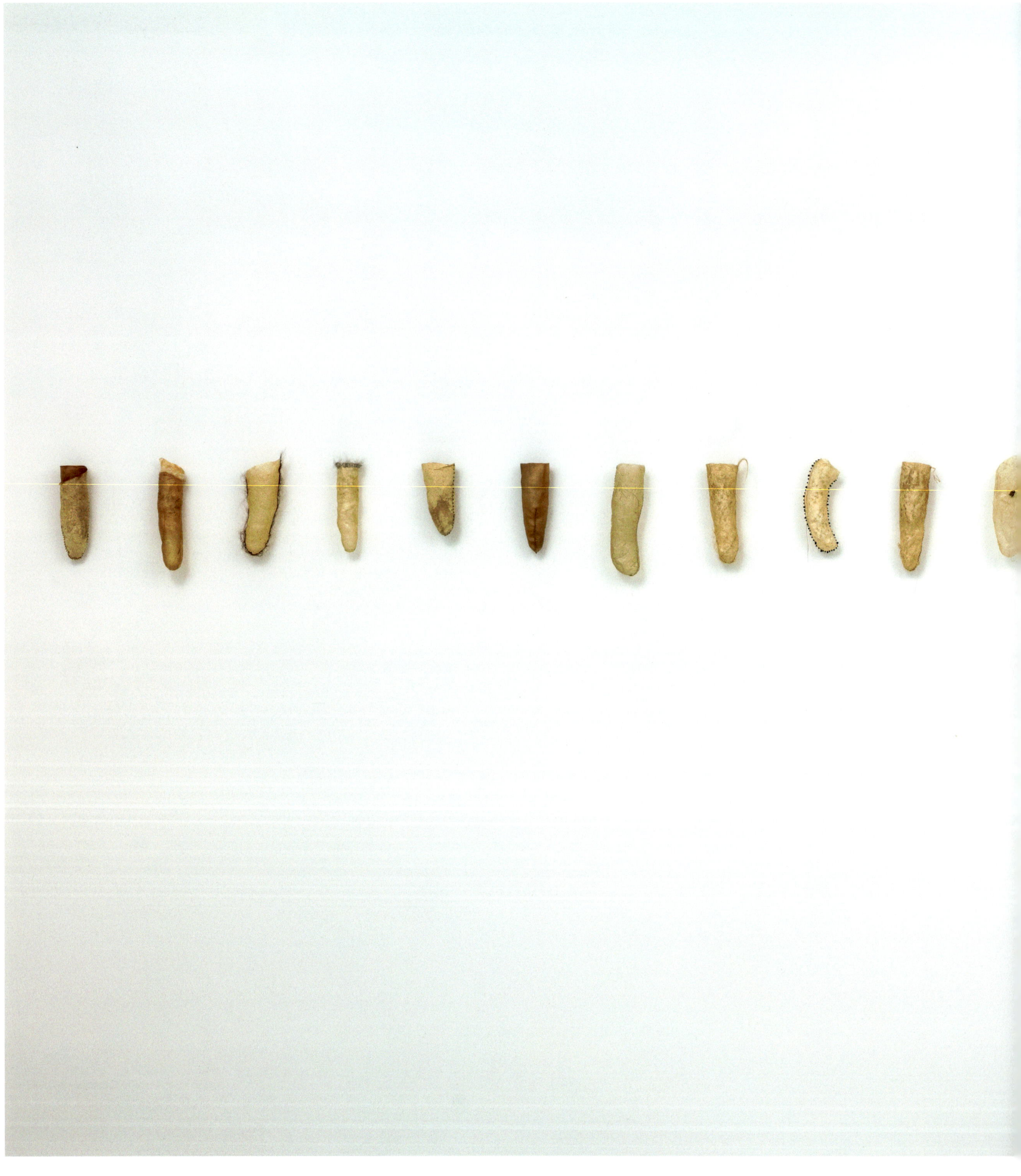

Large Secrets

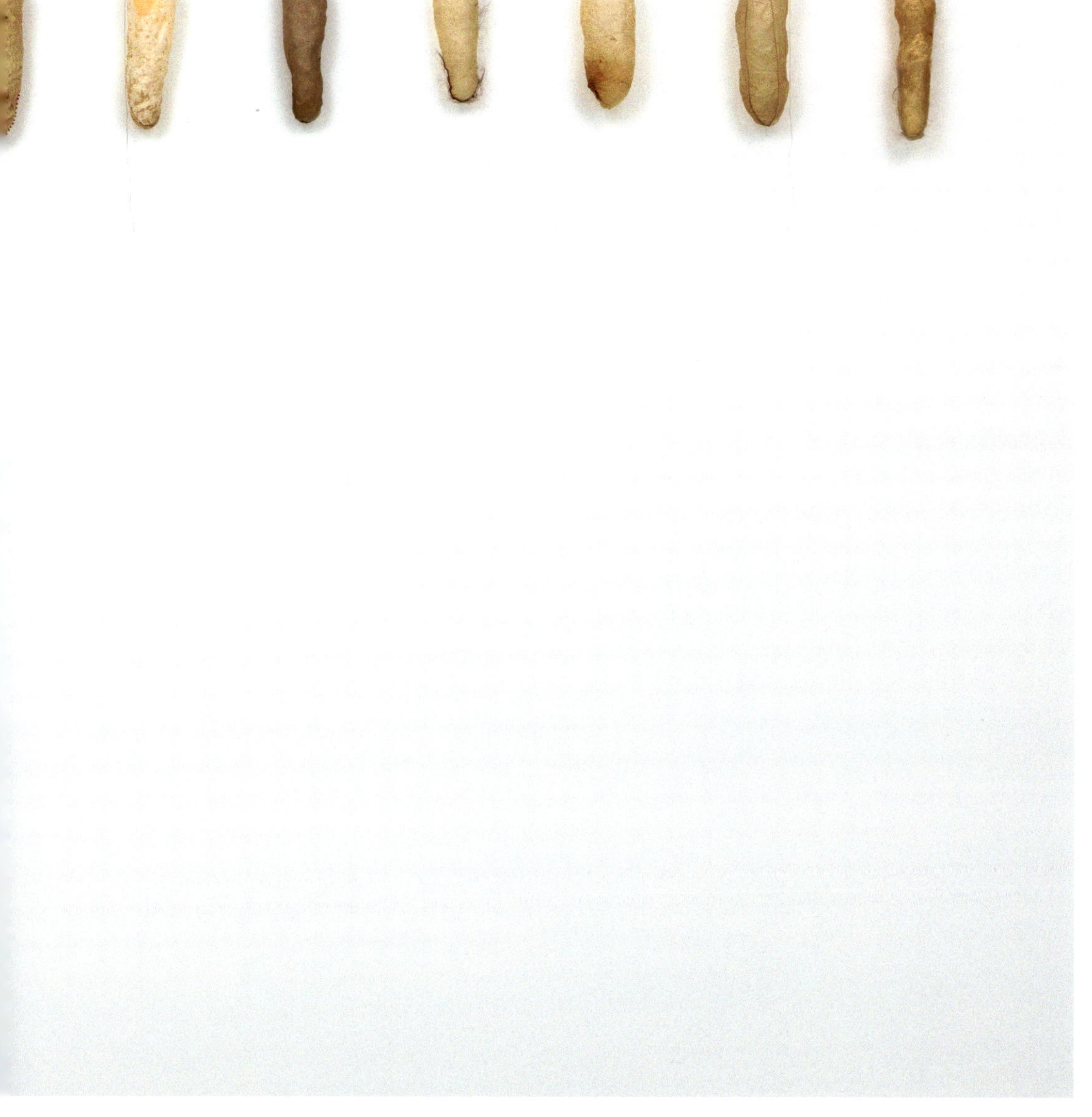

Large Secrets, 2017–2022. Reindeer and sheep rawhide, porcupine quills, walrus stomach, seal intestine, human hair, nylon thread, glass bead, cotton string, steel pins, dimensions variable. Photograph by Kevin Todora.

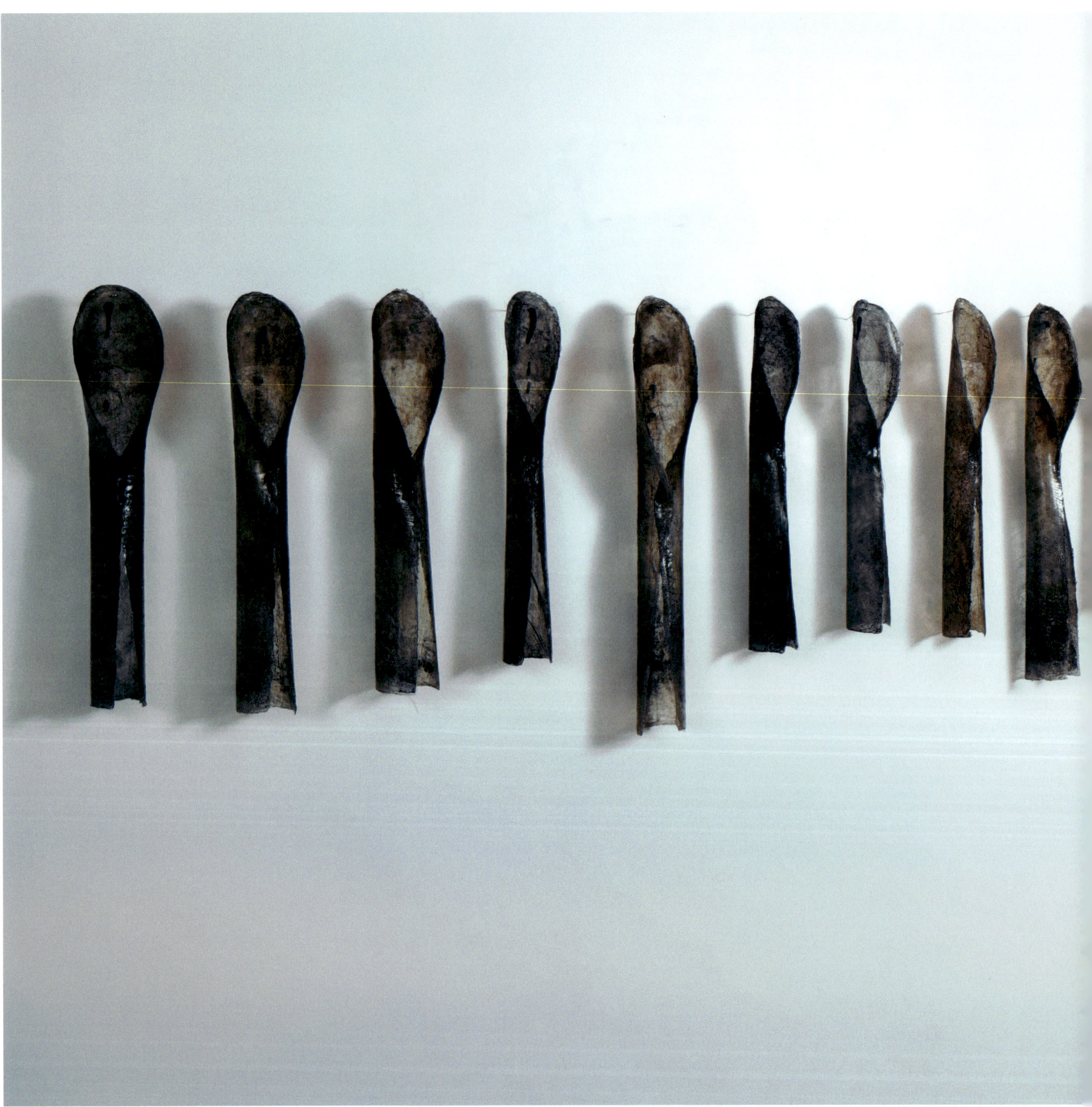

Grey Curl

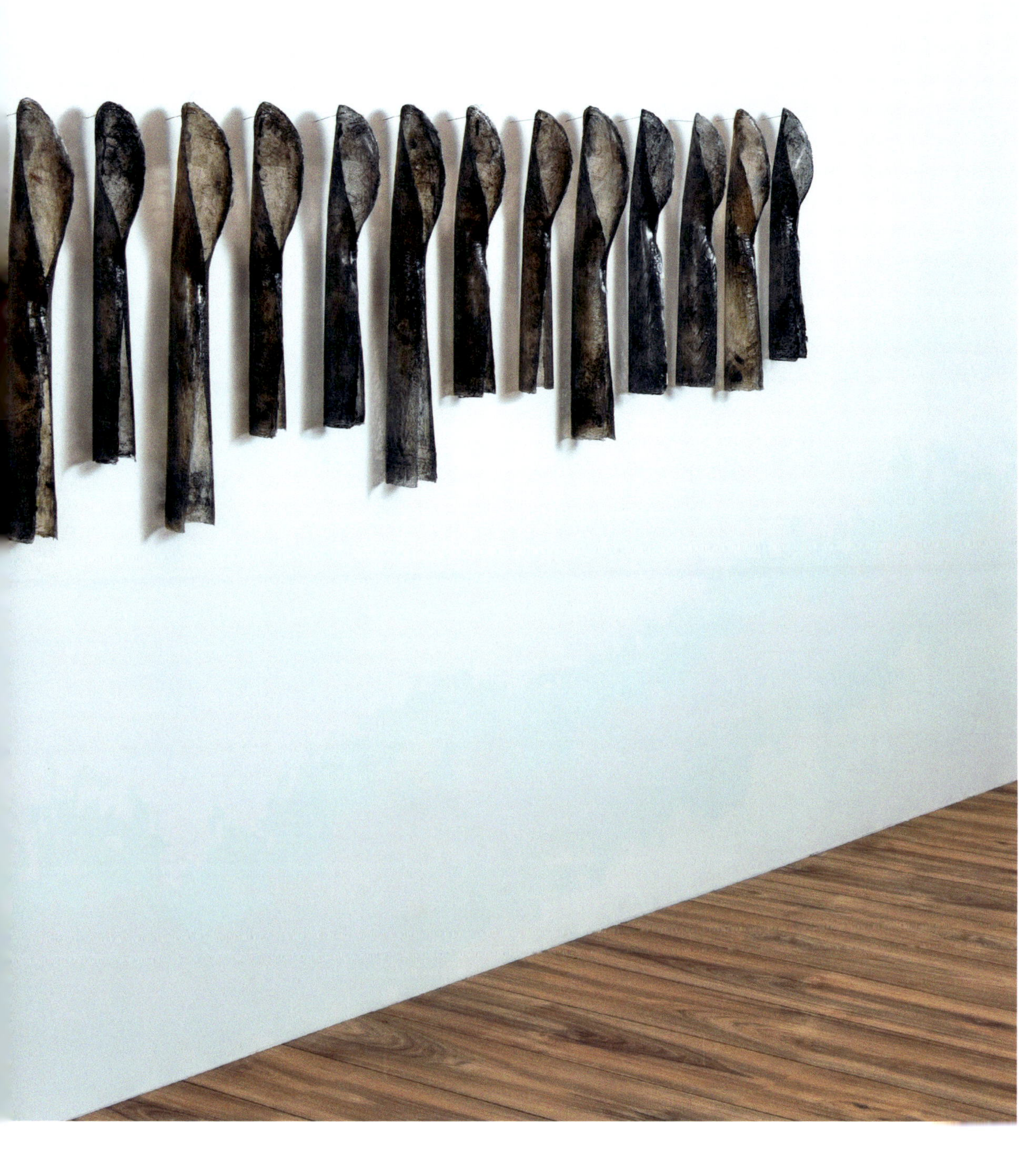

Grey Curl, 2013. Acrylic polymer, reindeer fur, human hair, nylon thread, steel pins, dimensions variable. Collection of the Museum of Contemporary Native Art, Santa Fe. Photograph by Chris Arend

Marrow Curl

Marrow Curl, 2013. Acrylic polymer, reindeer fur, human hair, nylon thread, steel pins, glass beads, paper, dimensions variable. Private collection. Photographs by Chris Arend.

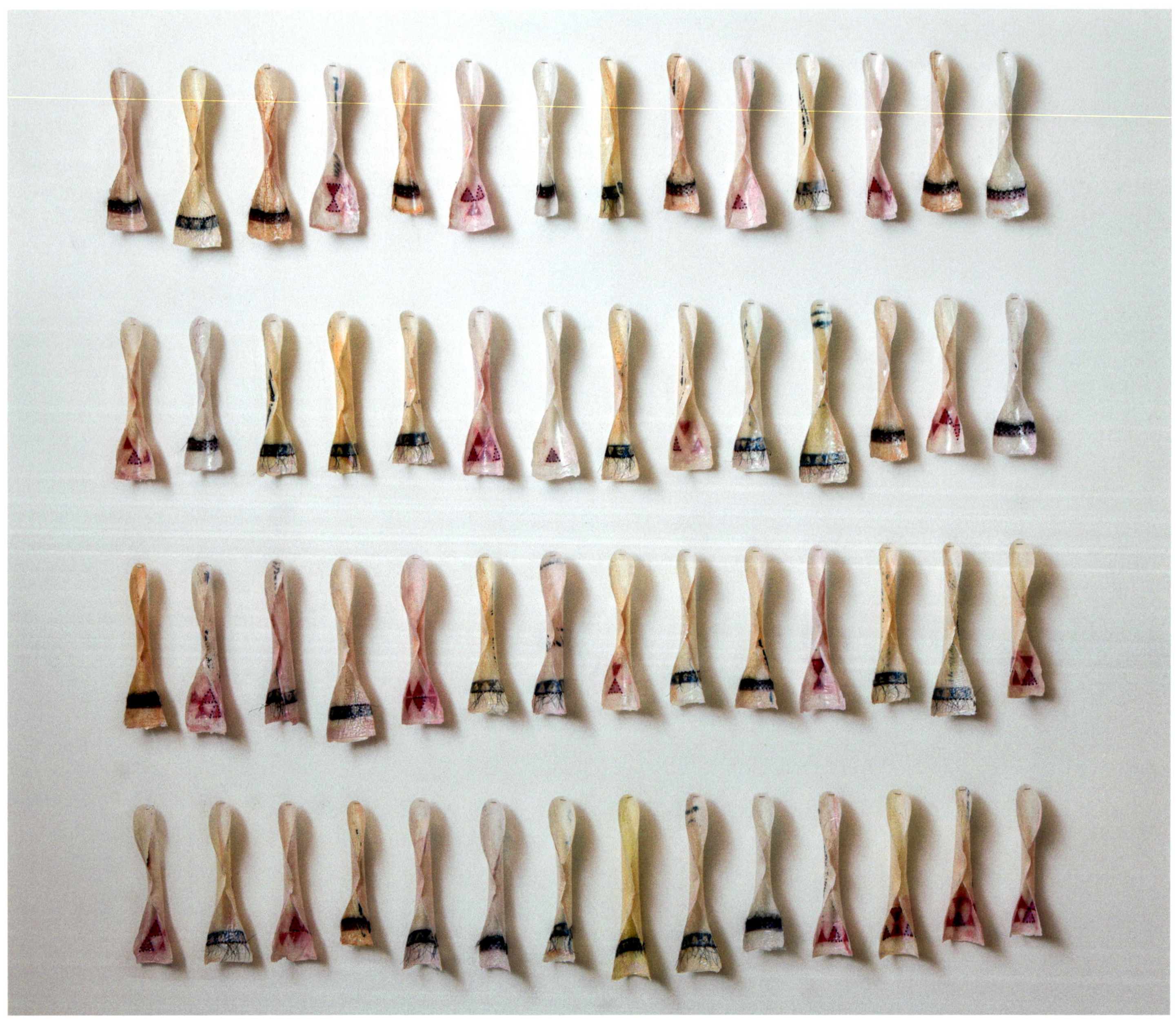

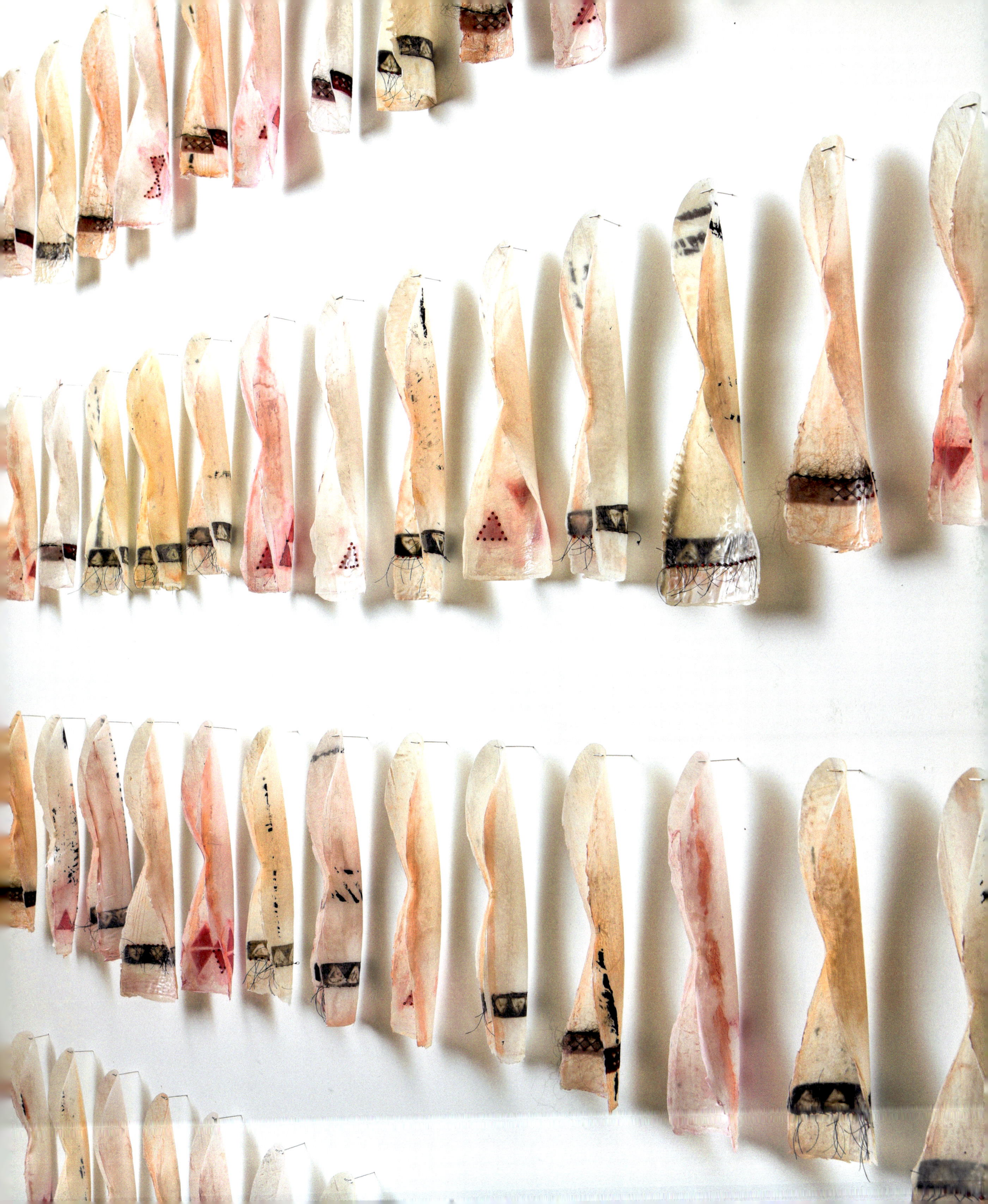

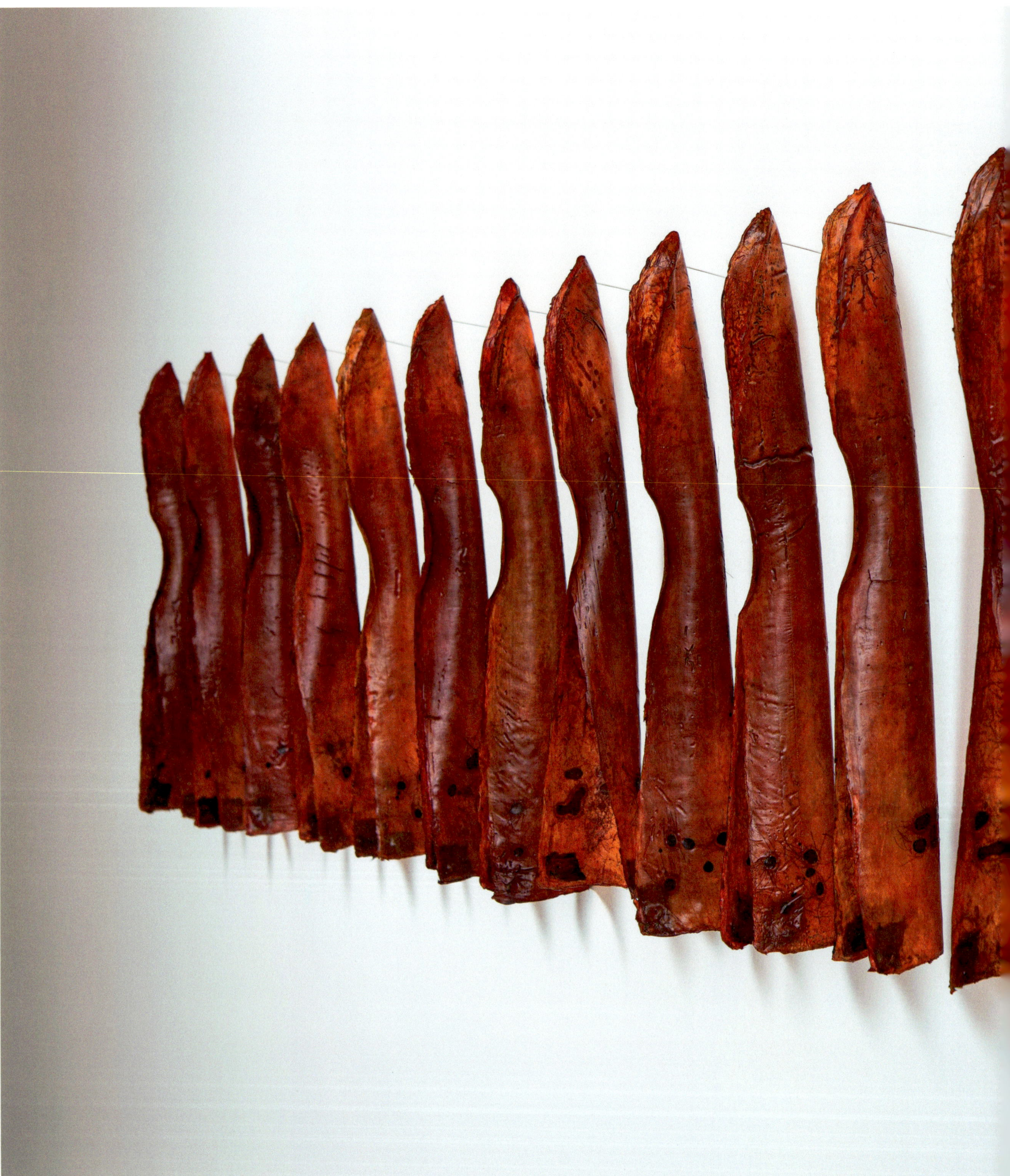

Orange Curl

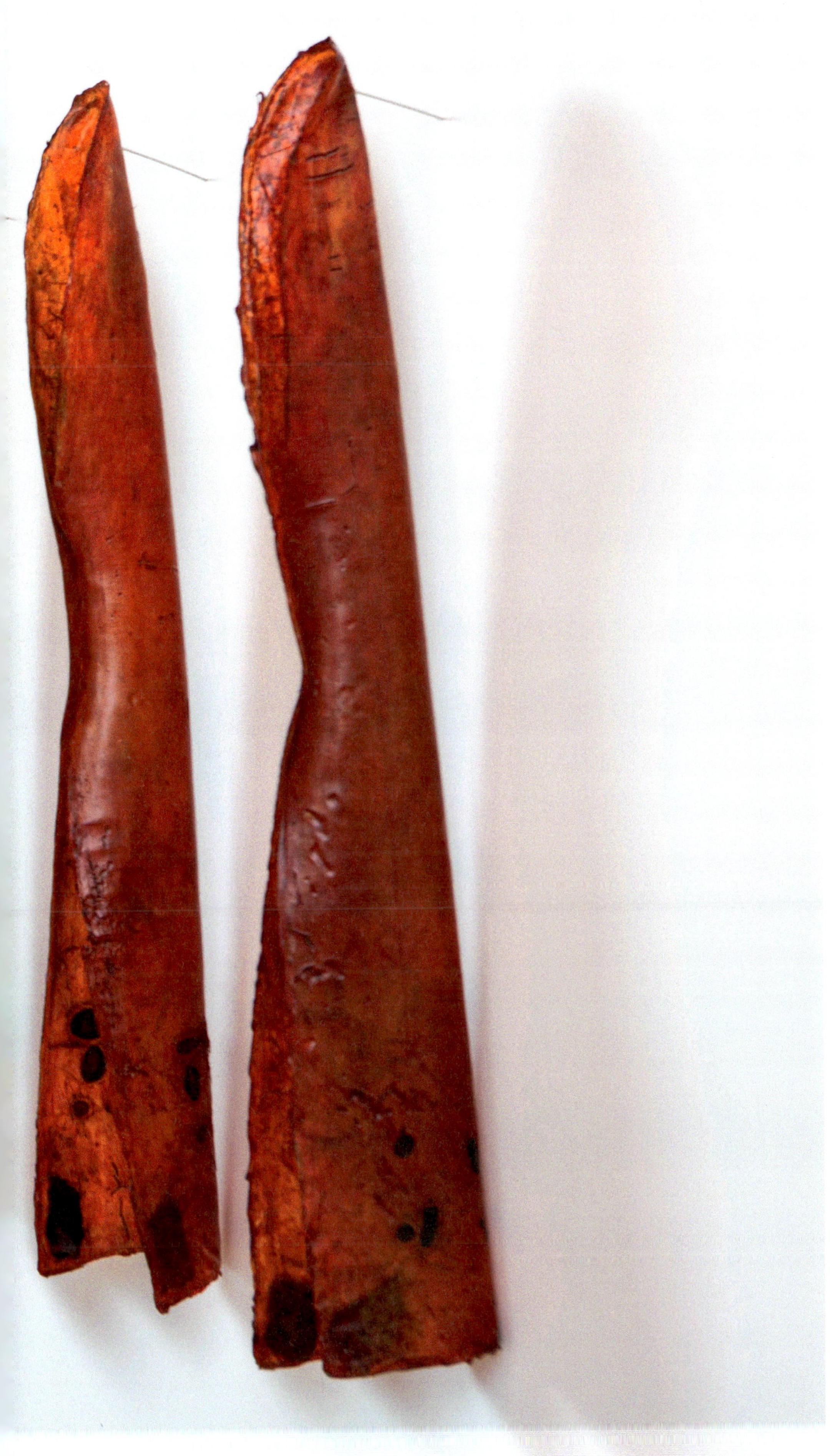

Orange Curl, 2013. Acrylic polymer, reindeer fur, nylon thread, fabric, steel pins, dimensions variable. Private collection. Photograph by Chris Arend

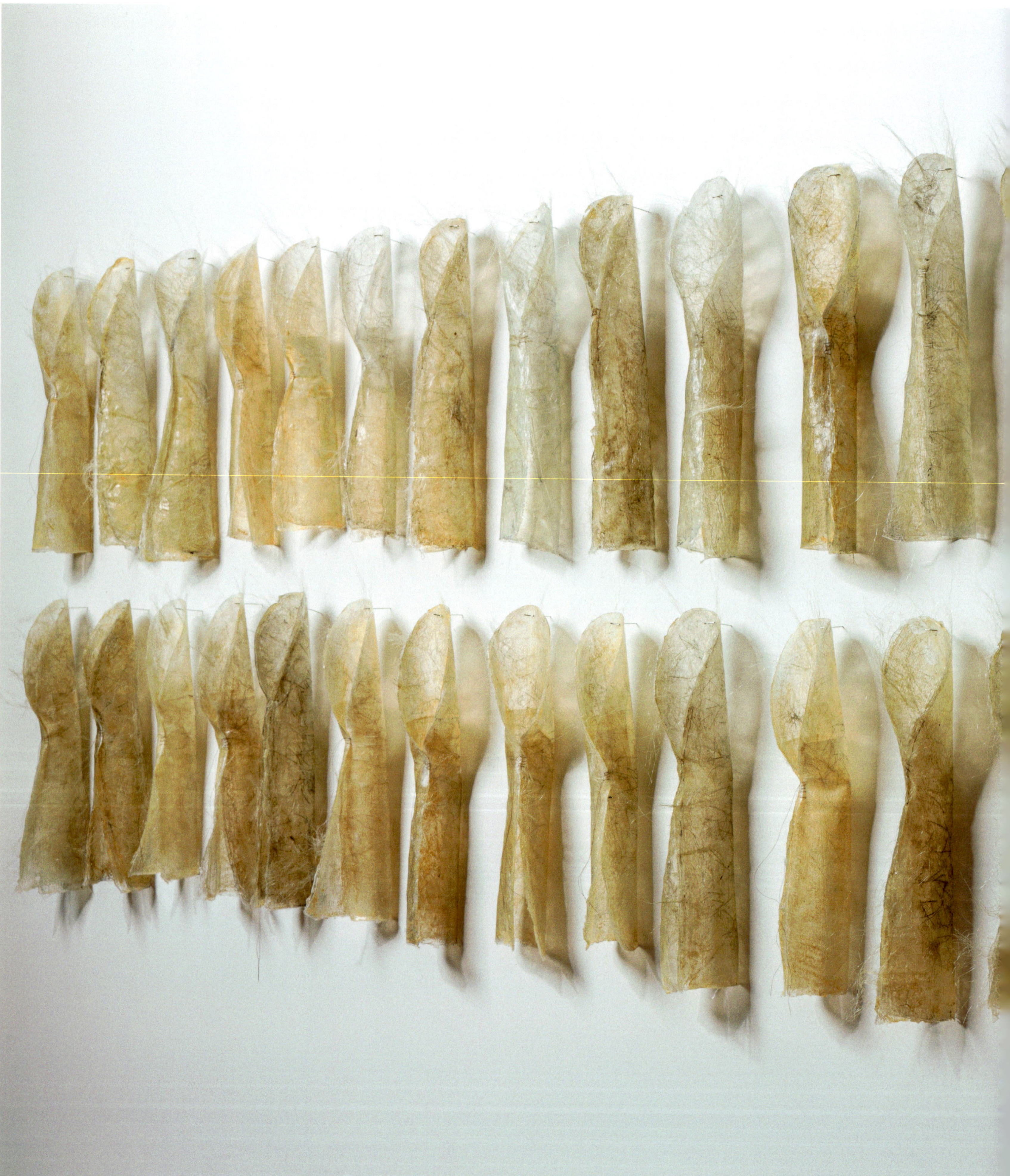

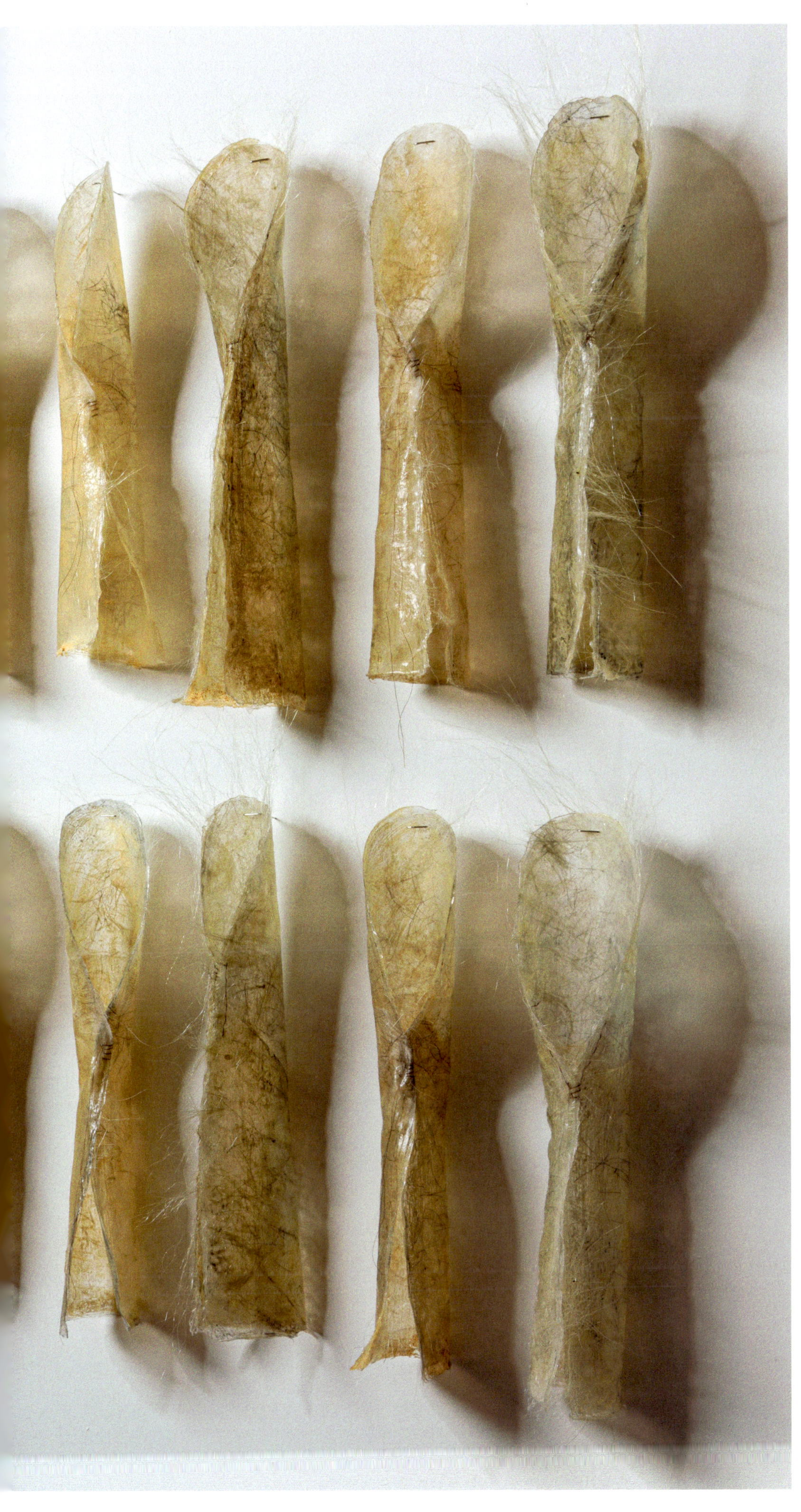

Polar Bear Curl

Polar Bear Curl, 2013. Acrylic polymer, polar bear fur, nylon thread, paper, steel pins, dimensions variable. Collection of the Whitney Museum of American Art. Photograph by Chris Arend

Red Curl I+II

Red Curl, a combination of synthetic and natural materials. The shape is loosely based on Iñupiaq parka sleeve patterns. Like the repetitive tasks of working on the land, the creative process is intimate, meditative–a continuum of generational connections to place. *Red Curl* mimics the form of strips of cold-drying sockeye salmon. The shapes are open-ended, allowing the spirit of the fish to return for future harvests. Use of repetitive forms is common in Kelliher-Combs' work. Each individual is part of the whole, evoking our relationships to one another and to the natural world.

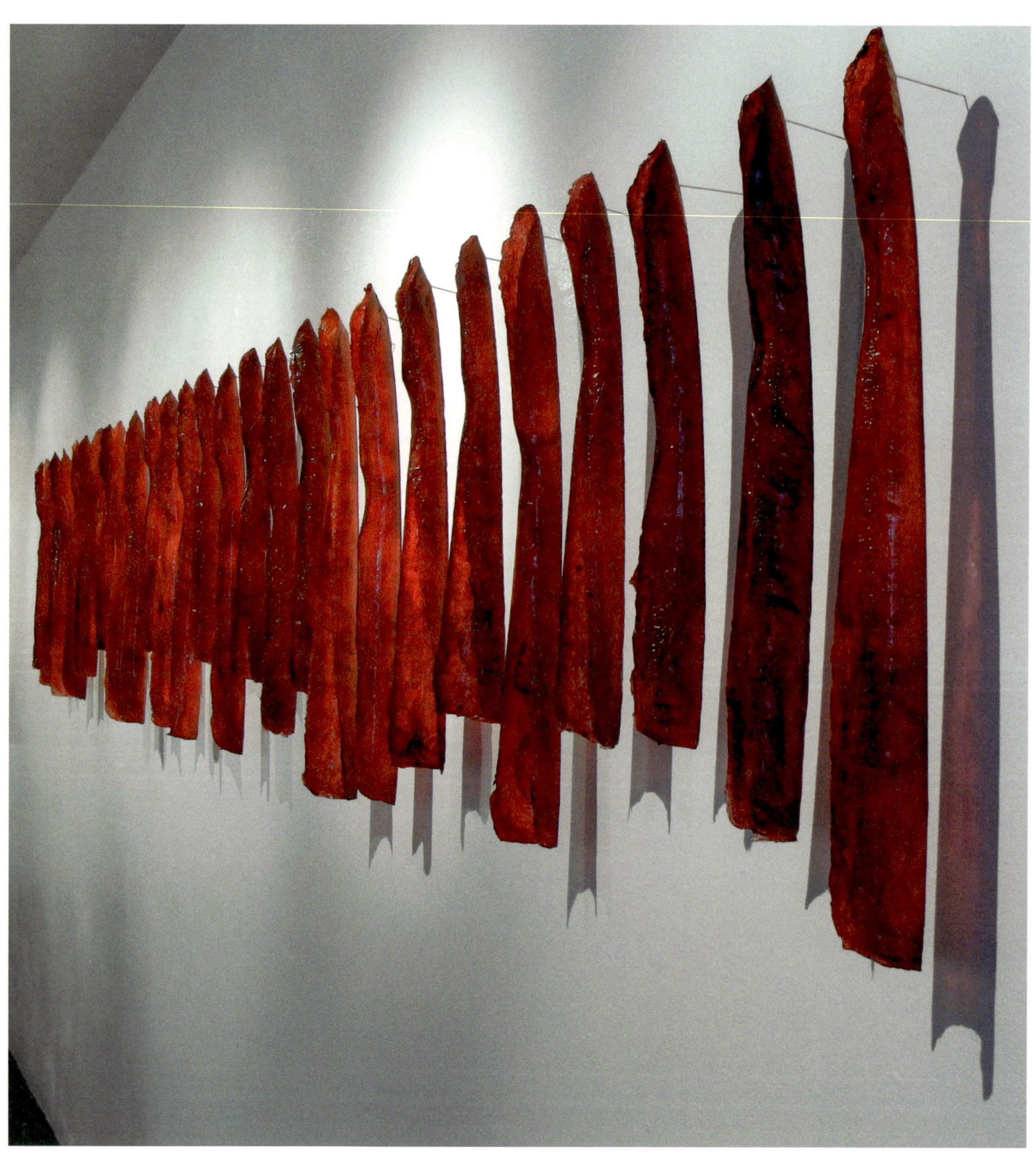

Red Curl I, 2011. Acrylic polymer, nylon thread, paper, steel pins, dimensions variable. Private collection. Photograph by Kevin G. Smith.

Red Curl II, 2017. Acrylic polymer, nylon thread, paper, reindeer fur, steel pins, dimensions variable. Collection of the Anchorage Museum. Photograph by Chris Arend.

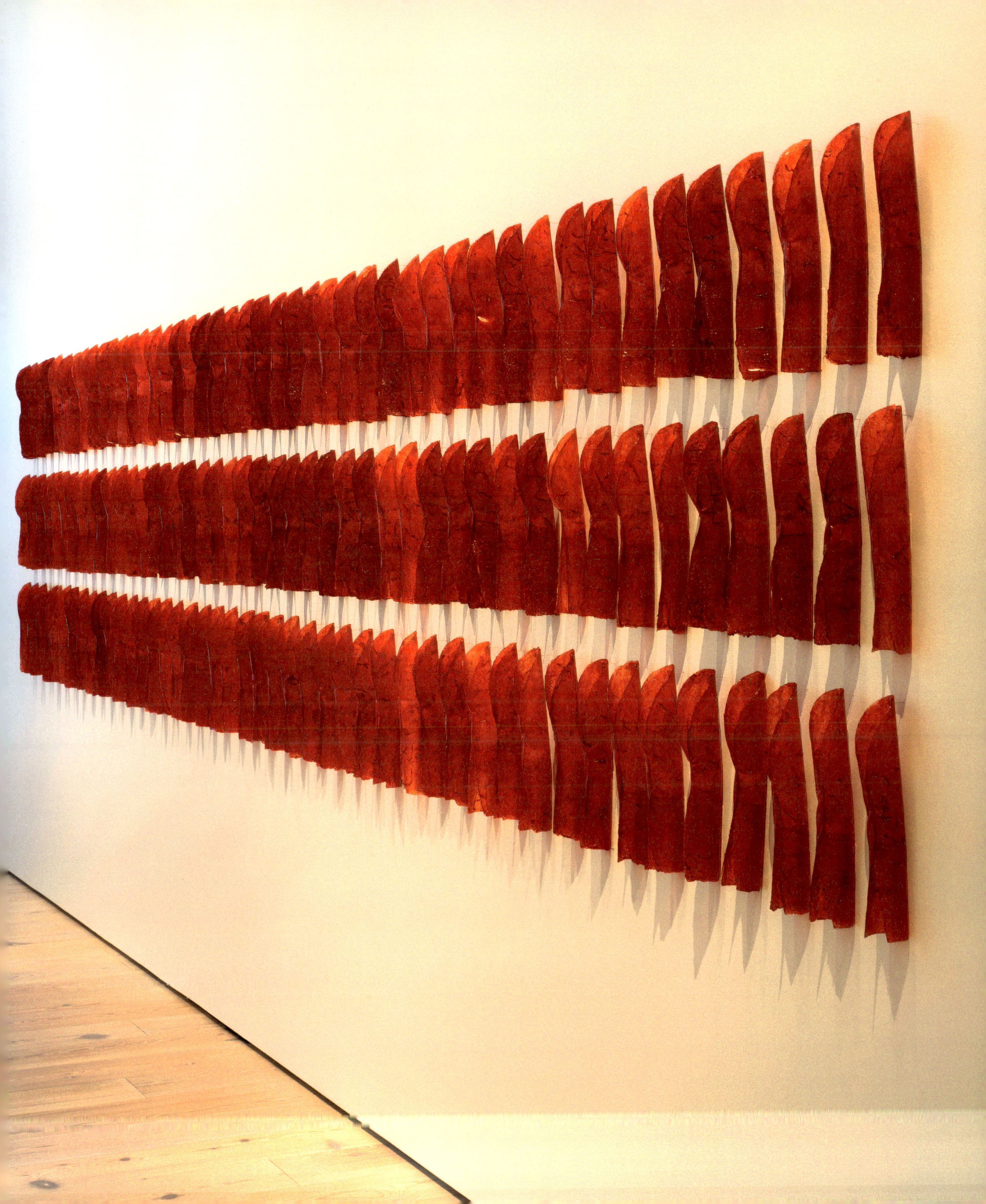

Rust Curl

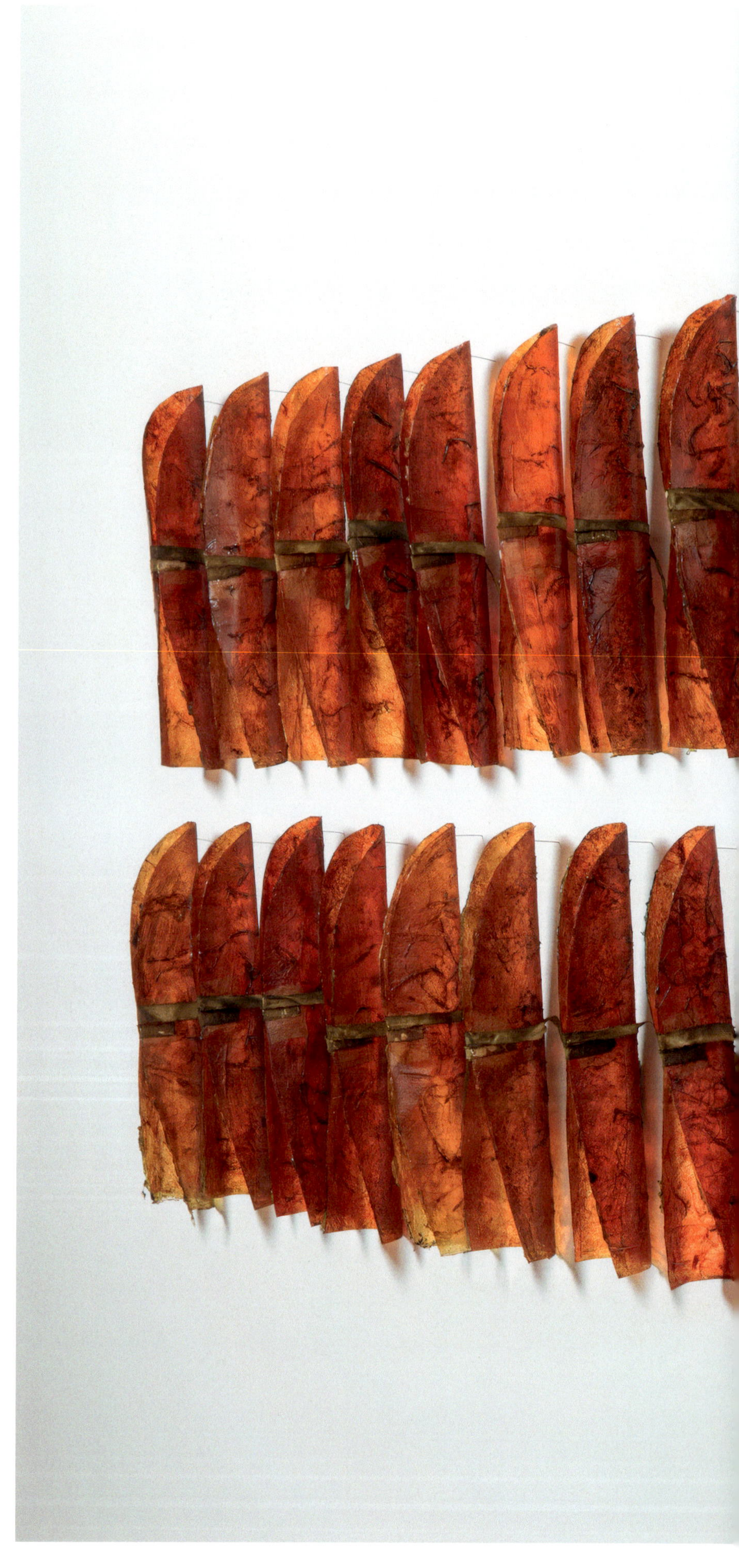

Rust Curl, 2017. Acrylic polymer, reindeer fur, nylon thread, paper, fabric ribbon, steel pins, dimensions variable. Private collection. Photograph by Chris Arend.

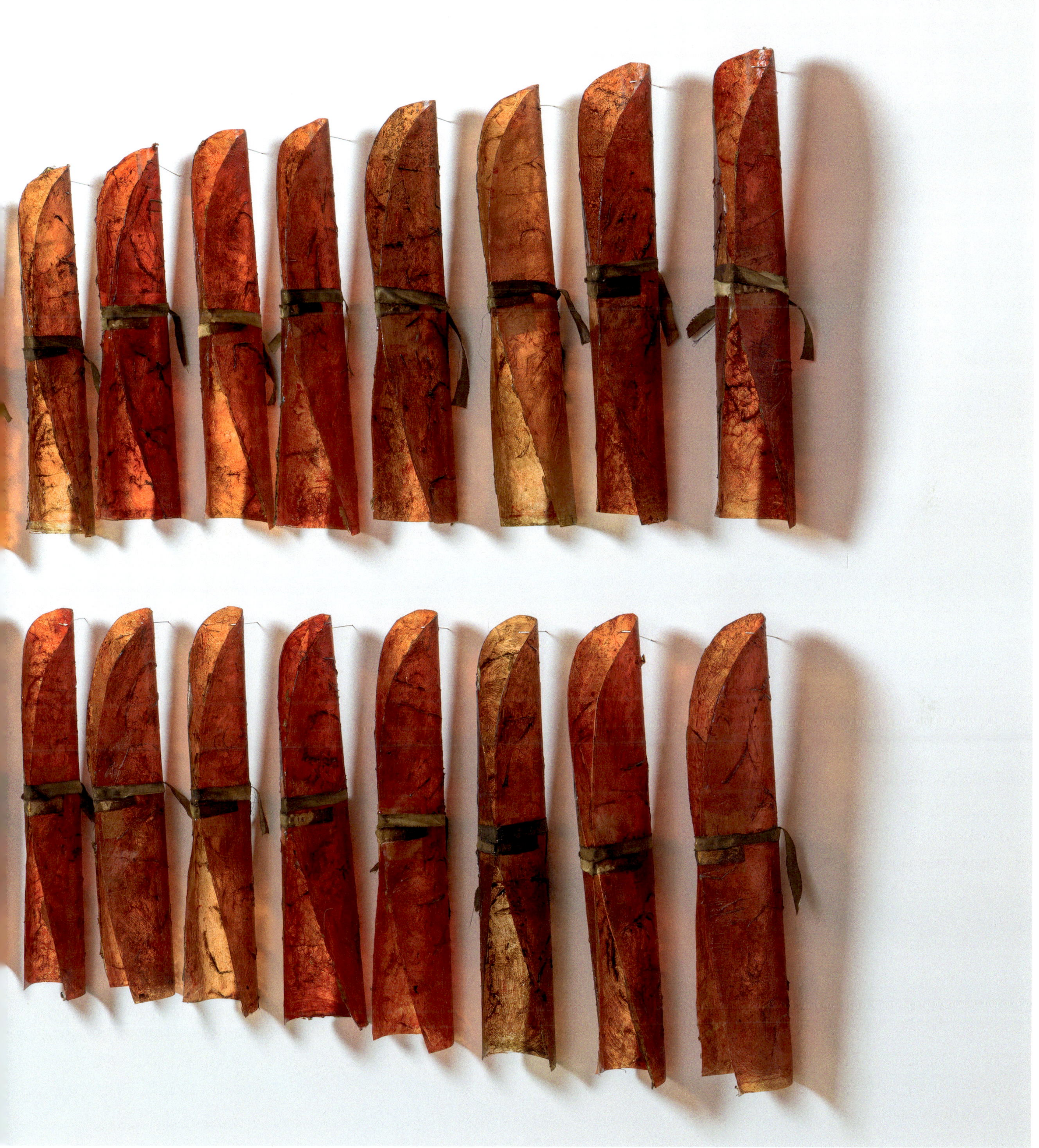

New Artifact

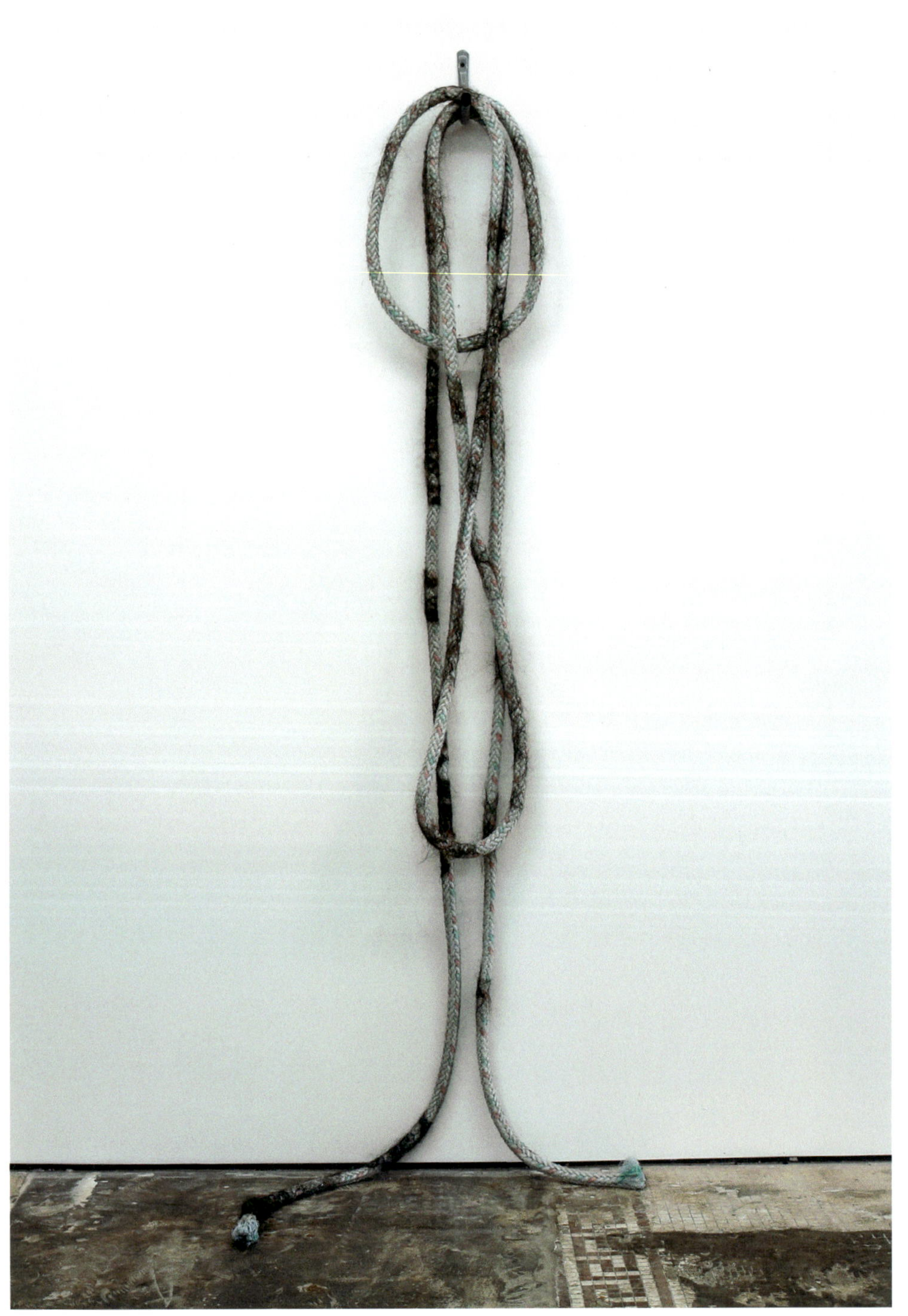

New Artifact (Tether), 2023. Found object, human hair, nylon thread, metal hook. Photograph by Greg Meza.

New Artifact (White), 2023. Found object, auto body paint. Photograph by Kevin Todora.

New Artifact (Red), 2023. Found object, auto body paint. Photograph by Kevin Todora.

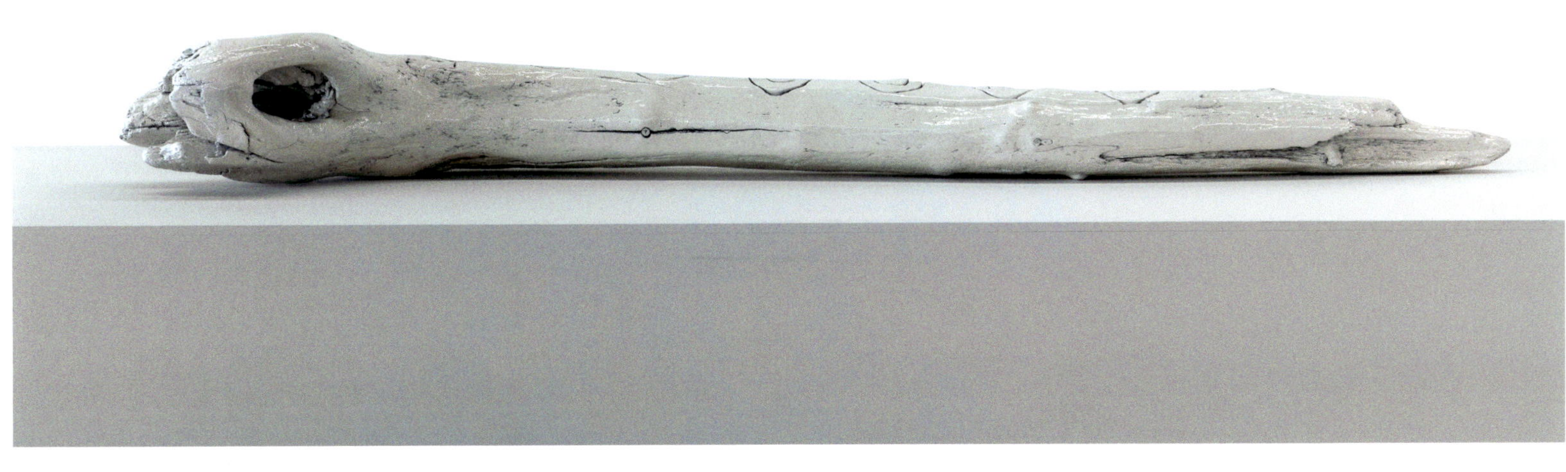

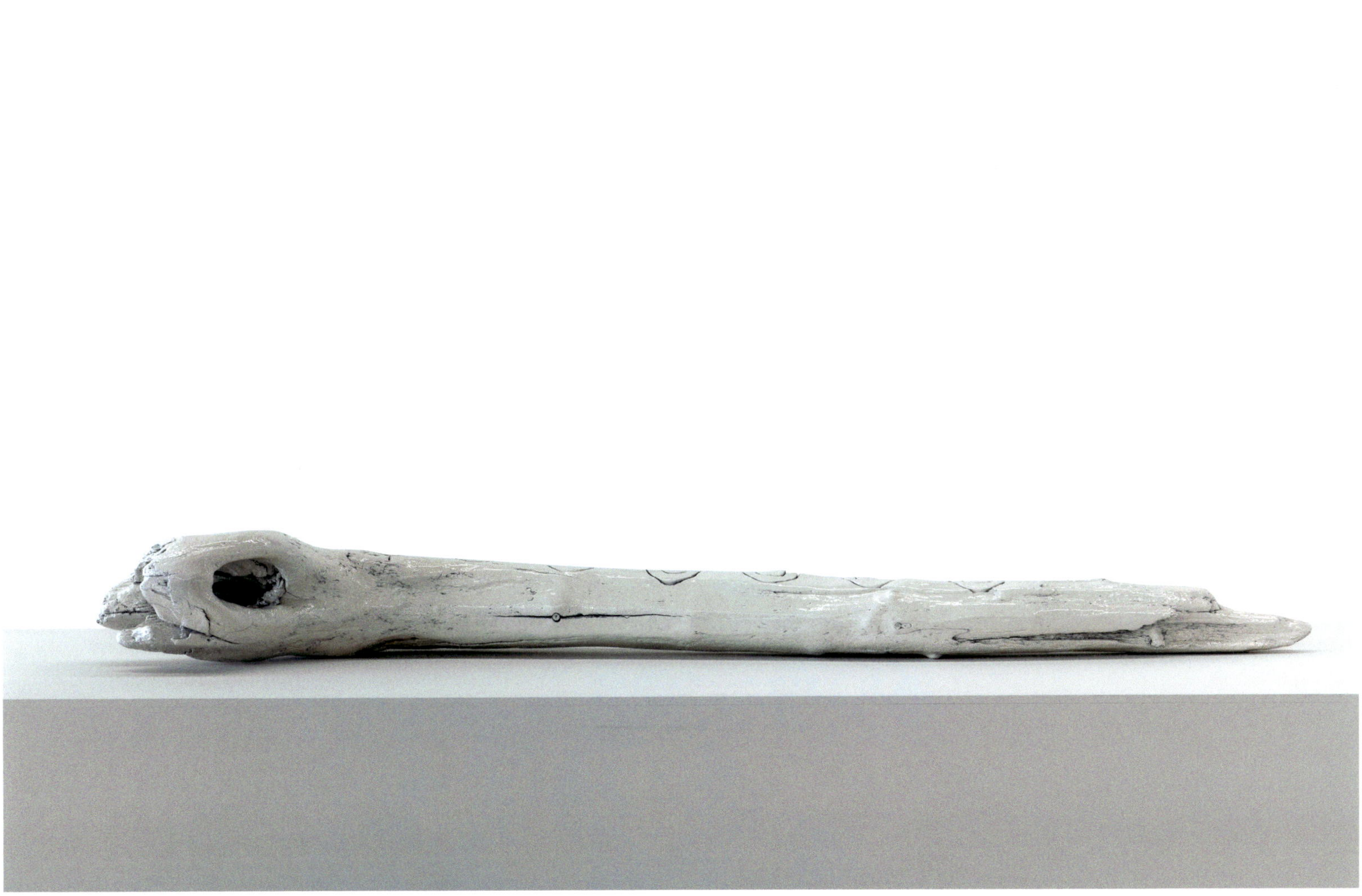

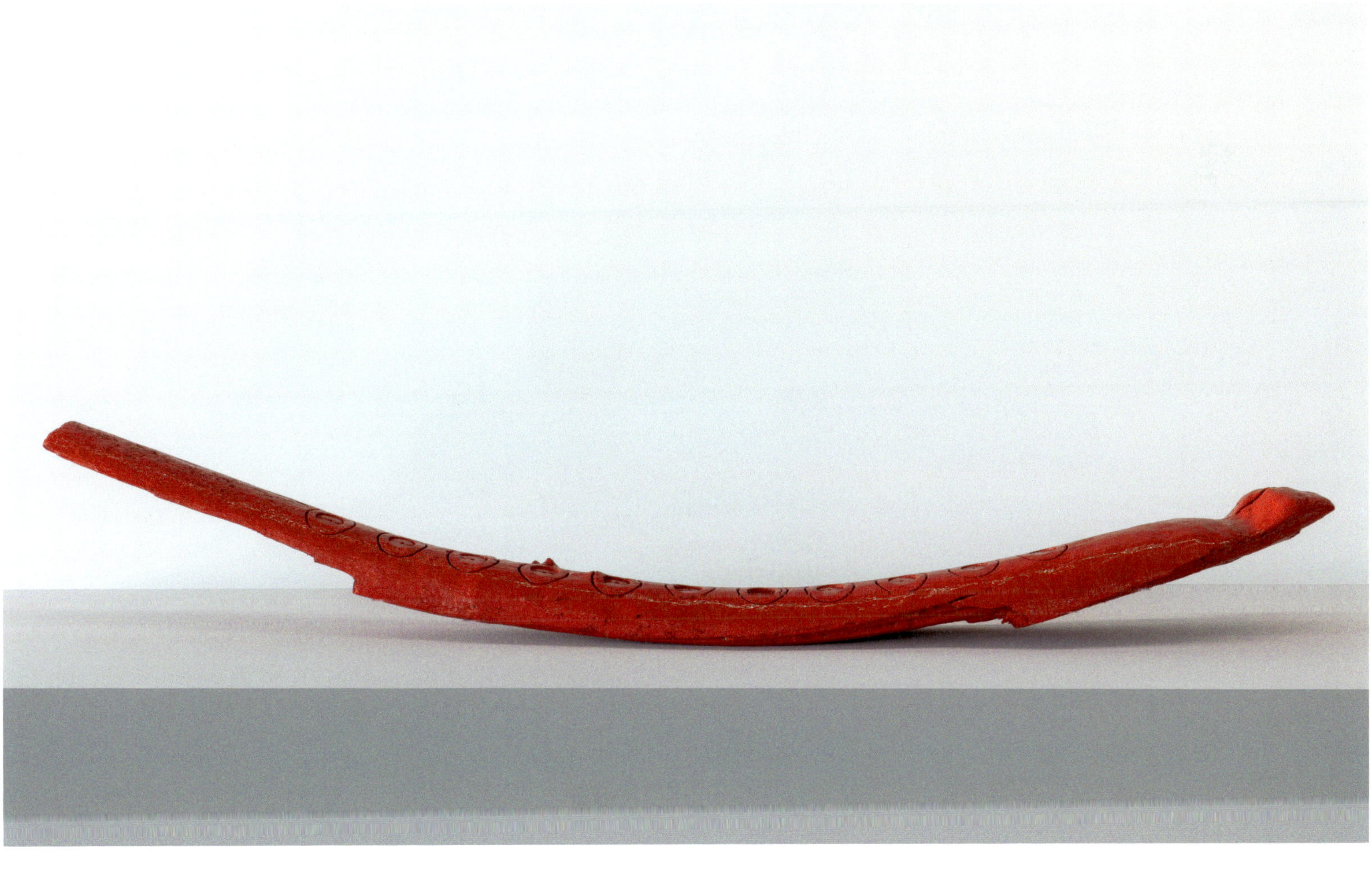

Portable Secrets

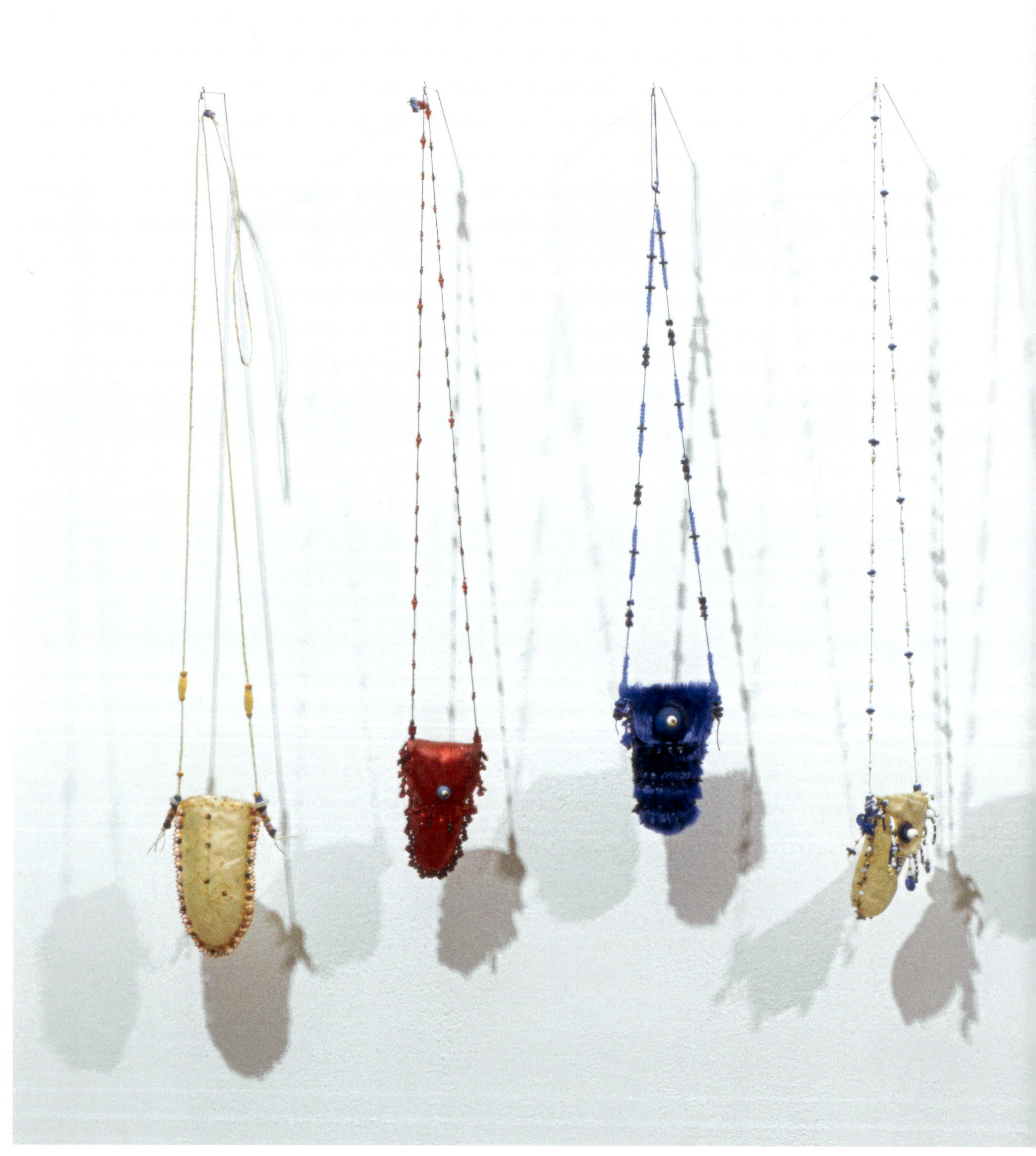

Portable Secrets, 2004. Seal skin, walrus stomach, seal intestine, glass bead, nylon thread, walrus ivory, synthetic sinew, dimensions variable. Private collection. Photograph by Kevin G. Smith.

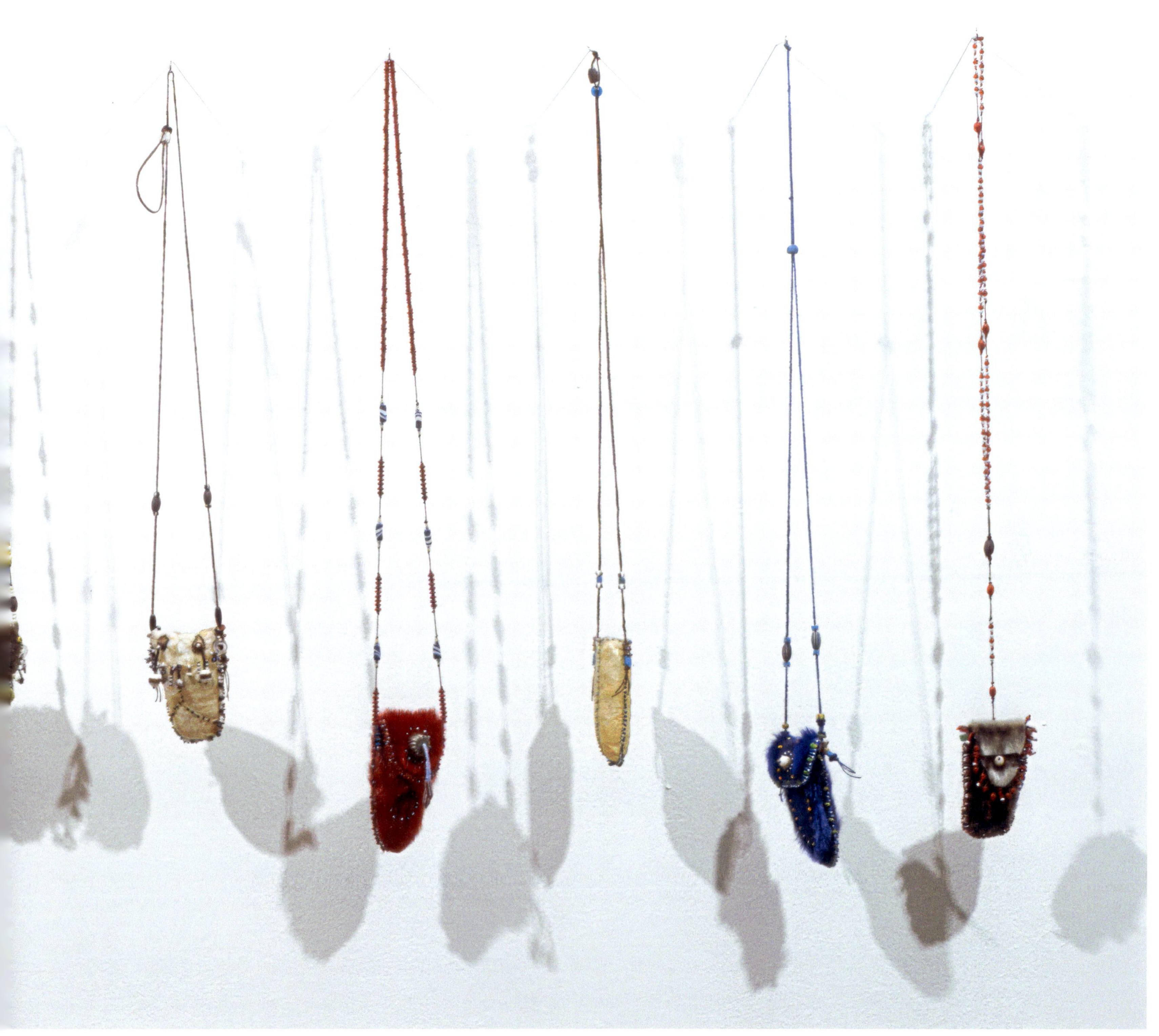

Prick

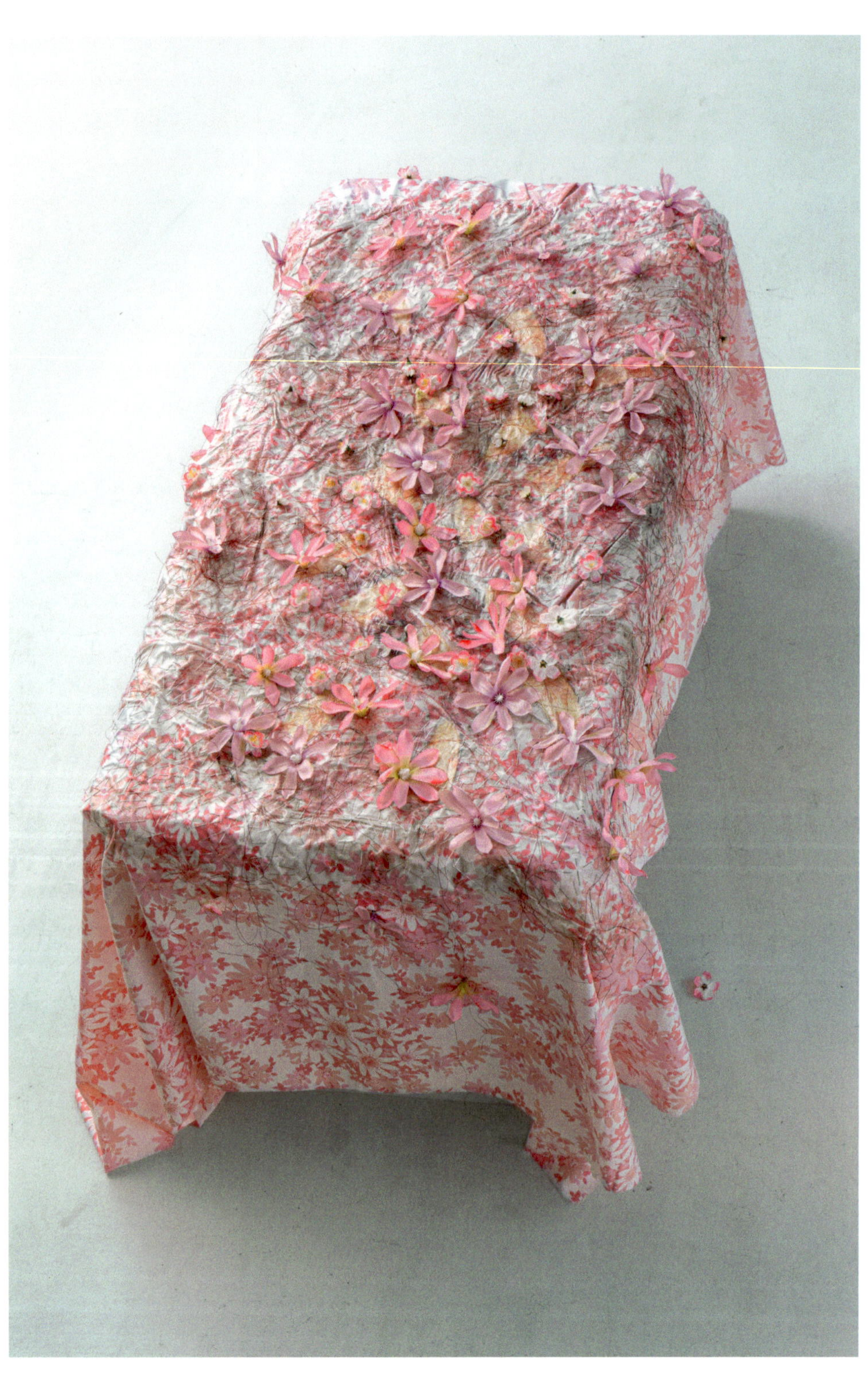

Prick, 2018. Found fabric, synthetic flowers, steel needles, collagen sausage casing, acrylic polymer, polyurethane, dimensions variable. Photographs by Chris Arend.

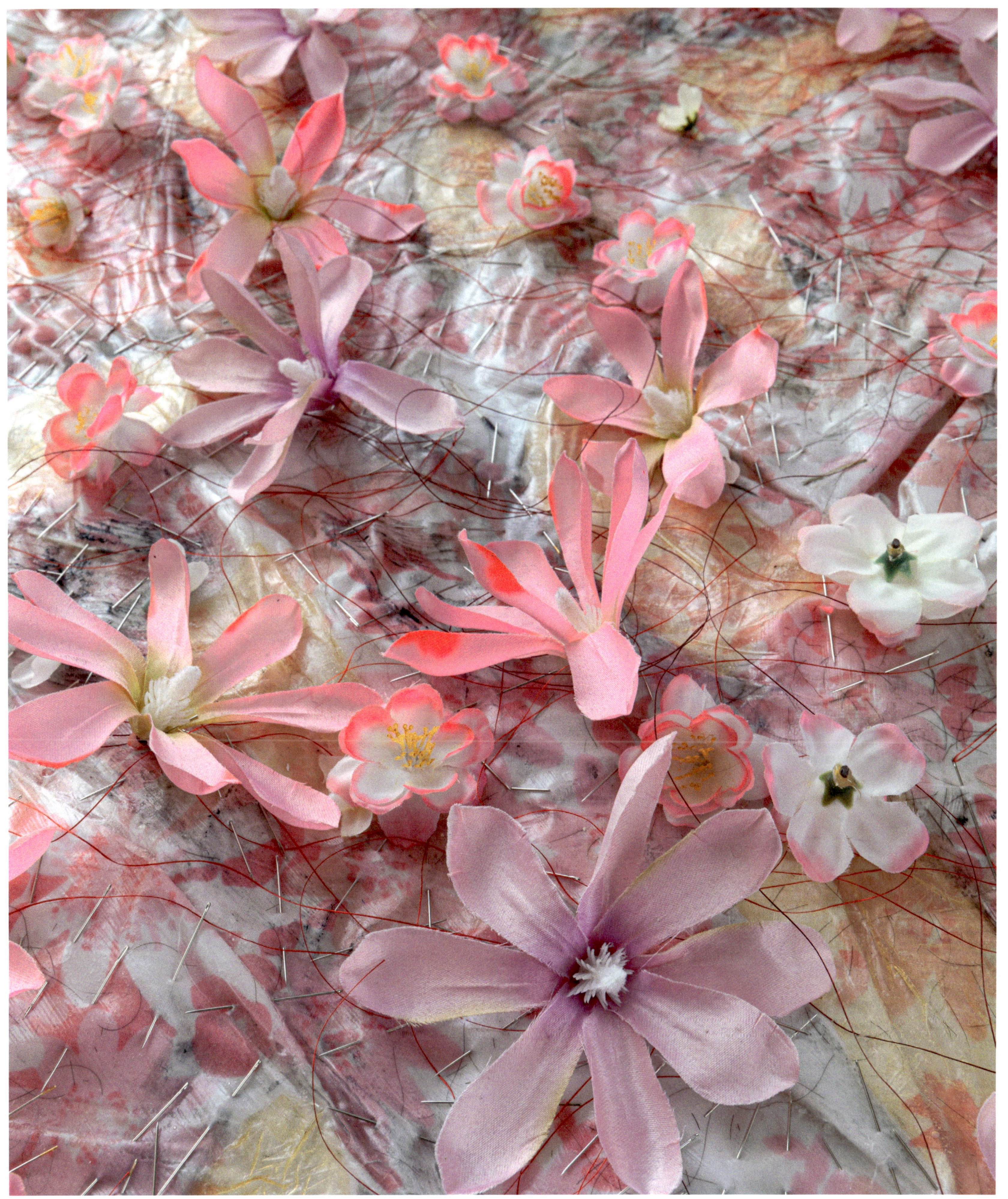

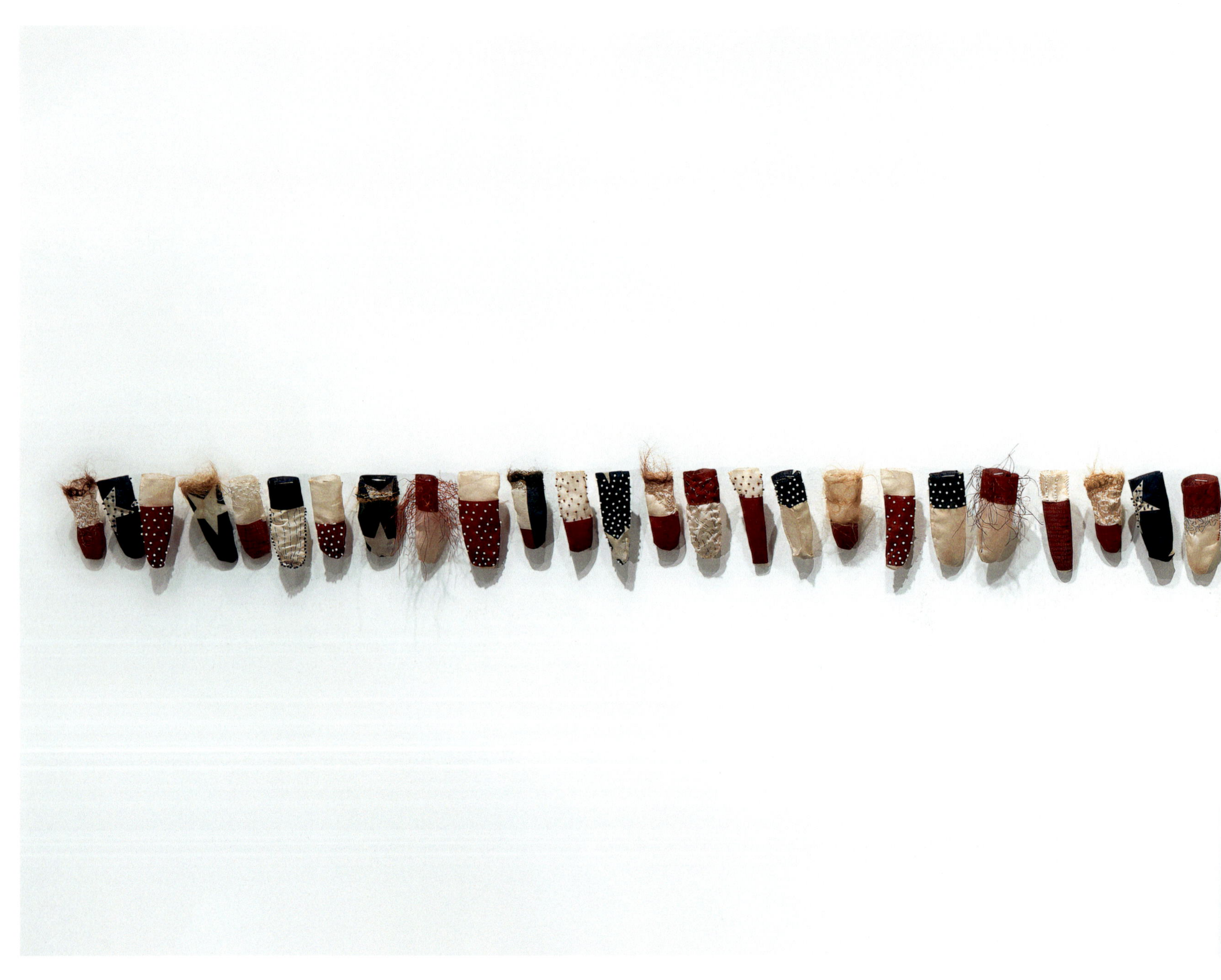

Red, White and Blue Small Secrets, 2019-present. Cotton fabric, human hair, glass bead, nylon thread, steel pins, dimensions variable. Private collection. Photograph courtesy of the Minus Space Gallery.

Red White and Blue
Small Secrets

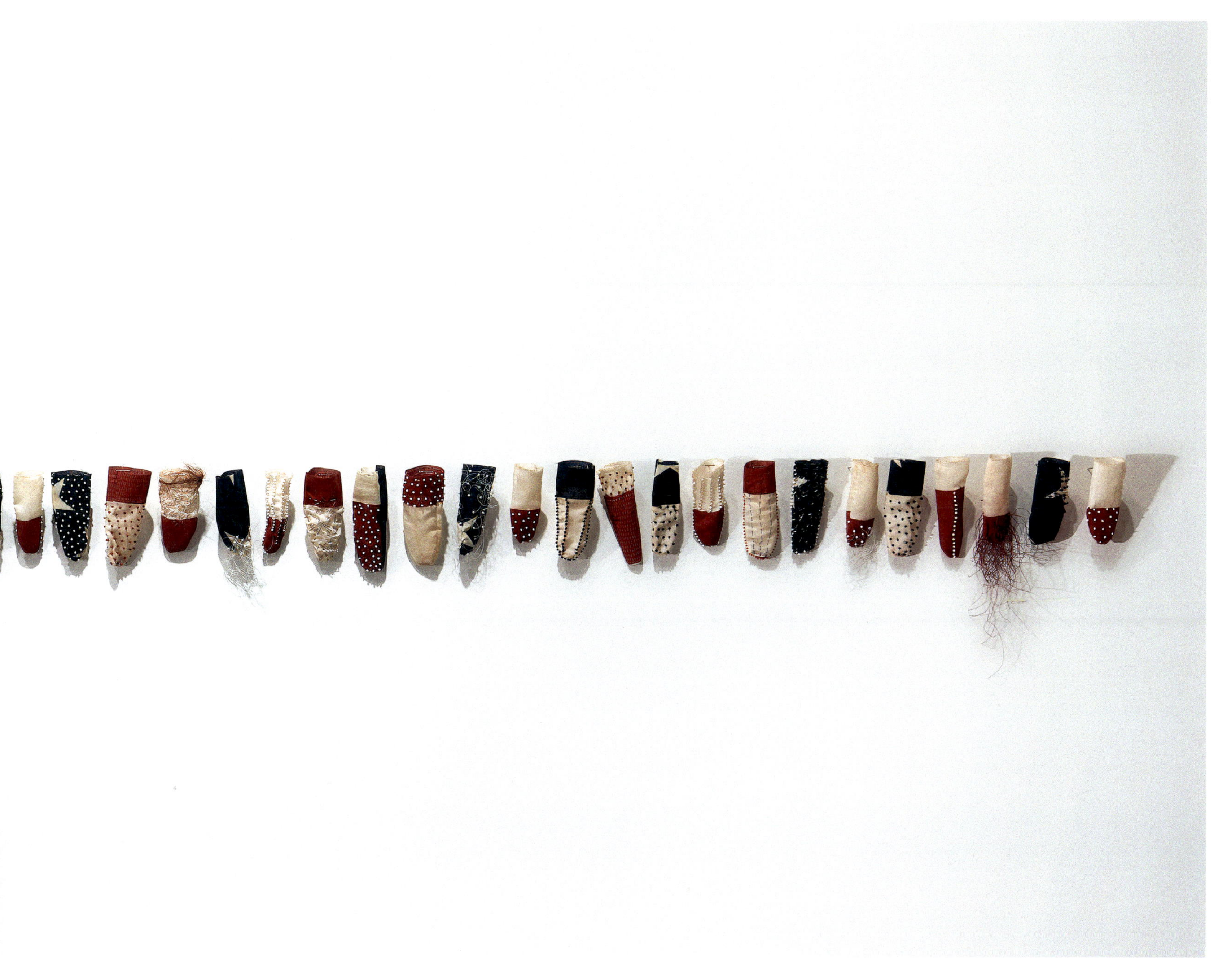

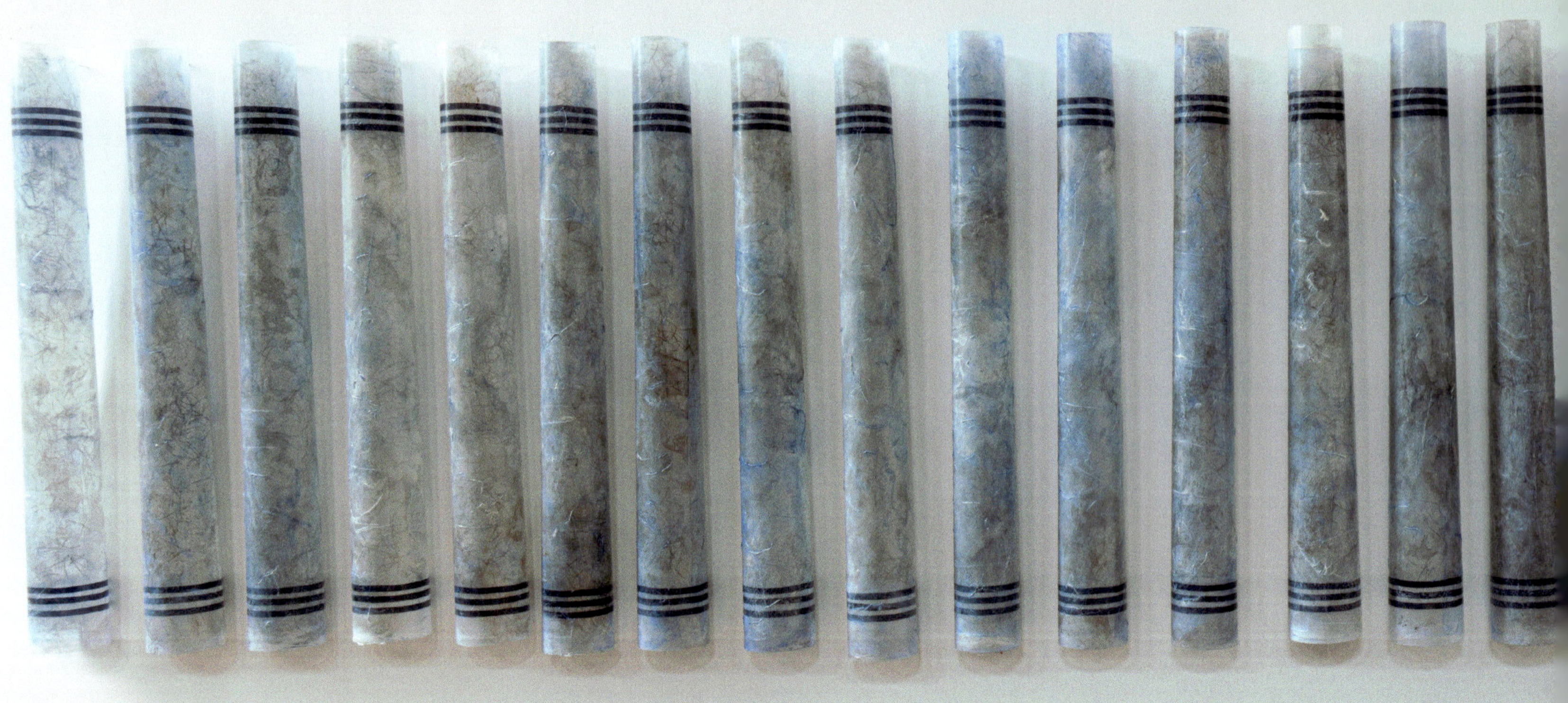

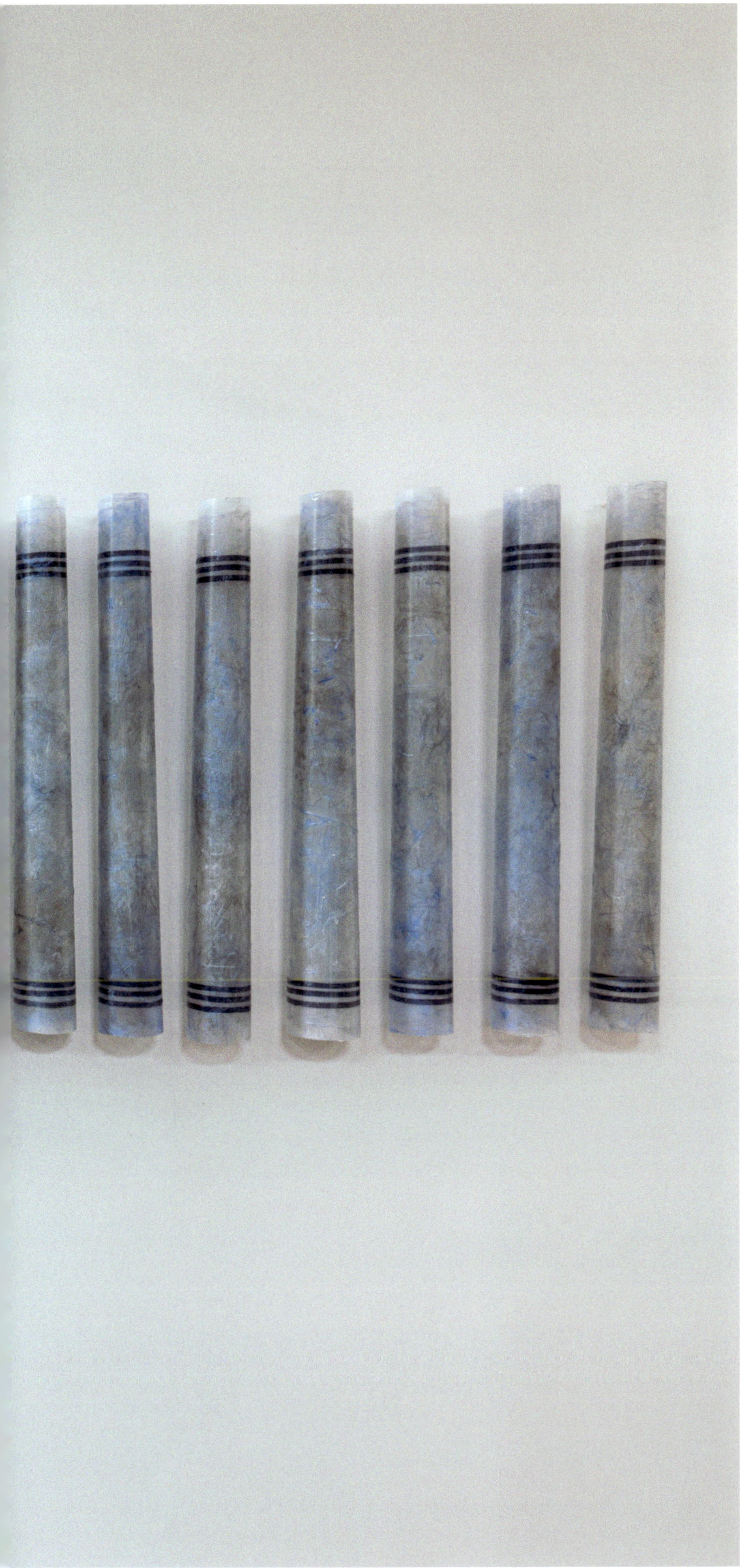

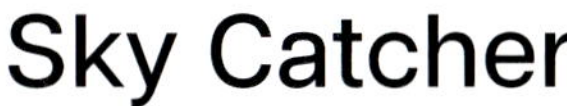

Sky Catcher

Sky Catcher, 2017. Archival mylar, acrylic polymer, reindeer fur, steel pin, nylon thread, dimensions variable. Photograph by Chris Arend.

Small Secrets

Small Secrets, 2018. Reindeer and sheep rawhide, glass bead, human hair, acrylic paint, steel pins, nylon thread, dimensions variable. Collection of the Anchorage Museum. Photographs by Chris Arend.

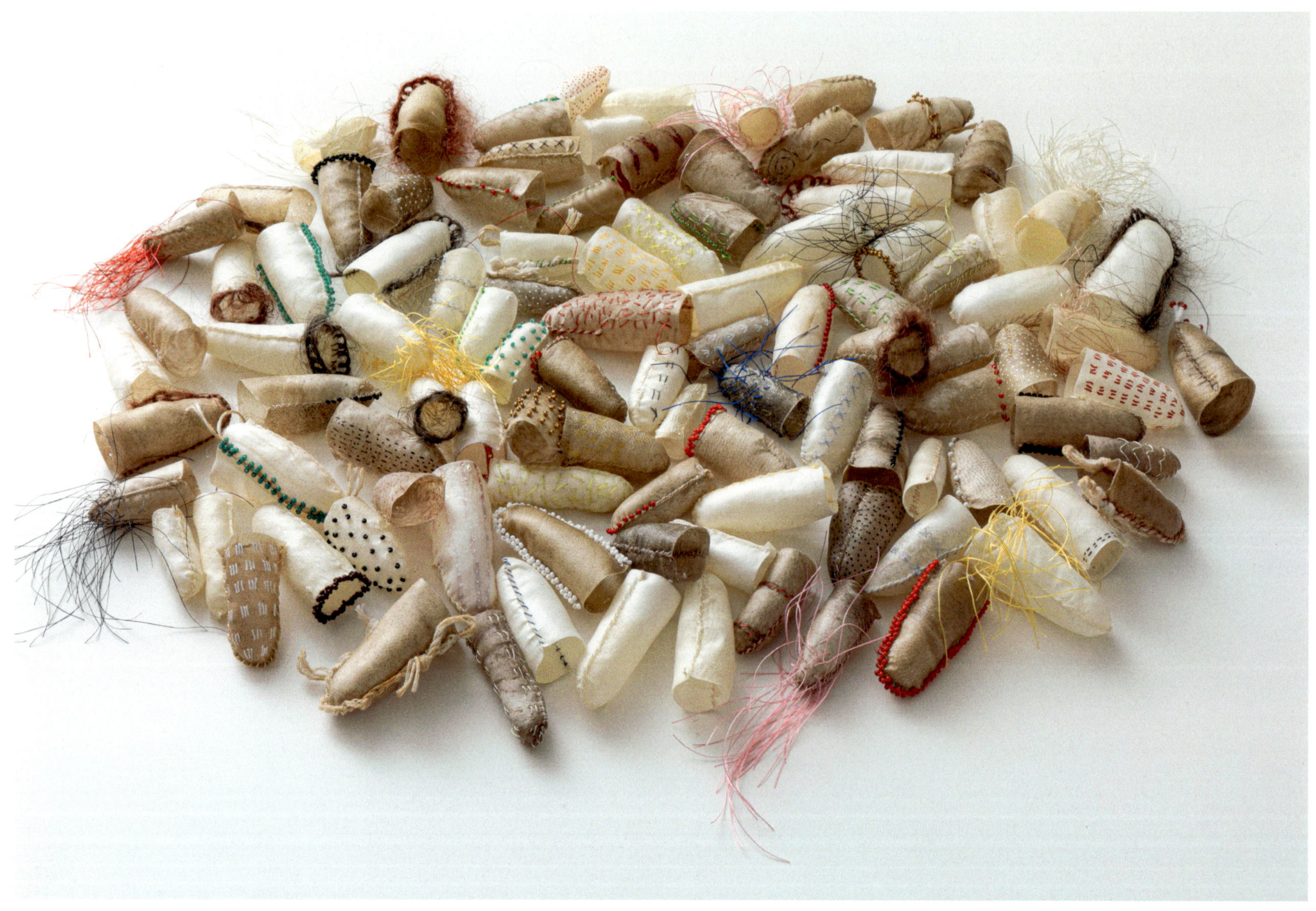

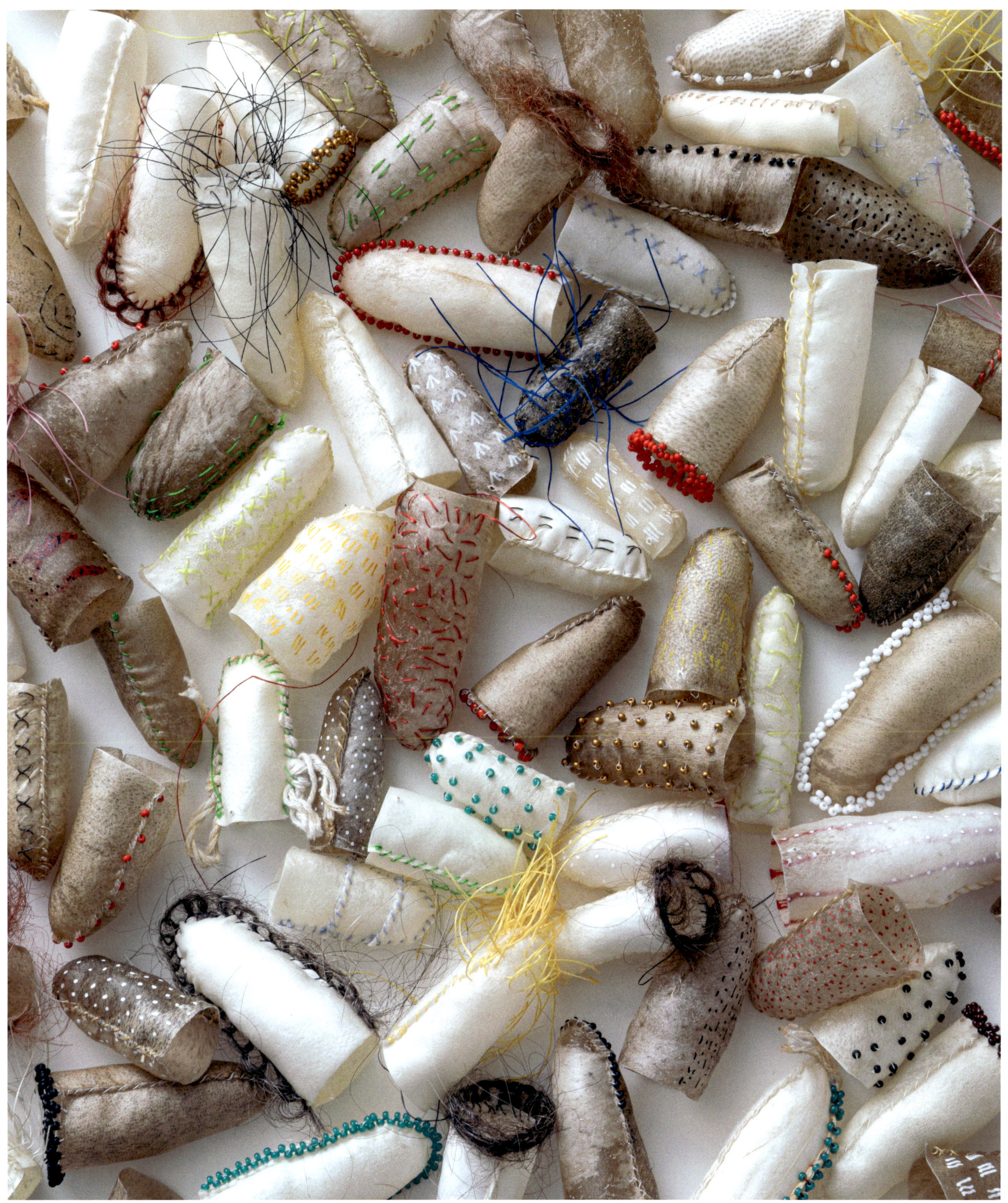

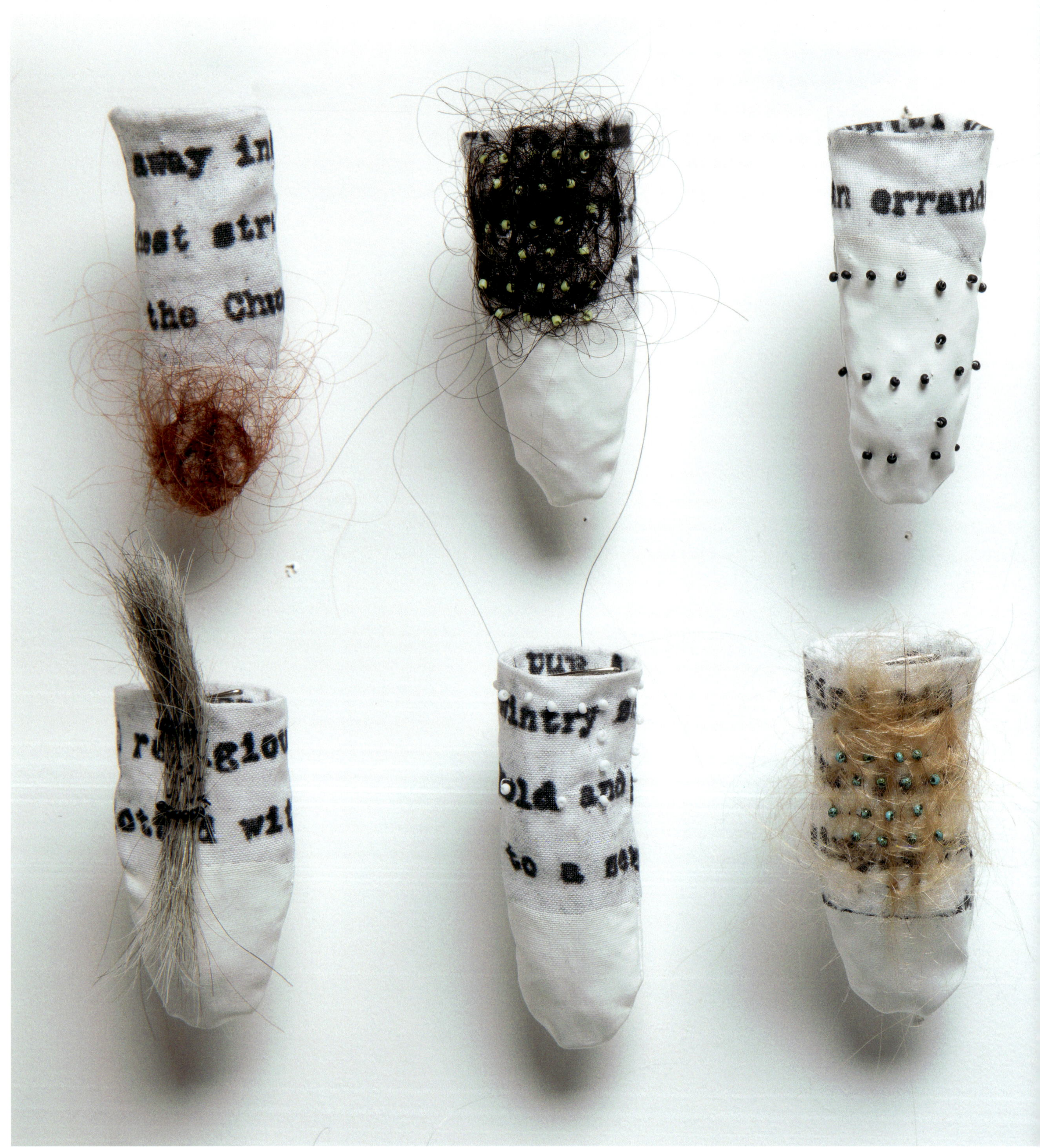

Small Secrets Sheldon Jackson

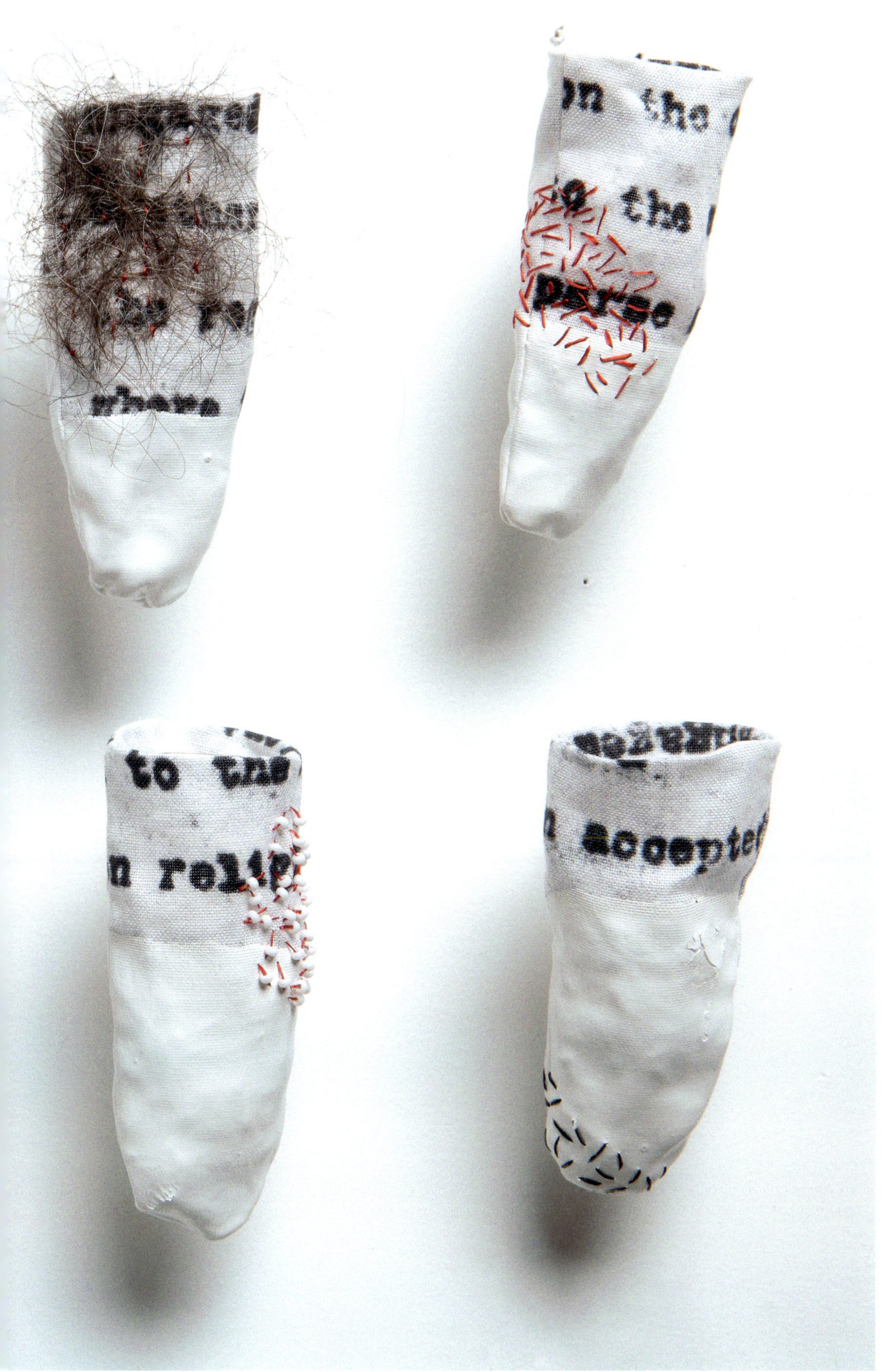

Small Secrets Sheldon Jackson, 2021. Painted fabric, glass bead, human hair, steel pins, nylon thread. Collection of Union College, Schenectady, NY. Photograph by Chris Arend.

Small Secrets
Sheldon Jackson

The sculpture *Small Secrets: Sheldon Jackson* began when curator Julie Lohnes invited Kelliher-Combs to participate in a project involving the archival records of Sheldon Jackson, the larger-than-life Presbyterian missionary who was credited with saving a "simple race from extinction" in the state of Alaska. Today we know his and others' approach to the education and assimilation of the First Peoples of the United States has had far-reaching negative consequences. He wielded influence in the United States government, ignoring the separation of church and state to create a system of education that initiated the systematic erasure of entire generations of Alaska Native histories, languages, customs, and families. As he set about educating Alaska Natives through menial labor, sending some as far away as the Indian Industrial School in Carlisle, Pennsylvania, he collaborated with other religious denominations in dividing up the state of Alaska to right the "heathen" ways of Alaska Native peoples. These missions often harbored sex offenders who abused their congregation.

The trauma of this history is still fresh. Kelliher-Combs is a daughter of parents who were educated at boarding schools, thousands of miles away from their homes and families. Her family has seen and experienced firsthand the results of Jackson's and others' policies. Often historical trauma creates "secrets," and despite the challenging and negative taboo of talking about these issues, they must be voiced in order to promote healing and awareness and to break the cycle of abuse.

Small Secrets Sheldon Jackson, 2021. Painted fabric, glass bead, human hair, steel pins, nylon thread. Collection of Union College, Schenectady, NY. Photograph by Chris Arend.

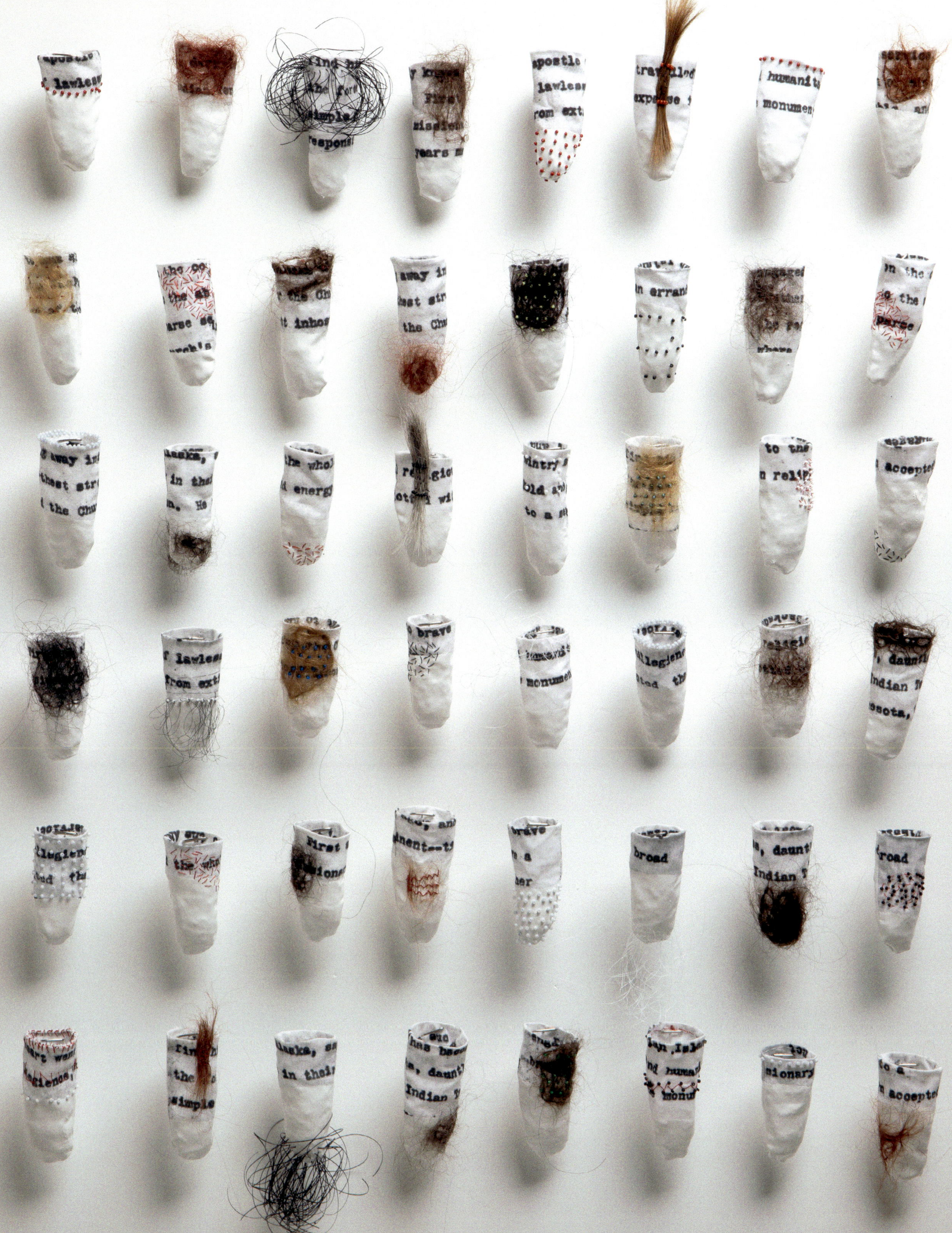

Small White Secrets

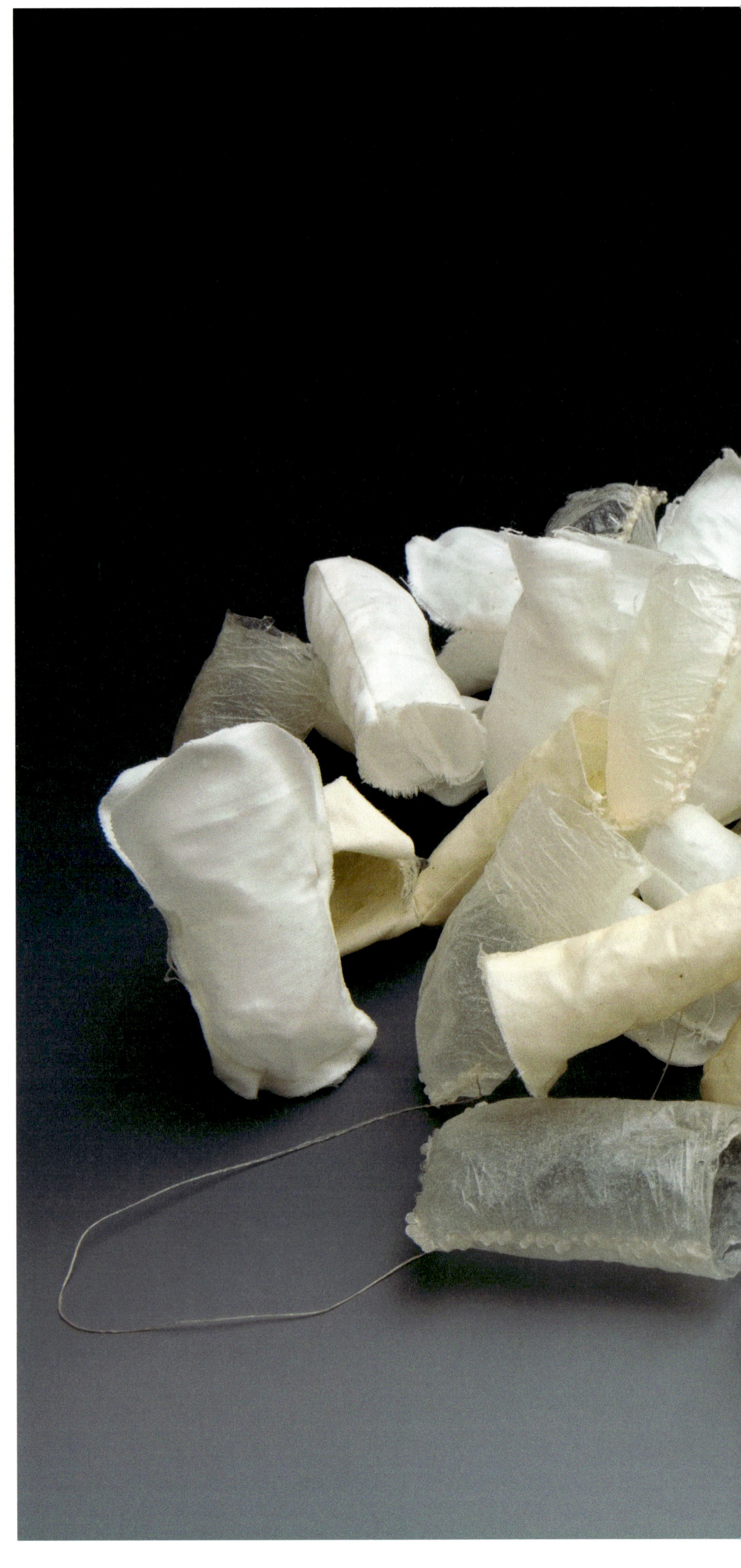

Small White Secrets, 2006. Painted fabric, glass bead, human hair, steel pins, nylon thread. Private collection. Photograph by Chris Arend.

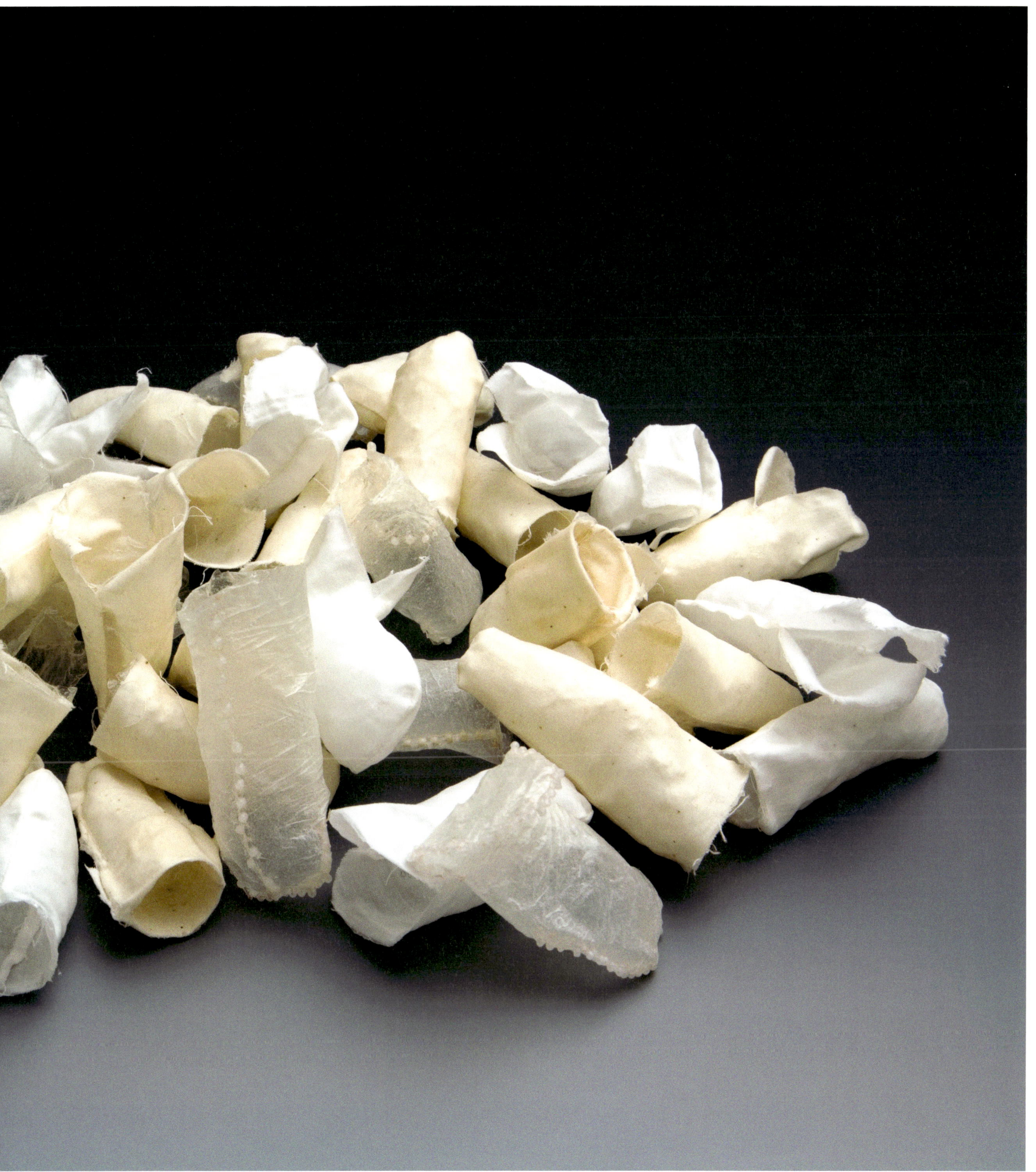

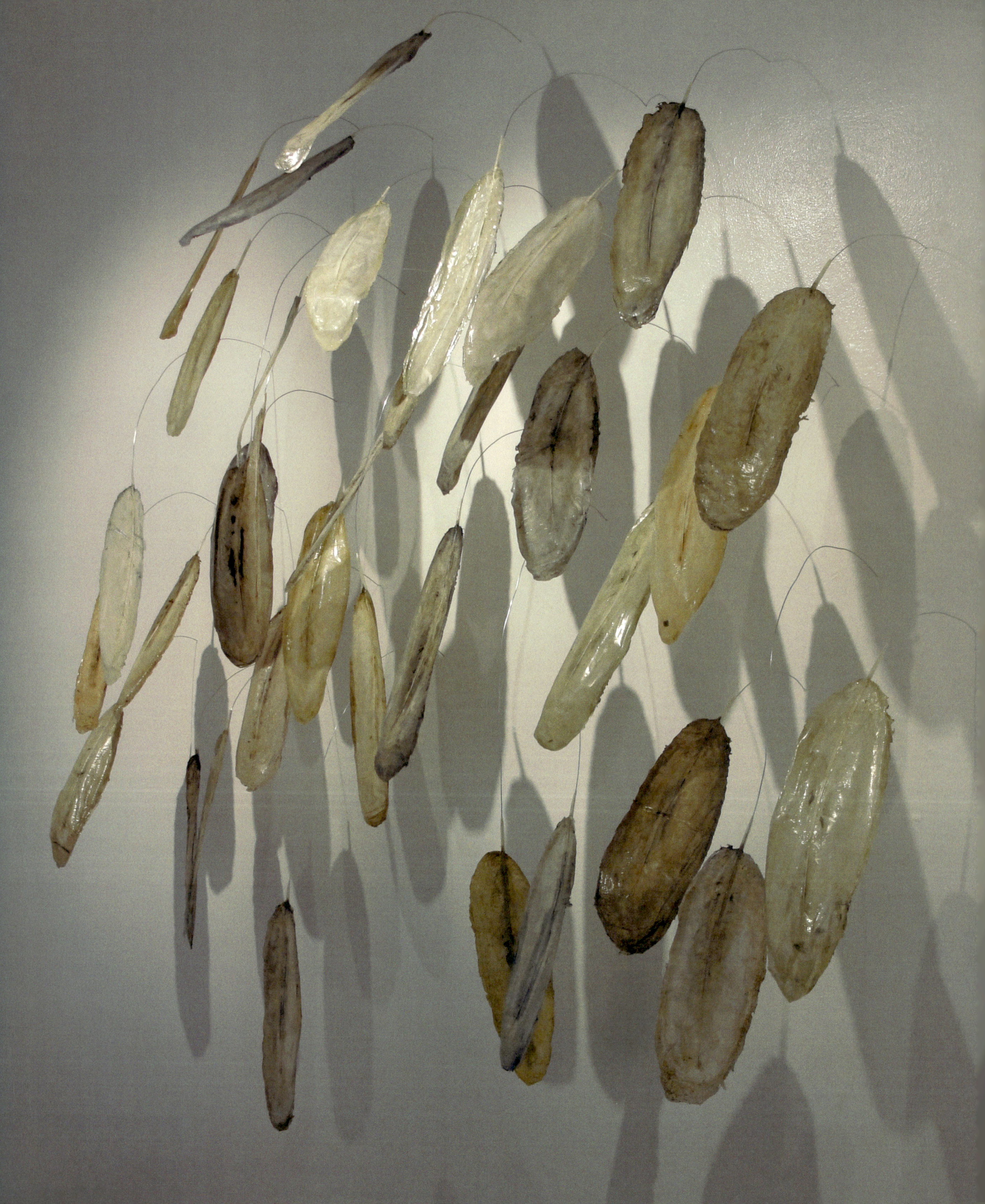

INSTALLATIONS

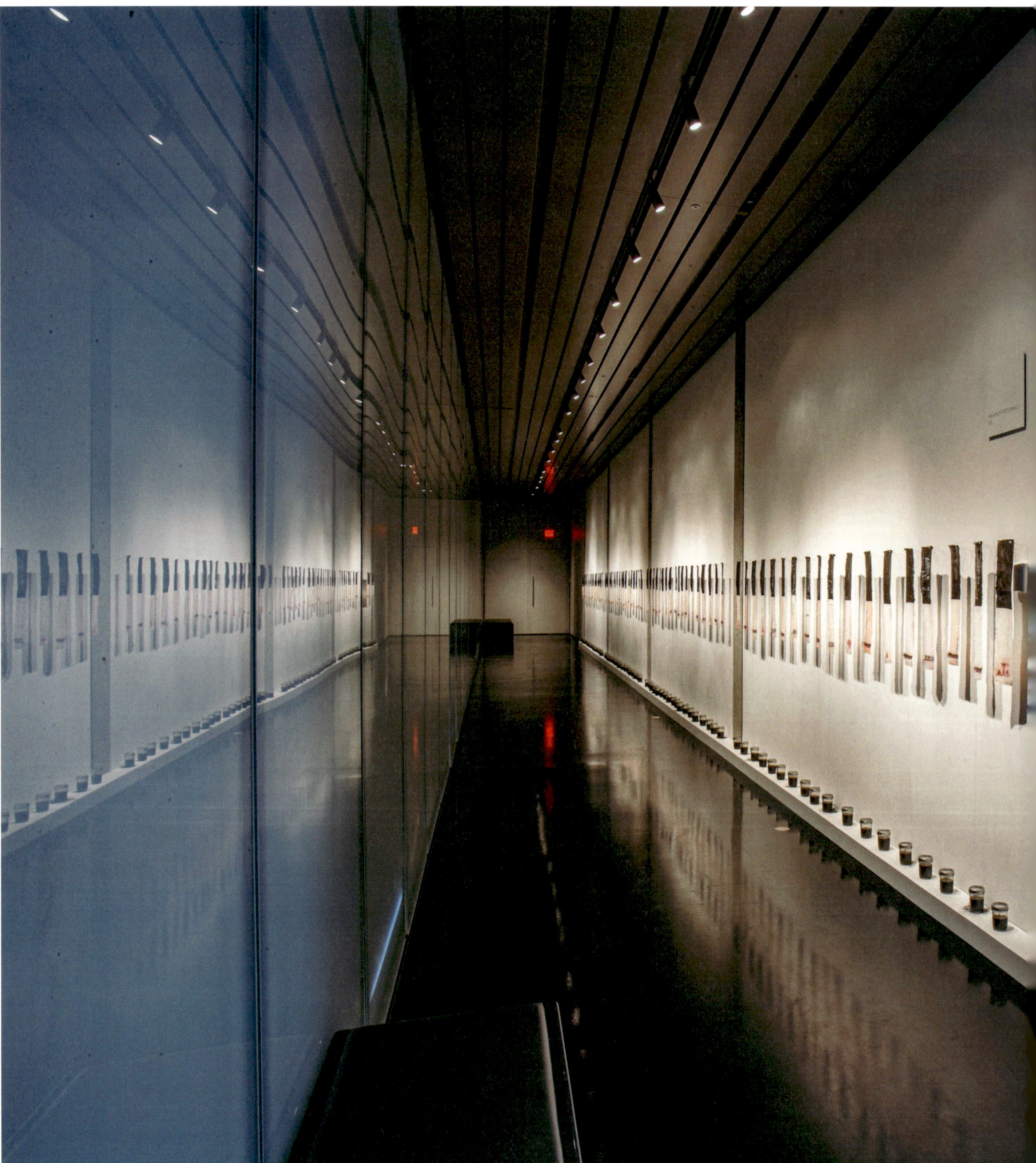

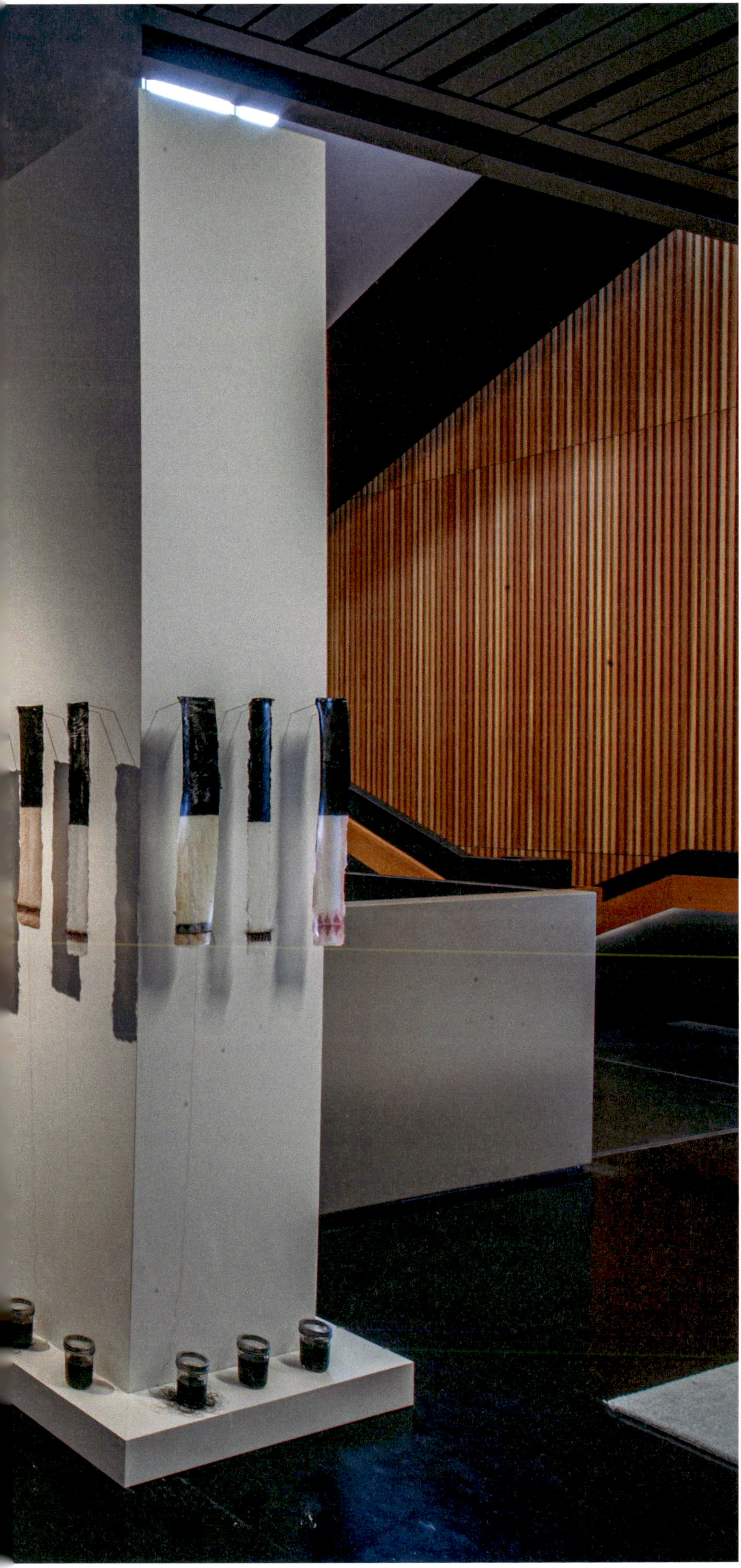

Black and White

As a child, Kelliher-Combs grew up with the teaching that the land would provide. Today, new ideas about that sentiment abound. *Black and White* is a comment on new subsistence practices. The imagery is inspired by maktaaq—whale blubber and skin, a common food for Iñupiaq and Athabascan people. The stitched, synthetic skin is adorned with glass trade beads and human hair. The qupak patterns are from Iñupiaq and Athabascan parka trim. Each maktaaq strip is hung over a glass canning jar. The meats, berries, fish, and other foods these jars usually contain have been replaced with used motor oil, representing the new subsistence that exists through our dependence on oil extraction. Three generations of Alaskans have worked on the oil fields of Alaska's North Slope, extracting crude to feed and house their families. *Black and White* illustrates a paradoxical situation: relying on the western economic model, but through an Indigenous worldview. It is not a black and white world.

Black and White installation at the Anchorage Museum, 2012. Acrylic polymer, glass beads, human hair, paper, canning jar, nylon thread, used motor oil, steel pins, dimensions variable. Photograph by the artist.

Black and White

▾ *Black and White* installation at the Anchorage Museum, 2012. Acrylic polymer, glass beads, human hair, paper, canning jar, nylon thread, used motor oil, steel pins, dimensions variable. Photograph by the artist.

▸ Detail of *Black and White* installation at the Anchorage Museum, 2012. Acrylic polymer, glass beads, human hair, paper, canning jar, nylon thread, used motor oil, steel pins, dimensions variable. Photograph by the artist.

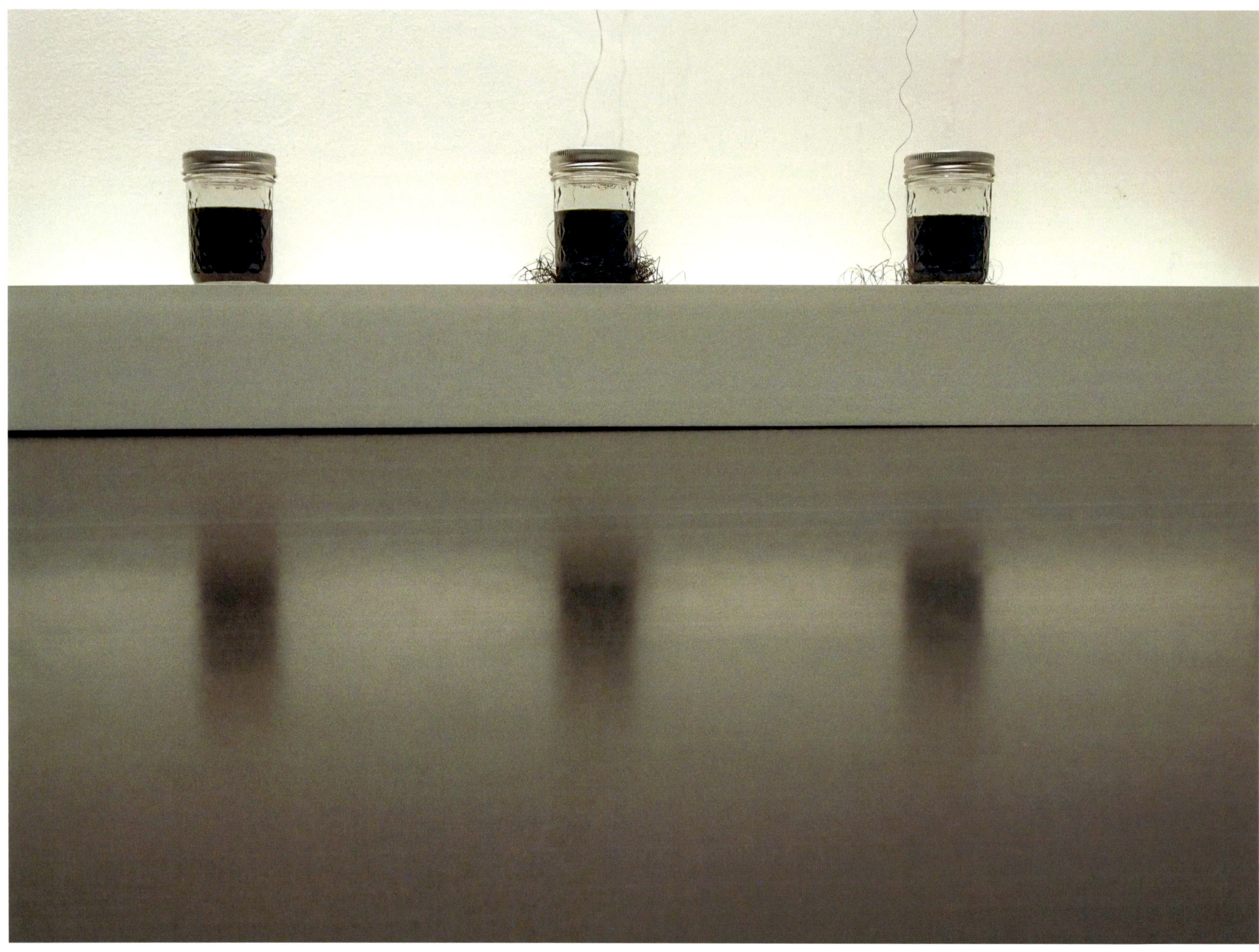

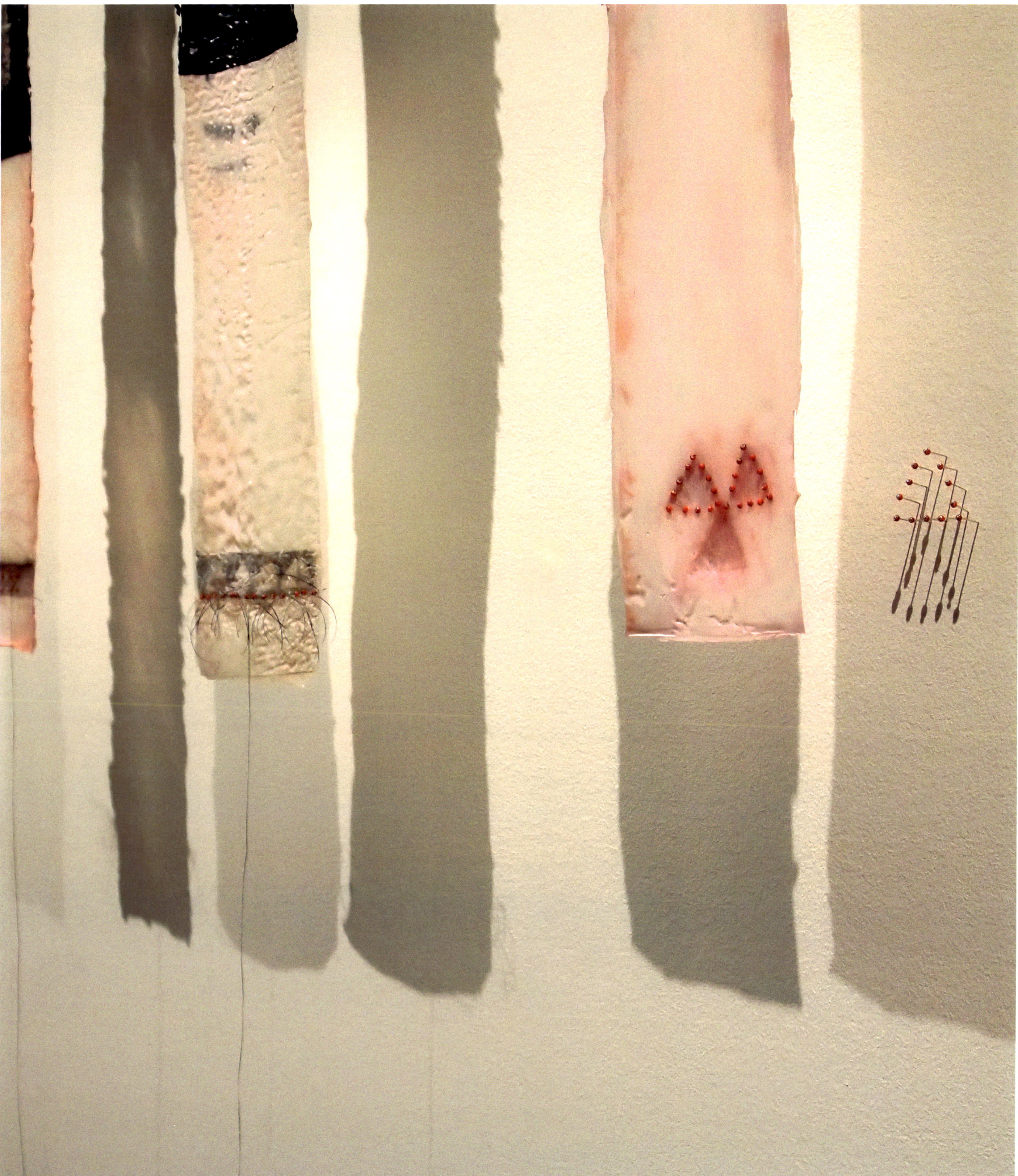

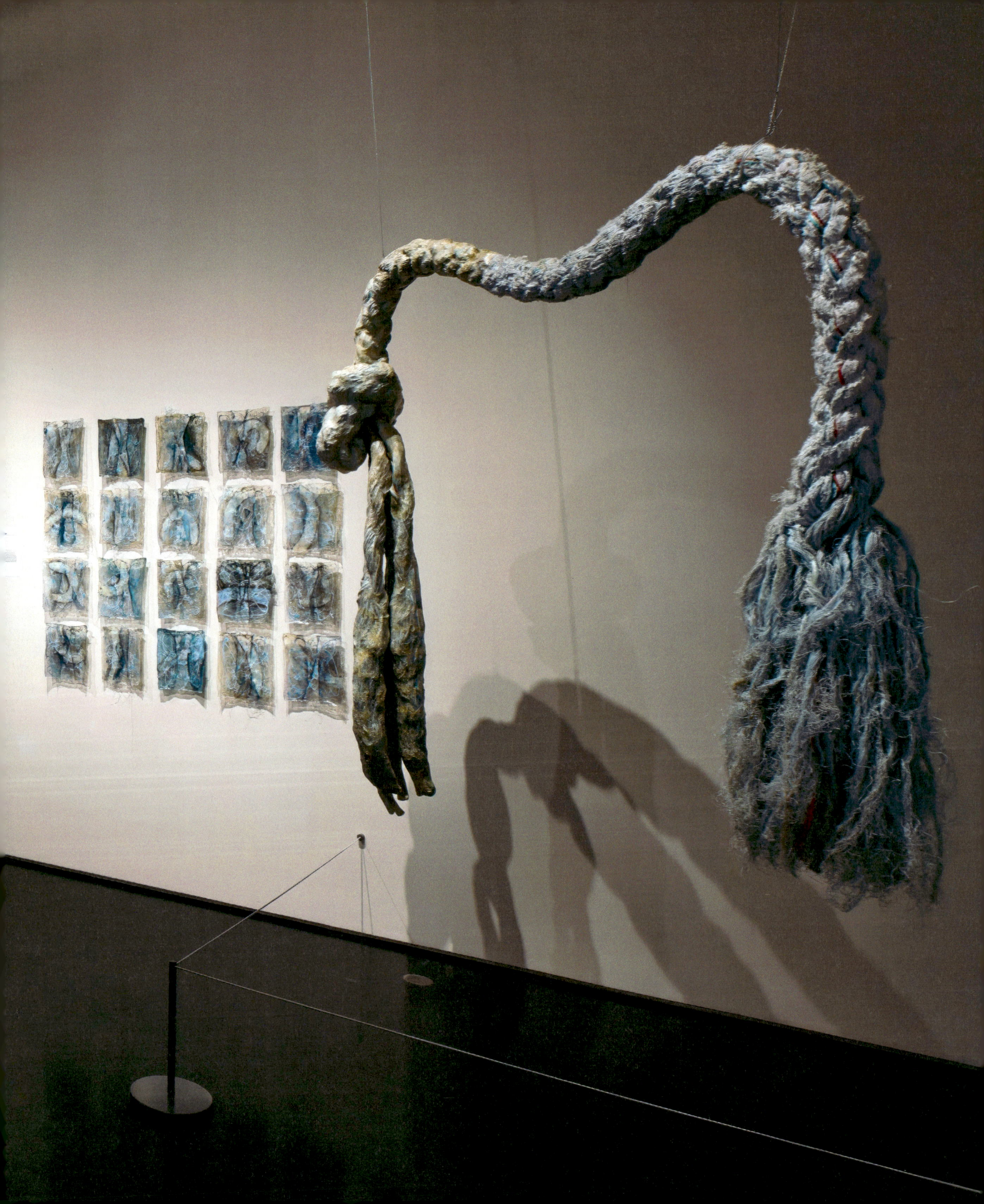

Sea Woman by Taqralik Partridge

you are always looking to climb
up, up above the tallest tree
up, up past the highest peak
up, up beyond the clouds to the stratosphere
to your own glory you would build yourself a monument
as high as the edge of the sky

but I, I bring the clouds to the ground
I, I am always traveling down

In your mother's womb I held you
of your thirst I quenched you
in your hunger, you were fed
through all your years I carry you
and when your days are over
I will take back your dead

I am lowly water
poured out on the ground
I have no voice but what the wind gives me,
what the moon pulls out of me,
what the rush down, down, down
into the earth can tell

my tributaries and my estuaries
my lakes, my creeks, my rivers
my disappearing glaciers
my mark upon the shore
the rain upon your face
the early morning dew

the sleet, the snow, the hail
the tide, the flood, the sneaking mouth
of cracks climbed up in the ice
the mist lain heavy in the valley
my deepest sweetest wells
all these are me and I
am them
from my fathoms to my swells

I will take your effluent
I swallow your brackish waste
I will wash through your greed
suck up your grief
course through your desire
the slick of your industry I let rest
upon my seas
your tailings in my ponds
your poisons in my streams
in my depths I harbour particles
of every discarded treasure
you thought you could never live without

I, I bring the clouds to the ground
I, I am always traveling down

build your monuments
climb your towers
pour me and pour me and pour me again
you will have your due
and I, I will have mine

◂ *Blue Aeon* installation at the Anchorage Museum, 2014. Mixed media, dimensions variable. Private collection. Photograph courtesy of the Anchorage Museum.

Goodbye

Goodbye is a memorial to those who have lost their lives to suicide. This personal and deeply wounding experience is tragically common. Within this exhibit are single gloves and mittens representing the many who have taken their own lives. Alaska is two times above the national average in the rate of suicide, and Alaska Natives are three times above the national average.

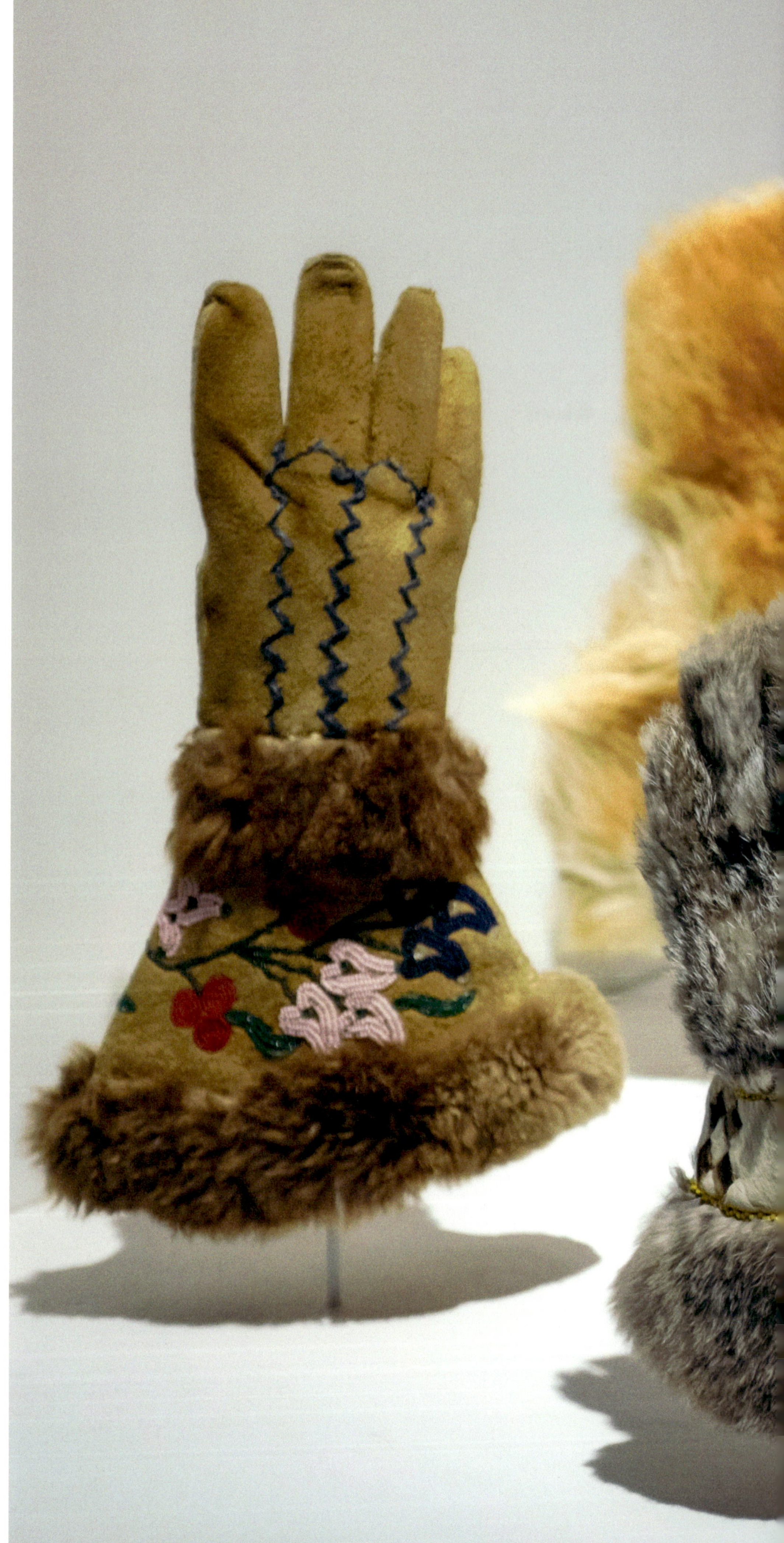

Goodbye, 2018. Installation of cultural belongings from the Anchorage Museum's collection at the Korundi Museum, Rovaniemi, Finland. Photograph by the artist.

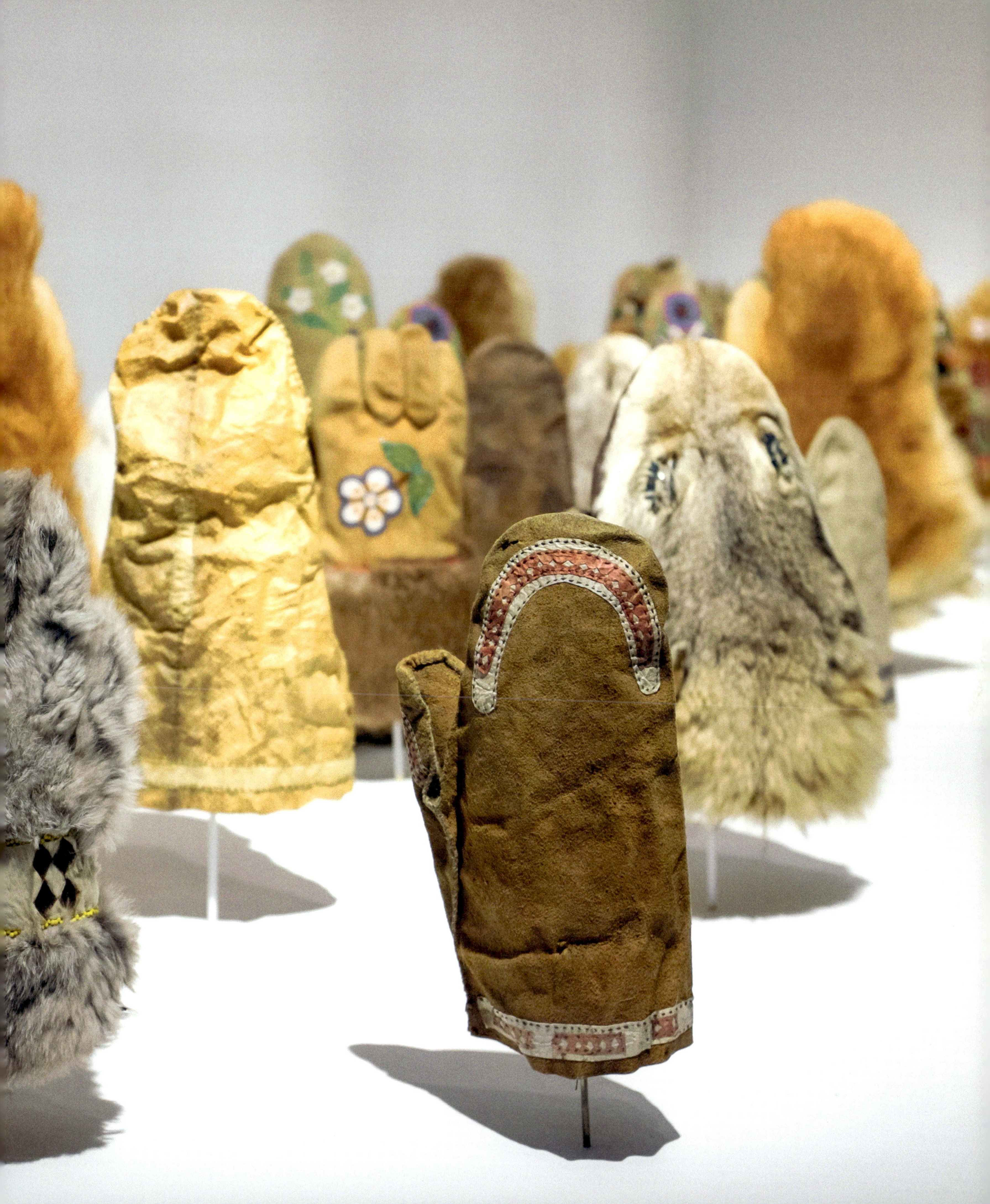

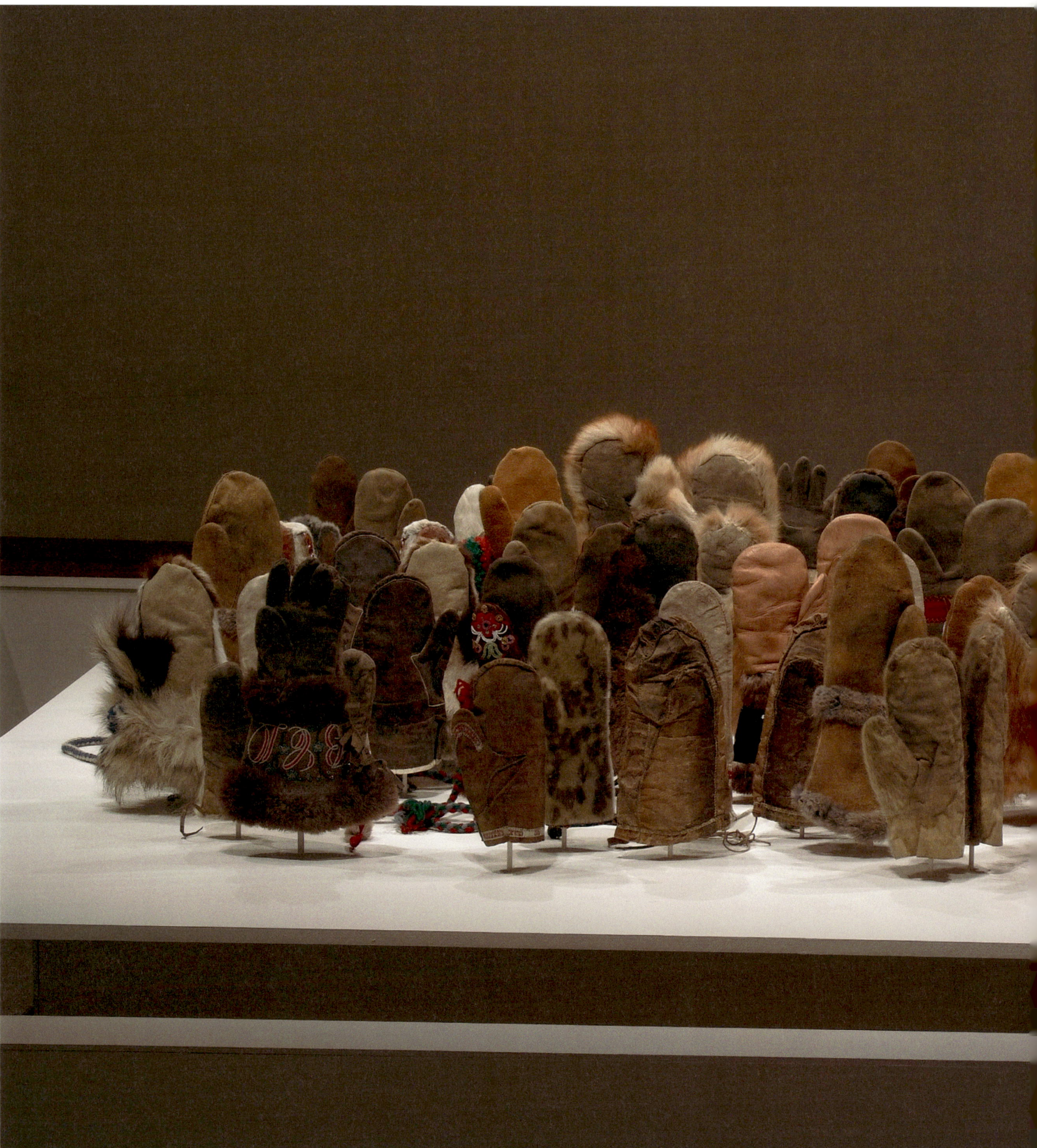

Goodbye

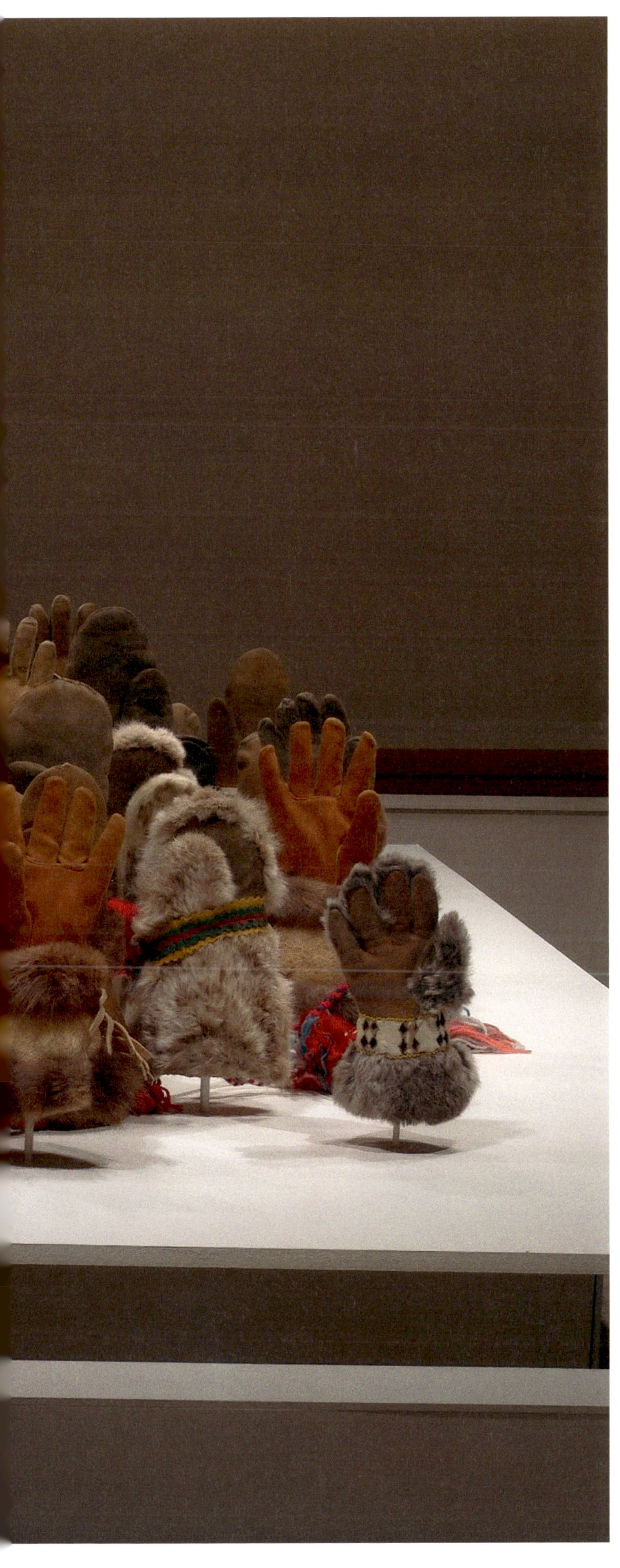

Goodbye, 2007. Installation of cultural belongings from the collection of the Anchorage Museum. Photograph by the artist.

Credible Idiot Strings

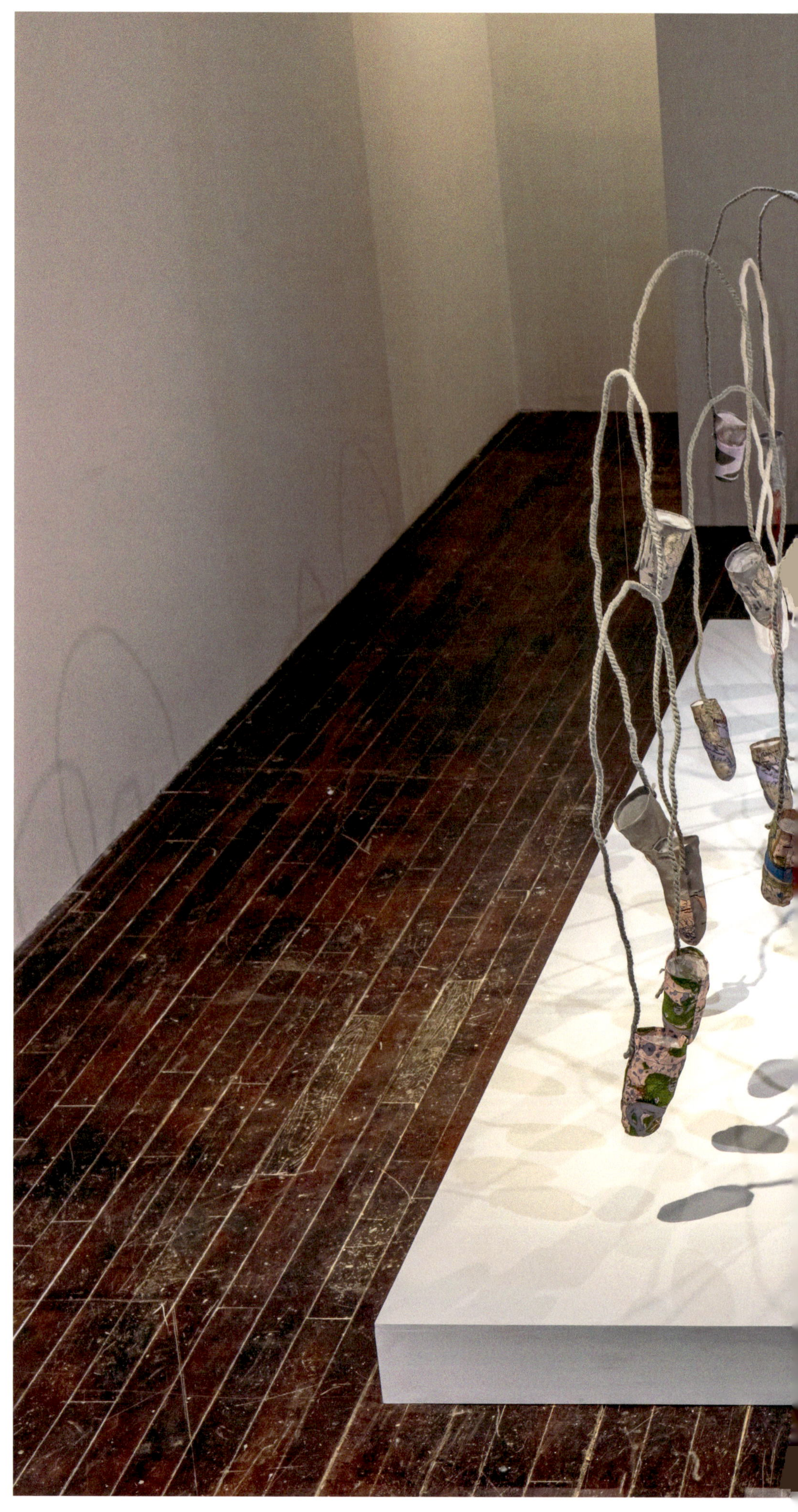

Credible Idiot Strings installation, 2022. Printed maps, wool yarn, steel wire, polyurethane, glass beads, nylon thread. Private collection. Photograph courtesy of the Mattress Factory.

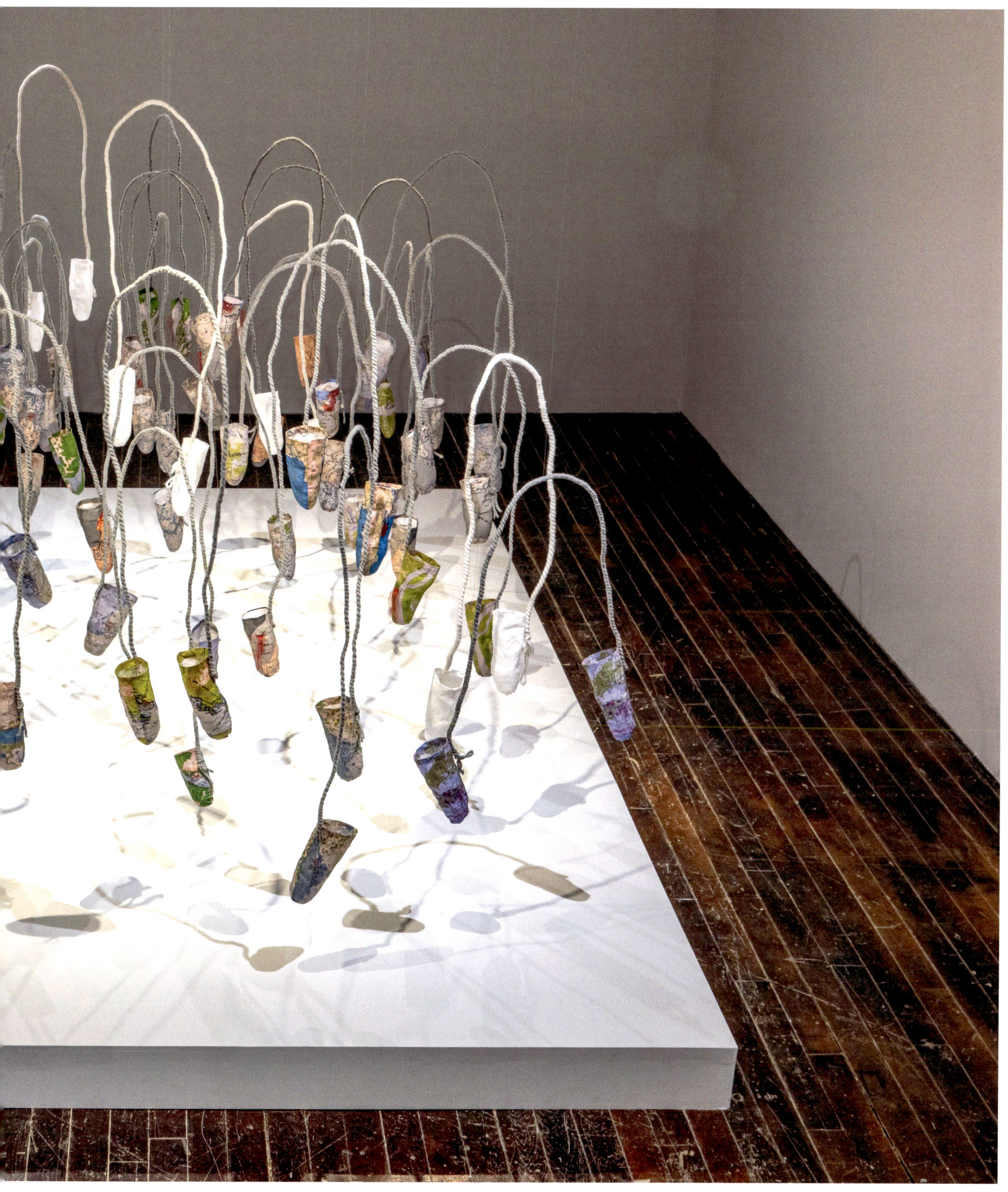

Credible Idiot Strings

Credible Idiot Strings II, installation at the Power Plant Gallery, Toronto, 2022. Printed maps, wool yarn, steel wire, polyurethane, glass beads, nylon thread. Tia Collection, Santa Fe, NM Photograph courtesy of the Power Plant Gallery.

Credible Idiot Strings (detail), 2022. Installation at the Mattress Factory, Pittsburg PA. Printed maps, wool yarn, steel wire, polyurethane, glass bead, nylon thread. Private collection. Photograph courtesy of the Mattress Factory.

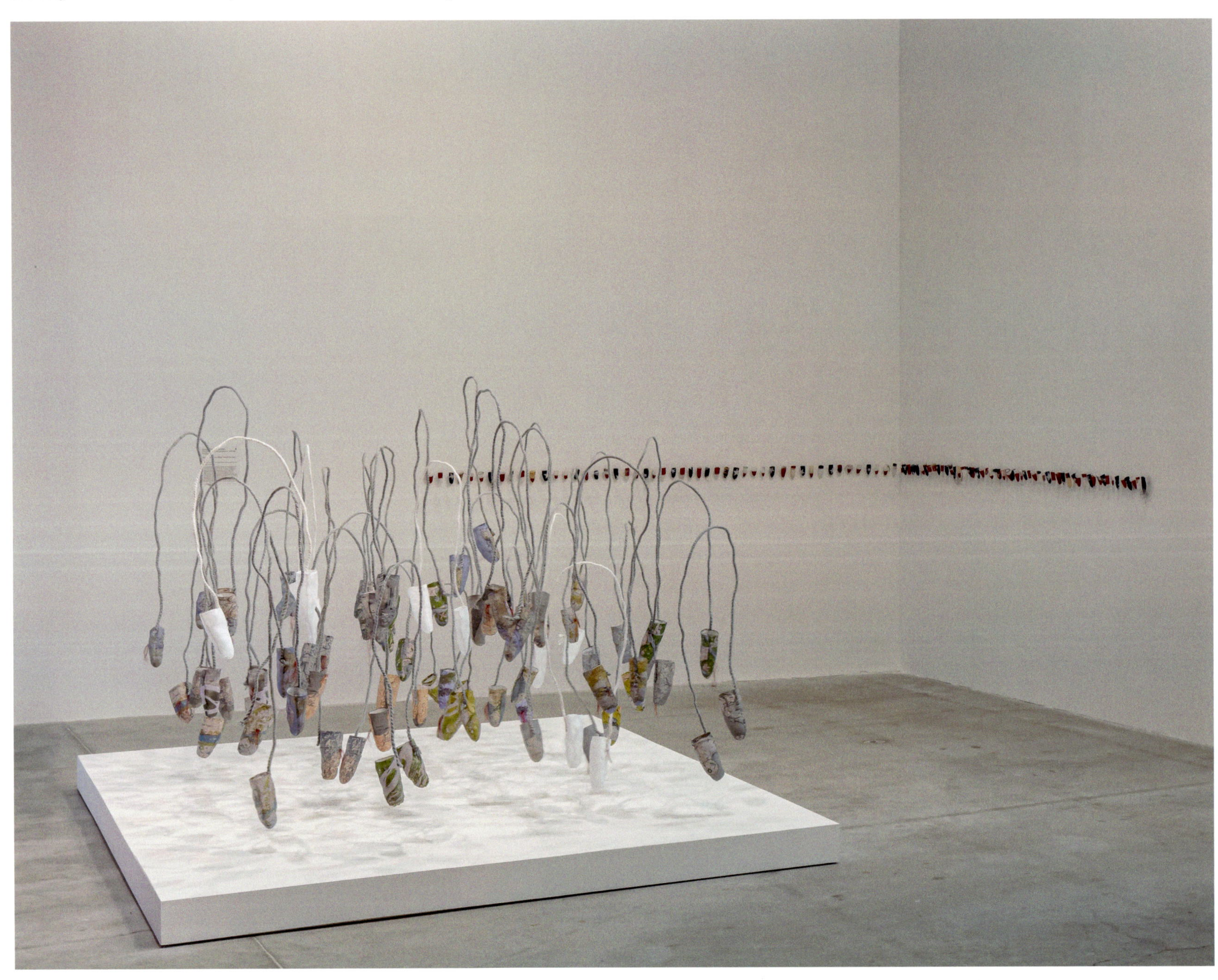

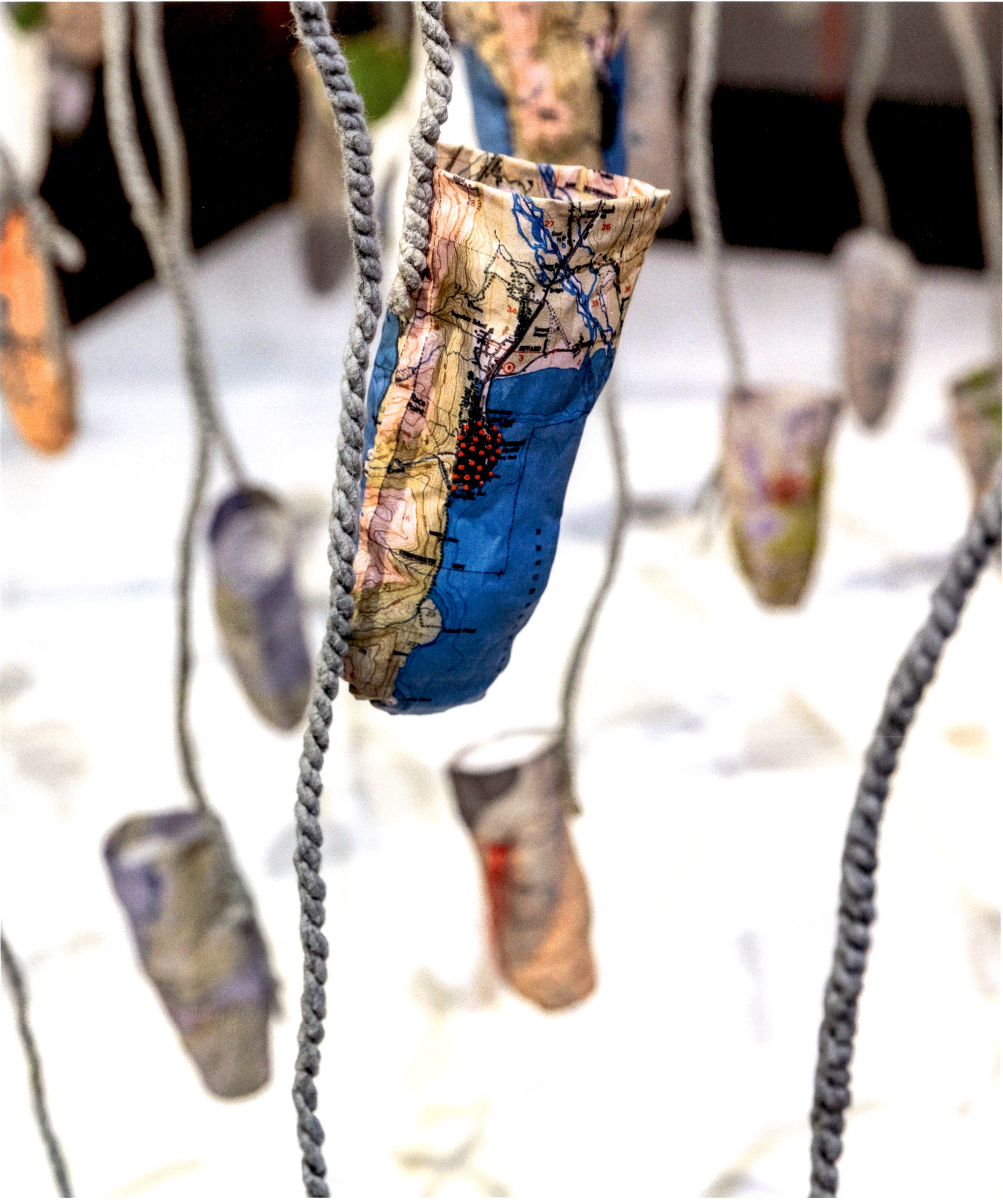

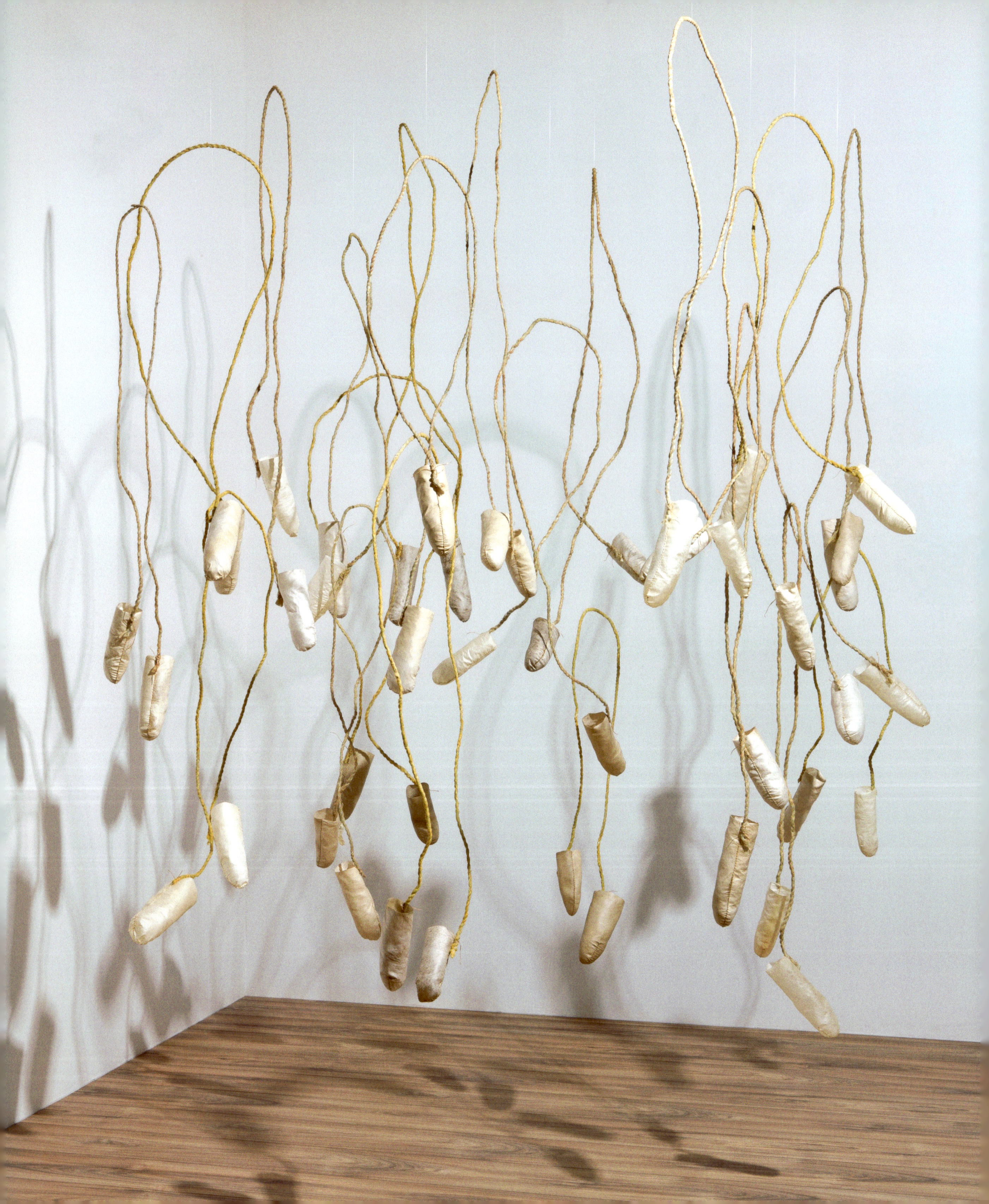

Gold Idiot Strings

Gold Idiot Strings, 2013. Wool yarn, steel wire, beeswax, nylon thread, sheep and reindeer rawhide. Collection of the Alaska State Museum. Photographs by Chris Arend.

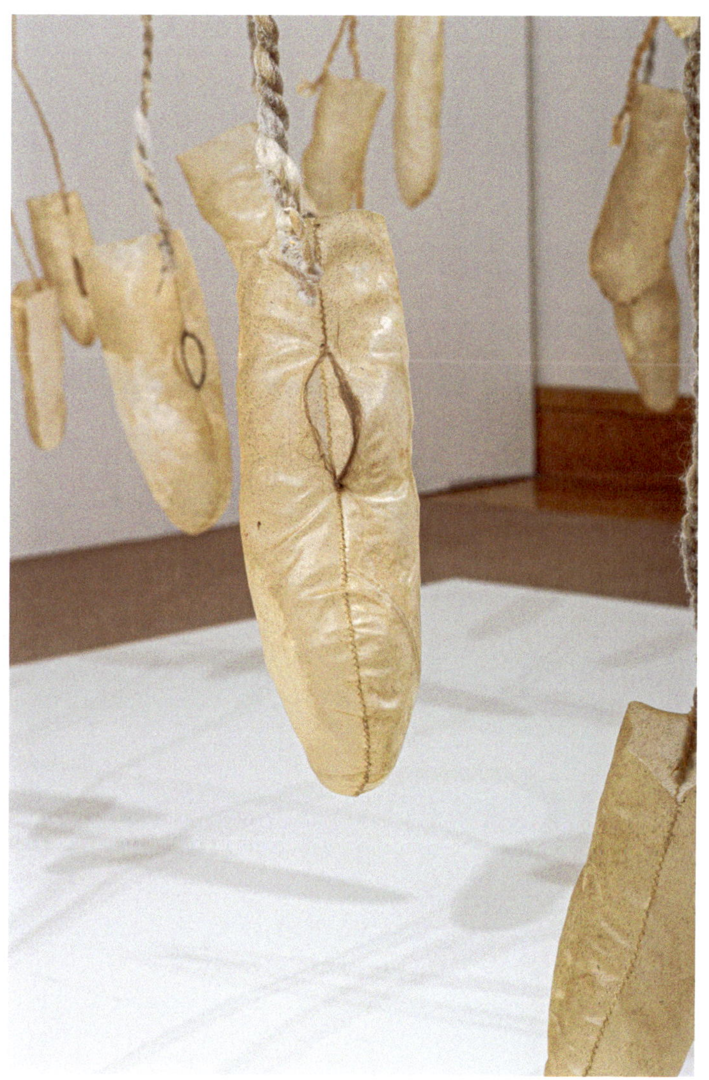

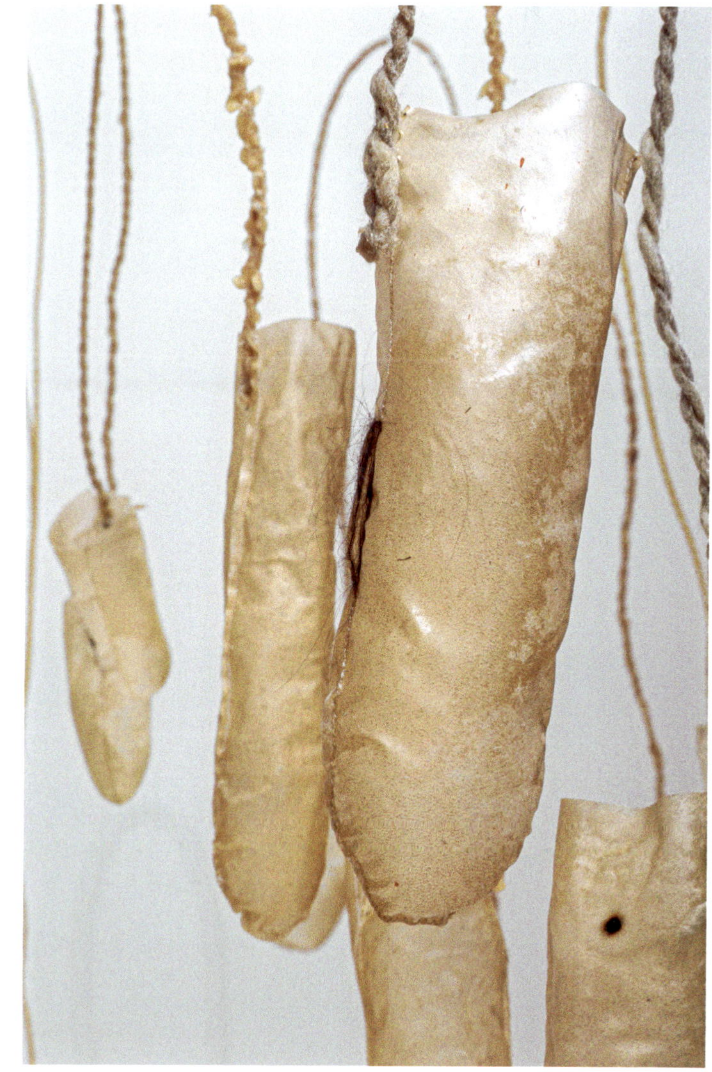

Idiot Strings with Pore

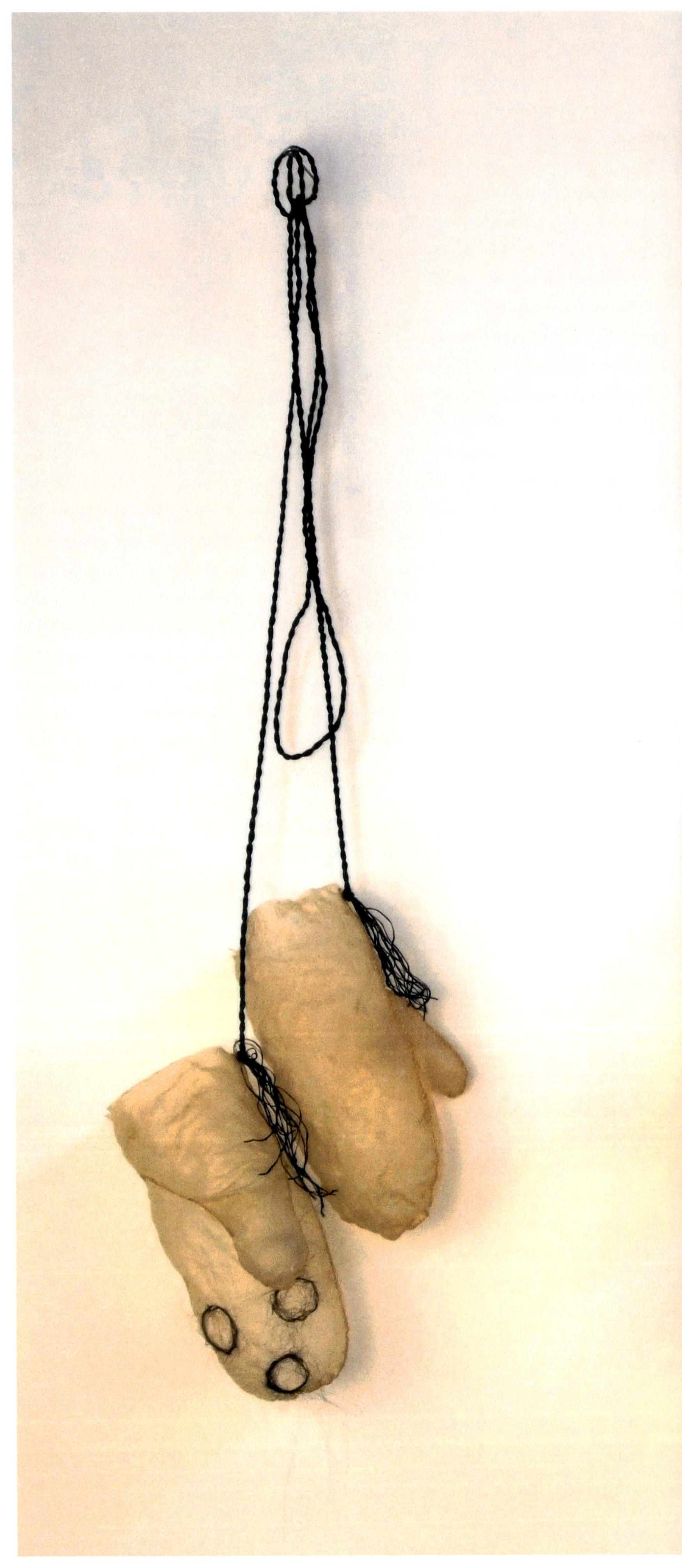

Idiot Strings with Pore, 2000. Synthetic sinew, walrus stomach, human hair, nylon thread. Private collection. Photograph by the artist.

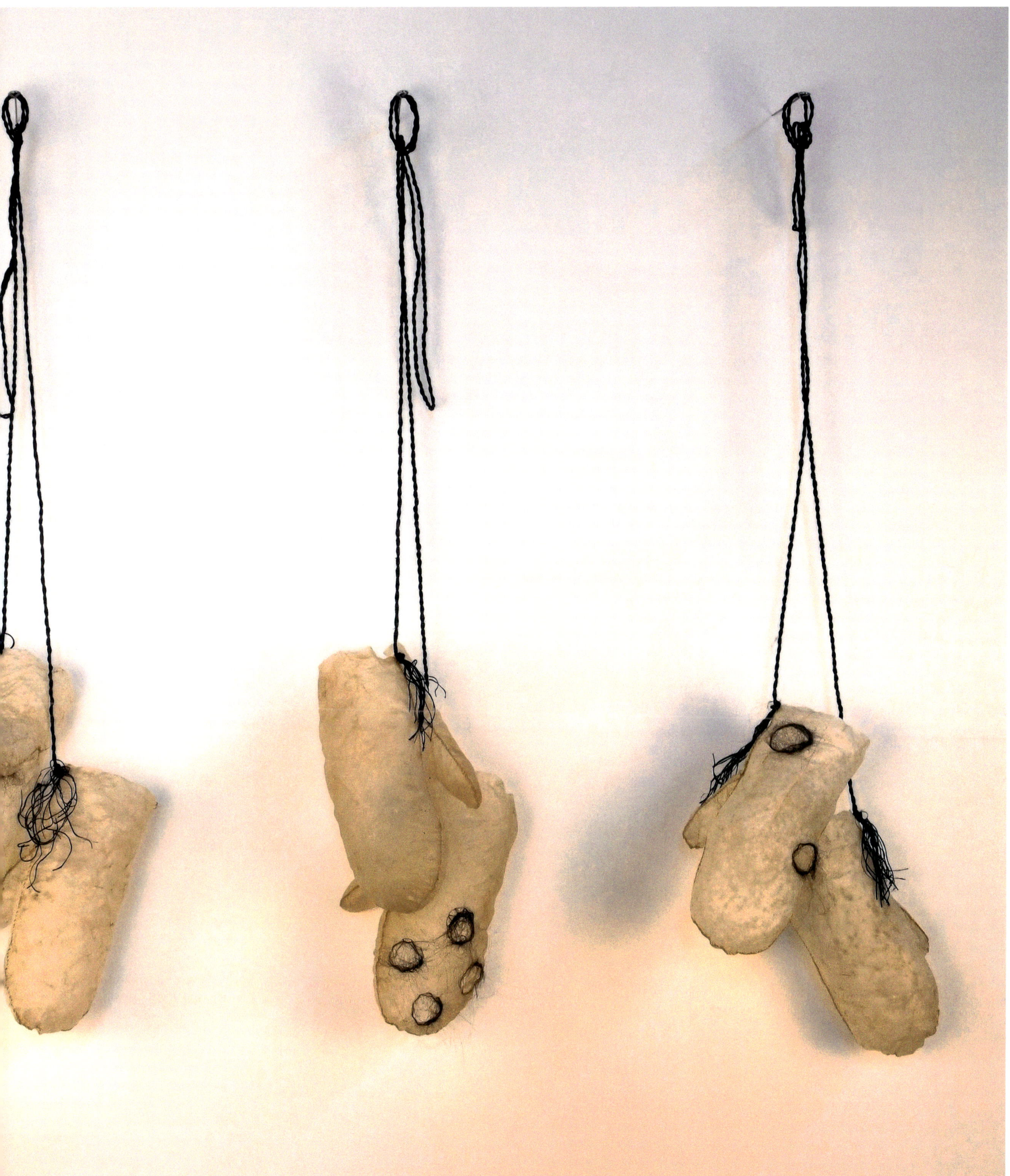

Idiot Strings, Things We Carry

This series originated as a memorial to the loss of three uncles who tragically took their own lives. This works draws attention to the staggering elevated rates of suicide amongst Alaska Native and Native American peoples. Alaska Natives are three times more likely to take their life than the rest of the nation. In both material and form, these pouches and ties evoke the body and suggest its absence. Casting overlapping shadows through line and movement demonstrate that one loss touches many. Kelliher-Combs states: "Despite the negative taboo of talking about this issue, although challenging, must be voiced in order to transform and promote healing and awareness. We must always remember those whom we have lost and continue to heal from the historical traumas of colonization."

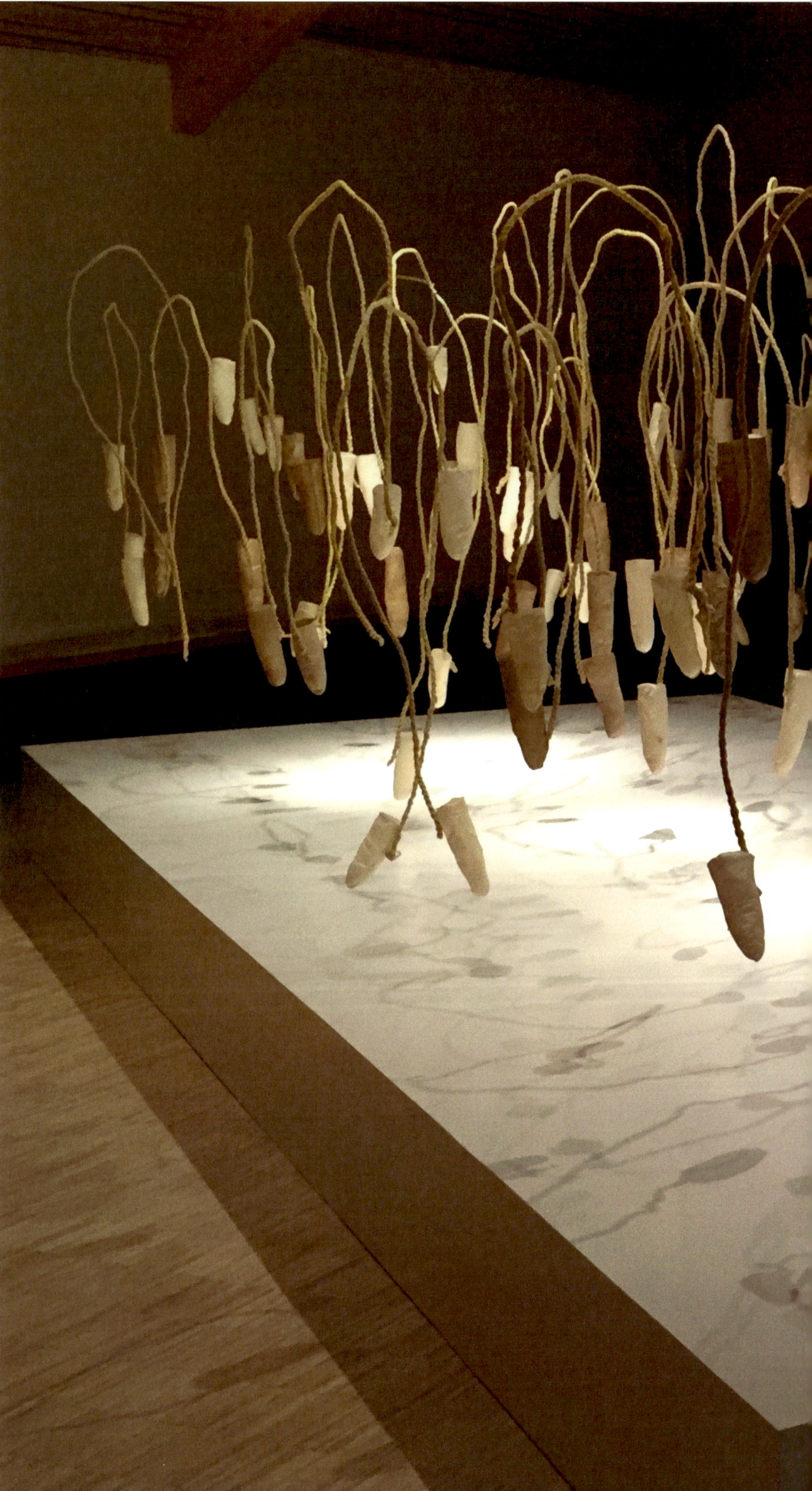

Idiot Strings, Things We Carry, 2018. Installation at the Svalbard Museum, Svalbard, Norway. Wool yarn, steel wire, beeswax, nylon thread, sheep and reindeer rawhide. Collection of the Princeton University Art Museum. Photograph by Kjetil Rydland.

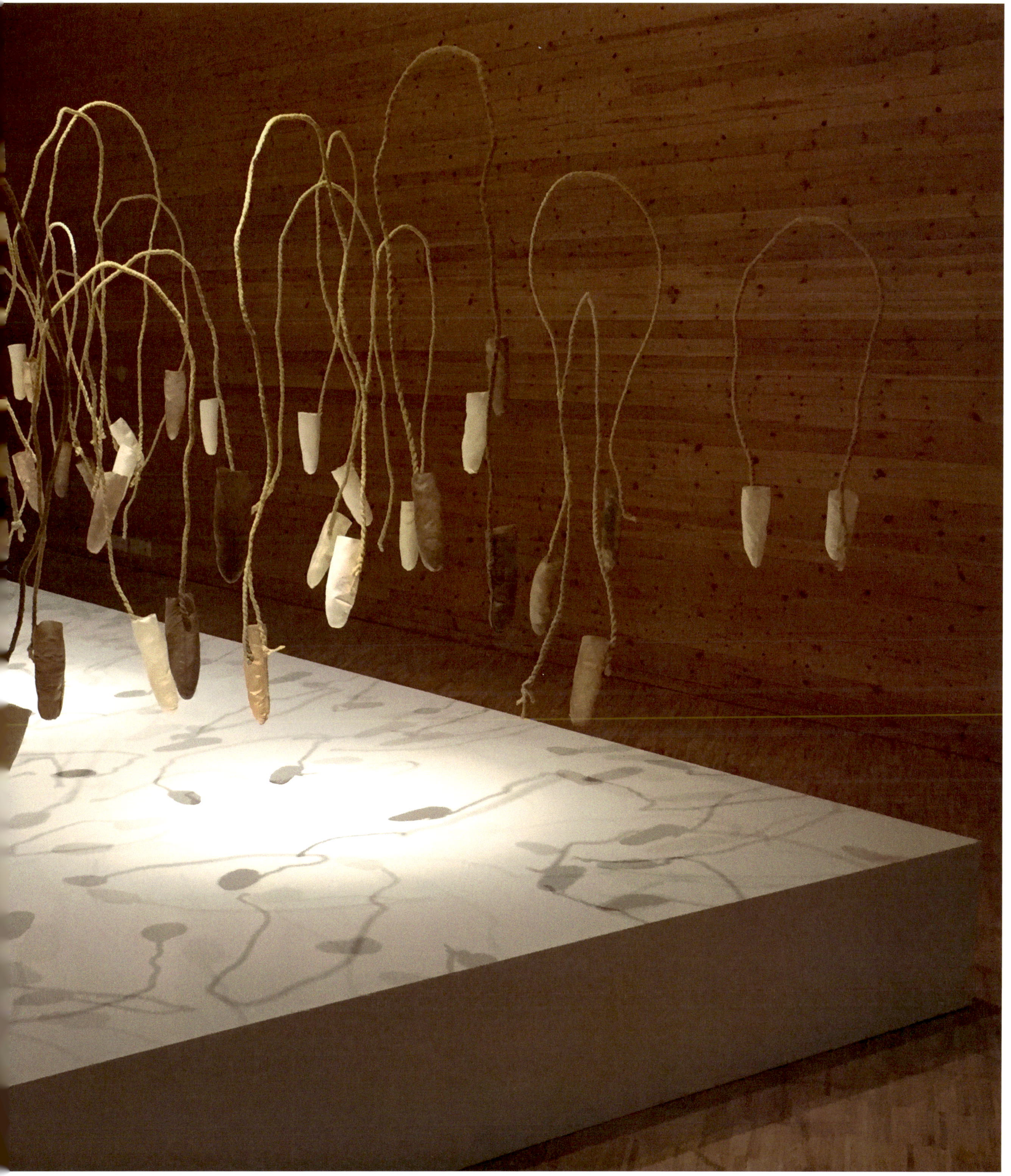

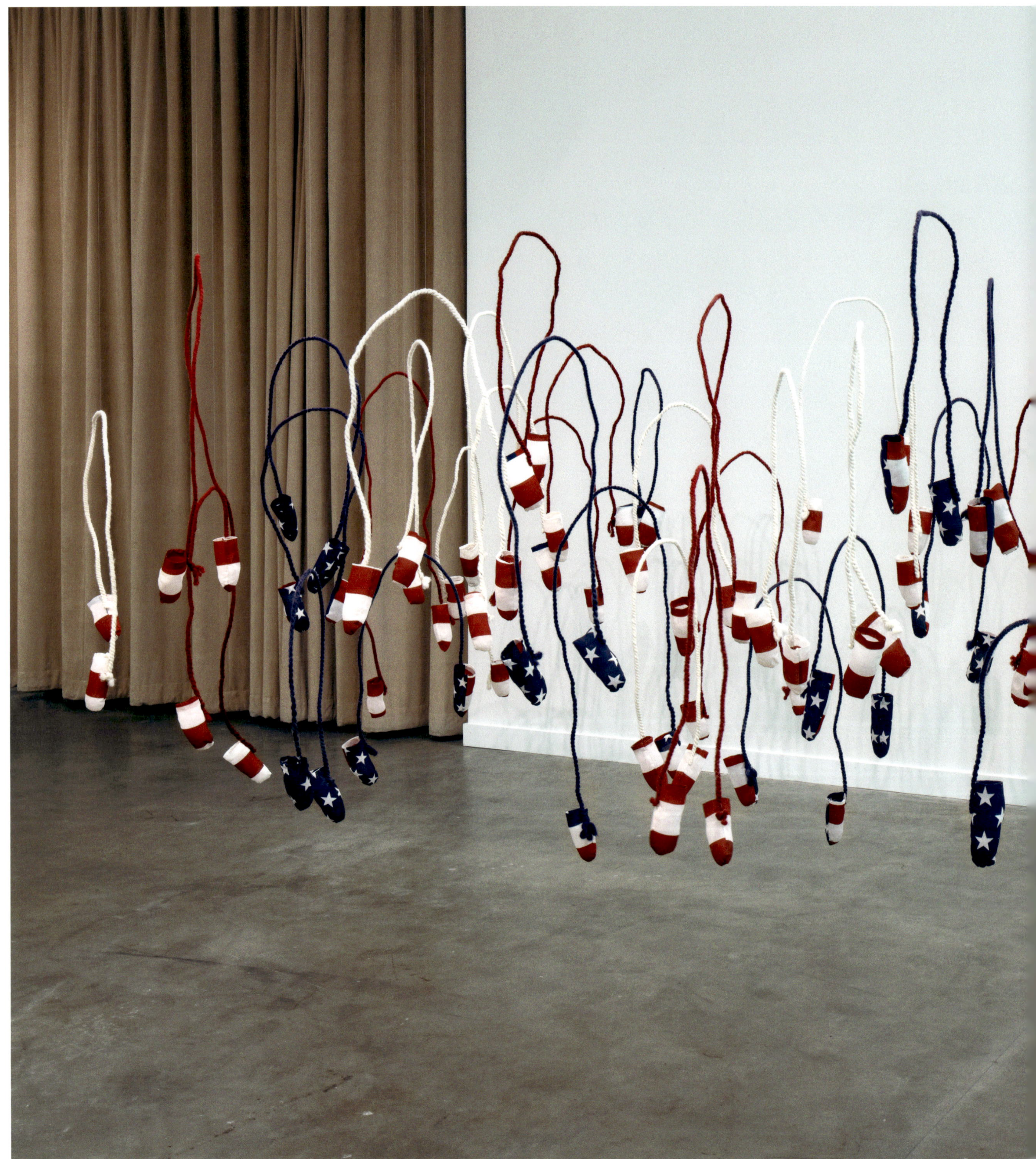

Red, White and Blue Idiot Strings

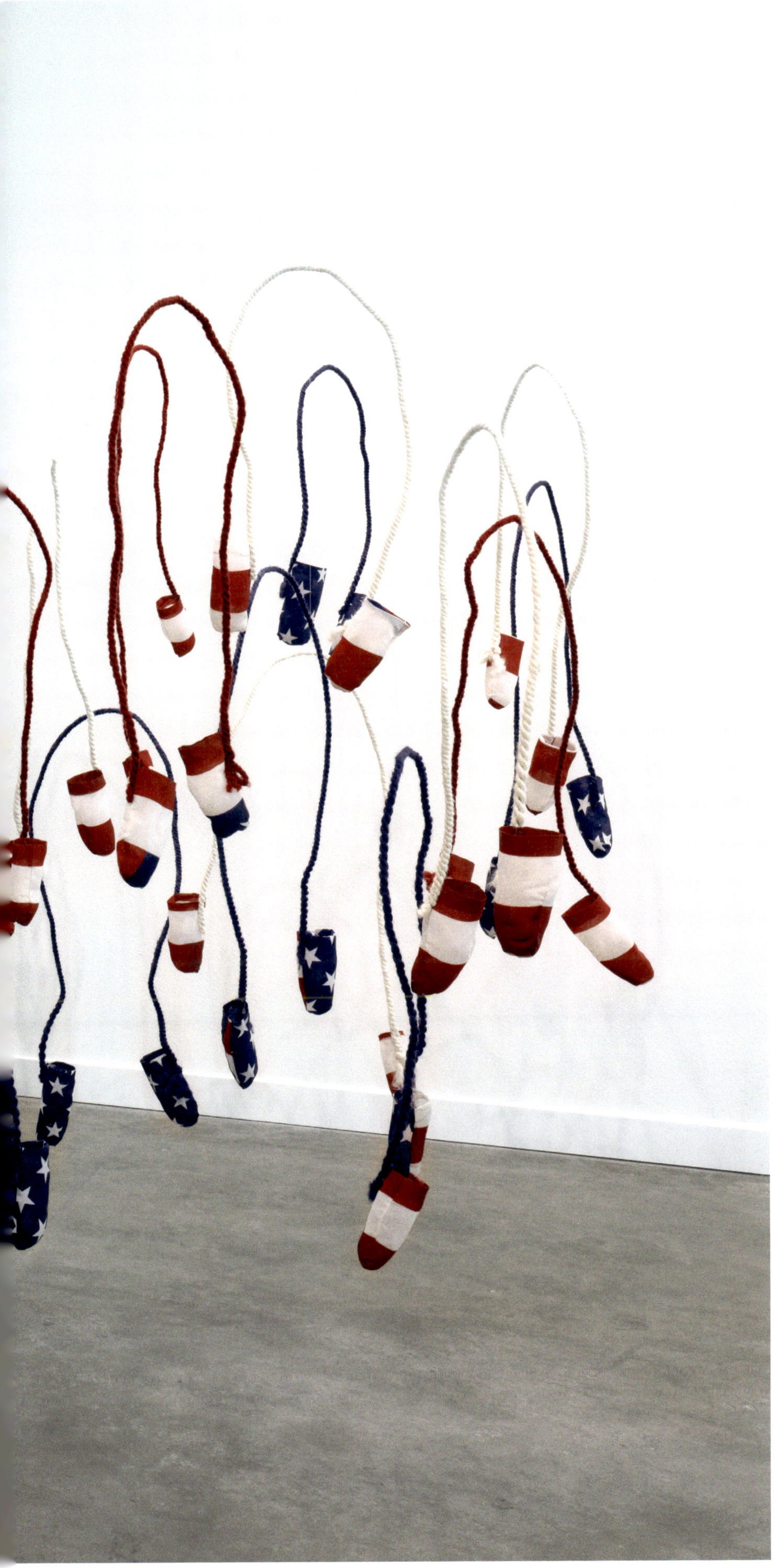

Red, White and Blue Idiot Strings, 2023. Wool yarn, steel wire, polyurethane, cotton and rayon fabric, nylon thread, dimensions variable. Photographs by Paul Salveson.

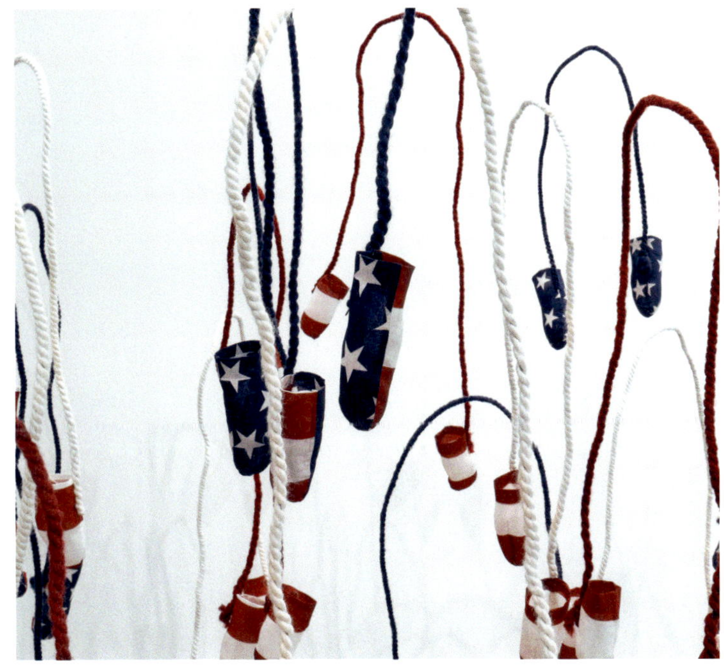

Red Idiot Strings

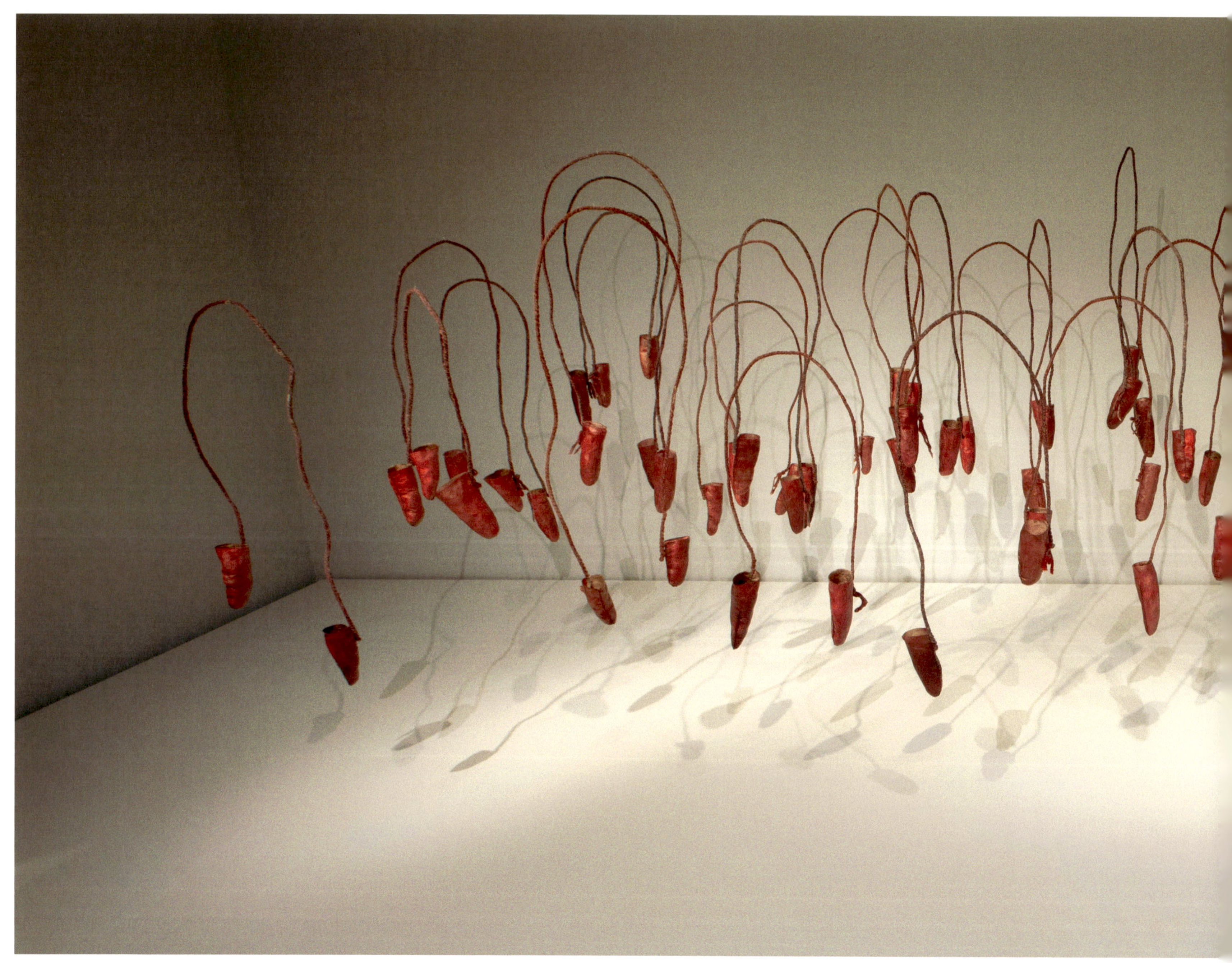

Red Idiot Strings, 2018. Wool yarn, steel wire, beeswax, nylon thread, sheep and reindeer rawhide, and acrylic polymer, dimensions variable. Collection of the Anchorage Museum. Photograph by Chris Arend.

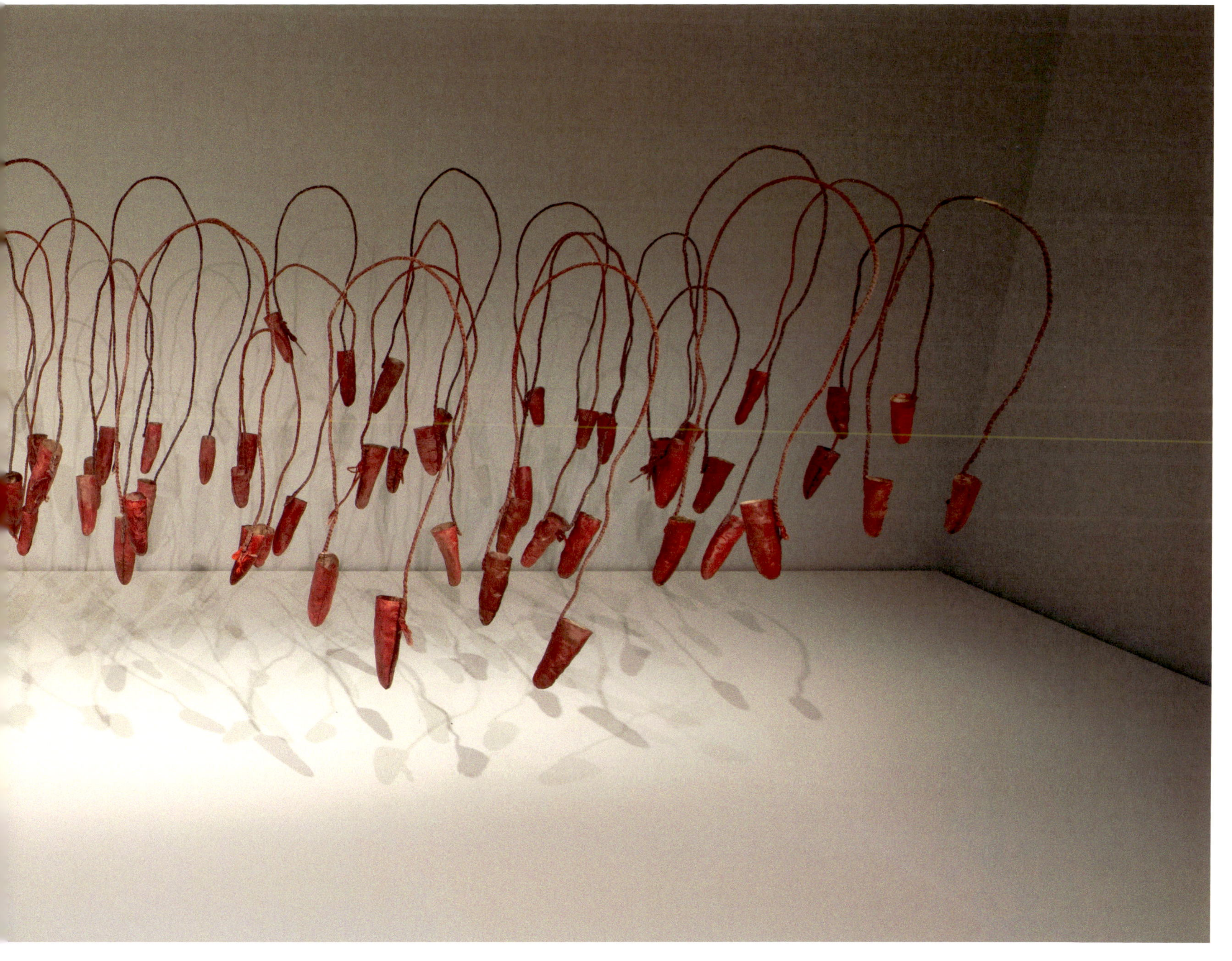

Shedding Skin

Shedding Skin, 2014. Installation at the Hood Museum, Dartmouth College, Hanover, NH. Nylon thread, steel pins, dimensions variable. Photographs by Case Hathaway Zepeda.

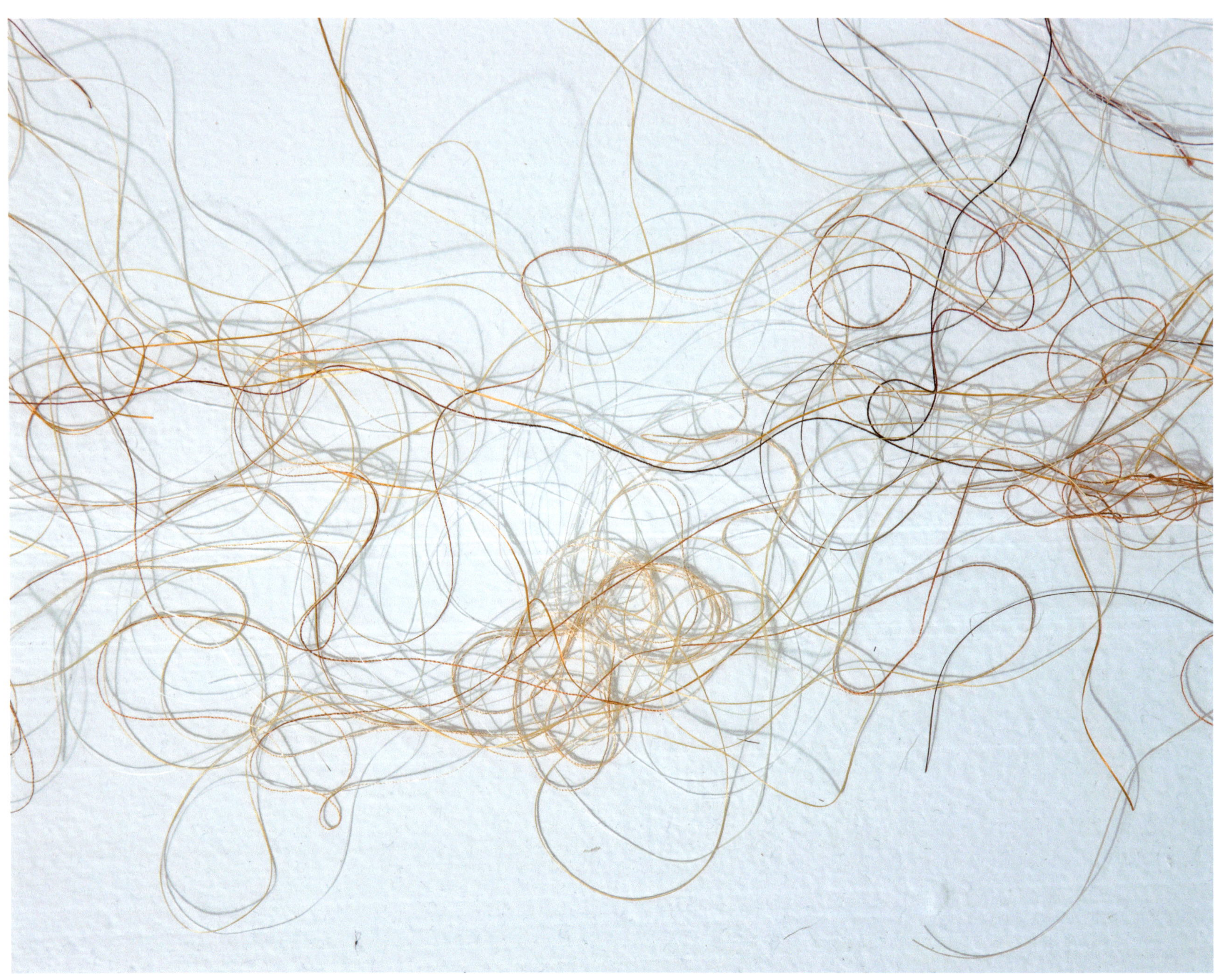

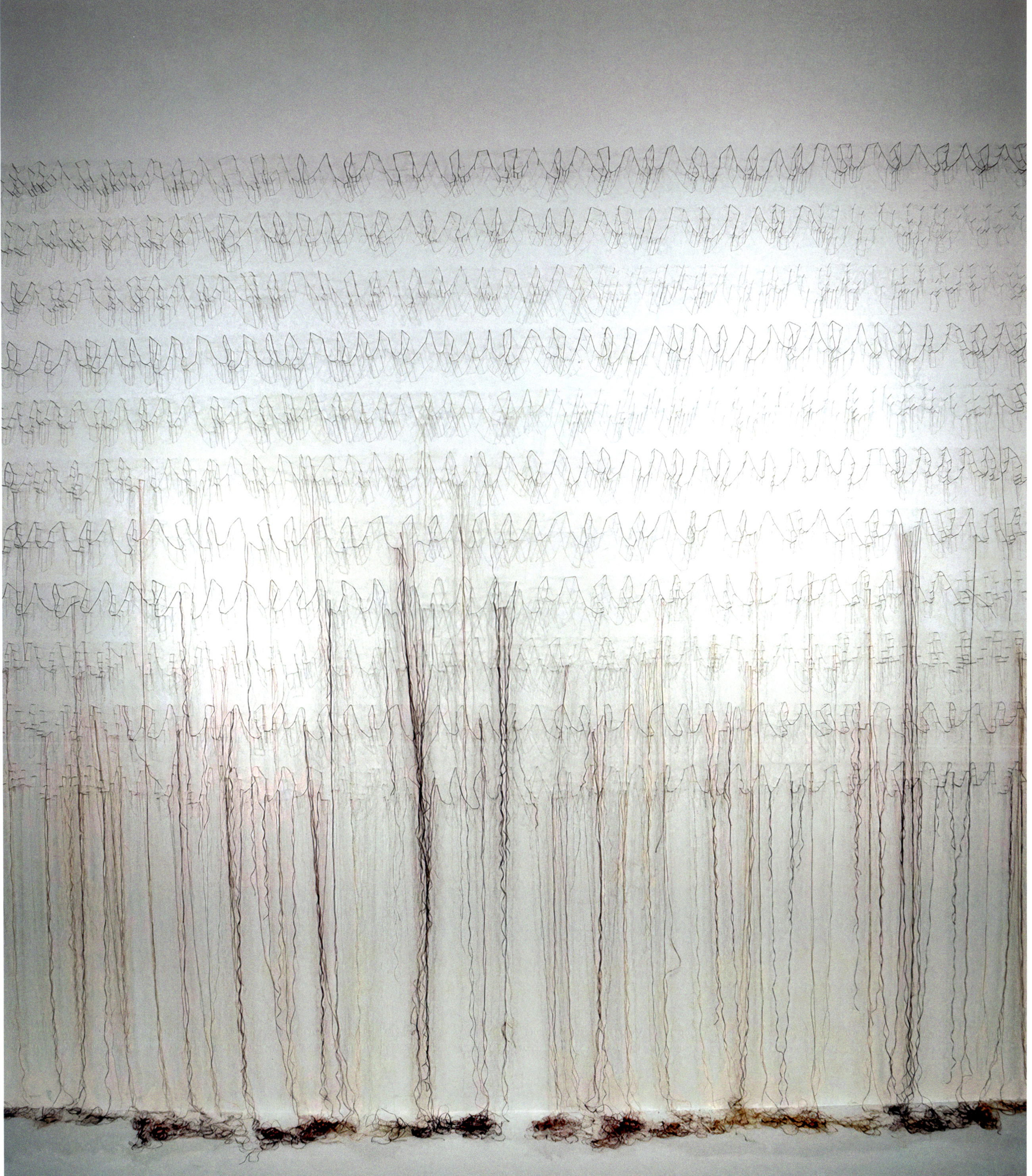

Shedding Skin

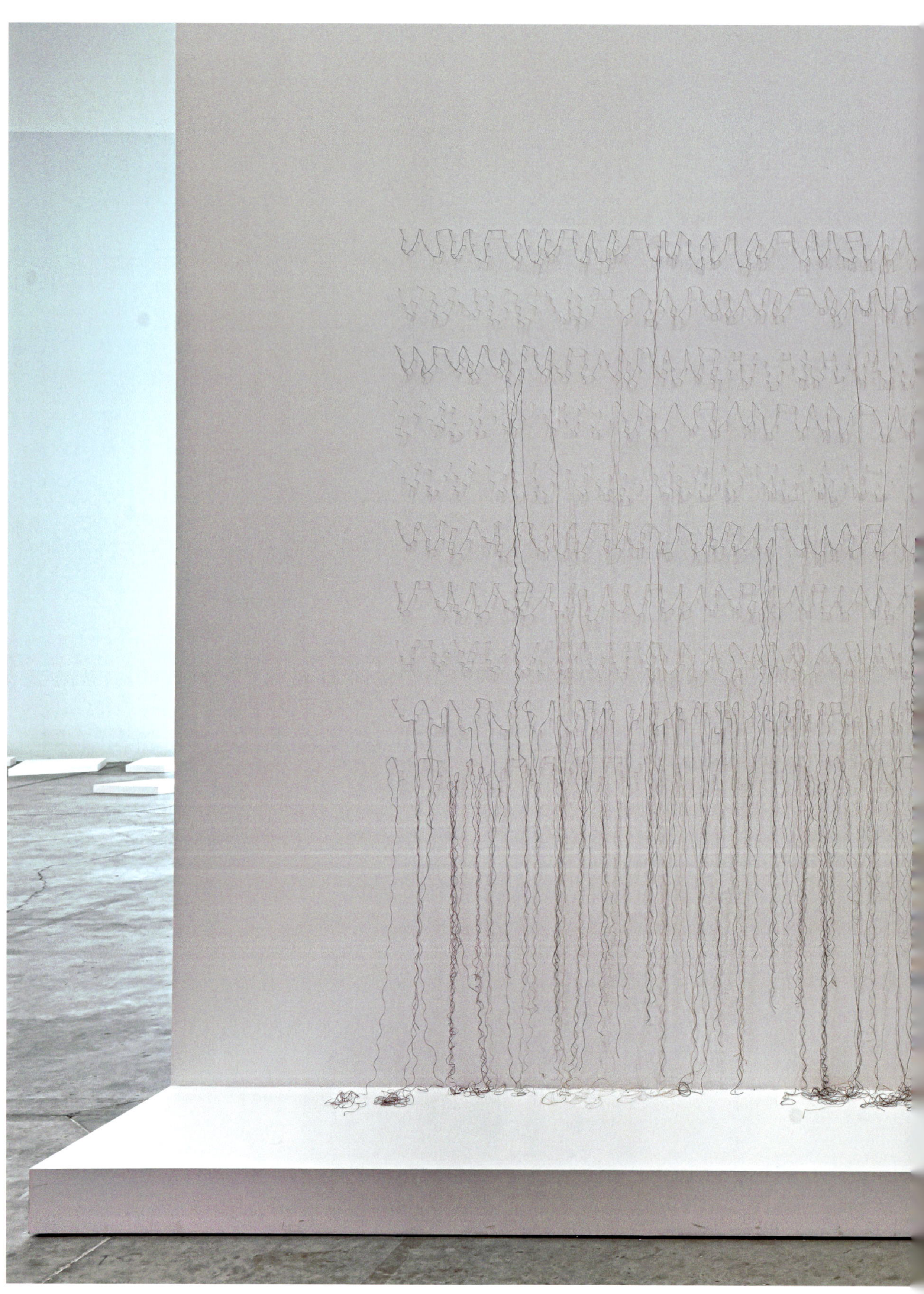

Shedding Skin, 2022. Installation at the Power Plant Gallery, Toronto, Canada. Nylon thread, steel pins, dimensions variable. Photograph courtesy of the Power Plant Gallery.

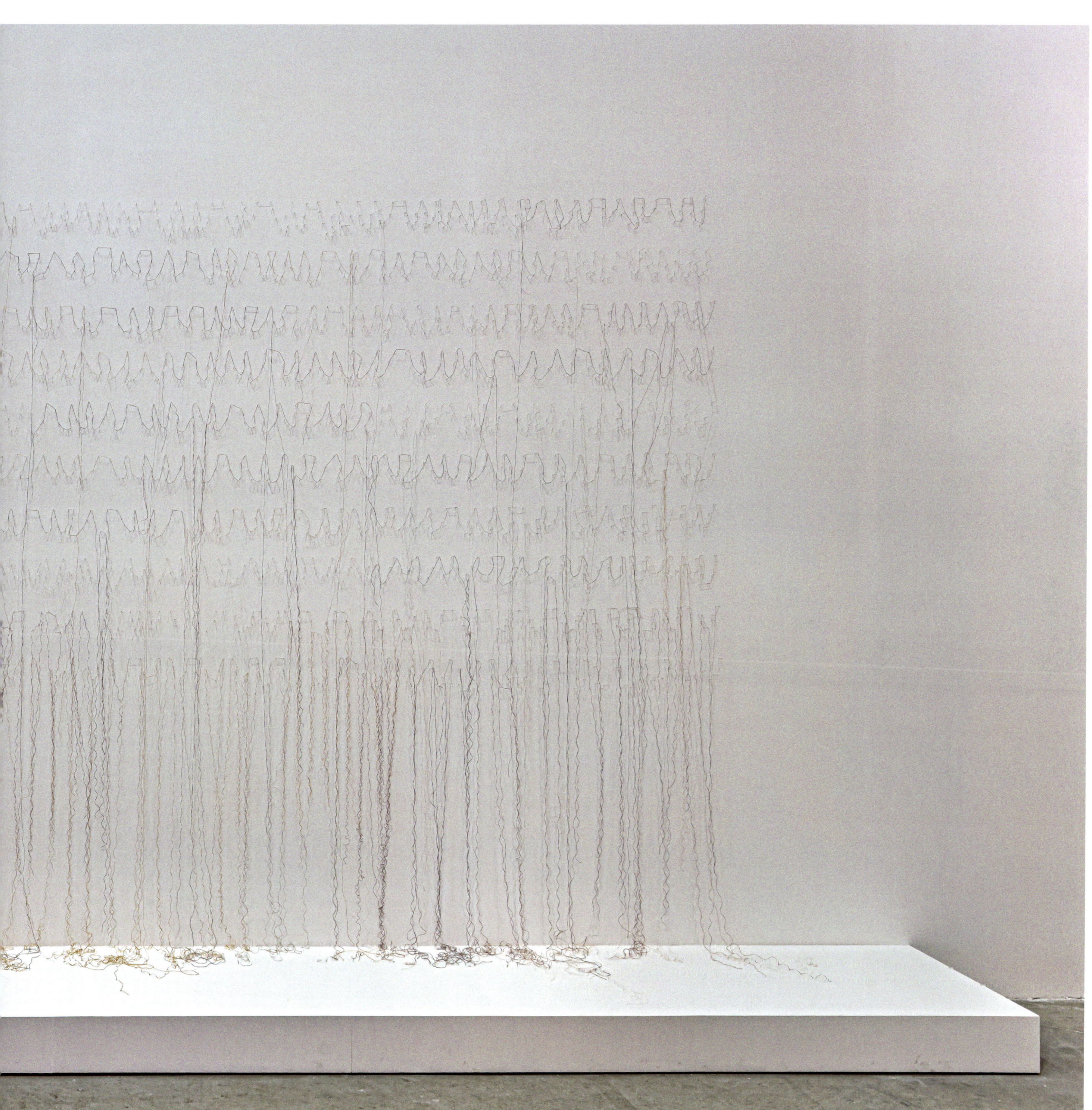

Red Luck Strings

Red Luck Strings, 2009. Installation at the Fairbanks International Airport, Alaska. Steel wire, aluminum mesh, spray paint, dimensions variable. Photographs by Kevin G. Smith.

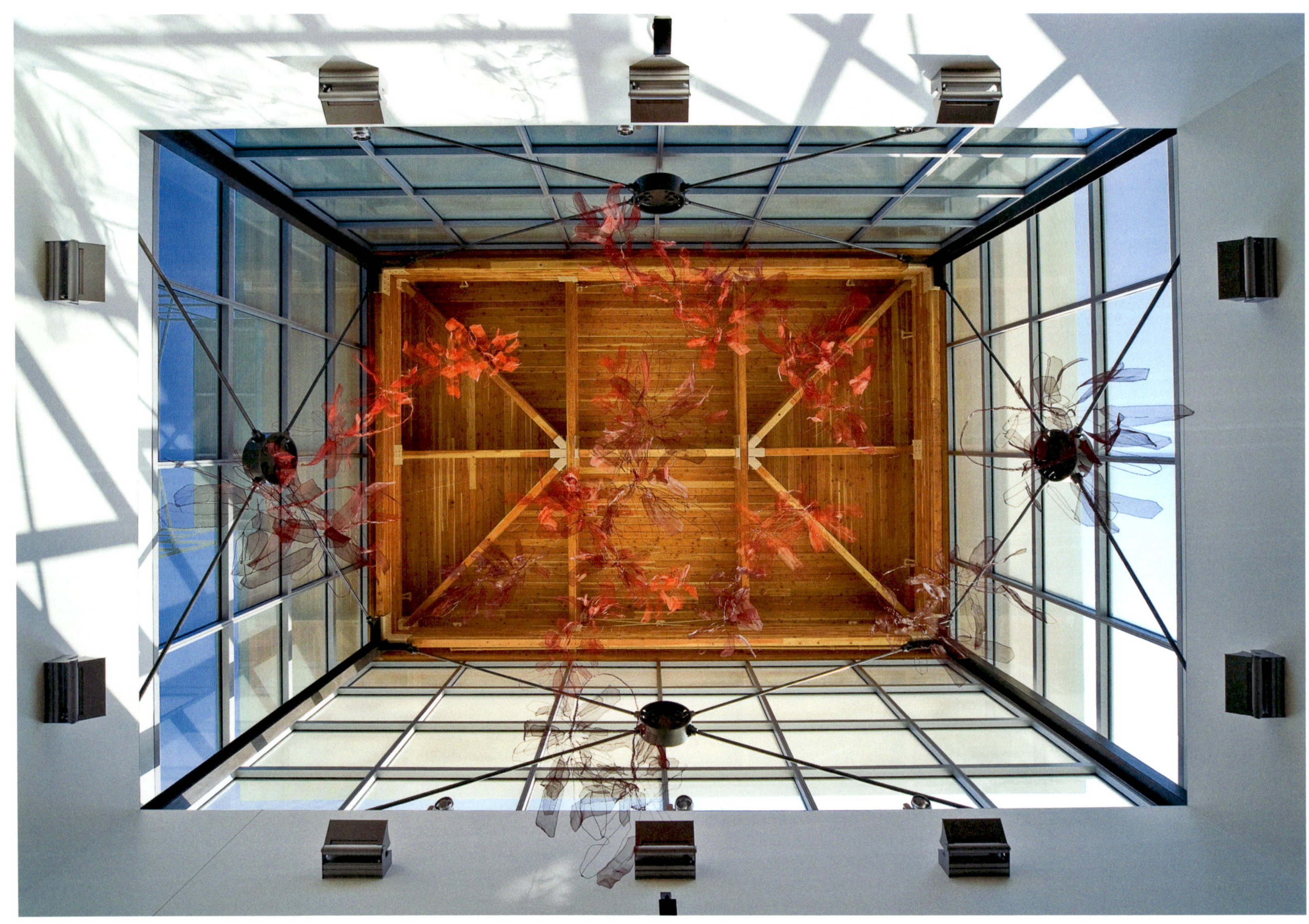

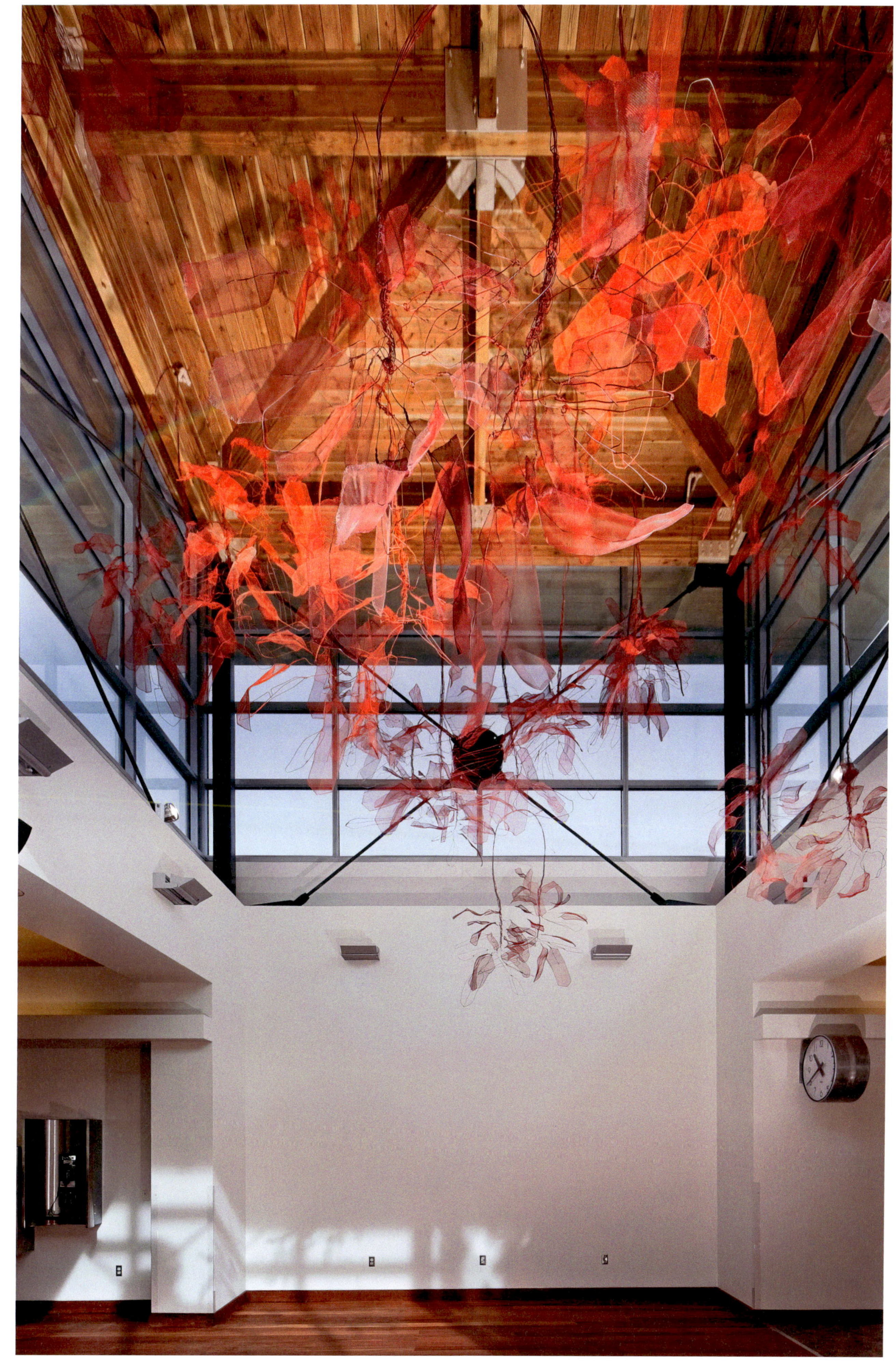

Trim

Trim, 2015. Installation. Nylon thread, steel needles, dimensions variable. Photograph by Kevin G. Smith.

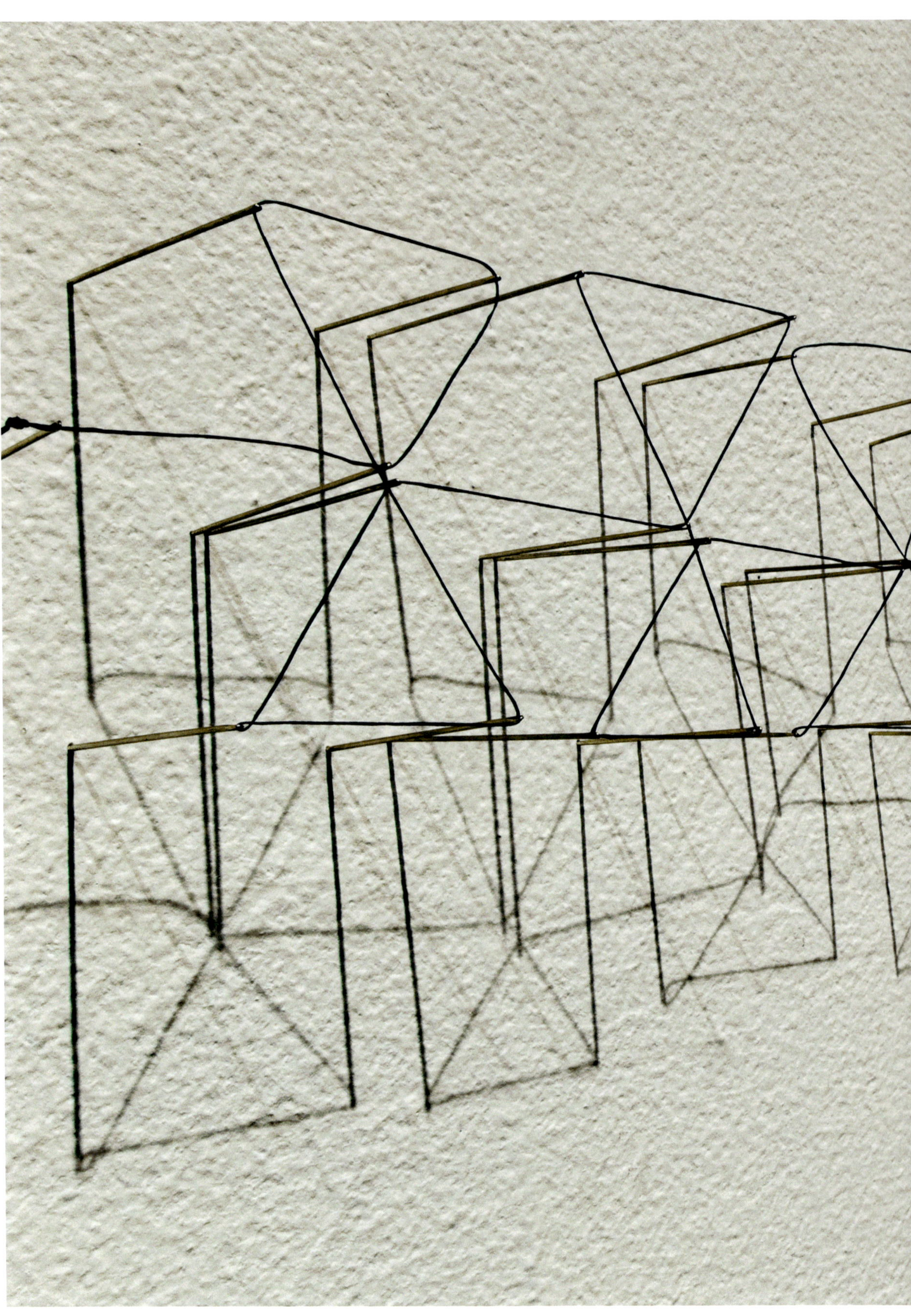

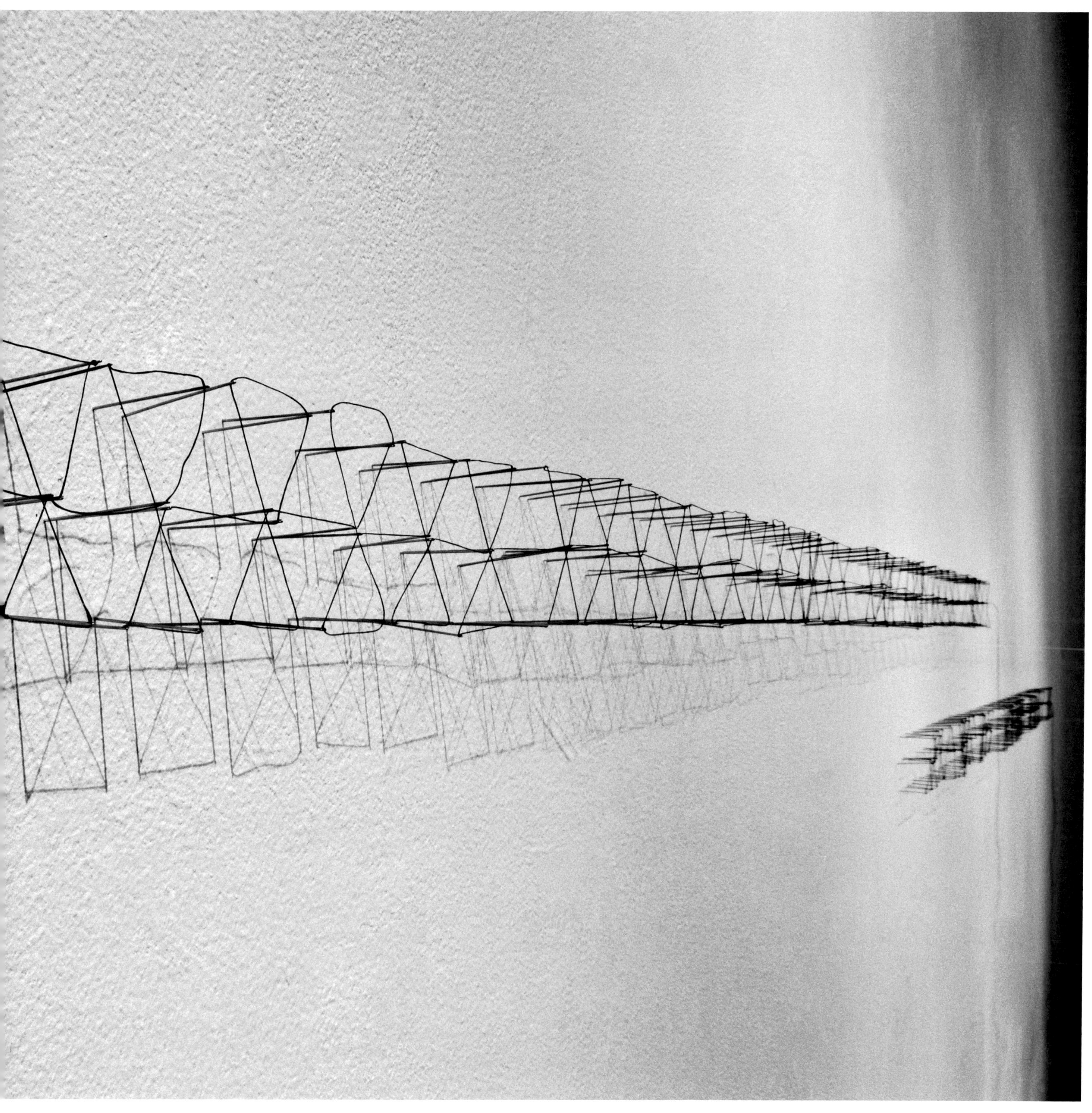

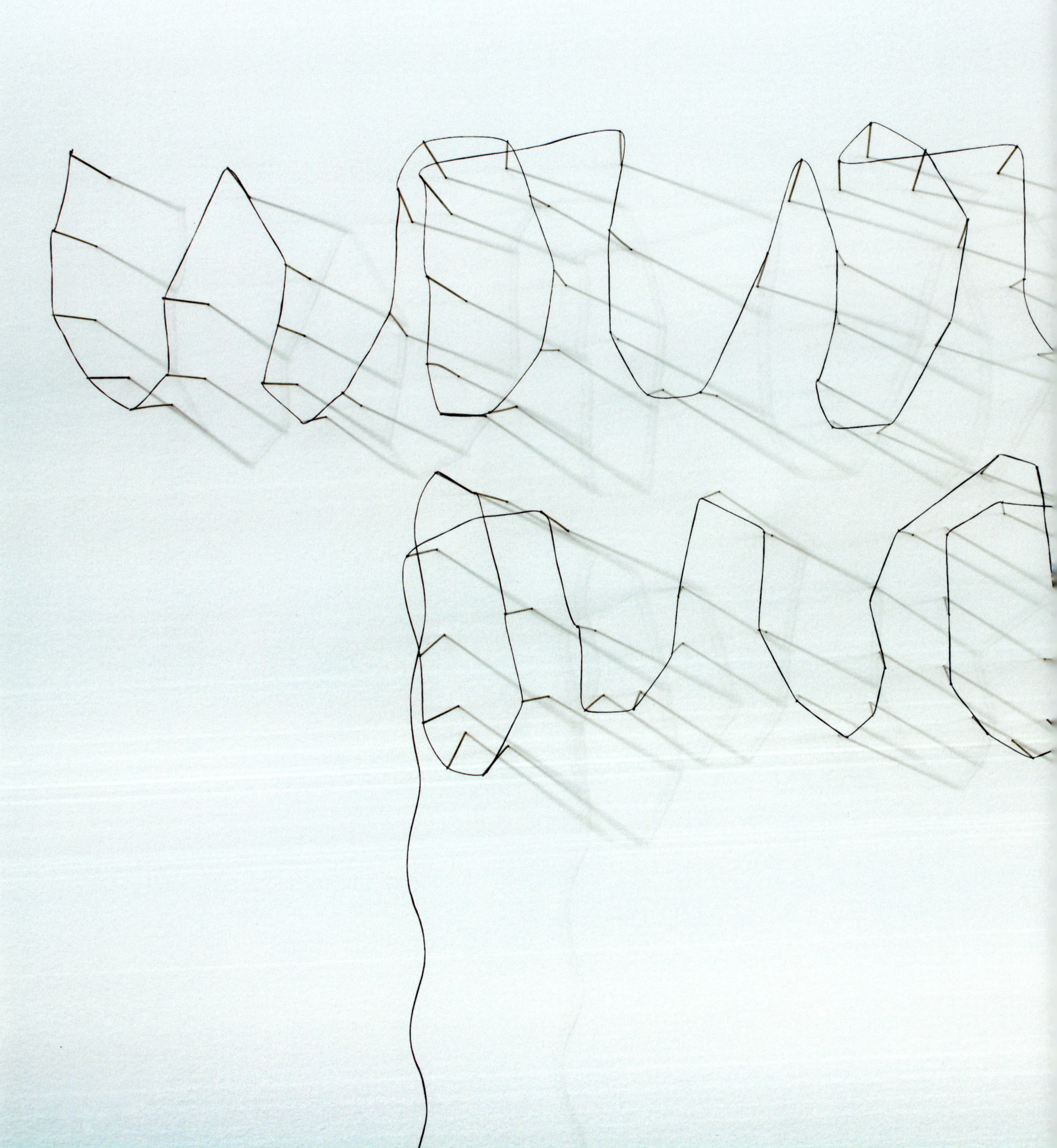

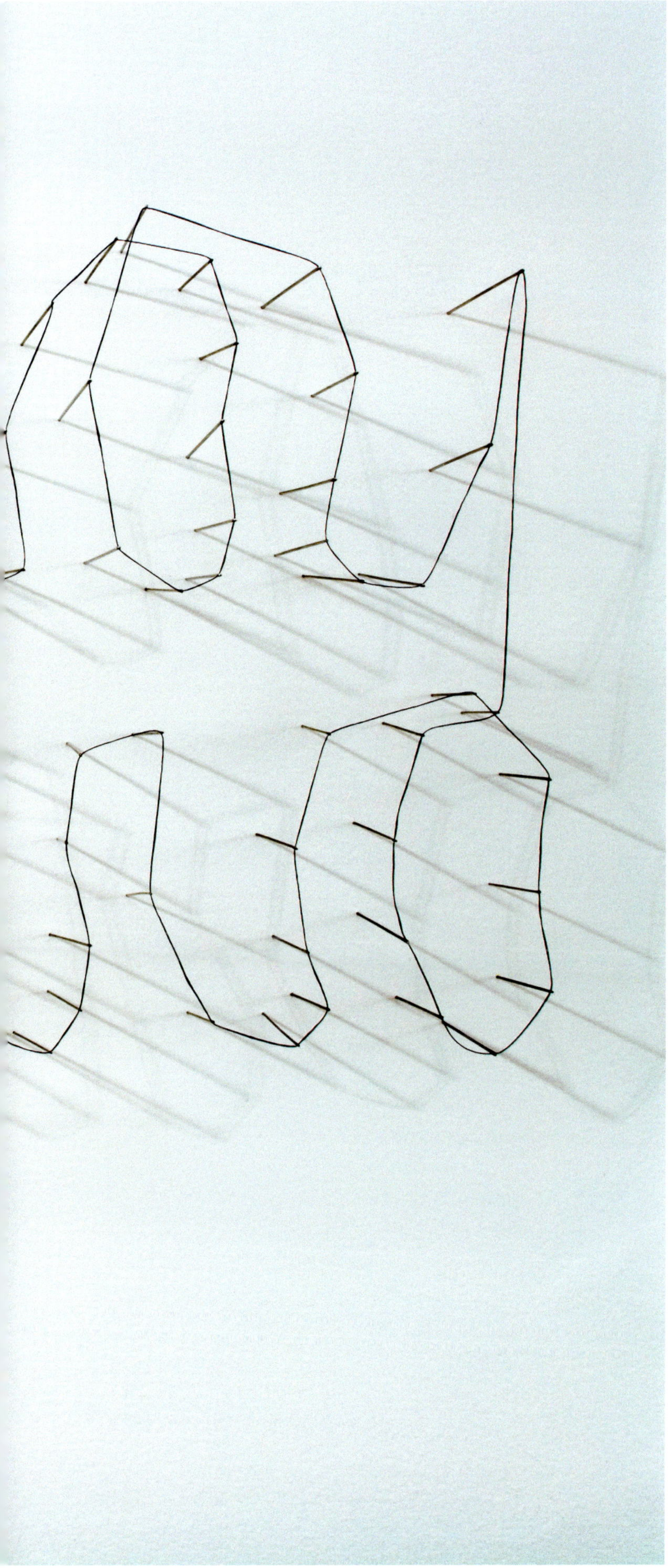

Unraveled Secrets

Unraveled Secret, 2006. Installation at the Museum of Contemporary Native Art, Santa Fe, NM. Nylon thread, steel pins, dimensions variable. Photograph by the artist.

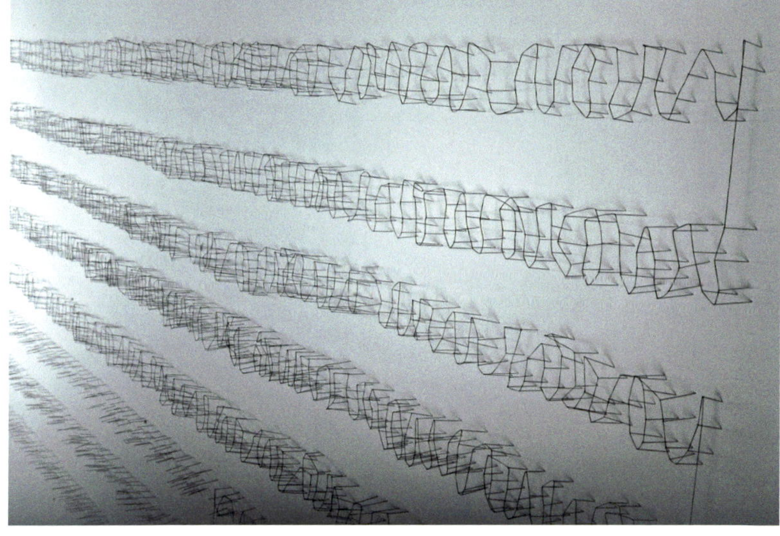

White Idiot Strings

White Idiot Strings, 2019. Wool yarn, steel wire, beeswax, Tyvek, ink, dimensions variable. Photograph by Chris Arend.

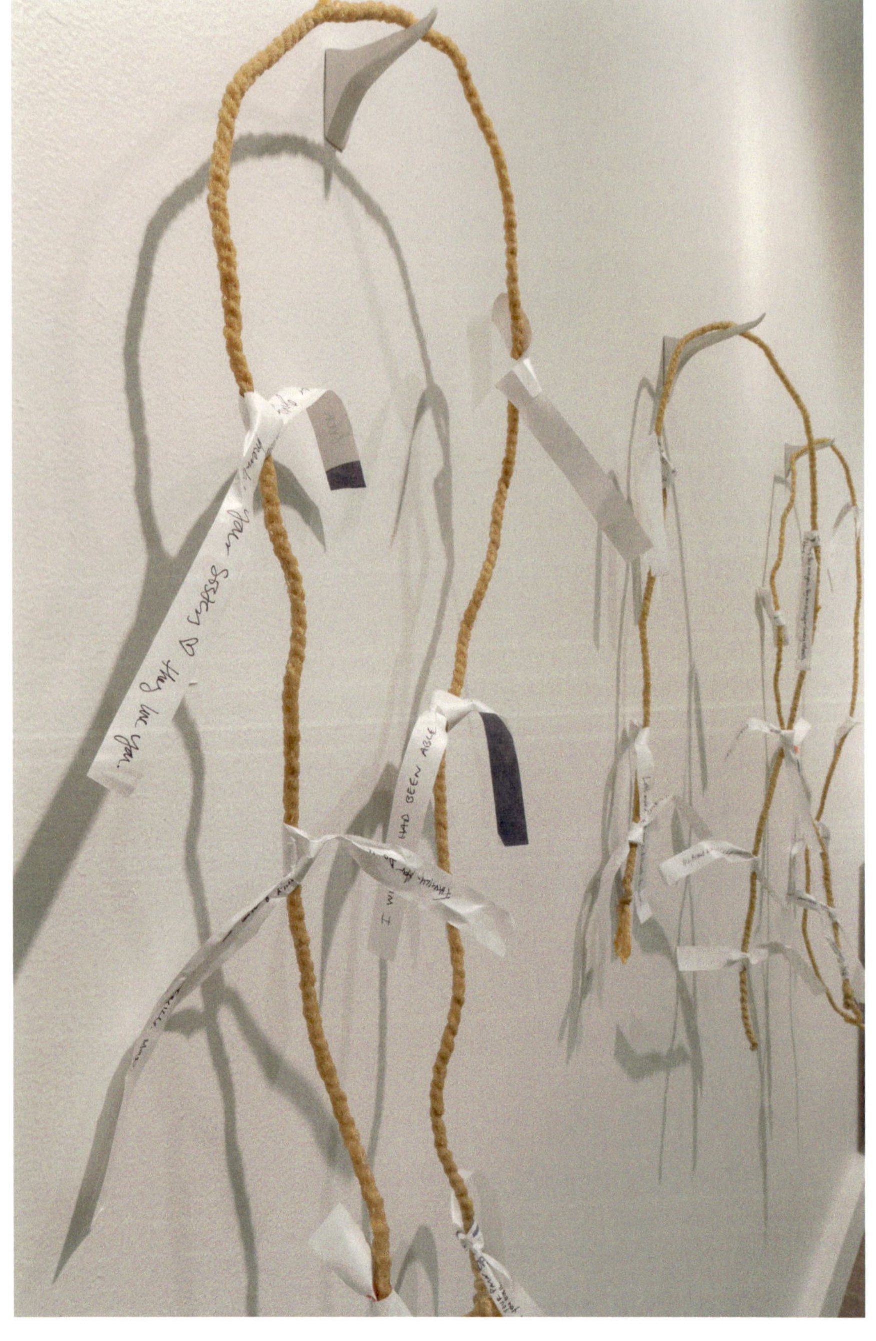

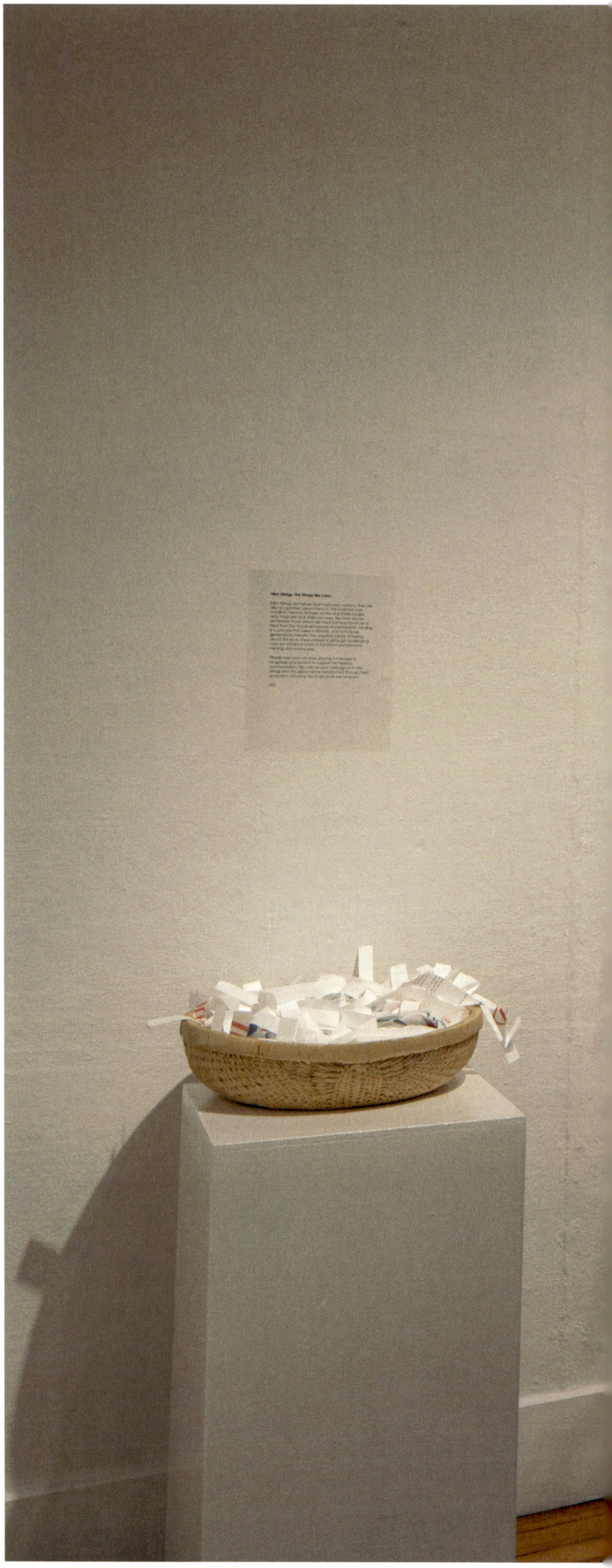

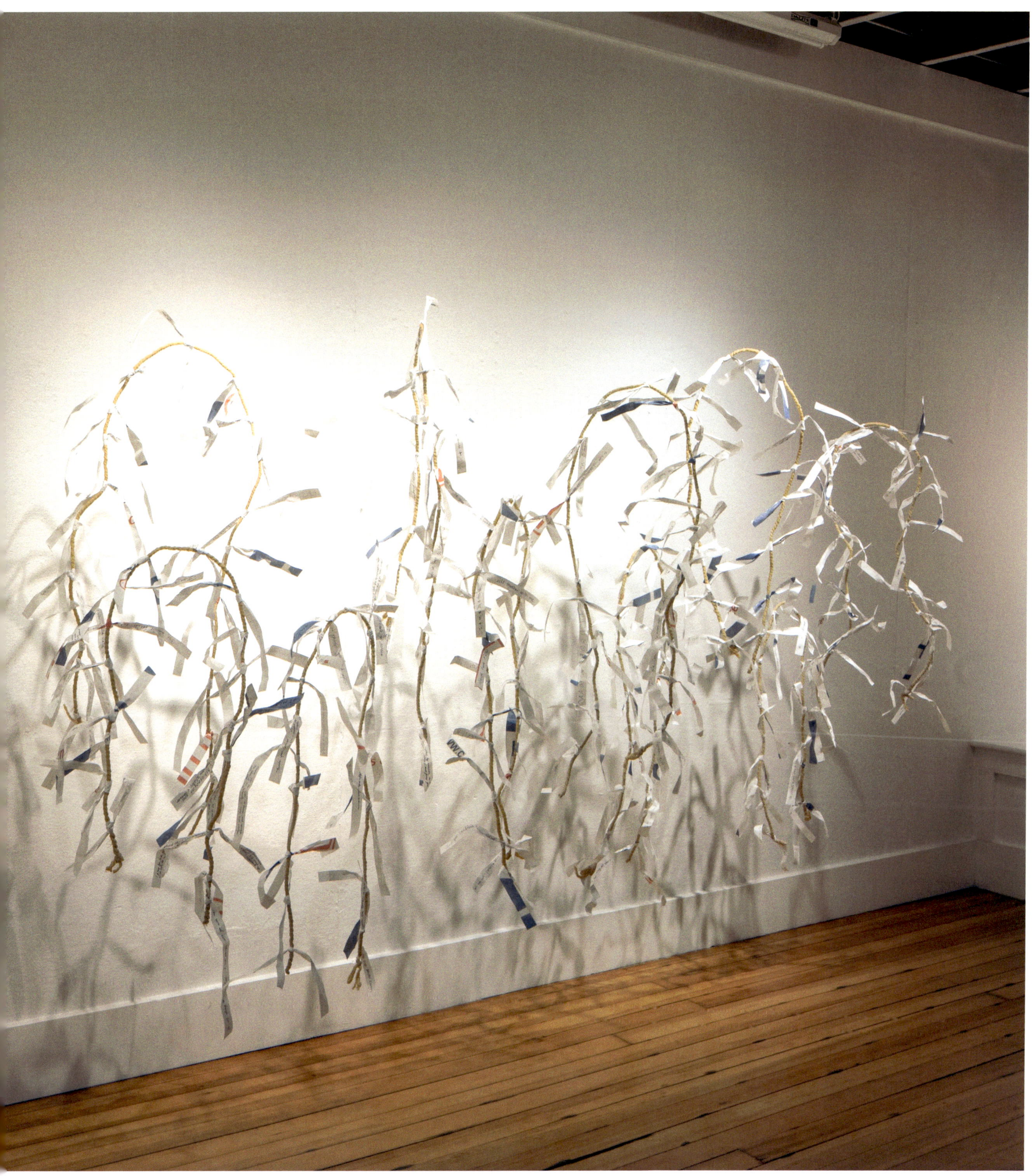

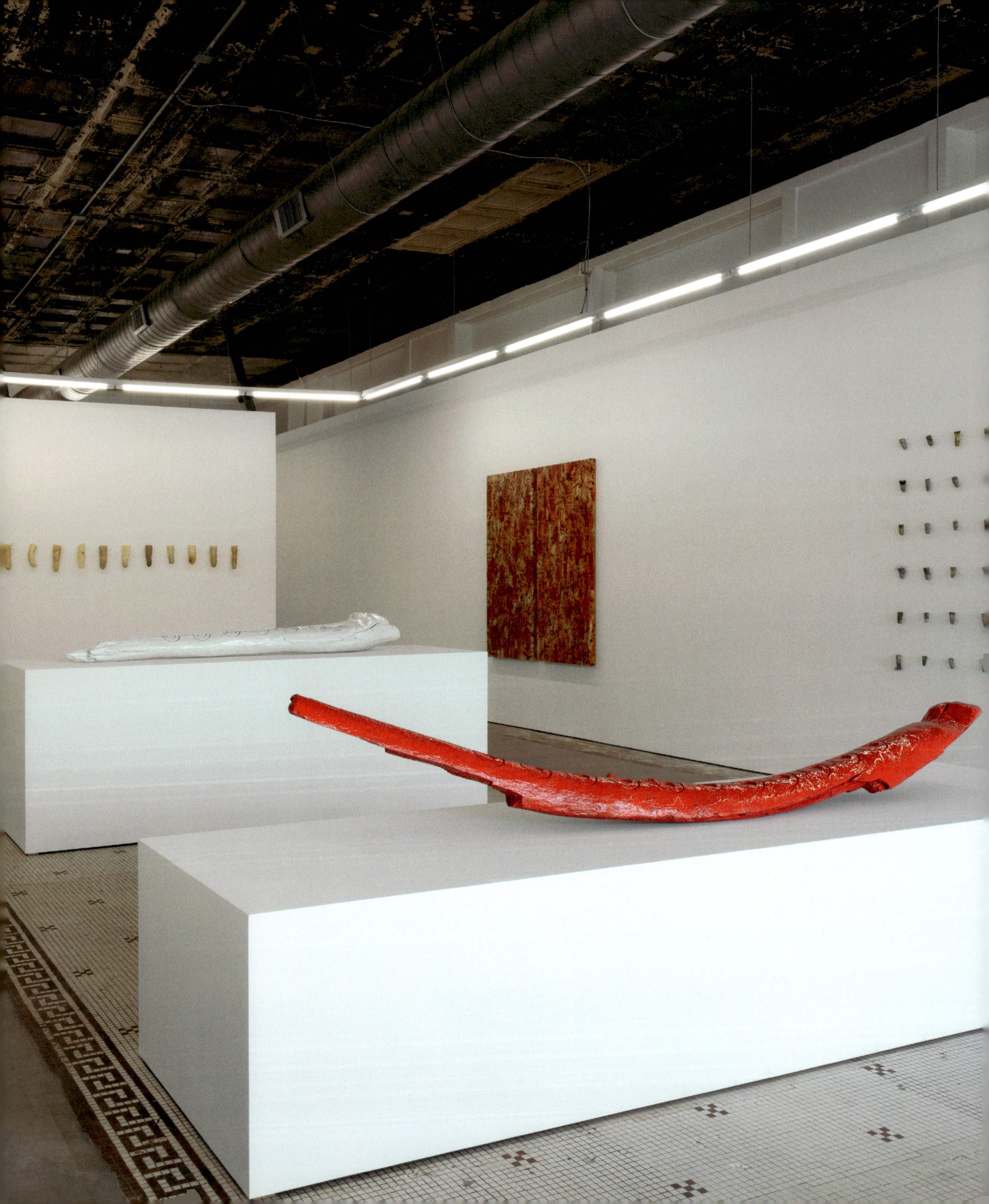

Exhibitions

Selected Solo Exhibitions

2023 *Mark*, STARS gallery, Los Angeles, CA
Mark, Tureen gallery, Dallas, TX
Visceral: Verity, Legacy, Identity – Alaska Native Gut Knowledge and Perseverance, Alaska State Museum, Juneau, AK

2019 *Mark*, Minus Space, Brooklyn, NY
Goodbye: The Things We Carry, Yukon Arts Center, Whitehorse, YT, Canada
Sonya Kelliher-Combs, Bunnell Street Arts Center, Homer, AK

2018 *Recent Work*, Cyrano's ArtSpace Gallery, Anchorage, AK
The Things We Carry, Kunsthall Svalbard, Northern Norway Art Museum, Svalbard, Norway

2017 *New Work*, Kenai Arts Center, Kenai, AK
Remnant, Peters Projects, Santa Fe, NM

2016 *Sonya Kelliher-Combs*, Carrie McLain Museum, Nome, AK

2015 *Stitch: Line*, International Gallery of Contemporary Art, Anchorage, AK

2014 *Recent Work*, Jaffe-Friede Gallery, Dartmouth College, Hanover, NH

2012 *Qupak*, Pratt Museum, Homer, AK
Where They Overlap, Gorman Museum of Native American Art, UC Davis, Davis, CA

2011 *Hide*, IAIA Museum of Contemporary Native Arts, Santa Fe, NM

2010 *Hide*, National Museum of Indian Art, New York, NY

2008 *Walrus Family Portrait*, International Gallery of Contemporary Art, Anchorage, AK

2007 *New Secrets*, Well Street Art Company, Fairbanks, AK
Unraveled Secret, Bunnell Street Arts Center, Homer, AK

2006 *Unraveled Secret*, Institute of American Indian Arts, Santa Fe, NM
Secret, Modo Gallery, Hudson, NY

2005 *Untitled Secrets*, Well Street Art Company, Fairbanks, AK
Untitled, Anchorage Museum Solo Exhibition Series, Anchorage, AK

2002 *1000 Secrets*, Decker/Morris Gallery, Anchorage, AK

2001 *Idiot Strings: Catch and Release*, Alaska State Museum, Juneau, AK

2000 *New Works*, Decker/Morris Gallery, Anchorage, AK

1998 *Asianggataq*, Harry Wood Art Gallery, Arizona State University, Tempe, AZ

1994 *Formline*, Carrie McLain Museum, Nome, AK
Transformation, University of Alaska Fine Arts Gallery, Fairbanks, AK

1990 *Sonya Kelliher-Combs*, Carrie McLain Museum, Nome, AK

Selected Group Exhibitions

2023 *Young Elder*, James Fuentes Gallery, New York, NY
The Inseparables, STARS gallery, Los Angeles, CA

2022–23 *Arctic Highways*, Swedish Embassy, Washington, DC; traveling exhibition, Yukon Arts Centre, Whitehorse, YT, Canada; Swedish American Museum, Chicago, IL; Scandinavia House, New York,

NY; National Nordic Museum, Seattle, WA
Arctic/Amazon, Power Plant Gallery, Toronto, ON, Canada
Alakkaajut, SAW Gallery/Nordic Lab, Ottawa, ON, Canada; Urban Shaman Contemporary Aboriginal Art Gallery, Winnipeg, MB, Canada
Object Relations: Indigenous Belongings, Wallach Art Gallery, Columbia University, New York, NY
Agency: Feminist Art and Power, Museum of Sonoma County, Sonoma, CA
Addenda, Mandeville Gallery, Union College, Schenectady, NY

2021 *Climate Change and Struggle: Indigenous Ecology in Contemporary Art*, Herbert F. Johnson Museum of Art, Cornell University, NY
Another Crossing, Fuller Craft Museum, Brockton, MA

2020 *Ecofeminism(s),* Thomas Erben Gallery, New York, NY
Settlement, online exhibition due to COVID-19; originally slated to be in Central Park, Plymouth, England
Allegories of Transformation, PACE Center, Parker, CO

2020 *Place of Origin*, Korundi Museum, Rovaniemi, Finland
Art for a New Understanding: Native Voices, 1950's to Now, Crystal Bridges, Fayetteville, AR; Nasher Museum, Duke University, Durham, NC
The Un-heroic Act: Representations of Rape in Contemporary Women's Art in the U.S., Anya and Andrew Shiva Gallery, John Jay College of Criminal Justice, New York, NY

2019–20 *Hearts of Our People: Native Women Artists*, Minneapolis Institute of Art, Minneapolis, MN; Frist Art Museum, Nashville, TN; Renwick Gallery, Smithsonian American Art Museum, Washington, DC; Philbrook Museum of Art, Tulsa, OK

2018–20 *Among All These Tundras*, Leonard & Bina Ellen Art Gallery, Montréal, QC, Canada; Esker Foundation, Calgary, AB, Canada; Onsite Gallery, Toronto, ON, Canada; Pātaka Art + Museum, Porirua, New Zealand

2017 *Subsistence*, Gallery of Northern Norway, Harstad, Norway, organized by the Nordnorsk Kunstmuseum and the Anchorage Museum in conjunction with the Arctic Art Festival
Native Art Now, Eiteljorg Museum of American Indians and Western Art, Indianapolis, IN

2016 *SITElines: New Perspectives on Art of the Americas*, SITE Santa Fe Biennial, Santa Fe, NM

2015 *Fifth World*, Mendel Art Gallery, Saskatoon, SK, Canada
Gyre: The Plastic Ocean, David J. Sencer CDC Museum, Atlanta, GA

2014 *Annual Group Show,* Zane Bennett Contemporary Art, Santa Fe, NM
Native Art Now – Contemporary Indigenous Art from North America, Nordamerika Native Museum, Zurich, Switzerland
Gyre: The Plastic Ocean, Anchorage Museum, Anchorage, AK

2013 *Masks and Transparencies: Contemporary Artists of Alaska*, Orenda Art International, Paris, France
Sakahàn: International Indigenous Art, National Gallery of Canada, Ottawa, ON, Canada
This Is Not a Silent Movie, Los Angeles Craft and Folk Art Museum, Los Angeles, CA; Museum of Contemporary Craft, Portland, OR; University of Montana, Missoula, MT, in collaboration with the Anchorage Museum

2012 *True North*, Anchorage Museum, Anchorage, AK

2010–11 *This Is Displacement*, Edge Center for the Arts, Bigfork, MN; Northrop theatre, Minneapolis, MN; Diverse Works, Houston, TX; American Indian Community House, New York, NY

2010 *Contemporary Inuit Art,* Katuaq Cultural Center, Nuuk, Greenland

2009 *Dry Ice*, Robeson Center for the Arts, Princeton, NJ
50/50: Fifty Years of Alaska's History, statewide touring exhibition

2008 *Native Voices: Contemporary Indigenous Art*, FiveMyles gallery, Brooklyn, NY

2007 *Diversity and Dialogue: The Eiteljorg Fellowship*, Eiteljorg Museum of American Indians and Western Art, Indianapolis, IN

2005 *Changing Hands: Art Without Reservation, Part 2*, Museum of Arts and Design, New York, NY
Cheongju International Craft Biennial, Cheongju Arts Center, Cheongju, South Korea
Alaska Native Art and Culture Festival, Smithsonian Museum of Natural History, Washington, DC
Defiant Objects, Anchorage Museum, Anchorage, AK

2004 *Works from Spenard 4215*, International Gallery of Contemporary Art, Anchorage, AK
Alaska Native Art: People of a Place, Art of a People, Sotheby's Institute of Art, New York, NY
Grand Opening, The Center, Anchorage, AK

2003 *Points of View*, Anchorage Museum, Anchorage, AK

2002 *The 8th Native American Fine Art Invitational*, Heard Museum, Phoenix, AZ

2001 *Ceremony of Healing*, Alaska Pacific University, Anchorage, AK
State of the Art Biennial, Parkland College, Champaign, IL

2000 *Invitational 7*, Decker/Morris Gallery, Anchorage, AK

1993 *Arts from the Arctic*, Anchorage Museum, Anchorage, AK

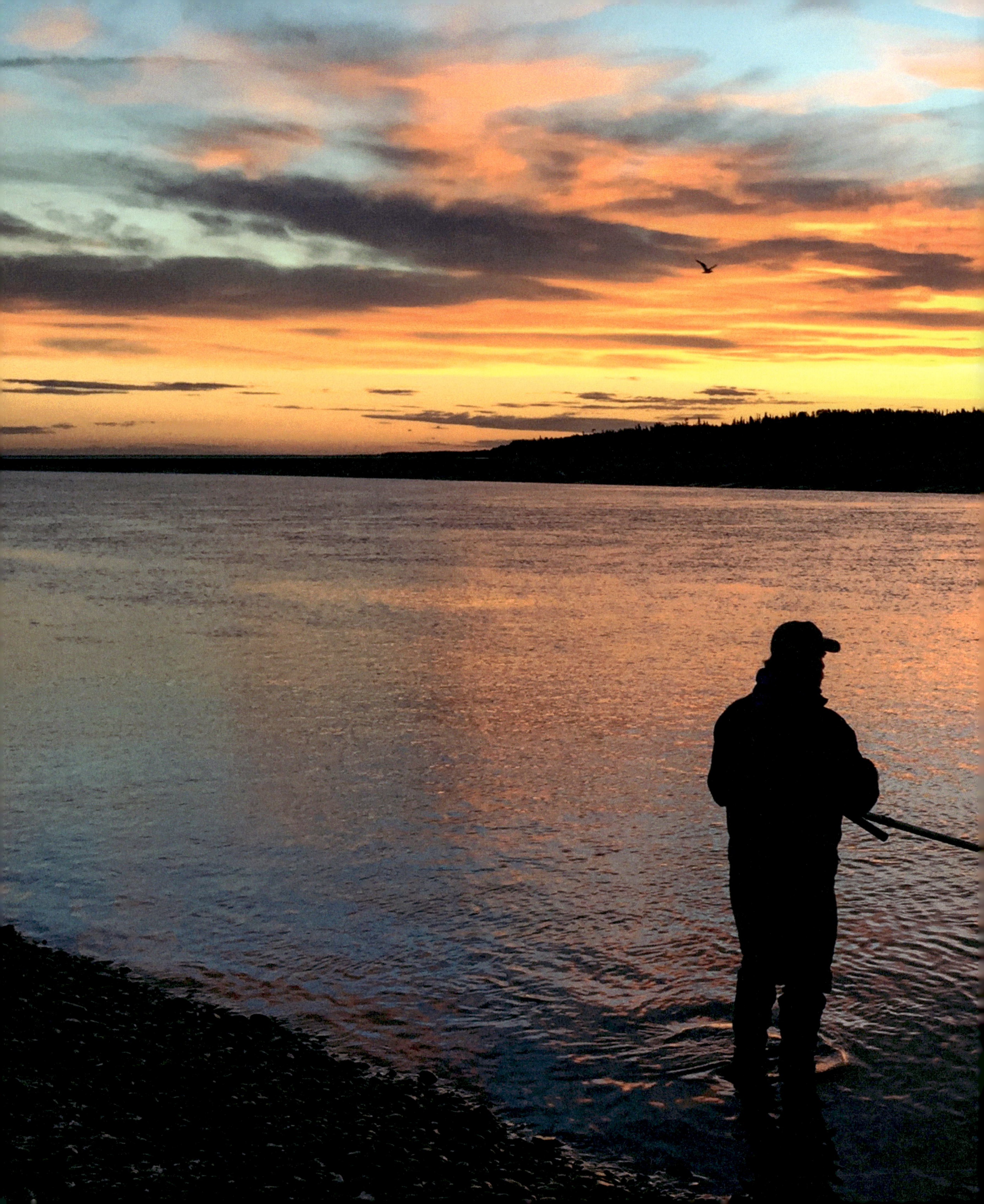

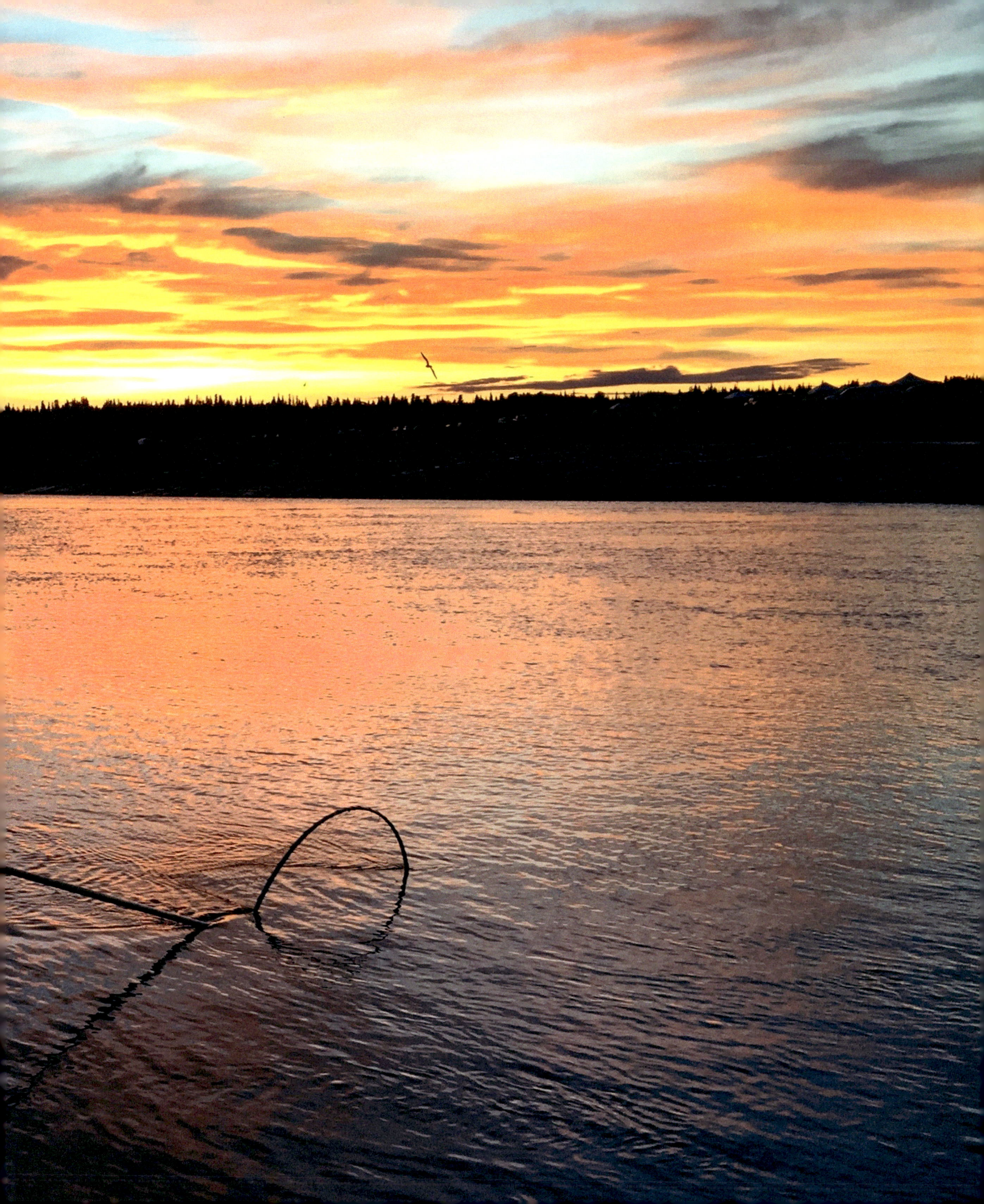

Acknowledgements

Special thanks to:

Tanya Aguiñiga
Edna and Francis Alvanna
Kathleen Ash-Milby
Judy Baletka
Sissel M. Bergh
Susie Bevins-Ericsen
Dawn Biddison
Carmen Bydalek
Ellen Carrlee
The CIRI Foundation
Tomas Colbengtson
Shaun Combs
Don Decker
Julie Decker
Matthew Deleget
Angela Demma
Rachelle Dowdy
Lisa Favero
Zach Feuer
Alex Fitzgerald
Cody Fitzsimmons
Carla and Scott Gingrich
Becky and David Gochman
Anna Gologergan
Shan Goshorn
Maureen Gruben
Gunvor Guttorm
Candice Hopkins
Heather Igloliorte
Inuit Art Foundation
Edna Jackson
Allison Kelliher
Peggy and Maurice Kelliher
Trudy and Patrick Kelliher
Jessie Kleemann
Harry Koozata
Andrew Kreps
Tanya Lukin Linklater
James Luna
Britta Marakatt-Labba
Barry McWayne
David Mollett
David Winfield Norman
Taqralik Partridge
Laura Phipps
Rasmuson Foundation
Marie Saclamana
Dottie Sanders
Jim Schoppert
Christopher Schwartz
Christopher Scott
Ronald Senungetuk
Nadia Sethi
Melissa Shaginoff
Lacie Stiewing
James and Karoline Stotts
Mary and Harry Stotts
Marie Watt
Amber Webb
Jocelyn Young

Thank you to Edna Ahgeak MacLean (Iñupiaq) translation) Simonetta Mignano, Eliza Jones and Susan Paskvan (Athabascan translation) as well as Cindy Burrill and Annika Morris, for your assistance with this publication.

Thank you to the countless others who have helped me throughout the years.

Quyanna!

Additional Captions

Cover *Guarded Secrets*, 2013. Reindeer and sheep rawhide, porcupine quill, archival glue, nylon thread. Dimensions variable. Collection of the Anchorage Museum.
front- and endpapers *Three Sisters* (details), 1998. (see pp. 86, 87)
p. 2 *Small Red, White and Blue Secrets on Pink*, Whitewashed, 2023. Acrylic polymer, reindeer fur, nylon thread, fabric, glass bead, airplane fabric, 36.25 × 29.75 × 2.5 in. Private collection. Photograph by Kunning Huang.
p. 6 Sonya Kelliher-Combs in her studio. Photograph by Chris Arend.
pp. 10–11 Artist's studio in Anchorage, Alaska. Photograph by the artist.
p. 12 Sonya Kelliher-Combs at work in her studio. Photograph by Reginald Eldridge.
pp. 14–15 *Legacy: Resilience*, 2023. 35 cultural belongings with gut from the collection of the Alaska State Museum, with plastic rosaries, plastic bag, dimensions variable. Alaska State Museum Collection. Photograph by Brian Wallace.

Resilience:
1. The power or ability of a material to return to its original form or position.
2. The ability of a person to adjust and recover readily from illness, adversity, major life changes, etc.

These 35 vessels were historically used in the gathering, preparation, and storage of foods and materials. In some of the vessels, the sustenance has been replaced by plastic rosaries. This installation builds upon Kelliher-Combs' series *Forgive You, Father, For You Have Sinned*. Contemporary Alaska Native people have experienced both positive and negative exposure to religion and have lived with historical trauma as well as loss of identity. These vacancies are often replaced by negative life patterns, including addiction, suicide, violence, and mental illness. This installation is for those who have suffered the wounds of abuse by clergy and the church. These traumas have become intergenerational, affecting multiple generations. It is hard to talk about these issues, but it is important to allow space and dialogue for healing and recovery of all that has been taken through the traumas of colonization.
pp. 24–25 *Credible, Alaska*, 2022–23. Projected and painted video installation. Photograph by Brian Wallace.
pp. 32–33 *Credible Secrets with Red* (detail), 2023. (see pp. 142, 143)
pp. 40–41 *Secret Portraits* and *A Million Tears*, installation at Urban Shaman Gallery, Winnipeg, Canada, 2021. Photograph courtesy of the Urban Shaman Gallery.
pp. 46–47 *Legacy: Perseverance*, 2023. Perseverance: The quality that allows someone to continue trying to do something even though it is difficult. This installation is about the transmission of knowledge from one to another, whether it be through hand work, music, and dance, or through hunting, gathering, and preparing our foods and goods. Sharing and helping one another is an everyday value.
35 cultural belongings with gut from the collection of the Alaska State Museum, dimensions variable. Alaska State Museum Collection. Photograph by Brian Wallace.
pp. 60–61 *A Million Tears* (detail), 2021. Mixed media, dimensions variable. Photograph by Chris Arend.
p. 62 *Secret Portraits* (detail), 2005. Mixed media, dimensions variable. Private collection. Photograph by Kevin G. Smith.
p. 78 *Watermelon Walrus Family Portrait*, 2013. Mixed media, 30 × 40 in. Private collection. Photograph by Kevin G. Smith.
p. 148 *Small Secrets Sheldon Jackson* (detail), 2021. Painted fabric, glass beads, human hair, steel pins, nylon thread. Collection of Union College, Schenectady, NY. Photograph by Chris Arend.
p. 194 *Natural Luck*, 2015. Steel wire, paper, acrylic polymer. Private collection. Photograph by Kevin G. Smith.
p. 232 *Mark* exhibition, 2023. Tureen Gallery, Dallas, TX. Photograph by Kevin Todora.
pp. 236–237 Dipnetting on the Kasilof River, Alaska, 2020. Photograph by the artist.

Imprint

Published by
Hirmer Verlag
Bayerstraße 57–59
80335 Munich
Germany

Anchorage Museum
625 C Street
Anchorage, AK 99501
USA
ANCHORAGE MUSEUM

Supported, in part, by grants from:

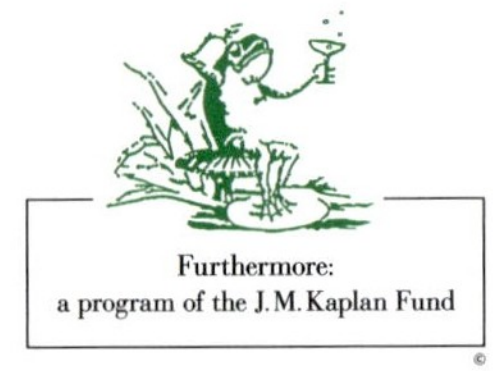

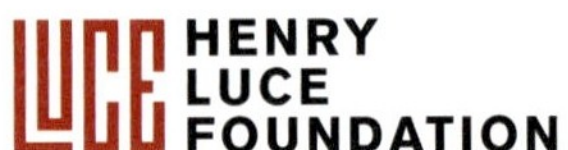

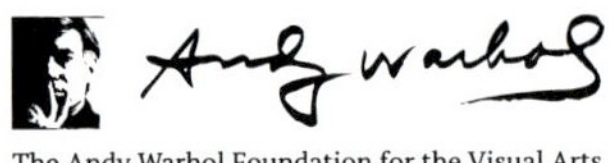

Becky and David Gochman

And support from private contributions

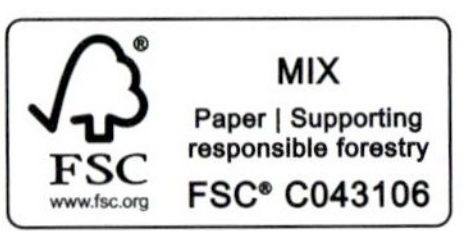

Editor
Julie Decker
Copyediting and proofreading
Mike Pilewski
Layout and typesetting
Hannes Halder
Hirmer Publishers Senior Editor
Elisabeth Rochau-Shalem
Hirmer project management
Rainer Arnold
Prepress
Repromayer, Reutlingen
Paper
Gardamatt Ultra 150 g/m²
Printing and binding
Cuno Druck, Calbe

Printed in Germany

The Deutsche Nationalbibliothek lists this publication in the Deutsche Nationalbibliografie; detailed bibliographic data is available on the Internet at https://dnb.de.

www.hirmerpublishers.com

ISBN 978-3-7774-4254-9

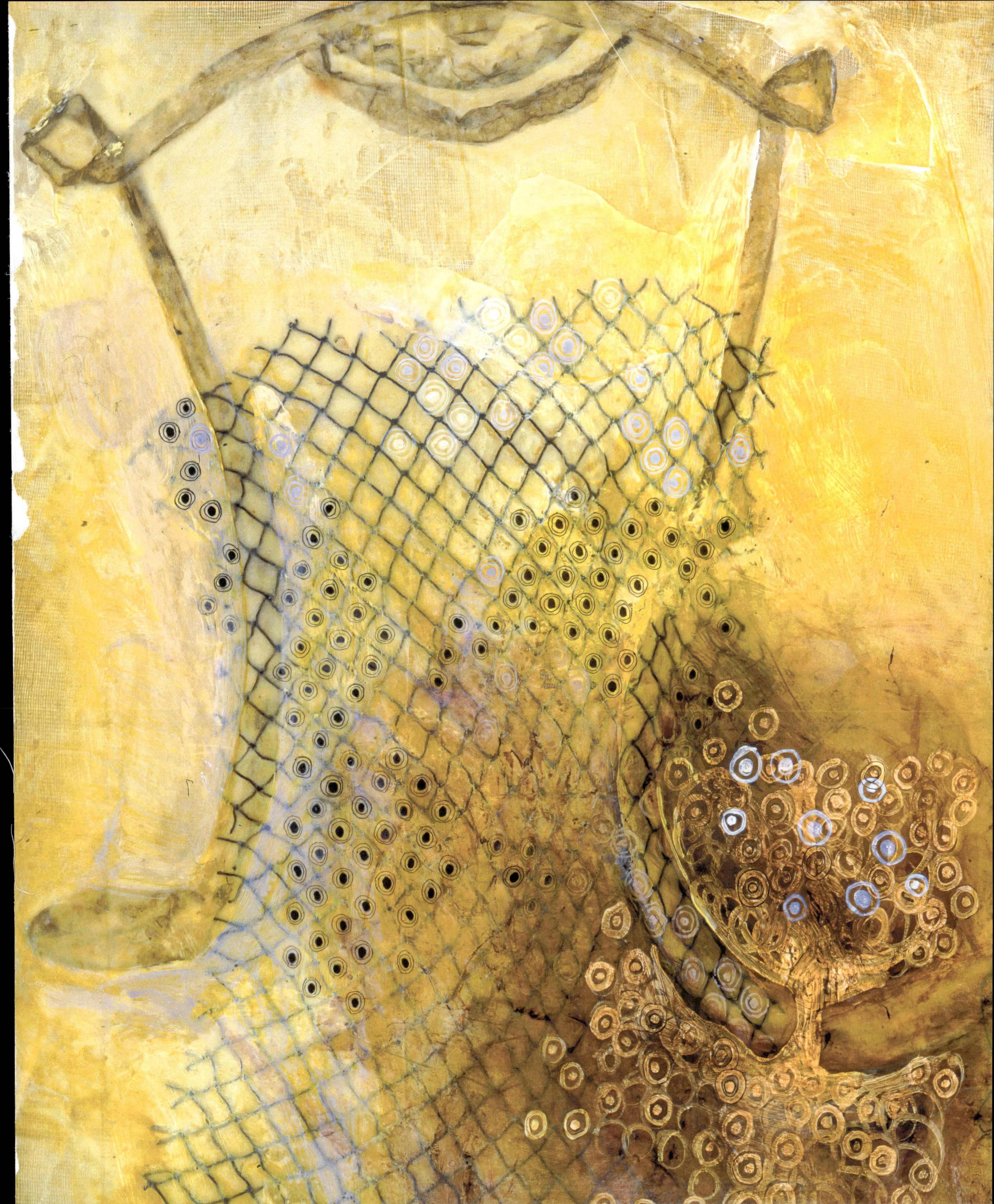

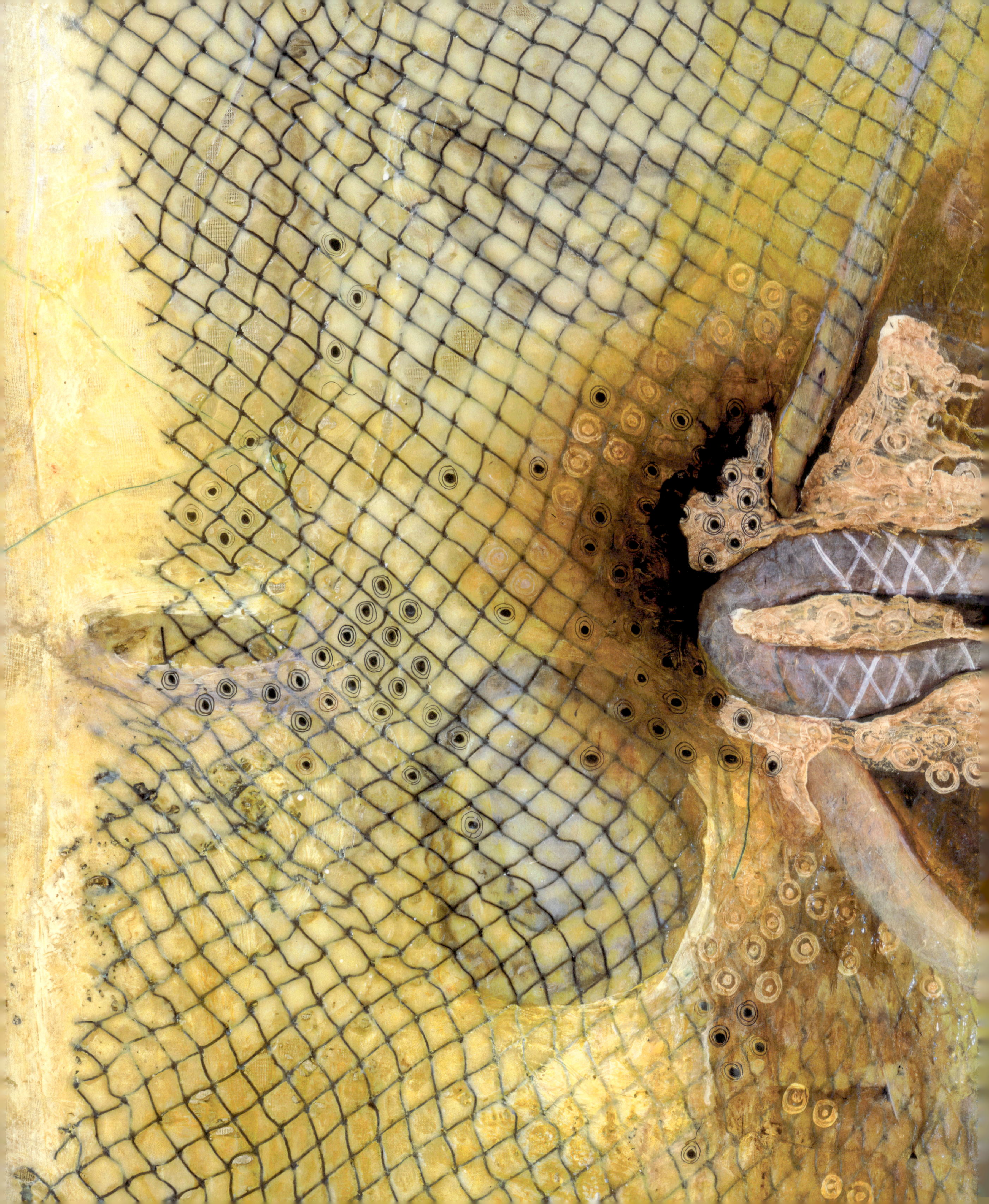